Archaeology
Essentials

Archae
Essent

Colin Renfrew • Paul Bahn

ology
ials

THIRD EDITION

Theories / Methods / Practice

With 295 illustrations

Thames & Hudson

First published in 2007 in paperback in the United States of America by Thames & Hudson Inc., 500 Fifth Avenue, New York, New York 10110

thamesandhudsonusa.com

Third edition 2015

Library of Congress Catalog Card Number 2014944450

ISBN 978-0-500-29159-7

Printed and bound in Canada by TC Transcontinental Printing

Contents

DIGITAL RESOURCES

We offer additional resources for instructors and students on the *Archaeology Essentials* webpage at:

thamesandhudsonusa.com/books/college

Our website for instructors provides a test bank and images in Jpeg format to be shown in class; projects to support key learning objectives; and five videos on specific subjects of related interest. Our student website offers chapter summaries, self-test quizzes, flash cards to revise terminology and concepts, a glossary, and useful internet links.

EBOOK

Archaeology Essentials is also available as an ebook. Visit nortonebooks.com for more information.

Preface

Archaeology Essentials is designed for college students taking an introductory course in archaeology. It aims to convey some of the excitement of archaeology in the 21st century and to give students a concise and readable account of the ways in which modern archaeologists investigate and understand our remote past. Archaeologists usually make the headlines when they find something spectacular: in 2013, for example, the discovery of the skeleton of the English King Richard III, buried in what remained of the former church of Greyfriars in Leicester, now a parking lot, created a sensation. Here were the remains of Richard "Crouchback" (the deformity in the spine clearly visible), the last English monarch to die in battle, at Bosworth Field in 1485. However, most archaeologists spend their time engaged in research that rarely makes the news, but is nevertheless vitally important for our understanding of the past.

Archaeology is still often a matter of painstaking excavation of an ancient site, but today archaeologists can use new techniques that sometimes avoid the need for excavation altogether. Advances in the methods for analyzing and evaluating archaeological finds mean that archaeologists can reach conclusions that would have been impossible just 15 or 20 years ago.

This book will introduce students to the methods, new and old, used by archaeologists: from the traditional shovel and trowel to satellite imaging, laser-based mapping using LIDAR (Light Detection and Ranging), and ground-based remote sensing. New technology has affected the work of archaeologists in the laboratory as well as in the field: we cover, for example, the use of genetic evidence. But the story of modern archaeology is not just about technology. There have been enormous advances in the questions archaeologists ask and in the assumptions and theoretical models they apply to archaeological evidence. Some questions, which an earlier generation of archaeologists might have considered closed, have now been opened up for new examination.

In other words, whatever the focus of an individual college course, it is our intention that students will find in this book an authoritative, concise, and clear explanation of modern archaeological practice.

Introduction
The nature and aims of archaeology

About 5300 years ago, a 40-year-old man made his last journey on a mountain path in the European Alps. He lay undisturbed until his body was discovered by hikers in September 1991. Archaeologists were able to determine not only his age, but also the contents of his last meal: meat (probably ibex and venison), plants, wheat, and plums. The Iceman suffered from arthritis, and analysis of a fingernail showed that he had suffered serious illness 4, 3, and 2 months before he died. At first it was thought that he died from exhaustion in a fog or blizzard. However, later analysis revealed what may be an arrowhead in his left shoulder and cuts on his hands, wrists, and ribcage, as well as a blow to the head, so he may well have died a violent death. These observations are just a sample of what archaeologists were able to learn about this long-dead man.

The thrill of discovery and the ability of **archaeology** to reveal at least some of the secrets of our past have been the theme of many famous novels and movies: notably Steven Spielberg's Indiana Jones series. But although many discoveries in archaeology are far less spectacular than either the Iceman or those represented in fiction – perhaps a collection of broken pieces of pottery – these kinds of remains too can tell us a lot about the past, through careful collection and analysis of the evidence.

Archaeology is unique in its ability to tell us about the whole history of humankind from its beginnings more than 3 million years ago. Indeed, for more than 99 percent of that huge span of time, archaeology – the study of past **material culture** – is the only source of information. The archaeological record is the only way that we can answer questions about the **evolution** of our species and the developments in **culture** and society that led to the emergence of the first civilizations and to the more recent societies that are founded upon them.

This book provides a brief introduction to the ways in which archaeologists uncover and collect evidence about our past (an impression of the extraordinary diversity of modern archaeological work is given by the images overleaf), how they analyze it (often using sophisticated scientific methods), and how they interpret it (both for fellow scholars and members of the public).

The Discipline of Archaeology

Many archaeologists consider themselves as part of the broader discipline of **anthropology**. Anthropology in the most general sense is the study of humanity: our physical characteristics as animals, and our unique non-biological characteristics. Anthropology is thus a broad discipline – so broad that it is often broken down into different fields:

- **Physical** or **biological anthropology**: the study of human biological or physical characteristics and how they evolved.
- **Cultural anthropology**: the study of human culture and society.
- Linguistic anthropology: the study of how speech varies with social factors and over time.
- Archaeology: the study of former societies through the remains of their material culture and, in the case of such literate cultures as those of Mesopotamia or Mesoamerica, such written records as have survived.

Archaeologists who are interested in the societies of ancient Greece and Rome, their empires and neighboring territories, consider themselves Classical archaeologists. They study the material remains of the Greek and Roman worlds, but can also take into account the extensive written records (literature, history, official records, and so on) that survive.

Similarly, biblical archaeologists work in much the same way as anthropological archaeologists, but with reference to the events set out in the Bible. Archaeology has some aspects in common with both history and with science. Like history, archaeology is concerned with documenting and understanding the human past, but archaeologists operate in a time frame much larger than the periods studied by historians. Conventional historical sources begin only with the introduction of written records in around 3000 BC in Western Asia, and much later in most other parts of the world (not until AD 1788 in Australia, for example). The period before written records and history (meaning the study of the past using written evidence) is known as **prehistory**.

Although archaeologists spend much of their time studying **artifacts** and buildings, it is worth emphasizing that archaeology is about the study of humans and, in that sense, like history, it is a humanity. But although it uses written history, it differs from the study of written history in a fundamental way. Historical records make statements, offer opinions, and pass judgments (even if those statements and judgments themselves need to be interpreted). The objects that archaeologists discover, on the other hand, tell us nothing directly in themselves. It is *we* today who have to make sense of these things. In this respect the practice of archaeology is rather like a science. The scientist collects data, conducts experiments, formulates a hypothesis (a proposition to account for the data), tests the hypothesis against more data, and then devises a model

The diversity of modern archaeology:

This page: (Right) Urban archaeology: excavation of a Roman site in the heart of London. (Below left) Working in the on-site archaeobotanical laboratory on finds from Çatalhöyük in Turkey. (Below right) An ethnoarchaeologist in the field in Siberia, sharing and studying the lives of modern Orochen people, here making blood sausages from the intestines of a recently butchered reindeer.

Opposite page: (Above right) Underwater archaeology: a huge Egyptian statue found in the now-submerged ruins of an ancient city near Alexandria. (Below left) An Inca "mummy," now known as the "Ice Maiden," is lifted from her resting place high up on the Ampato volcano in Peru (see p. 56). (Center right) Piecing together fragments of an elaborate mural from the early Maya site of San Bartolo in Guatemala. (Below right) Salvaged in advance of development: a 2000-year-old Western Han Dynasty tomb is excavated at a construction site in Guangzhou, China.

(a description that seems best to summarize the pattern observed in the data). The archaeologist has to develop a picture of the past, just as the scientist has to develop a coherent view of the natural world. It is not found ready made.

Archaeology, in short, is a science as well as a humanity. That is one of its fascinations as a discipline: it reflects the ingenuity of the modern scientist as well as the modern historian. The technical methods of archaeological science are the most obvious, from **radiocarbon dating** to studies of food residues in pots. Equally important are scientific methods of analysis: archaeology is just as much about the analytical concepts of the archaeologist as the instruments in the laboratory.

The Important Questions of Archaeology

Because the evidence of archaeology cannot speak for itself, it is important that archaeologists ask the right questions of the evidence. If the wrong questions are asked, the wrong conclusions will be drawn. For example, early explanations of the unexplained mounds found east of the Mississippi river assumed that they could not have been built by the indigenous American peoples of the region; it was believed instead that the mounds had been built by a mythical and vanished race of Moundbuilders. Thomas Jefferson, later in his career the third President of the United States, decided to test this hypothesis against hard evidence and dug a trench across a mound on his property. He was able to show that the mound had been used as a burial place on many occasions and found no evidence that it could not have been built by the indigenous peoples. In other words, Jefferson asked questions about what the evidence suggested: he did not simply reach a conclusion that fitted his prejudices and assumptions.

Traditional approaches tended to regard the objective of archaeology mainly as reconstruction: piecing together the puzzle. But today it is not enough simply to recreate the material culture of remote periods: how people lived and how they exploited their environment. We also want to know *why* they lived that way, why they had certain patterns of behavior, and how their material culture came to take the form it did. We are interested, in short, in explaining change.

How to Use This Book

This book is organized around some of the most important questions that archaeologists ask. Chapter 1 looks at the history of archaeology, the kinds of questions asked by archaeologists in the past and the methods they used. In Chapter 2 we ask the question What Is Left?: the evidence with which archaeologists work. The next chapter examines the important question Where? Archaeologists can learn a good deal from the **context** in which evidence is found, and have developed many techniques for locating and recovering evidence.

In Chapter 4 the question is When?: how can we know whether something dates from a few hundred years or many thousands of years ago? Chapter 5 examines the fascinating question of How Were Societies Organized? In Chapter 6 we look at the world in which ancient people lived: What Was the Environment and What Did They Eat? Technology was an important factor in changing society and the lives of our ancestors, as were contact and trade with other ancient peoples: the key question for Chapter 7 is How Were Artifacts Made, Used, and Distributed?

Chapter 8 looks at the archaeology of people: What Were They Like? The next chapter addresses some of the more difficult questions that modern archaeologists are trying to answer: the ways ancient peoples thought about their world and issues of identity. In other words, What Did They Think? An equally difficult question is Why Did Things Change?, the subject of Chapter 10. In Chapter 11 we address the often controversial question: Whose Past? The past may be remote in time but it can be very relevant today if it touches on the beliefs, identity, and wishes of the descendants of those who lived long ago. Finally, in Chapter 12 we look at both the practice of applied archaeology (a profession that now employs more people than the academic archaeology pursued in universities) and more generally The Future of the Past. At the end of that chapter we also include a new section on Building a Career in Archaeology.

If you follow the questions examined in this book you will understand how archaeologists work, think, analyze, and seek to understand the past. You will also discover that not all questions can be answered, or perhaps that there might be more than one answer.

To help you understand how archaeology works, we have provided some special features in this book. Case studies in boxes throughout the text show you archaeology in action and will help you understand the issues that archaeologists deal with in their research and fieldwork. Key Concept and Key Fact boxes summarize and review important concepts, methods, or facts about archaeology. At the end of every chapter there is a summary to recap what you have read and a suggested reading list that will guide you to the most important and helpful publications if you want to research any subject further. Archaeological terms in the text that are defined in the glossary are highlighted in bold (e.g. **excavation**) when they first occur in a chapter.

The Searchers
The history of archaeology

The Speculative Phase

- The First Excavations

The Beginnings of Modern Archaeology

- The Antiquity of Humankind and the Concept of Evolution
- The Three Age System
- Ethnography and Archaeology
- Discovering the Early Civilizations
- 19th-Century North American Pioneers
- The Development of Field Techniques

Classification and Consolidation

- The Ecological Approach
- The Rise of Archaeological Science

A Turning Point in Archaeology

- The Birth of the New Archaeology
- The Postprocessual Debate of the 1980s and 1990s
- Pluralizing Pasts
- The Development of Public Archaeology
- Indigenous Archaeologies

Study Questions
Summary
Further Reading

The history of archaeology is commonly seen as the history of great discoveries: the tomb of Tutankhamun in Egypt, the lost Maya cities of Mexico, the painted caves of the Paleolithic, such as Lascaux in France, or the remains of our human ancestors buried deep in the Olduvai Gorge in Tanzania. But even more than that it is the story of how we have come to look with fresh eyes at the material evidence for the human past, and with new methods to aid us in our task.

It is important to remember that just a century and a half ago, most well-read people in the Western world – where **archaeology** as we know it today was first developed – believed that the world had been created only a few thousand years earlier (in the year 4004 BC, according to the then-standard interpretation of the Bible), and that all that could be known of the remote past had to be gleaned from the earliest historians, notably those of the ancient Near East, Egypt, and Greece. There was no awareness that any kind of coherent history of the periods before the development of writing was possible at all.

But today we can indeed penetrate the depths of the remote past. This is not simply because new discoveries are being made. It is because we have learned to ask some of the right questions, and have developed some of the right methods for answering them. The material evidence of the archaeological record has been lying around for a long time. What is new is our awareness that the methods of archaeology can give us information about the past, even the prehistoric past (before the invention of writing). The history of archaeology is therefore in the first instance a history of ideas, of theory, of ways of looking at the past. Next it is a history of developing research methods, employing those ideas, and investigating those questions. And only thirdly is it a history of actual discoveries.

In this chapter and in this book it is the development of the questions and ideas that we shall emphasize, and the application of new research methods. The main thing to remember is that every view of the past is a product of its own time: ideas and theories are constantly evolving, and so are methods. When we describe the archaeological research methods of today we are simply speaking of one point on the trajectory of the subject's evolution. In a few decades' or even a few years' time these methods will certainly look old-fashioned and out of date. That is the dynamic nature of archaeology as a discipline.

The Speculative Phase

Humans have always speculated about their past, and most **cultures** have their own foundation myths to explain why society is how it is. Most cultures, too, have been fascinated by the societies that preceded them. The Aztecs exaggerated their Toltec ancestry, and were so interested in Teotihuacan – the huge Mexican city abandoned hundreds of years earlier, which they mistakenly linked with the Toltecs – that they incorporated ceremonial stone masks from that **site** in the foundation deposits of their own Great Temple. A rather more detached curiosity about the relics of bygone ages developed in several other early civilizations, where scholars and even rulers collected and studied objects from the past.

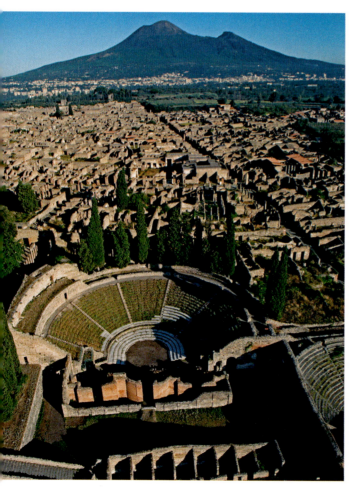

The Roman city of Pompeii lies in the shadow of Mount Vesuvius in Italy. When the volcano erupted in AD 79, the entire city was buried, all but forgotten until excavations began in the mid-18th century. Such spectacular discoveries generated huge interest in the past, and greatly influenced the arts.

During the revival of learning in Europe known as the Renaissance (14th to 17th centuries), princes and people of refinement began to form "cabinets of curiosities," in which curios and ancient **artifacts** were displayed rather haphazardly with exotic minerals and all manner of specimens illustrative of what was called "natural history." During the Renaissance also, scholars began to study and collect the relics of ancient Greece and Rome. And they began too in more northern lands to study the local relics of their own remote past. At this time these were mainly the field monuments – those conspicuous sites, often made of stone, which immediately attracted attention, such as Stonehenge. Careful scholars, such as the Englishman William Stukeley, made systematic studies of some of these monuments, with accurate plans that are still useful today. Stukeley and his colleagues successfully demonstrated that these monuments had not been constructed by giants or devils, as suggested by such local names as the Devil's Arrows, but by people in antiquity. Stukeley was also successful in phasing field monuments, demonstrating that, since Roman roads cut barrows, the former must have been built after the latter.

The First Excavations

In the 18th century more adventurous researchers initiated **excavation** of some of the most prominent sites. The Roman city of Pompeii in Italy was one of the first of these. Buried under meters of volcanic ash after the cataclysmic eruption of nearby Mount Vesuvius, Pompeii was only rediscovered in 1748. Although to begin with the motivation of the excavators was to find valuable ancient masterpieces, it was not long before published finds from Pompeii were attracting enormous international attention, influencing **styles** of furniture and interior decoration, and even inspiring several pieces of romantic fiction. Not until 1860, however, did well-recorded excavations begin.

The credit for conducting what has been called "the first scientific excavation in the history of archaeology" traditionally goes to Thomas Jefferson (later in his career third President of the United States), who in 1784 dug a trench or section across a burial mound on his property in Virginia. Jefferson's work marks the beginning of the end of the Speculative Phase.

In Jefferson's time people were speculating that the hundreds of unexplained mounds known east of the Mississippi river had been built not by the indigenous Americans, but by a mythical and vanished race of "Moundbuilders." Jefferson adopted what today we would call a scientific approach, that is, he tested ideas about the mounds against hard evidence – by excavating one of them. His methods were careful enough to allow him to recognize different layers (or **stratigraphy**) in his trench, and to see that the many human bones present were less well preserved in the lower layers. From this he deduced that the mound had been reused as a place of burial on many separate occasions. Although Jefferson admitted, rightly, that more evidence was needed to resolve the Moundbuilder question, he saw no reason why ancestors of the present-day Native Americans themselves could not have raised the mounds.

Jefferson was ahead of his time. His sound approach – logical **deduction** from carefully excavated evidence, in many ways the basis of modern archaeology – was not taken up by any of his immediate successors in North America. In Europe, meanwhile, extensive excavations were being conducted, for instance by the Englishman Richard Colt Hoare, who dug into hundreds

"The First Excavation"

- Thomas Jefferson, later to become President of the United States, conducted the "first scientific excavation" in Virginia in 1784

- By carefully digging a trench across a Native American burial mound he was able to observe different layers and to draw reasoned conclusions from the data

Early excavations: Richard Colt Hoare and William Cunnington direct a dig north of Stonehenge in 1805.

of burial mounds in southern Britain during the first decade of the 19th century. None of these excavations, however, did much to advance the cause of knowledge about the distant past, since their interpretation was still within the biblical framework, which insisted on a short span for human existence.

The Beginnings of Modern Archaeology

It was not until the middle of the 19th century that the discipline of archaeology became truly established. Already in the background there were the significant achievements of the newly developed science of geology. The study of the **stratification** of rocks (their arrangement in superimposed layers or strata) established principles that were to be the basis of archaeological excavation, as foreshadowed by Jefferson. It was demonstrated that the stratification of rocks was due to processes that were still going on in seas, rivers, and lakes. This was the principle of "**uniformitarianism**": that geologically ancient conditions were in essence similar to, or "uniform with," those of our own time, introduced by the great geologist Sir Charles Lyell. This idea could be applied to the human past also, and it marks one of the fundamental notions of modern archaeology: that in many ways the past was much like the present.

The Antiquity of Humankind and the Concept of Evolution

These advances in geology did much to lay the groundwork for what was one of the most significant events in the intellectual history of the 19th century (and an indispensable one for the discipline of archaeology): the establishment of the antiquity of humankind. It had become widely agreed that earth's origins extended far back into a remote past, so that the biblical notion of the creation of the world and all its contents just a few thousand years before our own time

Charles Darwin caricatured as an ape, published in 1874. The drawing was captioned with a line from William Shakespeare's *Love's Labour's Lost*: "This is the ape of form."

could no longer be accepted. The possibility of a **prehistory** of humankind, indeed the need for one, was established.

This harmonized well with the findings of Charles Darwin, whose fundamental work, *On the Origin of Species*, published in 1859, established the concept of **evolution** to explain the origin and development of all plants and animals. The idea of evolution itself was not new – earlier scholars had suggested that living things must have changed or evolved through the ages. What Darwin demonstrated was how this change occurred. The key mechanism was, in Darwin's words, "natural selection," or the survival of the fittest. In the struggle for existence, environmentally better-adapted individuals of a particular species would survive (or be "naturally selected"), whereas less well-adapted ones would die. The surviving individuals would pass on their advantageous traits to their offspring and gradually the characteristics of a species would change to such an extent that a new species emerged. This was the process of evolution. The implications were clear: that the human species had emerged as part of this same process. The search for human origins in the material record, using the techniques of archaeology, could begin.

Darwin's work on evolution also had an immediate impact on archaeologists who were laying the foundations for the study of artifacts and how they develop over time. But his influence on social thinkers and anthropologists has been even more significant. The principles of evolution can also be applied to social organization, for culture can be seen as learned and passed on between generations, albeit in a more general way than in biological evolution.

The Three Age System

As we have noted, some archaeological techniques, notably those in the field of excavation, were already being developed. So too was another conceptual device that proved very useful for the progress of European prehistory: the **Three Age System**. As early as 1808, Colt Hoare had recognized a sequence of stone, "brass," and iron artifacts within the barrows he excavated, but this was first systematically studied in the 1830s by the Danish scholar C.J. Thomsen. He proposed that prehistoric artifacts could be divided into those coming from a Stone Age, a Bronze Age, and an Iron Age, and this **classification** was soon found useful by scholars throughout Europe. Later a division in the Stone Age was established – between the **Paleolithic** or Old Stone Age and the **Neolithic** or New Stone Age.

These terms were less applicable to Africa, where bronze was not used south of the Sahara, or to the Americas, where bronze was less important and iron was not in use before the European conquest. But it was conceptually significant. The Three Age System established the principle that by studying and classifying prehistoric artifacts, they could be ordered chronologically. Archaeology was moving beyond mere speculation about the past, and becoming instead a discipline involving careful excavation and the systematic study of the artifacts unearthed. Although superseded by modern dating methods, the Three Age System remains one of the fundamental divisions of archaeological materials today.

Ethnography and Archaeology

Another important strand in the thought of the time was the realization that the study by ethnographers of living communities in different parts of the world could be a useful starting point for archaeologists seeking to understand something of the lifestyles of their own early native inhabitants, who clearly had comparably simple tools and crafts. For example, as early as the 16th century, contact with native communities in North America provided antiquarians and historians with models for tattooed images of Celts and Britons.

Soon ethnographers and anthropologists were themselves producing schemes of human progress. Strongly influenced by Darwin's ideas about evolution, the British anthropologist Edward Tylor and his American counterpart Lewis Henry Morgan both published important works in the 1870s arguing that human societies had evolved from a state of savagery (primitive hunting) through barbarism (simple farming) to civilization (the highest form of society). Morgan's work was partly based on his great knowledge of living Native Americans.

Discovering the Early Civilizations

By the 1880s, then, many of the ideas underlying modern archaeology had been developed. But these ideas themselves took shape against a background of major 19th-century discoveries of ancient civilizations in the Old World and the New.

The splendors of ancient Egyptian civilization had already been brought to the attention of an avid public after Napoleon's military expedition there of 1798–1800. It was the discovery by one of his soldiers of the Rosetta Stone that eventually provided the key to understanding Egyptian hieroglyphic writing. Inscribed on the stone were parallel texts written in both Egyptian and Greek scripts. The Frenchman Jean-François Champollion used this bilingual inscription finally to decipher the hieroglyphs in 1822, after 14 years' work. A similar piece of brilliant scholarly detection helped unlock the secrets of cuneiform writing, the script used for many languages in ancient Mesopotamia.

Egypt and the Near East also held a fascination for the American lawyer and diplomat John Lloyd Stephens, but it was in the New World that he was to make his name. His travels in Yucatan, Mexico with the English artist Frederick Catherwood, and the superbly illustrated books they produced together in the early 1840s, revealed for the first time to an enthusiastic public the ruined cities

Frederick Catherwood's accurate, if somewhat romantic, drawing of a stela at Copan; at the time of his visit to the site, in 1840, Maya glyphs had not been deciphered.

of the ancient Maya. Unlike contemporary researchers in North America, who continued to argue for a vanished white race of Moundbuilders as the architects of the earthworks there, Stephens rightly believed that the Maya monuments were, in his own words, "the creation of the same races who inhabited the country at the time of the Spanish conquest." Stephens also noted that there were similar hieroglyphic inscriptions at the different sites, which led him to argue for Maya cultural unity – but no Champollion was to emerge to decipher the glyphs until the 1960s.

19th-Century North American Pioneers

In North America, two themes dominated 19th-century archaeology: the enduring belief in a vanished race of Moundbuilders; and the search for "glacial man" – the idea that human fossils and Stone Age tools would be found in the Americas in association with extinct animals, as they had been in Europe. Ephraim Squier, for example, an Ohio newspaperman who excavated more than 200 mounds in the 1840s, considered the mounds beyond the capabilities of any Native Americans, who were "hunters averse to labor," maintaining the myth of the Moundbuilders. His work does still have some use, though, since the plans and records he made are now the best record there is of the many mounds that were destroyed as settlers moved westward.

Samuel Haven, Librarian of the American Antiquarian Society, produced a remarkable synthesis in 1856, *The Archaeology of the United States*, which is considered a foundation stone of modern American archaeology. In it, he argued persuasively that the Native Americans were of great antiquity, and, through cranial and other physical characteristics, he pointed to their probable links with Asiatic races. Disagreeing strongly with Squier and others, he concluded that the mysterious mounds had been built by the ancestors of living Native Americans.

Plan of Serpent Mound, Ohio, as prepared by Squier (with the help of Edwin Davis, an Ohio physician) in 1846.

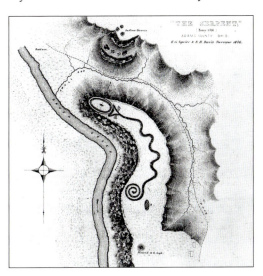

Ephraim Squier.

Samuel Haven.

Part of a 348-ft long painting used by lecturer Munro Dickeson in the 19th century to illustrate his mound excavations.

John Wesley Powell.

Cyrus Thomas.

Another scholar, John Wesley Powell, had spent much of his youth digging into mounds and learning geology. Eventually he was appointed director of the U.S. Geographical and Geological Survey of the Rocky Mountain region. He published a wide range of information on the rapidly dwindling Native American cultures. Moving to Washington, Powell also headed the Bureau of American Ethnology, an agency he set up to study the Native Americans. A fearless campaigner for native rights, he recommended the setting up of reservations, and also began the recording of tribal oral histories.

In 1881 Powell recruited Cyrus Thomas to head the Bureau's archaeology program, and to settle the Moundbuilder question once and for all. After 7 years of fieldwork and the investigation of thousands of mounds, Thomas proved that the Moundbuilder race had never existed: the monuments had been erected by the ancestors of modern Native Americans.

The Development of Field Techniques

It was only in the late 19th century that a sound methodology of scientific excavation began to be generally adopted. From that time some major figures stand out, who in their various ways have helped create the modern field methods we use today.

General Augustus Lane-Fox Pitt-Rivers, for much of his life a professional soldier, brought long experience of military methods, survey, and precision to impeccably organized excavations on his estates in southern England. Plans, sections, and even models were made, and the exact position of every object

General Pitt-Rivers, excavator of Cranborne Chase, and pioneer in recording techniques. To the right is his meticulous plan of a barrow on Cranborne Chase.

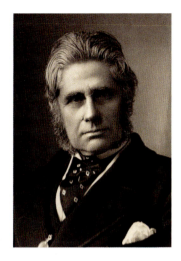

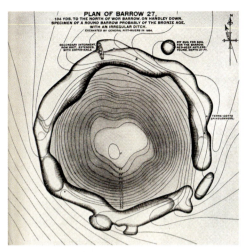

was recorded. He was not concerned with retrieving beautiful treasures, but with recovering all objects, no matter how mundane. He was a pioneer in his insistence on total recording, and his four privately printed volumes, describing his excavations on Cranborne Chase from 1887 to 1898, represent the highest standards of archaeological publication.

A younger contemporary of Pitt-Rivers, Sir William Flinders Petrie was likewise noted for his meticulous excavations and his insistence on the collection and description of everything found, not just the fine objects, as well as on full publication. He employed these methods in his exemplary excavations in Egypt, and later in Palestine, from the 1880s until his death.

Flinders Petrie outside the tomb in which he lived in Giza, Egypt, in the early 1880s.

Sir Mortimer Wheeler, and his excavation at Arikamedu, India, 1945.

Julio Tello, arguably the greatest Native American social scientist of the 20th century – he was a Quechua Indian – and the father of Peruvian archaeology.

Sir Mortimer Wheeler fought in the British army in both world wars and, like Pitt-Rivers, brought military precision to his excavations, notably through such techniques as the grid-square method of dividing and digging a site. He is particularly well known for his work at British hillforts, notably Maiden Castle. Equally outstanding, however, was his achievement as Director-General of Archaeology in India, where he held training schools in modern field methods, and excavated at many important sites.

Julio Tello, "America's first indigenous archaeologist," was born and worked in Peru, began his career with studies in Peruvian linguistics, and qualified as a medical doctor before taking up anthropology. He did much to awaken an awareness of the archaeological heritage of Peru, and was the first to recognize the importance of the key site of Chavín de Huantar and indeed of such other major sites as Sechín Alto, Cerro Sechín, and Wari. He was one of the first to stress the autonomous rise of civilization in Peru, and he also founded the Peruvian National Museum of Archaeology.

Alfred Kidder was the leading Americanist of his time. As well as being a major figure in Maya archaeology, he was largely responsible for putting the Southwest on the archaeological map with his excavations at Pecos Ruin, a large pueblo in northern New Mexico, from 1915 to 1929. His survey of the

Key Early Advances

- The rejection of a literal interpretation of the biblical account of early human history and the establishment of the antiquity of humankind

- Charles Darwin's theories of evolution and natural selection

- The establishment of the Three Age System that divided prehistory into a Stone Age followed by a Bronze Age and an Iron Age

- The development of archaeological field techniques

1 The Searchers

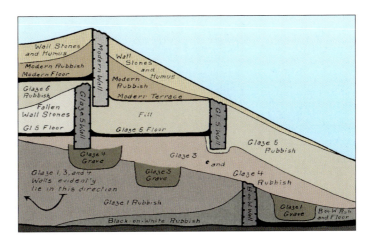

Alfred Kidder (above) and his cross-sectional drawing (above right) of the stratigraphy at the Pecos pueblo site.

region, *An Introduction to the Study of Southwestern Archaeology* (1924), has become a classic. Kidder was one of the first archaeologists to use a team of specialists to help analyze artifacts and human remains. He is also important for his "blueprint" for a regional strategy: (1) reconnaissance; (2) selection of criteria for ranking the remains of sites chronologically; (3) organizing them into a probable sequence; (4) stratigraphic excavation to elucidate specific problems; followed by (5) more detailed regional survey and dating.

Classification and Consolidation

As we have seen, well before the end of the 19th century many of the principal features of modern archaeology had been established and many of the early civilizations had been discovered. There now ensued a period, lasting until about 1960, that has been described as the "classificatory-historical period." Its central concern was chronology. Much effort went into the establishment of regional chronologies, and the description of the development of culture in each area.

It was scholars studying the prehistoric societies of Europe and North America who made some of the most significant contributions to the subject. In the United States there was a close link between anthropologists and archaeologists studying the Native Americans. The anthropologist Franz Boas reacted against the broad evolutionary schemes of his predecessors and demanded much greater attention to the collection and classification of information in the field. Huge inventories of cultural traits, such as pot and basket designs or types of moccasins, were built up. This tied in with the so-called "direct historical approach" of the archaeologists, who attempted to trace modern Native American pottery and other styles "directly" back into the distant past. By the 1930s the number of separate regional sequences was so great that a group of scholars led by W.C. McKern devised what became known as the "**Midwestern Taxonomic System**," which correlated sequences in the Midwest by identifying similarities between artifact collections.

Professor Gordon Childe at the site of the Neolithic settlement at Skara Brae, Orkney, in 1930.

Meanwhile, Gordon Childe, a brilliant Australian based in Britain and a leading thinker and writer about European prehistory, had almost single-handedly been making comparisons of this sort between prehistoric sequences in Europe. Both his methods and the Midwestern Taxonomic System were designed to order the material, to answer: To what period do these artifacts date? and also: With which other materials do they belong? This latter question usually carried with it an assumption that Childe made explicit: that a constantly recurring collection or "**assemblage**" of artifacts (a "culture" in his terminology) could be attributed to a particular group of people. This approach thus offered the hope of answering, in a very general sense, the question: to whom did these artifacts belong?

But Childe went beyond merely describing and correlating the culture sequences, and attempted to account for their origin. In the late 19th century scholars had argued that all the attributes of civilization, from stone architecture to metal weapons, had spread or "diffused" to Europe from the Near East by trade or migration of people. With the much greater range of evidence available to him, Childe modified this approach and argued that Europe had undergone some indigenous development – but he nevertheless attributed the major cultural changes to Near Eastern influences.

Later Childe went on to try and answer the much more difficult question: Why had civilization arisen in the Near East? Himself influenced by Marxist ideas and the relatively recent Marxist revolution in Russia, he proposed that there had been a **Neolithic Revolution** that gave rise to the development of farming, and later an Urban Revolution, which led to the first towns and cities. Childe was one of the few archaeologists of his generation bold enough to address this whole broad issue of why things happened or changed in the past. Most of his contemporaries were more concerned with establishing chronologies and cultural sequences. But after World War II scholars with new ideas began to challenge conventional approaches.

The Ecological Approach

One of the most influential new thinkers in North America was the anthropologist Julian Steward. Like Childe he was interested in explaining cultural change, but he brought to the question an anthropologist's understanding of how living cultures work. Moreover he highlighted the fact that cultures do not interact simply with each other, but with the environment as well. Steward christened the study of ways in which adaptation to the environment could cause cultural change "**cultural ecology**." Perhaps the most direct archaeological impact of these ideas can be seen in the work of Gordon Willey, one of Steward's graduate associates, who carried out a pioneering investigation in the Virú Valley, Peru, in the late 1940s. This study of some 1500 years of pre-Columbian occupation involved a combination of observations from detailed maps and aerial photographs, survey at ground level, and excavation and surface potsherd

- The early 20th-century establishment of regional chronologies and sequences of artifacts

- The development of scientific aids for archaeology, notably radiocarbon dating

- The post-World War II development of an environmental or ecological explanation for past change

- Increasing collaboration with specialists in other disciplines, such as animal or plant studies

- Gordon Childe's bold questioning of why things happened or changed in the past

collection to establish dates for the hundreds of prehistoric sites identified. Willey then plotted the geographical distribution of these many sites in the valley at different periods and set the results against the changing local environment.

Quite independently of Steward, however, the British archaeologist Grahame Clark developed an ecological approach with even more direct relevance for archaeological fieldwork. Breaking away from the artifact-dominated "culture history" approach of his contemporaries, he argued that by studying how human populations adapted to their environments we can understand many aspects of ancient society. Collaboration with new kinds of specialists was essential: for example, specialists who could identify animal bones or plant remains in the archaeological record could help build up a picture not only of what prehistoric environments were like, but also what foods prehistoric peoples ate.

The Rise of Archaeological Science

The other striking development of the period immediately after World War II was the rapid development of scientific aids for archaeology. We have already seen how pioneers of the ecological approach forged an alliance with specialists from the environmental sciences. Even more important, however, was the application to archaeology of the physical and chemical sciences.

The greatest breakthrough came in the field of dating. In 1949 the American chemist Willard Libby announced his invention of **radiocarbon dating**. It was not until well over a decade later that the full impact of this momentous technical achievement began to be felt, but the implications were clear: here at last archaeologists might have a means of directly determining the age of undated sites and finds anywhere in the world without complicated cross-cultural comparisons. Traditionally, prehistoric Europe had been dated by supposed contacts with early Greece and hence (indirectly) with ancient Egypt, which could itself be dated historically. The radiocarbon method now promised a completely independent chronology for ancient Europe. It also meant that to establish a date was no longer one of the main end products of research. It was still important, but it could now be done much more efficiently, allowing the archaeologist to go on to ask more challenging questions than merely chronological ones.

Archaeological applications for scientific techniques now include plant and animal studies, and methods for analyzing human remains and artifacts. Over the past decade developments in biochemistry and molecular genetics have led to the emergence of the new disciplines of molecular archaeology and archaeogenetics. Sensitive techniques in the field of chemistry are beginning to allow the precise identification of organic residues and are giving fresh insights into both diet and nutrition. The study of **DNA**, both modern and ancient, has offered novel approaches to the study of human evolution, and is now beginning to give the study of plant and animal domestication a systematic, molecular basis.

A Turning Point in Archaeology

The 1960s mark a turning point in the development of archaeology. By this time some archaeologists were dissatisfied with the way research in the subject was being conducted. These dissatisfactions were not so much with excavation techniques, or with the newly developed scientific aids in archaeology, but with the way conclusions were drawn from them – how archaeologists explain things.

The fundamental cause for dissatisfaction with the traditional archaeology was that it never seemed to explain anything, other than in terms of migrations of peoples and supposed "influences." Already in 1948 the American archaeologist Walter W. Taylor had argued for an approach that would take into consideration the full range of a culture system. And in 1958 Gordon Willey and Philip Phillips argued for a greater emphasis on the social aspect, for a broader study of the general processes at work in culture history (a "processual interpretation").

That was all very well, but what would it mean in practice?

The Birth of the New Archaeology

In the United States the answer was provided, at least in part, by a group of younger archaeologists, led by Lewis Binford, who set out to offer a new approach to the problems of archaeological interpretation, which was soon dubbed "the **New Archaeology**." Binford and his colleagues argued against trying to use archaeological data to write a kind of "counterfeit history." They maintained that the potential of the archaeological evidence was much greater than had been realized for the investigation of social and economic aspects of past societies. It was a more optimistic view than that of many of their predecessors.

They also argued that archaeological reasoning should be made explicit. Conclusions should be based not simply on the authority of the scholar making the interpretation, but on an explicit framework of logical argument. Thus conclusions, if they are to be considered valid, must be open to testing.

These processual archaeologists sought to explain rather than simply to describe, and to do so, as in all sciences, by seeking to make valid generalizations.

Lewis Binford, the founder of the "New Archaeology," lecturing on his work among the Nunamiut hunters of Alaska.

1 The Searchers

Key Concepts
Processual Archaeology

In the early days of the New Archaeology, its principal exponents were very conscious of the limitations of the older, traditional archaeology. The following contrasts were among those that they often emphasized:

The Nature of Archaeology:
Explanatory vs Descriptive

- Archaeology's role was now to explain past change, not simply to reconstruct the past and how people had lived. This involved the use of explicit theory.

Explanation:
Culture process vs Culture history

- Traditional archaeology was seen to rely on historical explanation: the New Archaeology, drawing on the philosophy of science, would think in terms of culture process, of how changes in economic and social systems take place. This implies generalization.

Reasoning:
Deductive vs Inductive

- Traditional archaeologists saw archaeology as resembling a jigsaw puzzle: the task was one of "piecing together the past." Instead, the appropriate procedure was now to formulate hypotheses, constructing models, and deducing their consequences.

Validation:
Testing vs Authority

- Hypotheses were to be tested, and conclusions should not be accepted on the basis of the authority or standing of the research worker.

Research Focus:
Project design vs Data accumulation

- Research should be designed to answer specific questions economically, not simply to generate more information, which might not be relevant.

Choice of Approach:
Quantitative vs Simply qualitative

- Quantitative data allowed computerized statistical treatment, with the possibility of sampling and significance testing. This was often preferred to the purely verbal traditional approach.

Scope:
Optimism vs Pessimism

- Traditional archaeologists often stressed that archaeological data were not well suited to the reconstruction of social organization or cognitive systems. The New Archaeologists were more positive, and argued that it would never be known how hard these problems were until archaeologists had tried to solve them.

They tried to avoid the rather vague talk of the "influences" of one culture upon another, but rather to analyze a culture as a system that could be broken down into subsystems (such as technology, trade, or ideology), which could be studied in their own right. They placed much less emphasis on artifact **typology** and classification.

In order to fulfill these aims, the New Archaeologists to a large extent turned away from the approaches of history toward those of the sciences. There was a great willingness to employ more sophisticated quantitative techniques and to draw on ideas from other disciplines, notably geography.

In their enthusiasm to use a battery of new techniques, the New Archaeologists drew also on a range of previously unfamiliar vocabularies, which their critics tended to dismiss as jargon. Indeed in recent years, several critics have reacted against some of those aspirations to be scientific. But there can be no doubt that archaeology will never be the same again. Most workers today, even the critics of the early New Archaeology, implicitly recognize its influence when they agree that it is indeed the goal of archaeology to explain what happened in the past as well as to describe it. Most of them agree too that in order to practice good archaeology it is necessary to make explicit, and then to examine, our underlying assumptions.

Increasingly also there has been a readiness to apply the techniques of archaeological investigation to more recent times. In the United States James Deetz made significant contributions, and, more widely, medieval archaeology and industrial archaeology are now recognized fields.

The Postprocessual Debate of the 1980s and 1990s

Post-modernist currents of thought in the 1980s and 1990s encouraged a great diversity of approaches to the past. While many field archaeologists were relatively untouched by theoretical debates, and the processual tradition established by the New Archaeology rolled on, there were several new approaches, sometimes collectively termed "postprocessual," which dealt with interesting and difficult questions.

Influential arguments, some of them first advanced by the archaeologist Ian Hodder and his students, have stressed that there is no single, correct way to undertake archaeological inference, and that the goal of objectivity is unattainable. However, this well-justified critique of the scientism of the early New Archaeology sometimes overlooks more recent developments in scientific methodology. It can also lead to charges of relativism, where one person's view has to be regarded as as good as another's, and where, in interpretive matters, "anything goes," and where the borderlines between archaeological research and fiction (or science fiction) may be difficult to define.

For its early proponents, postprocessual archaeology represented so radical a critique of processual archaeology as to establish a new beginning in archaeological theory. However, others saw "postprocessualism" as simply a development of some of the ideas and theoretical problems introduced by the New Archaeology. To these critics it brought in a variety of approaches from other disciplines, so that the term "postprocessual" was a shade arrogant in presuming to supersede what it might quite properly claim to complement.

Key Influences
Postprocessual Archaeology

Postprocessualism is a collective term for a number of approaches to the past, all of which have roots in the post-modernist current of thought that developed in the 1980s and 1990s.

- The **neo-Marxist** element has a strong commitment to social awareness: that it is the duty of the archaeologist not only to describe the past, but also to use such insights to change the present world. This contrasts quite strikingly with the aspirations towards objectivity of many processual archaeologists.

- The **post-positivist** approach rejects the emphasis on the systematic procedures of scientific method that are such a feature of processual archaeology, sometimes seeing modern science as hostile to the individual, as forming an integral part of the "systems of domination" by which the forces of capitalism exert their "hegemony."

- The **phenomenological** approach lays stress on the personal experiences of the individual and on the way in which encounters with the material world and with the objects in it shape our understanding of the world. In landscape archaeology, for example, the archaeologist sets out to experience the humanly shaped landscape as it has been modified and formed by human activities.

- The **praxis** approach lays stress upon the central role of the human "agent" and upon the primary significance of human actions (praxis) in shaping social structure. Many social norms and social structures are established and shaped by habitual experience (and the notion of **habitus** similarly refers to the unspoken strategy-generating principles employed by the individual, which mediate between social structure and practice). The role of the individual as a significant agent is thus emphasized.

- The **hermeneutic** (or interpretive) view rejects generalization, another feature of processual archaeology. Emphasis is laid, rather, upon the uniqueness of each society and culture and on the need to study the full context of each in all its rich diversity. A related view stresses that there can be no single correct interpretation: each observer or analyst is entitled to his or her own opinion about the past. There will therefore be a diversity of opinions, and a wide range of perspectives – which is why the emphasis is on interpretive archaeologies (plural).

The term "interpretive archaeologies" (plural) has been suggested as a more positive label than "postprocessual."

In recent times, the majority of postprocessual archaeologists have taken a less aggressively anti-scientific tone, and the emphasis has instead been upon the use of a variety of personal and often humanistic insights to develop a range of different fields and interests, recognizing the varied perspectives of different social groups. Ian Hodder's work at the early farming site of Çatalhöyük in

Turkey provides a good example of this approach in action. It is now recognized that there is no single or coherent postprocessual archaeology, but rather a whole series of interpretive approaches and interests.

One of the strengths of the interpretive approach is to bring into central focus the actions and thoughts of individuals in the past. It argues that in order to understand and interpret the past, it is necessary to "get inside the minds" and think the thoughts of the people in question. This might seem a logical goal when examining symbolic systems (for example figurative artworks employing a complex **iconography**) but there is in reality no easy way to get into other people's minds, especially past minds.

Whatever the methodological problems, the consequence of the various debates has been to broaden the range of archaeological theory in a positive manner and to emphasize the symbolic and cognitive aspects of human endeavor in a way that the early New Archaeology failed to do.

Pluralizing Pasts

The postprocessual archaeologists are certainly right in arguing that our own interpretation and presentation of the past involve choices that depend less on an objective assessment of the data than on the feelings and opinions of the researchers and of the clients whom they aim to please. The great national museum in the United States, the Smithsonian Institution in Washington, D.C., found it almost impossible to mount an exhibition in 1995 dealing with the destruction of Hiroshima 50 years earlier, without exciting the anger both of ex-servicemen and of liberals respectful of Japanese sensibilities.

It is evident that archaeology cannot avoid being caught up in the issues of the day, social and political as well as intellectual. An example is the influence of feminist thinking and the growth of feminist archaeology, which overlaps with the relatively new field of gender studies. A pioneer in the emphasis of the importance of women in prehistory was Marija Gimbutas. Her research in the Balkans led her to create a vision of an "Old Europe" associated with the first farmers whose central focus was (or so she argued) a belief in a great Mother Goddess figure. Although many feminist archaeologists today would take issue with certain aspects of Gimbutas' approach, she has certainly helped foster the current debate on gender roles.

In an article of 1984, Margaret Conkey and Janet Spector drew attention to the androcentrism (male bias) of the discipline of archaeology. As Margaret Conkey pointed out, there existed a need "to reclaim women's experience as valid, to theorize this experience, and to use this to build a program of political action."

The deeply pervasive nature of androcentric thinking in most interpretations of the past should not be underestimated: the gender-specific terminology of "Man the Toolmaker," even when swept away with every reference to "mankind" corrected to "humankind," does in fact conceal further, widely held assumptions or prejudices – for instance that Paleolithic stone tools were mainly made by men rather than women, for which there is little or no evidence.

The box overleaf describes some of the more high-profile female archaeologists who have made important contributions to the discipline, but feminist archaeologists can with justice point to the imbalances between female and male professionals among archaeologists today; the goal of "political action" may be seen as justified by current social realities. In the 1990s feminist concern over androcentrism became one voice among many questioning the supposed objectivity and political neutrality of archaeology.

The Development of Public Archaeology

A further turning point came during the later 20th century with the development of public archaeology – that is to say archaeology supported through resources made available as a public obligation. This came with the growing realization that the potential knowledge about the historic (or prehistoric) past embedded in the archaeological record – the material remains of that past – is a resource of public importance, both nationally and internationally. And that the destruction of that past without adequate record should be prevented.

From these realizations came the widespread acceptance that these material remains of the past should be protected and conserved. Moreover, if commercial development sometimes required damage or destruction to that resource, steps should be taken to mitigate that damage through conservation and through recording. There are three key principles here:

- The material record of the past is a public resource that should be managed for the public good;
- When practical circumstances make inevitable some damage to that record, steps should be taken to mitigate the impact through appropriate survey, excavation, and research;
- The developer pays: the persons or organizations initiating the eventual impact (usually through building works undertaken for economic reasons) should fund the necessary actions in mitigation.

The nations of the world have in practice developed different legal frameworks to deal with these problems. They vary from country to country. In France the approach is termed "preventive archaeology," in Britain "**rescue archaeology**," and in the United States "**Cultural Resource Management**."

These issues are worth emphasizing. In those countries with legislation protecting the material record of the past, a large proportion of the resources devoted toward archaeology come through these practices of conservation and mitigation, as governed by national legislation. The protective system in place is influential for the way archaeology is conducted and for the way students are trained. We return to these important issues in Chapter 12.

Women Pioneers of Archaeology

The story of many early women archaeologists was one of exclusion and lack of recognition or promotion – or even employment. Furthermore, many brilliant academic women accepted that, after marriage, professional careers were no longer possible, and they were left to support the academic work of their husbands with little public recognition. This has remained so until the present time, so the achievements of the following pioneers, spanning the 19th and 20th centuries, stand out all the more.

Harriet Boyd Hawes

This well-educated American majored in Classics and was fluent in Greek. Just after graduating, in her early twenties, she spent several seasons riding around Crete on muleback, in dangerous territory, alone or in the company of a woman friend, looking for prehistoric sites. In 1901 she discovered the Bronze Age site of Gournia – the first Minoan town site ever unearthed – which she excavated for the next three years, supervising a hundred local workmen. She published her findings in exemplary fashion in a lavishly illustrated report that is still consulted today.

Gertrude Caton-Thompson

A wealthy British researcher who followed courses in prehistory and anthropology at Cambridge, Caton-Thompson subsequently became well known for her pioneering inter-disciplinary project of survey and excavation in the Faiyum of Egypt; and later, perhaps most famously, at Great Zimbabwe, where her excavations in 1929 unearthed datable artifacts from a stratified context, and confirmed that the site represented a major culture of African origin.

Dorothy Garrod

In 1937 Dorothy Garrod became the first woman professor in any subject at Cambridge, and probably the first woman prehistorian to achieve professorial status anywhere in the world. Her excavations at Zarzi in Iraq and Mount Carmel in Palestine provided the key to a large section of the Near East, from the Middle Paleolithic to the Mesolithic, and found fossil human remains crucial to our knowledge of the relationship

Dorothy Garrod, one of the first to study the prehistoric Near East systematically.

Harriet Boyd Hawes (in 1892), discoverer of the Minoan town site of Gournia, Crete.

Gertrude Caton-Thompson – her work at Great Zimbabwe confirmed that the site was the work of a major African culture.

Anna O. Shepard (above left) was an acknowledged expert in the ceramics of the American Southwest and Mesoamerica.

Kathleen Kenyon (above center) was a great excavator and worked at two of the most important and complex sites in the Near East, Jericho and Jerusalem.

Tatiana Proskouriakoff (above right) – her work on Maya glyphs contributed greatly to their final decipherment.

between Neanderthals and *Homo sapiens*. With her discovery of the Natufian culture, the predecessor of the world's first farming societies, she posed a series of new problems still not fully resolved today.

Anna O. Shepard

An American who studied archaeology as well as a wide range of hard sciences, Shepard subsequently became a specialist in ceramics, as well as Mesoamerican and Southwestern archaeology. She was one of the pioneers of petrographic analysis of archaeological pottery, focusing on sherd paste, paint, and temper. She published extensively on the technology of New World pottery, and wrote a standard work, *Ceramics for the Archaeologist*.

Kathleen Kenyon

A formidable British archaeologist, Kenyon trained on Roman sites in Britain under Sir Mortimer Wheeler, and adopted his method, with its close control over stratigraphy. She subsequently applied this approach in the Near East at two of the most complex and most excavated sites in Palestine: Jericho and Jerusalem. At Jericho, in 1952–58, she found evidence that pushed back the date of occupation to the end of the Ice Age, and uncovered the walled village of the Neolithic farming community commonly referred to as "the earliest town in the world."

Tatiana Proskouriakoff

Born in Siberia, Proskouriakoff moved with her family to Pennsylvania in 1916. Unemployed after graduating as an architect in 1930 during the Great Depression, she ended up working as a museum artist in the University of Pennsylvania. A visit to the Maya site of Piedras Negras led her to devote the rest of her life to Maya architecture, art, and hieroglyphs.

Mary Leakey

A cigar-smoking, whisky-drinking, British archaeologist who, together with her husband Louis, transformed their chosen field. They worked for almost half a century at many sites in East Africa, carrying out meticulous excavations, most notably at Olduvai Gorge, Tanzania, and at Laetoli, where she excavated the famous trails of fossilized hominin footprints, made 3.7 million years ago.

Mary Leakey worked for almost half a century at various early hominin sites in East Africa, transforming our knowledge of human development.

Indigenous Archaeologies

Comparable questions have continued to emerge in the developing indigenous archaeologies in the territories of former colonies, now freed from the previous imperial power. The appropriate policy for cultural heritage management, and indeed the very nature of the cultural heritage itself, are often contested, sometimes along ethnic lines. Marginalized groups, such as the Australian Aborigines, have sought to achieve more influence in the heritage sphere, and have often found their interests overlooked and misunderstood.

Deeper questions arise, however, about the nature of the "globalization" process, itself the outcome of technological advances developed in the West, and whether the very notion of "cultural heritage," as commonly understood, may not be a product of Western thought. The Western-conceived notion of Cultural Heritage Management has been seen by post-colonial thinkers as an imposition of Western values, with officially endorsed notions of "heritage" perhaps leading to homogenization and the undervaluation of cultural diversity. Even the UNESCO-sponsored listing of "World Heritage Sites," from the standpoint of this critique, is dominated by Western-formulated notions of "heritage."

While some aspects of archaeology at the beginning of the new millennium were inevitably controversial, they were also in some ways very positive. They emphasized the value and importance of the past for the contemporary world, and they led to the realization that the cultural heritage is an important part of the human environment, and can be as fragile as the natural environment. They imply, then, that the archaeologist has an important role to play in achieving a balanced view also of our present world, which is inescapably the product of the worlds that have preceded it. The task of interpretation is now seen as very much more complex than it once seemed.

Today, archaeology – once largely the preserve (and the product) of white, upper class, European or North American males – has changed. Many active archaeologists are women. All nationalities are represented. Indigenous archaeologists play an increasing role. Yet the 19th- and 20th-century origins of the discipline are still all too evident today.

Study Questions

- Why is the study of stratification important to archaeology?
- Why was the invention of radiocarbon dating so momentous?
- How did the New Archaeology differ from classificatory-historical archaeology?
- What are some postprocessual approaches to archaeology?
- What is feminist archaeology?
- Why has "public archaeology" become important in recent decades?

Summary

- The history of archaeology is a history of new ideas, methods, and discoveries. Modern archaeology took root in the 19th century with the acceptance of three key concepts: the great antiquity of humanity, Darwin's principle of evolution, and the Three Age System for ordering material culture.

- Many of the early civilizations, especially in the Old World, had been discovered by the 1880s, and some of their ancient scripts deciphered. This was followed by a long phase of consolidation – of improvements in fieldwork and excavation, and the establishment of regional chronologies.

- After World War II the pace of change in the discipline quickened. New ecological approaches sought to help us understand human adaptation to the environment. New scientific techniques introduced among other things reliable means of dating the prehistoric past. The New Archaeology of the 1960s and 1970s turned to questions not just of what happened when, but also why, in an attempt to explain processes of change. Meanwhile, pioneer fieldworkers studying whole regions opened up a truly world archaeology in time and space – in time, back from the present to the earliest toolmakers, and in space, across all the world's continents.

- More recently a diversity of theoretical approaches, often grouped under the label postprocessual, highlighted the variety of possible interpretations and the sensitivity of their political implications.

- Today archaeology plays a significant role in the establishment of national and ethnic identity, and heritage tourism is a profitable business.

- Precisely how archaeologists are continuing to push back the frontiers of knowledge about our planet's human past forms the subject of the rest of this book.

Further Reading

Good introductions to the history of archaeology include:

Bahn, P.G. (ed.). 1999. *The Cambridge Illustrated History of Archaeology*. Cambridge University Press: Cambridge & New York.

Bahn, P. G. (ed.). 2014. *The History of Archaeology. An Introduction*. Routledge: London.

Daniel, G. & Renfrew, C. 1988. *The Idea of Prehistory*. Edinburgh University Press: Edinburgh; Columbia University Press: New York.

Deetz, J. 1996. *In Small Things Forgotten: An Archaeology of Early American Life* (2nd ed.). Anchor Books: New York.

Fagan, B.M. 2004. *A Brief History of Archaeology: Classical Times to the Twenty-First Century*. Prentice Hall: Upper Saddle River, N.J.

Johnson, M. 2010. *Archaeological Theory, an Introduction* (2nd ed.). Wiley-Blackwell: Oxford.

Lowenthal, D. 1999. *The Past is a Foreign Country*. Cambridge University Press: Cambridge & New York.

Trigger, B.G. 2006. *A History of Archaeological Thought* (2nd ed.). Cambridge University Press: Cambridge & New York.

Renfrew, C. & Bahn, P. (eds). 2004. *Key Concepts in Archaeology*. Routledge: London & New York.

Willey, G.R. & Sabloff, J.A. 1993. *A History of American Archaeology* (3rd ed.). Freeman: New York.

[See p. 345 for a list of useful websites]

What Is Left?
The variety of the evidence

Basic Categories Of Archaeological Evidence

- The Importance of Context

Formation Processes

Cultural Formation Processes – How People Have Affected What Survives In The Archaeological Record

Natural Formation Processes – How Nature Affects What Survives In The Archaeological Record

- Inorganic Materials
- Organic Materials
- Preservation of Organic Materials: Extreme Conditions

Study Questions
Summary
Further Reading

The relics of past human activity are all around us. Some of them were deliberate constructions, built to last, for example the pyramids of Egypt, the Great Wall of China, or the temples of Mesoamerica and India. Others, such as the remains of the Maya irrigation systems of Mexico and Belize, are the visible relics of activities, the aim of which was not primarily to impress the observer, but that still command respect today for the scale of the enterprise they document.

Most of the remains of **archaeology** are far more modest, however. They are the discarded garbage from the daily activities of human existence: the food remains, the bits of broken pottery, the fractured stone tools, the debris that is formed everywhere as people go about their daily lives.

In this chapter we define the basic archaeological terms, briefly survey the scope of the surviving evidence, and look at the great variety of ways in which it has been preserved for us. From the frozen soil of the Russian steppes, for instance, have come the wonderful finds of Pazyryk, those great chieftains' burials where wood and textiles and skins are splendidly preserved. From the dry caves of Peru and other arid environments have come remarkable textiles, baskets, and other remains that often perish completely. And by contrast, from wetlands, whether the swamps of Florida or the lake villages of Switzerland, further organic remains are being recovered, this time preserved not by the absence of moisture, but by its abundant presence to the exclusion of air.

Extremes of temperature and of humidity have preserved much. So too have natural disasters. The volcanic eruption that destroyed Pompeii in Italy is the most famous of them, but there have been others, such as the eruption of the Ilopango volcano in El Salvador in the 2nd century AD, which buried land surfaces and settlement remains in a large part of the southern Maya area.

Unfortunately most archaeological **sites** are not in areas subjected to extremes of climate or volcanic activity, and levels of preservation can vary enormously. Our knowledge of the early human past is dependent in this way on the human activities and natural processes that have formed the archaeological record, and on those further processes that determine, over long periods of time,

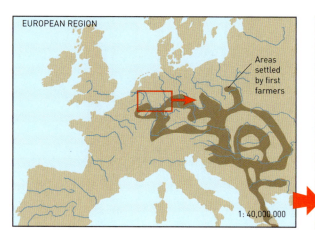

EUROPEAN REGION

Areas settled by first farmers

1: 40,000,000

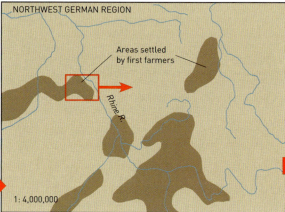

NORTHWEST GERMAN REGION

Areas settled by first farmers

Rhine R.

1: 4,000,000

what *is* left and what is gone for ever. Today we can hope to recover much of what is left, and to learn from it by asking the right questions in the right way.

Basic Categories of Archaeological Evidence

The evidence studied by archaeologists very often includes **artifacts** – objects used, modified, or made by people. But equally important is the study of organic and environmental remains – known as "**ecofacts**" – that, although not made by humans, can still be very revealing about many aspects of past human activity. Much archaeological research concentrates on the analysis of these artifacts and ecofacts that are found together on sites, which in turn are most productively studied together with their surrounding landscapes and grouped together into regions. Some of these different scales at which archaeologists operate, as well as the terminology they use, are illustrated above and opposite.

Artifacts are humanly made or modified portable objects, such as stone tools, pottery, and metal weapons. But artifacts provide evidence to help us answer all the key questions – not just technological ones – addressed in this book. A single clay vessel or pot can be analyzed in a number of different ways. The clay may be tested to produce a date for the vessel and thus perhaps a date for the location where it was found. It could also be tested to find the source of the clay and thus give evidence for the range and contacts of the group that made the vessel. Pictorial decoration on the pot's surface could help to form or be related to a sequence of design **styles** (a **typology**), and it could tell us something about ancient beliefs, particularly if it shows gods or other figures. And analysis of the vessel's shape and any food or other residues found in it can yield information about the pot's use, perhaps in cooking, as well as about ancient diet.

Some researchers broaden the meaning of the term "artifact" to include all humanly modified components of a site or landscape, such as hearths, postholes, and storage pits – but these non-portable artifacts are more usefully described as **features**. Such simple features as postholes may themselves,

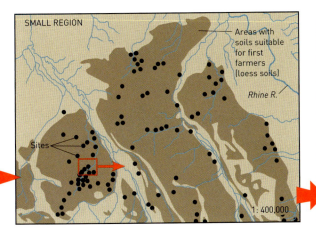

SMALL REGION

Areas with soils suitable for first farmers (loess soils)

Rhine R.

Sites

1: 400,000

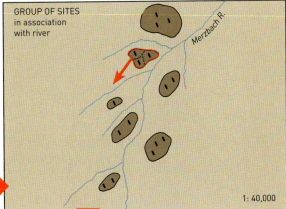

GROUP OF SITES
in association with river

Merzbach R.

1: 40,000

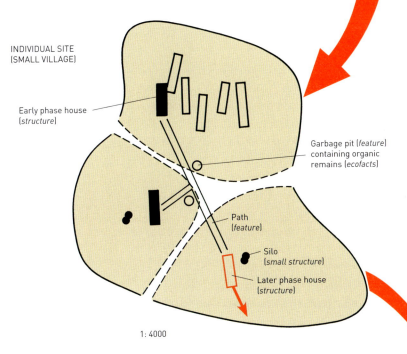

INDIVIDUAL SITE
(SMALL VILLAGE)

Early phase house
(*structure*)

Garbage pit (*feature*)
containing organic
remains (*ecofacts*)

Path
(*feature*)

Silo
(*small structure*)

Later phase house
(*structure*)

1: 4000

Different scales and terminology used in archaeology, from the continental region (opposite page, top left) to the individual structure (right). In this representation of the pattern of settlement of Europe's first farmers (5th millennium BC), the archaeologist might study – at the broader scale – the interesting association between sites and light, easily worked soils near rivers. At the smaller scale, the association – established by excavation – of houses with other houses and with such structures as silos for grain storage raises questions, for example about social organization and permanence of occupation at this period.

INDIVIDUAL STRUCTURE (HOUSE)

Scatter of *artifacts*

Posthole (*feature*)

1: 400

Artifacts and features are found
in association with the structure

2 What is Left?

41

Key Concepts
Types of Evidence

- *Artifacts*: portable objects used, modified, or made by humans

- *Ecofacts*: organic and environmental remains not made by humans

- *Features*: non-portable artifacts

- *Sites*: places where artifacts, ecofacts, and features are found together

or in combination with remains of hearths, floors, ditches, etc., give evidence for complex features or structures, defined as buildings of all kinds, from houses and granaries to palaces and temples.

Non-artifactual organic and environmental remains, or ecofacts, include human skeletons, animal bones, and plant remains, but also soils and sediments – all of which may shed light on past human activities. They are important because they can indicate, for example, what people ate or the environmental conditions under which they lived.

Archaeological sites may be thought of as the huge variety of places where artifacts, features, structures, and organic and environmental remains are found together. For working purposes we can simplify this still further and define sites as places where significant traces of human activity are identified. Thus a village or town is a site, and so too is an isolated monument, such as Serpent Mound in Ohio. Equally, a surface scatter of stone tools or potsherds may represent a site occupied for no more than a few hours, whereas a Near Eastern **tell** or mound is a site indicating human occupation over perhaps thousands of years.

The Importance of Context

In order to reconstruct past human activity at a site it is crucially important to understand the **context** of a find, whether artifact, ecofact, or feature. A find's context consists of its immediate **matrix** (the material surrounding it, usually some sort of sediment, such as gravel, sand, or clay), its **provenience** (horizontal and vertical position within the matrix), and its **association** with other finds (occurrence together with other archaeological remains, usually in the same matrix). In the 19th century the demonstration that stone tools were often associated with the bones of extinct animals in a sealed matrix helped establish the idea of the great antiquity of humankind.

Increasingly since then archaeologists have recognized the importance of identifying and accurately recording associations between remains on sites. This is why it is such a tragedy when looters dig up sites indiscriminately, looking for rich finds, without recording matrix, provenience, or associations. All the contextual information is lost. A looted vase may be an attractive object for a collector, but far more could have been learnt about the society that produced it had archaeologists been able to record where it was found (in a tomb, ditch, or house?) and in association with what other artifacts or organic remains (weapons, tools, or animal bones?). Much information about the Mimbres people of the American Southwest has been lost for ever because looters bulldozed their sites, hunting for the superbly painted – and highly sought after – bowls made by the Mimbres 1000 years ago.

When modern (or ancient) looters disturb a site, perhaps shifting aside material they are not interested in, they destroy that material's primary context. If archaeologists subsequently excavate that shifted material, they need to be able to recognize that it is in a secondary context. This may be straightforward for, say, a Mimbres site, looted quite recently, but it is much more difficult for a site disturbed in antiquity. Nor is disturbance confined to human activity: archaeologists dealing with the tens of thousands of years of the **Paleolithic** or Old Stone Age period know well that the forces of nature – encroaching seas or ice sheets, wind and water action – invariably destroy primary context. A great many of the Stone Age tools found in European river gravels are in a secondary context, transported by water action far from their original, primary context.

Formation Processes

In recent years archaeologists have become increasingly aware that a whole series of **formation processes** may have affected both the way in which finds came to be buried and what happened to them after they were buried. The study of these processes is called **taphonomy**.

A useful distinction has been made between cultural formation processes and noncultural or natural formation processes. Cultural formation processes involve the deliberate or accidental activities of human beings as they make or use artifacts, build or abandon buildings, plow their fields, and so on. Natural formation processes are natural events that govern both the burial and the survival of the archaeological record. The sudden fall of volcanic ash that covered Pompeii is an exceptional example; a more common one would be the gradual burial of artifacts or features by wind-borne sand or soil. Likewise the transporting of stone tools by river action, referred to on the previous page, or the activities of animals – burrowing into a site or chewing bones and pieces of wood – are also examples of natural formation processes.

At first sight these distinctions may seem of little interest to the archaeologist. In fact they are vital to the accurate reconstruction of past human activities. It can be important to know whether certain archaeological evidence is the product of human or non-human (cultural or natural) activity. If, for example, you are trying to reconstruct human woodworking activities by studying cutmarks on timber, then you should learn to recognize certain kinds of marks made by beavers using their teeth and to distinguish these from cutmarks made by humans using stone or metal tools.

Let us take an even more significant example. For the earliest phases of human existence in Africa, at the beginning of the Paleolithic or Old Stone Age period, theories about our primitive hunting ability have been based on the association between stone tools and animal bones found at archaeological sites. The bones were assumed to be those of animals hunted and slaughtered by the early humans who made the tools. But studies of animal behavior and cutmarks on animal bones suggest that in many cases the excavated bones are the remains of animals hunted and largely eaten by other predatory animals. The humans with their stone tools would have come upon the scene as mere scavengers, at the end of a pecking order of different animal species. By no means everyone agrees with this scavenging hypothesis. The point to emphasize here is that the issue can best be resolved by improving our techniques for distinguishing

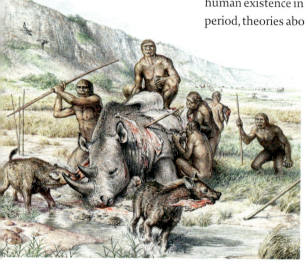

Early humans as mighty hunters (below) or mere scavengers (bottom)? Our understanding of formation processes governs the way in which we interpret associations of human tools with animal bones from the fossil record in Africa.

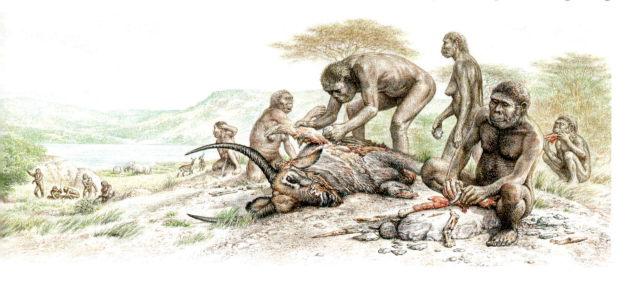

Experimental Archaeology

One effective way to study formation processes is through long-term experimental archaeology. An excellent example is the experimental earthwork constructed on Overton Down, southern England, in 1960.

The earthwork consists of a substantial chalk and turf bank, 21 m (69 ft) long, 7 m (25 ft) wide, and 2 m (6 ft 7 in) high, with a ditch cut parallel to it. The aim of the experiment has been to assess not only how the bank and ditch alter through time, but also what happens to materials, such as pottery, leather, and textiles, that were buried in the earthwork in 1960. Sections (trenches) have been – or will be – cut across the bank and ditch at intervals of 2, 4, 8, 16, 32, 64, and 128 years (in real time, 1962, 1964, 1968, 1976, 1992, 2024, and 2088): a considerable commitment for all concerned.

On this timescale, the project is still at a relatively early stage. But preliminary results are interesting.

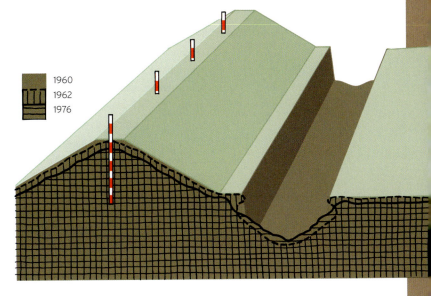

1960
1962
1976

In the 1960s the bank dropped some 25 cm (10 in) in height and the ditch silted up quite rapidly. Since the mid-1970s, however, the structure has stabilized. As for the buried materials, tests after 4 years showed that pottery was unchanged and leather little affected, but textiles were already becoming weakened and discolored.

The excavations in 1992 revealed that preservation was better in the chalk bank, which is less biologically active, than in the turf core, where textiles and some wood had completely

The bank and ditch as cut in 1960, together with the changes revealed by sections cut across the earthwork in 1962 and 1976.

disappeared. The structure itself had changed little since 1976, though there was considerable reworking and transport of fine sediment by earthworms.

The experiment has already shown that many of the changes that interest archaeologists occur within decades of burial, and that the extent of these changes can be far greater than had hitherto been suspected.

between cultural and natural formation processes – between human and non-human activity. Many studies are now focusing on the need to clarify how to differentiate cutmarks on bones made by stone tools from those made by the teeth of animal predators. Modern experiments using replica stone tools to cut meat off bones are one helpful approach. Other kinds of **experimental archaeology** can be most instructive about some of the formation processes that affect physical preservation of archaeological material (see box above).

The remainder of this chapter is devoted to a more detailed discussion of the different cultural and natural formation processes.

Cultural Formation Processes – How People Have Affected What Survives in the Archaeological Record

We may separate these processes rather crudely into two kinds: those that reflect the original human behavior and activity before a find or site became buried; and those (such as plowing or looting) that came after burial. Now of course most major archaeological sites are formed as the result of a complex sequence of use, burial, and reuse repeated many times over, so that a simple two-fold division of cultural formation processes may not be so simple to apply in practice. Nevertheless, since one of our main aims is to reconstruct original human behavior and activity, we must make the attempt.

Original human behavior is often reflected archaeologically in at least four major activities: for example, in the case of a tool (see diagram below) there may be

1 acquisition of the raw material;
2 manufacture;
3 use (and distribution); and finally
4 disposal or discard when the tool is worn out or broken. (The tool may of course be reworked and recycled, i.e. repeating stages 2 and 3.)

Similarly, a food crop, such as wheat, will be acquired (harvested), manufactured (processed), used (eaten), and discarded (digested and the waste products excreted) – here we might add a common intermediate stage of storage before

An artifact, a stone tool in this case, may have entered the archaeological record at any one of these four stages in its life cycle. The archaeologist's task is to determine which stage is represented by the find in question.

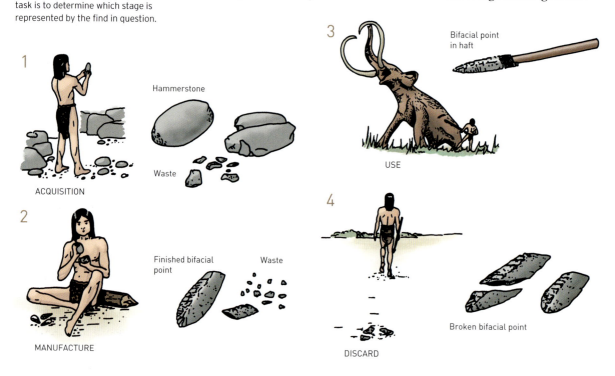

1 ACQUISITION — Hammerstone, Waste

2 MANUFACTURE — Finished bifacial point, Waste

3 USE — Bifacial point in haft

4 DISCARD — Broken bifacial point

use. From the archaeologist's point of view the critical factor is that remains can enter the archaeological record at any one of these stages – a tool may be lost or thrown out as inferior quality during manufacture, a crop may be accidentally burnt and thus preserved during processing. In order to reconstruct accurately the original activity it is therefore crucial to try to understand which one of the stages we are examining. It may be quite easy to identify, say, the first stage for stone tools, because stone quarries can often be recognized by deep holes in the ground, with piles of associated waste flakes and blanks, which survive well. But it is much more difficult to know beyond reasonable doubt whether a sample of charred plant remains comes from, say, a threshing area or an occupation area – and this may also make it difficult to reconstruct the true plant diet, since certain activities may favor the preservation of certain species of plant.

Deliberate burial of valuables is another major aspect of original human behavior that has left its mark on the archaeological record. In times of conflict or war people often deposit prized possessions in the ground, intending to reclaim them at a later date but sometimes for one reason or another failing to do so. These **hoards** are a prime source of evidence for certain periods, such as the European Bronze Age, for which hoards of metal goods are common, or later Roman Britain, which has yielded buried treasures of silver and other precious metals. The archaeologist, however, may not find it easy to distinguish between hoards originally intended to be recovered and valuables buried with no reclamation intended, perhaps to placate supernatural powers (placed for example at a particularly dangerous part of a crossing over a bog).

How archaeologists set about trying to demonstrate belief in supernatural powers and an afterlife will be seen in Chapter 9. Here we may note that, in addition to hoards, the major source of evidence comes from burial of the dead, whether in simple graves, elaborate burial mounds, or giant pyramids, usually with such grave-goods as ceramic vessels or weapons, and sometimes with painted tomb-chamber walls, as in ancient Mexico or Egypt. The Egyptians indeed went so far as to mummify their dead – to preserve them, they hoped, for eternity – as did the Incas of Peru, whose kings were kept in the Temple of the Sun at Cuzco and brought outside for special ceremonies.

Human destruction of the archaeological record might be caused by burials of the kind just described being dug into earlier deposits. But people in the past deliberately or accidentally obliterated traces of their predecessors in innumerable other ways. Rulers, for instance, often destroyed monuments or erased inscriptions belonging to previous chiefs or monarchs. Some human destruction meant to obliterate has inadvertently preserved material for the archaeologist to find. Burning, for example, may not always destroy. It can often improve the chances of survival of a variety of remains, such as of plants: the conversion into carbon greatly increases the powers of resistance to the ravages of time. Clay daubing and adobe usually decay, but if a structure has been fired, the mud is baked to the consistency of a brick. In the same way thousands of clay writing tablets from the Near East have been baked accidentally or deliberately in fires and thus preserved. Timbers too may char and survive in structures, or at least leave a clear impression in the hardened mud.

Today human destruction of the archaeological record continues at a frightening pace, through land drainage, plowing, building work, looting, etc. In Chapter 10 we discuss how this affects archaeology generally and what the potential implications are for the future.

Natural Formation Processes – How Nature Affects What Survives in the Archaeological Record

We saw above how natural formation processes, such as river action, can disturb or destroy the primary context of archaeological material. Here we will focus on that material itself, and the natural processes that cause decay or lead to preservation.

Practically any archaeological material can survive in exceptional circumstances. Usually, however, inorganic materials survive far better than organic ones.

Inorganic Materials

The most common inorganic materials to survive archaeologically are stone, clay, and metals.

Stone tools survive extraordinarily well – some are more than 2 million years old. Not surprisingly they have always been our main source of evidence for human activities during the Paleolithic period, even though wooden and bone tools (which are less likely to be preserved) may originally have equalled stone ones in importance. Stone tools sometimes come down to us so little damaged or altered from their primary state that archaeologists can examine microscopic patterns of wear on their cutting edges and learn, for example, whether the

Key Concepts
Survival of Inorganic Materials

- Stone tools, fired clay, and some metals, such as gold, silver, and lead, survive very well in nearly all environments

- Some metals, such as copper, can corrode depending on the soil conditions, and iron rarely survives in an uncorroded state

- Although inorganic materials, particularly stone tools and pottery, are very often found at archaeological sites, these objects may well have been equalled or superseded in abundance and importance by objects that usually do not survive, such as wooden tools or baskets

This bronze head from a statue of a Greek male athlete was found off the coast of Croatia in 2001. Bronze survives well in seawater, but some 2000 years of encrustation had to be painstakingly removed by restorers.

tools were used to cut wood or animal hides. This is now a major branch of archaeological inquiry.

Fired clay, such as pottery and baked mud brick or adobe, is virtually indestructible if well fired. It is therefore again not surprising that for the periods after the introduction of pottery making (some 16,000 years ago in Japan, and 9000 years ago in the Near East and parts of South America) ceramics have traditionally been the archaeologist's main source of evidence. As we saw earlier in this chapter, pots can be studied for their shape, surface decoration, mineral content, and even the food or other residues left inside them. Acid soils can damage the surface of fired clay, and porous or badly fired clay vessels or mud brick can become fragile in humid conditions. However, even disintegrated mud brick can help to assess rebuilding phases in, for instance, Peruvian villages or Near Eastern tells.

Such metals as gold, silver, and lead survive well. Copper, and bronze with a low-quality alloy, are attacked by acid soils, and can become so oxidized that only a green deposit or stain is left. Oxidation is also a rapid and powerful agent of destruction of iron, which rusts and may similarly leave only a discoloration in the soil.

The sea is potentially very destructive. Underwater remains can be broken and scattered by currents, waves, or tidal action. On the other hand, the sea can cause metals to be coated with a thick, hard casing of metallic salts from the objects themselves; this helps to preserve the artifacts. If the remains are simply taken out of the water and not treated, the salts react with air, and give off acid that destroys the remaining metal. But the use of **electrolysis** – placing the object in a chemical solution and passing a weak current through it – leaves the metal artifact clean and safe. This is a standard procedure in underwater archaeology and is used on all types of objects from cannons to the finds recovered from the *Titanic*.

Organic Materials

Survival of organic materials is determined largely by the matrix (the surrounding material) and by climate (local and regional) – with the occasional influence of such natural disasters as volcanic eruptions, which are often far from disastrous for archaeologists.

The matrix, as we saw earlier, is usually some kind of sediment or soil. These vary in their effects on organic material; chalk, for example, preserves human and animal bone well (in addition to inorganic metals). Acid soils destroy bones and wood within a few years, but will leave telltale discolorations where postholes or hut foundations once stood. Similar brown or black marks survive in sandy soils, as do dark silhouettes that used to be skeletons.

But the immediate matrix may in exceptional circumstances have an additional component, such as metal ore, salt, or oil. Copper can favor the preservation of organic remains, perhaps by preventing the activity of destructive micro-organisms. The prehistoric copper (and salt) mines of central and southeast Europe have many remains of wood, leather, and textiles.

A combination of salt and oil ensured the preservation of a woolly rhinoceros at Starunia, Poland, with skin intact, and the leaves and fruits of tundra vegetation around it. The animal had been carried by a strong current into a pool saturated with crude oil and salt from a natural oil seep, which prevented decomposition: bacteria could not operate in these conditions, while salt had permeated the skin and preserved it. Similarly, the asphalt pits of La Brea, Los Angeles, are world famous for the large quantities and fine condition of the skeletons of a wide range of prehistoric animals and birds recovered from them.

Climate plays an important role too in the preservation of organic remains. Occasionally the "local climate" of an environment, such as a cave, preserves finds. Caves are natural "conservatories" because their interiors are protected from outside climatic effects, and (in the case of limestone caves) their alkaline conditions permit excellent preservation. If undisturbed by floods or the trampling feet of animals and people, they can preserve bones and even such fragile remains as footprints.

More usually, however, it is the regional climate that is important. Tropical climates are the most destructive, with their combination of heavy rains, acid soils, warm temperatures, high humidity, erosion, and wealth of vegetation and insect life. Tropical rainforests can overwhelm a site remarkably quickly, with roots that dislodge masonry and tear buildings apart, while torrential downpours gradually destroy paint and plasterwork, and woodwork rots away completely. Archaeologists in southern Mexico, for example, constantly have to battle to keep back the jungle. On the other hand, jungle conditions can be positive, in that they hinder looters from easily reaching even more sites than they do already.

Temperate climates, as in much of Europe and North America, are not good, as a rule, for the preservation of organic materials; their relatively warm but variable temperatures and fluctuating rainfall combine to accelerate the processes of decay. In some circumstances, however, local conditions can counteract these processes. At the Roman fort of Vindolanda, near Hadrian's Wall in northern England, more than 1300 letters and documents, written in ink on wafer-thin sheets of birch and alderwood, have been found. The fragments, dating to about AD 100, have survived because of the soil's unusual chemical condition: clay compacted between layers in the site created oxygen-free pockets (the exclusion of oxygen is vital to the preservation of organic materials), while chemicals produced by bracken, bone, and other remains effectively made the land sterile in that locality, thus preventing disturbance by vegetation and other forms of life.

Natural disasters sometimes preserve sites, including organic remains, for the archaeologist. The most common are violent storms, such as the one that covered the coastal **Neolithic** village of Skara Brae, Orkney Islands, with sand; the mudslide that engulfed the prehistoric village of Ozette on America's Northwest Coast (see box on p. 59); or volcanic eruptions, such as that of Vesuvius, which buried and preserved Roman Pompeii under a blanket of ash. Another volcanic eruption, this time in El Salvador in about AD 595, deposited a thick and widespread layer of ash over a densely populated area of Maya settlement. Work here has uncovered a variety of organic remains at the site of Cerén, including palm and grass roofing, mats, baskets, stored grain, and even preserved agricultural furrows.

Apart from these special circumstances, the survival of organic materials is limited to cases involving extremes of moisture: that is, very dry, frozen, or waterlogged conditions.

Preservation of Organic Materials: Extreme Conditions
Dry Environments.   Great aridity or dryness prevents decay through the shortage of water, which ensures that many destructive micro-organisms are unable to flourish. Archaeologists first became aware of the phenomenon in Egypt (see Tutankhamun box, overleaf), where much of the Nile Valley has such a dry atmosphere that bodies of the Predynastic period (before 3000 BC) have survived intact, with skin, hair, and nails, without any artificial mummification or coffins – the corpses were simply placed in shallow graves in the sand. Rapid drying out, plus the draining qualities of the sand, produced such spectacular preservative effects that they probably suggested the practice of mummification to the later Egyptians of the Dynastic period.

The pueblo dwellers of the American Southwest (*c.* AD 700–1400) buried their dead in dry caves and rockshelters where, as in Egypt, natural desiccation took place: these are not therefore true, humanly created mummies, although they are often referred to as such. The bodies survive, sometimes wrapped in fur blankets or tanned skins, and in such good condition that it has been possible to study

Dry Preservation: The Tomb of Tutankhamun

The arid conditions that prevail in Egypt have helped preserve a wide range of ancient materials, ranging from numerous written documents on papyrus (made of the pith of a Nile water plant) to two full-size wooden boats buried beside the Great Pyramid at Giza. But the best-known and most spectacular array of objects was that discovered in 1922 by Howard Carter and Lord Carnarvon in the tomb at Thebes of the pharaoh Tutankhamun, dating to the 14th century BC.

Tutankhamun had a short reign and was relatively insignificant in Egyptian history, a fact reflected in his burial, a poor one by pharaonic standards. But within the small tomb, originally built for someone else, was a wealth of treasure. For Tutankhamun was buried with everything he might need in the next life. The entrance corridor and the four chambers were crammed with thousands of individual grave-goods. They include objects of precious metal, such as jewelry and the famous gold mask, and food and clothing. But wooden objects, such as statues, chests, shrines, and two of the three coffins, make up a large part of the tomb's contents.

The grave furniture was not all originally intended for Tutankhamun. Some of it had been made for other members of his family, and then

The outermost of Tutankhamun's three coffins was made of cypress wood, overlaid with gold foil.

hastily adopted when the young king died unexpectedly. There were also touching items, such as a chair the king had used as a child, and a simple reed stick mounted in gold labeled as "A reed which His Majesty cut with his own hand." Even wreaths and funerary bouquets had survived in the dry conditions, left on the second and third coffins by mourners.

A gilded ritual couch found remarkably well preserved among the contents of the tomb of Tutankhamun.

EGYPT
Thebes •

A cutaway view of the tomb and its treasures, as found in 1922.

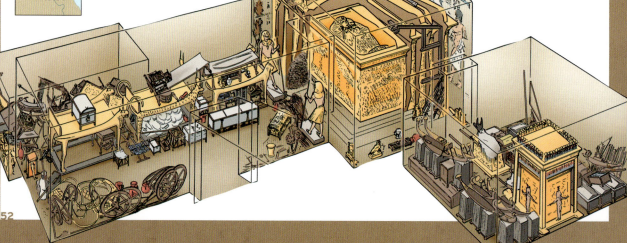

hair styles. Clothing (from fiber sandals to string aprons) also remains, together with a wide range of goods, such as basketry, feathered ornaments, and leather. Some far earlier sites in the same region also contain organic remains: Danger Cave, Utah (occupied from 9000 BC onward), yielded wooden arrows, trap springs, knife handles, and other wooden tools, while caves near Durango, Colorado, had preserved maize cobs, squashes, and sunflower and mustard seeds. Plant finds of this type have been crucial in helping to reconstruct ancient diet.

The coastal dwellers of central and southern Peru lived – and died – in a similarly dry environment, so that it is possible today to see the tattoos on their desiccated bodies, and admire the huge and dazzlingly colorful textiles from cemeteries at Ica and Nazca, as well as basketry and featherwork, and also maize cobs and other items of food. In Chile, the oldest deliberately made mummies have been found at Chinchorro, preserved again by the aridity of the desert environment.

A slightly different phenomenon occurred in the Aleutian Islands, off the west coast of Alaska, where the dead were kept and naturally preserved in volcanically warmed caves that were extremely dry. Here the islanders seem to have enhanced the natural desiccation by periodically drying the bodies by wiping or suspension over a fire; in some cases they removed the internal organs and placed dry grass in the cavity.

Cold Environments.   Natural refrigeration can hold the processes of decay in check for thousands of years. Perhaps the first frozen finds to be discovered were the numerous remains of mammoths encountered in the permafrost (permanently frozen soil) of Siberia, a few with their flesh, hair, and stomach contents intact. The unlucky creatures probably fell into crevices in snow, and were buried by silt in what became a giant deep-freeze. The best known are Beresovka, recovered in 1901, and baby Dima, found in 1977. Preservation can be still so good that dogs will eat the meat and they have to be kept well away from the carcasses.

The most famous frozen archaeological remains are those from the burial mounds of steppe nomads at Pazyryk in the Altai, southern Siberia, dating to the Iron Age, about 400 BC. They comprise pits dug deep into the ground, lined with logs, and covered with a low cairn of stones. They could only have been dug in the warm season, before the ground froze solid. Any warm air in the graves rose and deposited its moisture on the stones of the cairn; moisture also gradually infiltrated down into the burial chambers, and froze so hard there during the harsh winter that it never thawed during subsequent summers, since the cairns were poor conductors of heat and shielded the pits from the warming and drying effects of wind and sun. Consequently, even the most fragile materials have survived intact – despite the boiling water that had to be used by excavators to recover them.

Cold Preservation 1: The Iceman

The world's oldest fully preserved human body was found in September 1991 by German hikers near the Similaun glacier, in the Ötztaler Alps of South Tyrol. They spotted a human body, its skin yellowish-brown and desiccated, at an altitude of 3200 m (10,500 ft). The Iceman is the first prehistoric human ever found with his everyday clothing and equipment; other similarly intact bodies from prehistory have been either carefully buried or sacrificed.

The Iceman, the oldest fully preserved human, as found in 1991 (below right), emerging from the melting ice that had preserved him for more than 5000 years (below left).

The body was placed in a freezer in Austria, but subsequent investigation determined that the corpse – called Similaun Man, Ötzi, or simply the "Iceman" – had lain c. 90 m (300 ft) inside Italy, and he has been housed there, in a museum in Bolzano, since 1998. Fifteen radiocarbon dates have been obtained from the body, the artifacts, and the grass in the boots: they are all in rough agreement, averaging at 3300 BC.

It was initially thought the Iceman was overcome by exhaustion – perhaps caught in a fog or a blizzard. After death, he was dried out by a warm autumn wind, before becoming encased in ice. Since the body lay in a depression, it was protected from

the movement of the glacier above it for 5300 years, until a storm from the Sahara laid a layer of dust on the ice that absorbed sunlight and finally thawed it out.

He was a dark-skinned male, aged in his mid- to late 40s. Only about 1.56–1.6 m (5ft 2 in) tall, his size and stature fit well within the measurement ranges of Late Neolithic populations of Italy and Switzerland. Preliminary analysis of his DNA confirms his links to northern Europe.

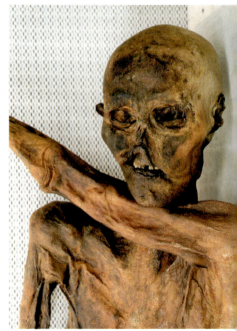

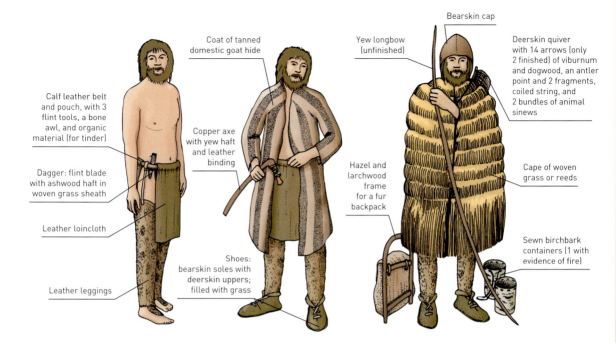

Bearskin cap

Coat of tanned domestic goat hide

Yew longbow (unfinished)

Deerskin quiver with 14 arrows (only 2 finished) of viburnum and dogwood, an antler point and 2 fragments, coiled string, and 2 bundles of animal sinews

Calf leather belt and pouch, with 3 flint tools, a bone awl, and organic material (for tinder)

Copper axe with yew haft and leather binding

Hazel and larchwood frame for a fur backpack

Cape of woven grass or reeds

Dagger: flint blade with ashwood haft in woven grass sheath

Leather loincloth

Sewn birchbark containers (1 with evidence of fire)

Leather leggings

Shoes: bearskin soles with deerskin uppers; filled with grass

The corpse currently weighs only about 54 kg (120 lb). His teeth are very worn, especially the front incisors, suggesting that he ate coarse ground grain, or that he regularly used them as a tool. When found he was bald, but hundreds of curly brownish-black human hairs, about 9 cm (3.5 in) long, were recovered from the vicinity of the body. These had fallen out after death, and it is possible he had a beard.

A body scan has shown that the brain, muscle tissues, lungs, heart, liver, and digestive organs are in excellent condition, though the lungs are blackened by smoke, probably from open fires, and he has hardening of the arteries and blood vessels. Traces of meat have been found in his colon (probably ibex and venison), along with wheat, plants, and plums.

Traces of chronic frostbite were noted in one little toe, and eight of his

ribs were fractured, though these had healed or were healing when he died.

Groups of tattoos, mostly short parallel vertical blue lines, were discovered on both sides of his lower spine, on his left calf and right ankle, his wrists, and he had a blue cross on his inner right knee. These marks, probably made with soot, may be therapeutic, aimed at relieving the arthritis that he had in his neck, lower back, and right hip.

His nails had dropped off, but one fingernail was recovered. Its analysis revealed not only that he undertook manual labor, but also that he experienced periods of reduced nail growth corresponding to episodes of serious illness – 4, 3, and 2 months before he died. The fact that he was prone to periodic crippling disease supported the view that he fell prey to adverse weather and froze to death.

The equipment and clothing of the Iceman are a virtual time-capsule of everyday life – more than 70 objects were found associated with him.

However, recent work has revealed what appears to be an arrowhead lodged in the Iceman's left shoulder, cuts on his hands, wrists, and ribcage, and a blow to the head – either from being struck or from falling – which is probably what killed him.

The items found with him constitute a unique "time-capsule" of everyday life. A great variety of woods and a range of sophisticated techniques of working with leather and grasses were used to create the collection of 70 objects, which add a new dimension to our knowledge of the period.

The Pazyryk bodies had been placed inside log coffins, with wooden pillows, and survived so well that their spectacular tattoos can still be seen. Clothing included linen shirts, decorated caftans, aprons, stockings, and headdresses of felt and leather. There were also rugs, wall-coverings, tables laden with food, and horse carcasses complete with elaborate bridles, saddles, and other trappings. A further well-preserved burial has been found in the region, containing a female accompanied by six horses, and grave-goods including a silver mirror and various wooden objects.

Similar standards of preservation have also been encountered in other regions, such as Greenland and Alaska. More southerly regions can produce the same effect at high altitude, for instance the Inca-period "mummies" found at a number of high-altitude sites in the Andes; or the 5300-year-old Iceman found preserved in the ice in the Alps near the border between Italy and Austria (see boxes on previous page and below).

Frozen conditions in southern Siberia helped to preserve many remarkable finds from the burial mounds of steppe nomads at Pazyryk, dating from about 400 BC, including this tattoo pattern on the torso and arms of a chieftain.

Cold Preservation 2: Mountain "Mummies"

Since the 1950s, sporadic discoveries have been made of frozen bodies high in the Andes mountains of South America – these finds have become known as mummies, even though they were preserved only by the cold, not by any process of artificial mummification. The Incas of the 15th–16th centuries AD built more than 100 ceremonial centers on many of the highest peaks in their empire, since they worshiped the snowcapped mountains, believing that they provided the water for irrigating their fields, and hence controlled fertility of crops and animals.

Among the offerings left for the mountain gods were food, alcoholic drinks, textiles, pottery ,and figurines – but also human sacrifices, often young children. In the 1990s, American archaeologist Johan Reinhard carried out a series of expeditions to high peaks in the Andes, and discovered some of the best-preserved ancient bodies ever found, thanks to this "extreme archaeology."

On the Ampato volcano, at 6312 m (20,708 ft), he found a bundle lying on the ice that contained an Inca girl – dubbed the "Ice Maiden" or "Juanita" – who had been ritually sacrificed (by a blow to the head) at the age of about 14, and buried with figurines, food, textiles, and pottery. The buried bodies of a boy and girl were later excavated at 5850 m (19,193 ft).

In 1999, on the peak of Llullaillaco – at 6739 m (22,109 ft) – he encountered a 7-year-old boy, and two girls of 15 and 6, all with figurines and textiles. So perfect is the preservation of all these bodies that detailed analyses can be carried out on their internal organs, their DNA, and their hair. For example, isotopes in the hair suggest that they chewed coca leaves, a common practice in the region even today.

The older, better-preserved Llullaillaco girl had neatly braided hair and wore a selection of ornaments.

Waterlogged Environments. A useful distinction in land archaeology (as opposed to archaeology beneath the sea) can be drawn between dryland and wetland sites. The great majority of sites are "dry" in the sense that moisture content is low and preservation of organic remains is poor. Wetland sites include all those found in lakes, swamps, marshes, fens, and peat bogs. In these situations organic materials are effectively sealed in a wet and airless environment that favors their preservation, as long as the waterlogging is more or less permanent up to the time of **excavation**. (If a wet site dries out, even only seasonally, decomposition of the organic materials can occur.)

It has been estimated that on a wet site often 75–90 percent, sometimes 100 percent, of the finds are organic. Little or none of this material, such as wood, leather, textiles, basketry, and plant remains of all kinds, would survive on most dryland sites. It is for this reason that archaeologists are turning their attention more and more to the rich sources of evidence about past human activities to be found on wet sites. Growing threats from drainage and peatcutting in the wetlands, which form only about 6 percent of the world's total land area, give this work an added urgency.

Wetlands vary a great deal in their preservative qualities. Acidic peat bogs preserve wood and plant remains, but may destroy bone, iron, and even pottery. The famous lake sites of the Alpine regions of Switzerland, Italy, France, and southern Germany, on the other hand, preserve most materials well. Sometimes other forces can help to preserve waterlogged remains, such as the mudslide that buried the Ozette site in Washington State (see box on p. 59).

Peat bogs, nearly all of which occur in northern latitudes, are some of the most important environments for wetland archaeology. The Somerset Levels in southern England, for example, have been the scene not only of excavations in the early 20th century to recover the well-preserved Iron Age lake villages of Glastonbury and Meare, but also of a much wider campaign in the last few decades that has unearthed numerous wooden trackways (including the world's "oldest road," a 6000-year-old 1.6-km (1-mile) stretch of track), and many details about early woodworking skills, and the ancient environment. On the continent of Europe, and in Ireland, peat bogs have likewise preserved many trackways – sometimes with evidence for the wooden carts that ran along them – and other fragile remains. Other types of European wetlands, such as coastal marshes, have yielded dugout logboats, paddles, even fish-nets and fish-weirs.

Bog bodies, however, are undoubtedly the best-known finds from the peat bogs of northwest Europe. Most of them date from the Iron Age. The degree of preservation varies widely, and depends on the particular conditions in which the corpses were deposited. Most individuals met a violent death and were probably either executed as criminals or killed as a sacrifice before being thrown into the bog. For example, in 2003 two partial Iron Age bodies were recovered from peat bogs in Ireland: Clonycavan Man had been killed with axe blows,

The surviving parts of Oldcroghan Man's body are superbly preserved, particularly his hands: the well-kept fingernails and absence of calluses suggest that he may have been an individual of relatively high status. Analysis of his stomach contents revealed a final meal of cereals and buttermilk.

and possibly disembowelled, while the huge (1.91 m (6 ft 3½ in) tall) Oldcroghan Man was stabbed, decapitated, and tied down to the bottom of a bog pool.

The best-preserved specimens, such as Denmark's Tollund Man, were in a truly remarkable state, with only the staining caused by bogwater and tannic acid as an indication that they were ancient rather than modern. Within the skin, the bones have often disappeared, as have most of the internal organs, although the stomach and its contents may survive. In Florida, prehistoric human brains have even been recovered.

Occasionally, waterlogged conditions can occur inside burial mounds. The oak-coffin burials of Bronze Age northern Europe, and most notably those of Denmark dating to about 1000 BC, had an inner core of stones packed round the tree-trunk coffin, with a round barrow built above. Water infiltrated the inside of the mound, and, by combining with tannin from the tree trunks, set up acidic conditions that destroyed the skeleton but preserved the skin (discolored like the bog bodies), hair, and ligaments of the bodies inside the coffins, as well as their clothing and such objects as birch-bark pails.

A somewhat similar phenomenon occurred with the ships that the Vikings used as coffins. The Oseberg ship in Norway, for example, held the body of a Viking queen of about AD 800, and was buried in clay, covered by a packing of stones and a layer of peat that sealed it in and ensured its preservation.

Lake-dwellings have rivaled bog bodies in popular interest ever since the discovery of wooden piles or house supports in Swiss lakes more than a century ago. The range of preserved material is astonishing, not simply wooden structures, artifacts, and textiles but, at Neolithic Charavines in France for example, even nuts, berries, and other fruits.

Wet Preservation: The Ozette Site

A special kind of waterlogging occurred at the Ozette site, Washington, on the US Northwest Coast. In about AD 1700, a huge mudslide buried part of a Makah Indian whale-hunting village. Ruins of huge cedar-plank houses lay protected by the mud for three centuries – but not forgotten, for the descendants kept the memory of their ancestors' home alive. Then the sea began to strip away the mud, and it seemed that the site might fall prey to looters. The Makah tribal chairman asked Washington State University archaeologist Richard Daugherty to excavate the site and salvage its remains. Clearing the mud with water pumped from the ocean and sprayed through hoses revealed a wealth of wood and fiber objects.

The houses, where several related families would have lived, were up to 21 m (68 ft 3 in) in length and 14 m (45 ft 6 in) wide. They had adzed and carved panels (with designs including wolves and thunderbirds), roof-support posts, and low partition walls. There were also hearths, sleeping platforms, storage boxes, mats, and baskets.

More than 55,000 artifacts – mostly wooden – were recovered. They had been preserved by the wet mud, which excluded oxygen. The most spectacular was a block of red cedar, a meter high, carved in the form of a whale's dorsal fin. Even leaves – still green – survived, together with many whale bones.

Field excavation and laboratory preservation continued non-stop for 11 years, an outstanding example of cooperation between archaeologists and indigenous people. Makah elders helped to identify artifacts; young Makah helped to excavate; and a museum now displays the results.

(Below left) A Makah Indian crew member measures a find in one of the Ozette houses.

(Below) A red cedar carving in the shape of a whale's dorsal fin, inlaid with 700 sea-otter teeth (some forming the shape of a thunderbird holding a serpent, which would stun the whale so that the thunderbird could pick it up in its claws).

Cleaning a basket holding a comb and a spindle whorl.

Ozette
UNITED STATES

Perhaps the greatest contribution to archaeology that lake-dwellings and other European wetland sites have made in recent years, however, is to provide abundant well-preserved timber for the study of tree-rings, the annual growth rings in trees, for dating purposes. In Chapter 4 we explore the breakthrough this has brought about in the establishment of an accurate tree-ring chronology for parts of northern Europe stretching back thousands of years.

Another rich source of waterlogged and preserved timbers can be found in the old waterfronts of towns and cities. Archaeologists have been particularly successful in uncovering parts of London's Roman and medieval waterfront, but such discoveries are not restricted to Europe. In the early 1980s archaeologists in New York excavated a well-preserved 18th-century ship that had been sunk to support the East River waterfront. Underwater archaeology itself is, not surprisingly, the richest source of all for waterlogged finds (see pp. 100–101).

The major archaeological problem with waterlogged finds, and particularly wood, is that they deteriorate rapidly when they are uncovered, beginning to dry and crack almost at once. They therefore need to be kept wet until they can be treated or freeze-dried at a laboratory. Conservation measures of this kind help to explain the enormous cost of both wetland and underwater archaeology. It has been estimated that "wet archaeology" costs four times as much as "dry archaeology." But the rewards, as we have seen above, are enormous.

The rewards in the future, too, will be very great. Florida, for example, has about 1.2 million ha (3 million acres) of peat deposits, and on present evidence these probably contain more organic artifacts than anywhere else in the world. So far the wetlands here have yielded the largest number of prehistoric watercraft from any one region, together with totems, masks, and figurines dating as far back as 5000 BC. In the Okeechobee Basin, for instance, a 1st-millennium BC burial platform has been found, decorated with a series of large carved wooden totem posts, representing an array of animals and birds. After a fire, the platform had collapsed into its pond. Yet it is only recently that wet finds in Florida have come to us from careful excavation rather than through the drainage that is destroying large areas of peat deposits and, with them, untold quantities of the richest kinds of archaeological evidence.

Study Questions

- What is the difference between an artifact and an ecofact?
- Why is it important for archaeologists to distinguish between cultural and natural formation processes?
- Why is the context of an artifact so very important to archaeologists?
- Why do inorganic materials survive better than organic materials?
- Why are archaeologists particularly interested in wet or waterlogged sites?
- What is experimental archaeology?

Summary

The archaeological evidence available to us depends on a number of important factors:

- What people, past and present, have done to it (cultural formation processes).

- What natural conditions, such as soil and climate, have preserved or destroyed (natural formation processes). Inorganic materials usually survive far better than organics, but the latter can be well preserved in a range of special environments – the dry, the cold, and the waterlogged.

- Our ability to find, recognize, recover, and conserve it.

- We can do nothing about the first two factors, being at the mercy of the elements and previous human behavior. But the third factor, which is the subject of this book, is constantly improving, as we understand better the processes of decay and destruction, and design research strategies and technical aids to make the most of what archaeological evidence actually survives.

Further Reading

Good introductions to the problems of differential preservation of archaeological materials can be found in:

Binford, L.R. 2002. *In Pursuit of the Past: Decoding the Archaeological Record*. University of California Press: Berkeley & London.

Coles, B. & J. 1989. *People of the Wetlands: Bogs, Bodies and Lake-Dwellers*. Thames & Hudson: London & New York.

Lillie, M.C. & Ellis, S. (eds). 2007. *Wetland Archaeology and Environments: Regional Issues, Global Perspectives*. Oxbow Books: Oxford.

Menotti, F. & O'Sullivan, M. 2012. *Oxford Handbook of Wetland Archaeology*. Oxford University Press: Oxford.

Schiffer, M.B. 2002. *Formation Processes of the Archaeological Record*. University of Utah Press: Salt Lake City.

Sheets, P.D. 2006. *The Ceren Site: An Ancient Village Buried by Volcanic Ash in Central America* (2nd ed.). Wadsworth: Stamford.

[See p. 345 for a list of useful websites]

Where?
Survey and excavation of sites and features

Locating Archaeological Sites and Features

- Ground Reconnaissance
- Aerial Survey
- Geographic Information Systems

Assessing the Layout of Sites and Features

- Site Surface Survey
- Subsurface Detection
- Ground-Based Remote Sensing

Excavation

- Stratigraphy
- Methods of Excavation
- Underwater Archaeology
- Recovery and Recording of the Evidence
- Processing and Classification

Study Questions
Summary
Further Reading

Traditionally, archaeologists are known for finding and excavating sites, but today, while **sites** and their **excavation** do remain of paramount importance, the focus has broadened. Archaeologists have become aware that there is a great range of "off-site" or "non-site" evidence, from scatters of **artifacts** to such **features** as plowmarks and field boundaries, that provides important information about the past. The study of entire landscapes by regional survey, for example, is now a major part of archaeological fieldwork.

It should also not be forgotten that suitable evidence for study often comes from new work at sites already the subject of fieldwork. Much potentially rich and rewarding material also lies locked away in museum and institution vaults, waiting to be analyzed by imaginative modern techniques. It is only recently, for example, that the plant remains discovered in Tutankhamun's tomb in the 1920s have received thorough analysis. Yet it remains true that the great majority of archaeological research is still dependent on the collection of new material by fresh fieldwork. The main way that archaeologists find this new material – in other words new sites and features – is by **reconnaissance survey**, either on the ground or from the air.

In the early days of **archaeology** the next step would have been to excavate. But when archaeologists excavate a site, digging through the layers of evidence, uncovering features and removing artifacts that may have been lying undisturbed for thousands of years, it is important to remember that this is essentially a destructive act – there is just one chance to record exactly what is found and the "experiment" can never be repeated. Excavation is also very expensive, but after the digging the excavators must be prepared to put considerable time, effort, and money into the conservation and storage of their finds, and into the interpretation and publication of their results. Non-destructive means of assessing the layout of sites and features, using, for example, site **surface survey** or **remote sensing** devices, have therefore taken on a new importance, often providing enough information for archaeologists to interpret features at a site, and making large-scale excavation unnecessary.

the search in the Near East for evidence of the places – as well as the people and events – described in the Old and New Testaments. Treated objectively as one possible source of information about Near Eastern sites, the Bible can be a rich source of documentary material, but there is certainly the danger that belief in the absolute religious truth of the texts can cloud an impartial assessment of their archaeological validity.

Much research in biblical archaeology involves attempting to link named biblical sites with archaeologically known ones. Place-name evidence, however, can also lead to actual discoveries of new archaeological sites. In southwest Europe, for example, many prehistoric stone tombs have been found thanks to old names printed on maps that incorporate local words for "stone" or "tomb."

Cultural Resource Management and "Applied Archaeology."   In this specialized work – discussed more fully in Chapter 12 – the archaeologist's role is to locate and record sites, in some cases before they are destroyed by new roads, buildings, or dams, or by peatcutting and drainage in wetlands.

In the USA a large number of sites are located and recorded in inventories every year under **Cultural Resource Management (CRM)** laws, which were considerably broadened and strengthened in the 1970s. Proper liaison with a developer should allow archaeological survey to take place in advance along the projected line of road or in the path of development. Important sites thus discovered may require excavation, and in some cases can even cause construction plans to be altered. Certain archaeological remains unearthed during the digging of subways in Rome and Mexico City, for instance, were incorporated into the final station architecture.

Reconnaissance Survey.   How does the archaeologist set about locating sites, other than through documentary sources and salvage work? A conventional and still valid method is to look for the most prominent remains in a landscape, particularly surviving remnants of walled buildings, and burial mounds, such as those in eastern North America or Wessex in southern Britain. But many sites are visible on the surface only as a scatter of artifacts and thus require more thorough survey – what we may call reconnaissance survey – to be detected.

Furthermore, in recent years, as archaeologists have become more interested in reconstructing the full human use of the landscape, they have begun to realize that there are very faint scatters of artifacts that might not qualify as sites, but that nevertheless represent significant human activity. Some scholars have therefore suggested that these "off-site" or "non-site" areas (that is, areas with a low density of artifacts) should be located and recorded, which can only be done by **systematic survey** work involving careful sampling procedures (see p. 69). This approach is particularly useful in areas where people leading a mobile way of life have left only a sparse archaeological record, as in much of Africa.

Reconnaissance survey has become important for another major reason: the growth of regional studies. Thanks to the pioneering researches of such scholars as Gordon Willey in the Virú Valley, Peru, and William T. Sanders in the Basin of Mexico, archaeologists increasingly seek to study settlement patterns – the distribution of sites across the landscape within a given region. The significance of such work for the understanding of past societies is discussed further in Chapter 5. Here we may note its impact on archaeological fieldwork: it is rarely enough now simply to locate an individual site and then to survey it and/or excavate it in isolation from other sites. Whole regions need to be explored, involving a program of reconnaissance survey.

In the last few decades, reconnaissance survey has developed from being simply a preliminary stage in fieldwork (looking for appropriate sites to excavate) to a more or less independent kind of inquiry, an area of research in its own right that can produce information quite different from that achieved by digging. In some cases excavation may not take place at all, perhaps because permission to dig was not forthcoming, or because of a lack of time or funds – modern excavation is slow and costly, whereas survey is cheap, quick, relatively non-destructive, and requires only maps, compasses, and tapes. Usually, however, archaeologists deliberately choose a surface approach as a source of regional data in order to investigate specific questions that interest them and that excavation could not answer.

Reconnaissance survey encompasses a broad range of techniques: no longer just the identification of sites and the recording or collection of surface artifacts, but sometimes also the sampling of natural and mineral resources, such as stone and clay. Much survey today is aimed at studying the spatial distribution of human activities, variations between regions, changes in population through time, and relationships between people, land, and resources.

Reconnaissance Survey in Practice.   For questions formulated in regional terms, it is necessary to collect data on a regional scale, but in a way that provides a maximum of information for a minimum of cost and effort. First, the region to be surveyed needs to be defined: its boundaries may be either natural (such as a valley or island), cultural (such as the extent of an artifact **style**), or purely arbitrary, though natural boundaries are the easiest to establish.

The area's history of development needs to be examined, not only to familiarize oneself with previous archaeological work and with the local materials but also to assess the extent to which surface material may have been covered or removed by natural processes. There is little point, for example, in searching for prehistoric material in sediments only recently laid down by river action. Other factors may have affected surface evidence as well. In much of Africa, for example, great animal herds or burrowing animals will often have disturbed surface material, so that the archaeologist may be able to examine only very broad distribution patterns. Geologists and environmental specialists can generally provide useful advice.

This background information will help determine the intensity of surface coverage of the survey. Other factors to take into consideration are the time and resources available, and how easy it is actually to reach and record an area. Arid (dry) and semi-arid environments with little vegetation are among the best for this type of work, whereas in equatorial rainforest, survey may be limited to soil exposures along river banks, unless time and labor permit the cutting of trails. Many regions, of course, contain a variety of landscapes, and more than one strategy for survey is often needed. Moreover, it must be remembered that some archaeological phases (with easily distinguishable artifacts or pottery styles, for example) are more "visible" than others, and that mobile **hunter-gatherer** or pastoral communities leave a very different – and generally sparser – imprint on the landscape than do agricultural or urban communities. All these factors must be taken into account when planning the search patterns and recovery techniques.

There are two basic kinds of reconnaissance survey: the unsystematic and the systematic. The former is the simpler, involving walking across each part of the area (for example, each plowed field), scanning a strip of ground, collecting or examining artifacts on the surface, and recording their location together with that of any surface features. It is generally felt, however, that the results may be biased and misleading. Walkers have an inherent desire to find material, and will therefore tend to concentrate on those areas that seem richer, rather than obtaining a sample representative of the whole area that would enable the archaeologist to assess the varying distribution of material of different periods or **types**. On the other hand, the method is flexible, enabling the team to focus greater efforts on the areas that have proved most likely to contain sites or finds.

Much modern survey is done in a systematic way, employing either a grid system or a series of equally spaced transects (straight paths) across the area. The area to be searched is divided into sectors, and these are walked systematically. Because of the constraints of time and money, it is often not possible to survey the entirety of an area in this way, so archaeologists have to employ a sampling strategy (see box opposite) where only certain sectors or transects are picked to be searched. Systematic survey also makes it easier to plot the location of finds since an exact position is always known.

For example, from 1992 to 1998 the Sydney Cyprus Survey Project, led by Bernard Knapp and Michael Given of the University of Glasgow, undertook an intensive archaeological survey in a 75-sq. km (29-sq. mile) area in the northern Troodos Mountains of Cyprus. This is an area famed for its copper sulphide ore deposits, exploited as early as the Bronze Age. The project examined the human transformation of the landscape over a period of 5000 years and placed it in its regional context. A first requirement for the systematic intensive survey strategy

Sampling Strategies

Archaeologists cannot usually afford the time and money necessary to investigate the whole of a large site or all sites in a given region, so they need to sample the area being researched. In a ground reconnaissance survey this will involve using one of the methods described below to choose a number of smaller areas to be searched, with the objective being to draw reliable conclusions about the whole area.

The way archaeologists use sampling is similar to the way it is employed in public opinion polls, which make generalizations about the opinions of millions of people using samples of just a few thousand. Surprisingly often the polls are more or less right. This is because the structure of sampled populations is well known – for example, we know their ages and occupations. We have much less background information to work with in archaeology, so must be more careful when we extrapolate generalizations from a sample. But as with opinion polls, in archaeological work the larger and better designed the sample, the more likely the results are to be valid.

Some sites in a given region, however, may be more accessible than others, or more prominent in the landscape, which may prompt a more informal sampling strategy. Long years of experience in the field will also give some archaeologists an intuitive "feel" for the right places to undertake work.

Types of Sampling

The simplest form is a simple random sample, where the areas to be sampled are chosen using a table of random numbers. However, the nature of random numbers results in some areas being allotted clusters of squares, while others remain untouched – the sample is, therefore, inherently biased.

One answer is the stratified random sample, where the region or site is divided into its natural zones (strata, hence the technique's name), such as cultivated land and forest, and squares are then chosen by the same random-number procedure, except that each zone has the number of squares proportional to its area. Thus, if forest comprises 85 percent of the area, it must be allotted 85 percent of the squares.

Another solution, systematic sampling, entails the selection of a grid of equally spaced locations – e.g. choosing every other square. By adopting such a regular spacing one runs the risk of missing (or hitting) every single example in an equally regular pattern of distribution – this is another source of potential bias.

A more satisfactory method is to use a stratified unaligned systematic sample, which combines the main elements from the other techniques. In collecting artifacts from the surface of a large tell or mound site at Giriki-i-Haciyan in Turkey, Charles Redman and Patty Jo Watson used a grid of 5-m squares, but orientated it along the site's main N-S/E-W axes, and the samples were selected with reference to these axes. The strata chosen were blocks of 9 squares (3 x 3), and one square in each block was picked for excavation by selecting its N-S/E-W coordinates randomly.

Transects vs Squares

In large-scale surveys, transects (straight paths) are sometimes preferable to squares, particularly in areas of dense vegetation, such as tropical rainforest. It is far easier to walk along a path than to locate accurately and investigate a square. In addition, transects can easily be segmented into units, whereas it may be difficult to locate or describe a specific part of a square; and transects are useful not merely for finding sites but also for recording artifact densities across the landscape. On the other hand, squares have the advantage of exposing more area to the survey, thus increasing the probability of intersecting sites. A combination of the two methods is often best: using transects to cover long distances, but squares when larger concentrations of material are encountered.

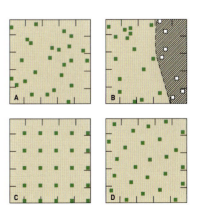

Types of sampling: (A) simple random; (B) stratified random; (C) systematic; (D) stratified unaligned systematic.

Systematic surface survey in the Egyptian desert: using GPS, archaeologists sample small areas spaced 100 m (330 ft) apart, looking for Middle Paleolithic stone tools. Finds are then processed in the field using electronic calipers and handheld computers.

was good maps. Enlarged aerial photographs were used to create a base map of the entire survey region. The main survey approach was a transect survey with the aim of obtaining a broad systematic sample of the area; areas with extensive evidence of early industrial, agricultural, or settlement activities, and locales with high densities of artifacts were investigated more closely. It took the team around 6 years to survey just 10 percent of the area. The survey identified 11 Special Interest Areas and 142 Places of Special Interest, which were investigated. The count in the field totalled 87,600 sherds of pottery, 8111 tile fragments, and 3092 lithics. About one third of these were collected and analyzed and entered into the project's database.

Results tend to be more reliable from long-term projects that cover a region repeatedly, since the visibility of sites and artifacts can vary widely from year to year or even with the seasons, thanks to vegetation and changing land-use. In addition, members of field crews inevitably differ in the accuracy of their observations, and in their ability to recognize and describe sites (the more carefully we look, and the more experience we have, the more we see); this factor can never be totally eliminated, but repeated coverage can help to counter its effects. The use of standardized recording forms makes it easy to put the data into a computer at a later stage; alternatively, handheld computers can be used in the field.

Finally, it may be necessary or desirable to carry out small excavations to supplement or check the surface data (particularly for questions of chronology, contemporaneity, or site function), or to test hypotheses that have arisen from the survey. The two types of investigation are complementary, not mutually exclusive. Their major difference can be summarized as follows: excavation tells us a lot about a little of a site, and can only be done once, whereas survey tells us a little about a lot of sites, and can be repeated.

Extensive and Intensive Survey.   Surveys can be made more extensive by combining results from a series of individual projects in neighboring regions to produce very large-scale views of change in landscape, land-use, and settlement through time – though, as with individual members of a field crew, the accuracy and quality of different survey projects may vary widely. Alternatively survey can be made more intensive by aiming at total coverage of a single large site or site-cluster. It is a paradox that some of the world's greatest and most famous archaeological sites have never, or only recently, been studied in this way, since attention has traditionally focused on the grander monuments rather than on any attempt to place them within even a local context. At Teotihuacan, near Mexico City, a major mapping project initiated in the 1960s has added hugely to our knowledge of the area around the great pyramid-temples (see pp. 84–85).

Ground reconnaissance survey has a vital place in archaeological work, and one that continues to grow in importance. In modern projects, however, it is usually supplemented (and often preceded) by reconnaissance from the air, one of the most important advances made by archaeology in the 20th century. In fact, the availability of air photographs can be an important factor in selecting and delineating an area for ground reconnaissance.

Aerial Survey

Archaeological survey using airborne or spaceborne remote sensing can be divided into two component parts: data collecting, which comprises taking photographs or images from aircraft or satellites; and data analysis, in which such images are analyzed, interpreted, and (often) integrated with other evidence from field survey, ground-based remote sensing, or documentary evidence. From the viewpoint of the photo interpreter or image analyst there is little difference between satellite images, multispectral/hyperspectral data, and traditional air photographs other than that of scale and resolution. The source itself is irrelevant and these data will collectively be referred to as "aerial images."

Millions of aerial images have already been taken: some of these are available for consultation in specialist libraries, and a lesser quantity is freely available online. Most result from "area survey" in which aerial images are taken in overlapping series to cover predefined areas, and a small number are taken each year by archaeologists who undertake prospective surveys using a light aircraft. It must be stressed that aerial images, even those resulting from prospective survey, are used for a wide range of archaeological purposes, from the discovery and recording of sites, to monitoring changes in them through time, photographing buildings, urban (and other) development – and, in fact, recording almost anything that "may not be there tomorrow." Nevertheless, the taking and analysis of aerial images from aircraft or satellite have led to a large number of archaeological discoveries, and the tally grows every year.

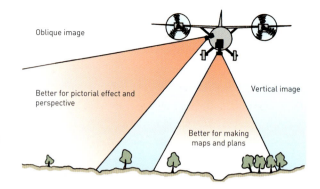

Oblique image

Better for pictorial effect and perspective

Vertical image

Better for making maps and plans

(Top) Aerial photographs are of two types: oblique and vertical. Obliques are easier to view and understand than verticals but may present more difficulty to the interpreter, who must transform the information to plan views.

(Above) An oblique aerial photograph of Newark earthworks, Ohio. An octagon and circle joined by a small strip of land are clearly visible, as are the small mounds just inside the octagon's corners.

How Are Aerial Images Used? Images taken from the air are merely tools; they are means to an end. Images do not themselves reveal sites – it is the image taker and the interpreter who do so, by examination of the terrain and the pictures. These are specialized skills. Long experience and a keen eye are needed to differentiate archaeological traces from other features, such as vehicle tracks, old river beds, and canals. Indeed, most military intelligence units during the final years of World War II had archaeologists on their staff as interpreters of air photographs.

Aerial images are of two types: oblique and vertical. Each has its advantages and drawbacks, but oblique images have usually been taken of sites observed from the air by an archaeologist and thought to be of archaeological significance, whereas most vertical images result from non-archaeological surveys (for instance, cartographic). Both types can be used to provide overlapping stereoscopic pairs of prints that enable a scene to be examined in three dimensions and so add confidence to any interpretation. Stereoscopic pictures taken of the ancient city of Mohenjodaro in Pakistan from a tethered balloon, for example, have enabled photogrammetric – accurately contoured – plans to be made of its surviving structures. Similarly, large areas can be surveyed with overlapping images, which are then processed into a very accurate photogrammetric base map of all the archaeological evidence identified from the air. Analytical ground survey can then proceed on a much surer basis.

Oblique images are often targeted on archaeological features that may show clearly, while vertical images may need to be more thoroughly examined by an interpreter seeking such information. Both types of image can be rectified or georeferenced using computer programs. This removes the scale and perspective distortions of oblique images and can correct for tilt and distortion in vertical views. After computer transformation the resulting image may be layered in graphics software or a **GIS** (**Geographic Information Systems** – see pp. 80–81) and interpreted by overdrawing the archaeological features that have been identified.

Mapping of individual sites from aerial photographs is often necessary in "applied archaeology" (see pp. 324–27) and also forms the beginning from which landscapes may be mapped and considered. For example, although it was known that prehistoric roadways existed within Chaco Canyon in the American Southwest, it was only when a major aerial reconnaissance project was undertaken by the National Park Service in the 1970s that the full extent of the system of roads was appreciated. Using the extensive coverage provided by the aerial images, a whole network of prehistoric roadways was identified and mapped. This was followed by selective ground surveys and some archaeological investigation. From the aerial coverage it has been estimated that the network, thought to date to the 11th and 12th centuries AD, extends some 2400 km (1500 miles), though of this only 208 km (130 miles) have been verified by examination at ground level.

Identifying Archaeological Sites From Above.

Successful identification of archaeological sites on aerial images requires knowledge of the types of feature that we may expect to be visible and of post-depositional (formation) processes that may have affected them since their abandonment. In general, for a site to be detected by any remote sensing method, it needs to have altered the soil or subsoil. These alterations can vary between holes cut into the ground (such as ditches and pits) and features placed upon it (such as banks, mounds, and walls), and these may now survive in relief – i.e. as lumps and bumps on the surface – or be completely buried under leveled cultivated land.

It is important to remember that similar holes and bumps may have been caused by natural disturbances or from recent human activity (leveling field boundaries or digging small quarries, for example), and an experienced image analyst should be able to identify these, and distinguish them from archaeological features, in an area with which they are familiar.

Aerial images record relief sites through a combination of highlight and shadow, so the time of day and season of the year are important factors in creating the most informative image of such sites. It may be necessary to obtain images taken at different times to maximize the information visible through light and shade (although to aid interpretation such new techniques as **LIDAR** (or ALS) allow a viewer to move the position of the sun at will; see pp. 75–76).

In some parts of the world, archaeological sites have been leveled and now lie in arable land. Although these sites have suffered a degree of destruction (and many continue to be destroyed by annual cultivation), these landscapes can be rewarding when examined on aerial images. In summer months, crops may grow differently above different soils and above different depths of soil and can thus indicate the presence of archaeological and natural features. These crop

How crop-marks are formed: crops grow taller and more thickly over sunken features, such as ditches (1), and show stunted growth over buried walls (2). Such variations may not be obvious at ground level, but are often visible from the air, as different-colored bands of vegetation.

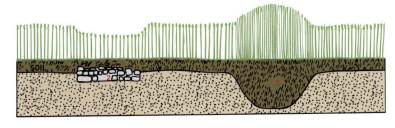

Features in relief on the left of this photograph show the remains of a Romano-British farm at Holbeach in the East Anglian fens of England. Ditches were cut to form field and other property boundaries, flank tracks, and drain the land. These features continue into the field on the right, where they have been filled and are now under a level field growing cereal. The track that runs across the upper part of the left field can be seen to the right, marked by a darker band where crop growth has been boosted by the deeper soil that fills the former ditch. Silted channels of former watercourses show as broad light-toned bands where the crop is growing sparsely in poorer soil. These differences illustrate how changes in crop growth can mark subsurface features.

differences, sometimes called crop-marks, have been the main way in which aerial survey has recorded the presence of archaeological features; indeed, more features have been discovered via crop-marks than with any other form of prospection.

Recent Developments. New technology is having an impact on aerial survey in different ways. Although the majority of existing images have been taken on film – black and white, color, or false color infrared – in the last few years digital sensors have become sufficiently good to be used in precision vertical cameras and the handheld cameras used by airborne archaeologists. For the latter, cameras taking images of sizes greater than 10 megapixels provide more than adequate resolution for most archaeological purposes. Modern flying, be this to capture a series of parallel overlapping strips of vertical photographs or to examine a chosen area by an archaeologist, is usually planned and recorded to take advantage of GPS (Global Positioning System) navigation.

The application of digital image analysis is still in its infancy. Just as in excavation and aerial survey, remote sensing research must be well planned and well executed, using a comprehensive methodology. Computerized image analysis may assist archaeological prospection to a limited degree, but will never lead to a fully automatic procedure, since data manipulation will vary greatly depending on the type of data, moment of image acquisition, atmospheric conditions, type of landscape, site characteristics, and the overall research goals of the project at hand. Field observations, archaeological interpretation, and human expertise remain indispensable.

LIDAR and SLAR. Use of LIDAR (Light Detection and Ranging) – also known as ALS (Airborne Laser Scanning) – has proved extremely valuable in the past few years. This technique uses an aircraft, whose exact position is known through use of GPS, carrying a laser scanner that rapidly pulses a series of beams to the ground. By measuring the time taken for these to return to the aircraft an accurate picture of the ground in the form of a digital elevation model (or digital surface model) is created. Software used with LIDAR provides archaeologists with two great advantages over conventional aerial photography: tree canopies can be eliminated by switching off the "first return," so the sensor can see into woodland; and the angle and azimuth of the sun can be moved to enable ground features to be viewed under optimal (and sometimes naturally impossible) lighting. Both facilities have been used to advantage in England where new sites – mostly enlargements to field systems – have been found, and locational corrections made to the existing record of the landscape around Stonehenge.

An excellent example of the practical application of LIDAR to an archaeological site comes from Caracol, a Maya city in Belize that flourished between AD 550 and 900. Arlen and Diane Chase of the University of Central Florida have been excavating at this site for more than 25 years, and during that time, despite the dense tropical forest, had managed to map 23 sq. km (9 sq. miles) of settlement. However, survey from the air enabled them within a few weeks to surpass the results of those 25 years, by covering a far larger area and discovering that the city actually extended over 177 sq. km (68 sq. miles). Images taken at the end of the dry season in 2009 took about 4 days (24 hours of flight time) to capture, the small aircraft passing back and forth over the city,

LIDAR in operation: the Iron Age hillfort of Welshbury in the Forest of Dean, England, is almost invisible in conventional aerial photographs (left). The initial LIDAR image shows little improvement (center) but once reflections from leaves and trees (the "first return") have been filtered out using a software algorithm the earthworks are clearly visible (right).

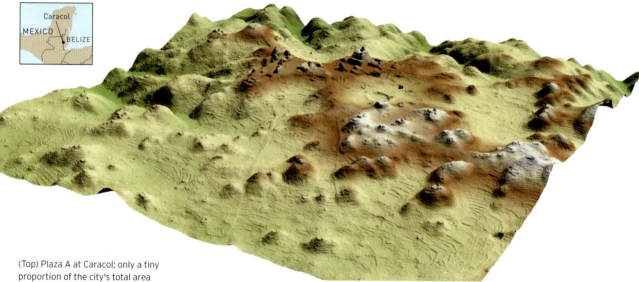

(Top) Plaza A at Caracol; only a tiny proportion of the city's total area has been cleared of jungle. (Above) A 3D projection of the Caracol LIDAR survey, showing the features beneath the jungle canopy; agricultural terraces show up as ripples in valleys and hillsides.

and making more than 4 billion measurements of the landscape below. This was then followed by 3 weeks of analysis by remote sensing experts.

Caracol's entire landscape can now be viewed in 3D, which has led to the discovery of new ruins, agricultural terraces, and stone causeways leading to more distant settlements. This was the first application of LIDAR to such a large archaeological site, and it is clear that the technique will radically transform research on sites in challenging environments of this kind. However, just as only excavation can verify the findings of ground-based remote sensing, so the data produced from the air at Caracol will need to be confirmed on the ground.

Another remote sensing technique, Sideways-Looking Airborne Radar (SLAR), has yielded evidence suggesting that Maya agriculture was more intensive than previously imagined. The technique involves recording in radar images the return of pulses of electromagnetic radiation sent out from a flying aircraft. Since radar will penetrate cloud cover and to some extent dense rainforest, Richard Adams and his colleagues were able to use SLAR from a high-flying NASA aircraft to scan 80,000 sq. km (31,200 sq. miles) of the Maya lowlands. The SLAR images revealed not only ancient cities and field systems, but also an enormous lattice of gray lines, some of which may have been canals, to judge by subsequent inspections by canoe. If field testing reveals that the canals are ancient, it will show that the Maya had an elaborate irrigation and water transport system.

Satellite Imagery and Google Earth. It is now routine to access Google Earth and use the high-resolution air photos and satellite cover there, or to buy copies of them. The high-resolution images available from the Ikonos (about 1 m resolution), QuickBird (60 cm), and GeoEye (40 cm) satellites offer data comparable with aerial photographs, while Google Earth has basic world cover from NASA's LANDSAT series (28.5 m) but includes blocks of Ikonos, QuickBird, and GeoEye images, some other satellite imagery, and some conventional aerial photographs. The data can be imported into remote sensing image-processing software, as well as into GIS packages for analysis.

The introduction of Google Earth has been a true "aerial revolution," since it offers every archaeologist the opportunity to examine the ground and look for archaeological sites – for example, it is being used by paleontologists in Africa to hunt for fossils, and in 2008 it revealed 500 new caves in South Africa, including the one that yielded the bones of *Australopithecus sediba* (see p. 134); and hundreds of new archaeological sites in Afghanistan are also being discovered by this method. But the same "rules" of visibility apply to those images as they do to conventional aerial photos, and absence of evidence on one particular date is

Two satellite images of the Urartian citadel of Erebuni, near Yerevan, Armenia, founded in 782 BC: on the left, with resolution of about 2 m (10 ft) is an image from the American CORONA series taken in 1971; on the right is a higher resolution screen shot from Google Earth of a QuickBird image taken in 2006. Both images are displayed with south to the top so that shadows assist photo-reading of topography and structures.

not evidence of absence. Most users have never been trained to interpret such images and many expect sites to be visible at all times.

QuickBird and Ikonos/GeoEye images can be taken to order, although the minimum cost may be high for some archaeological projects. Libraries of older images are lower in price. In parts of the world where maps are still regarded as secret or do not exist, an up-to-date satellite image may be the only way to provide a "base map" for archaeological investigations.

Much use has been made of the Cold War CORONA satellite photographs (at best about 2 m resolution), and these too provide a useful base map and allow provisional interpretation of sites that can later be checked by fieldwork – for example, CORONA images have led to the detection and detailed mapping of numerous kinds of archaeological remains, such as ancient roads, ruins, irrigation networks, and so forth.

(Below) CORONA photograph (with false color added) of radial trackways around Tell Brak, northeastern Syria, dating from around 2600 to 2000 BC. (Bottom) Thousands of miles of trackways in the region have been mapped by Jason Ur using a GIS database. The area shown below is about 80 km (50 miles) wide. Tell Brak is at center right, north of the Khabur River.

Jason Ur of Harvard University has used CORONA imagery to examine linear trackways ("hollow ways") across northern Mesopotamia (Syria, Turkey, and Iraq). These broad and shallow features were formed over time as people walked between settlements, and from settlements to fields and pasture. Because depressed features collect moisture and vegetation, they are easily visible on CORONA images. Some 6025 km (3750 miles) of premodern features have been identified, primarily dating to a phase of Bronze Age urban expansion from around 2600 to 2000 BC. Most commonly, trackways radiated out 2–5 km (1–3 miles) from sites, in a spoke-like pattern. Although there were several major centers, all movement was done by moving from place to place; no direct tracks existed between the major centers. From that we can deduce that political centralization and authority was probably weak.

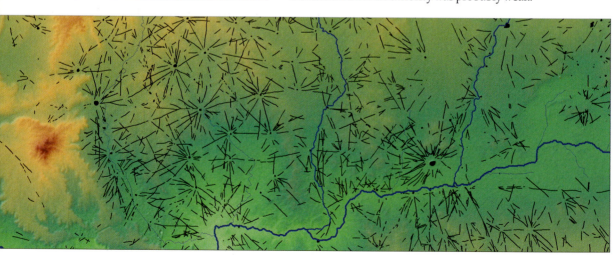

Key Concepts
Locating Sites Using Aerial Survey

- *Aerial Photography*: aerial photographs can be either oblique (better for pictorial effect and perspective) or vertical (better for maps and plans). Features visible from the air are classed as either earthworks, soil-marks, or crop-marks

- *LIDAR*: a new laser-scanning technique that can accurately map whole landscapes, even beneath tree cover. Resulting digital plans can be manipulated to reveal such subtle features as the remains of ancient field systems

- *Satellite Photography*: useful primarily at the largest scales, for example mapping very large sites or tracing ancient irrigation systems

Other Satellite Techniques. Another recent addition to the archaeologist's arsenal is SAR (Synthetic Aperture Radar), in which multiple radar images (usually taken from space, but also from aircraft) are processed to yield extremely detailed high-resolution results that can provide data for maps, databases, land-use studies, and so forth. SAR records height information and can provide terrain models of territory being surveyed. One of its many advantages is that, unlike conventional aerial photography, it provides results day or night and regardless of weather conditions. It can be used with multispectral data from satellites to make inventories of archaeological sites in a survey area – a rapid, non-destructive alternative to surface survey that does not involve the collection of artifacts and can thus save a great deal of time and effort in some circumstances.

The international Greater Angkor Project has found that the vast ruins of the 1000-year-old temple complex of Angkor in northern Cambodia may cover an area of up to 3000 sq. km (11,500 sq. miles). The ruins, shrouded in dense jungle and surrounded by landmines, have been the subject of studies using high-resolution SAR imagery obtained from NASA satellites. The resulting dark squares and rectangles on the images are stone moats and reflecting pools around the temples. The most important discovery for archaeologists so far has been the network of ancient canals surrounding the city (visible as light lines) that irrigated rice fields and fed the pools and moats. They were probably also used to transport the massive stones needed for constructing the complex.

ASTER (Advanced Spaceborne Thermal Emission and Reflection Radiometer) is an imaging instrument that flies on Terra, a satellite launched in 1999 as part of NASA's Earth Observing System (EOS), and is used to obtain detailed maps of land surface temperature, reflectance, and elevation.

Satellite remote sensing projects carried out by those with backgrounds in both remote sensing and archaeology have much to offer, but satellite

A satellite image of the huge ancient site of Angkor in Cambodia.

archaeology should not be regarded as a substitute for archaeological excavation or survey work. It is just one among a number of tools that archaeologists may want to employ in their research. Besides revealing the presence of (sub-) surface archaeological features (even in areas previously surveyed), satellite remote sensing can place archaeological sites in a much larger context, showing past social landscapes in all their complexity and helping greatly with quality assessment. Analysis of satellite imagery may further aid in determining where to excavate and may precede archaeological survey. Archaeologists will therefore need to rethink their surveying and excavation strategies in light of this new information, especially as image resolution continues to increase.

Geographic Information Systems

The standard approach to archaeological mapping is now the use of GIS (Geographic Information Systems), described in one official report as "the biggest step forward in the handling of geographic information since the invention of the map." GIS is a collection of computer hardware and software and of geographic data, designed to obtain, store, manage, manipulate, analyze and display a wide range of spatial information. A GIS combines a database with powerful digital mapping tools. GIS developed out of computer-aided design and computer-aided mapping (CAD/CAM) programs during the 1970s. Some CAD programs, such as AutoCAD, can be linked to commercial databases and have proved valuable in allowing the automatic mapping of archaeological sites held in a computer database. A true GIS, however, also incorporates the ability to carry out a statistical analysis of site distribution, and to generate new information.

A GIS may include an enormous amount of topographical and environmental data on relief, communications, hydrology, etc. To make the information easier to handle, it can be divided into different layers, each representing a single variable (see the illustration, left). Archaeological data may themselves be split into several layers, often so that each layer represents a discrete time-slice. As long as they can be spatially located, many different types of data can be integrated, including site plans, satellite images, aerial photographs, geophysical survey, as well as maps. A good example of many different types of data being incorporated into a GIS is the Giza Plateau Mapping Project in Egypt (see box overleaf).

The ability to incorporate aerial imagery can be particularly valuable for site reconnaissance, as it can provide detailed and current land-use information. Many topographic data already exist in the form of digital maps that can be taken directly into a GIS. Knowing exact ground coordinates is essential in archaeological practice for mapping purposes and learning about distribution patterns. This is done by means of a handheld GPS (Global Positioning System), which allows archaeologists to map their ground position (in some cases within as little as 3 cm) by connecting to a global satellite system. A minimum of four satellites has to be communicating with the GPS to provide close X and Y data,

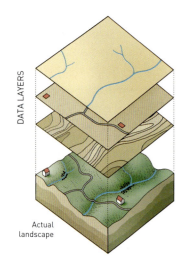

Diagram showing possible GIS data layers: from top to bottom, drainage, human activity, and relief.

DATA LAYERS

Actual landscape

which can display the received information in longitude/latitude (degrees minutes seconds), or to a UTM (Universal Transverse Mercator) coordinate system that provides data in eastings and northings. These data are extremely useful where a region is unmapped, or where the maps are old or inaccurate.

Once the basic outlines of a site have been mapped with reasonable accuracy by means of the GPS, and control points placed around the site, standard practice is to use a **total station** to record its more detailed features to a greater degree of accuracy. This instrument is an electronic theodolite integrated with an electronic distance meter, used to read distances to a particular point. Angles and distances are measured from the total station to points under survey and the coordinates (X, Y, Z, or northing, easting, and elevation) of the surveyed points relative to the total station positions are calculated. These data can then be downloaded from the total station to a computer to generate a map of the surveyed area. All the information is recorded and then submitted as GIS data to the client or sponsoring organization of the work as a matter of course.

Once data are stored within a GIS it is relatively straightforward to generate maps on demand, and to query the database to select particular categories of site to be displayed. Individual map layers, or combinations of layers, can be selected according to the subject under investigation.

One of the earliest, and most widespread, uses of GIS within archaeology has been the construction of predictive models of site locations. Most of the development of these techniques has taken place within North American archaeology, where the enormous spatial extent of some archaeological landscapes means that it is not always possible to survey them comprehensively. The underlying premise of all predictive models is that particular kinds of archaeological sites tend to occur in the same kinds of place. For example, certain settlement sites tend to occur close to sources of fresh water and on southerly aspects, because these provide ideal conditions in which humans can live (not too cold, and within easy walking distance of a water source). Using this information it is possible to model how likely a given location is to contain an archaeological site from the known environmental characteristics of that location. In a GIS environment this operation can be done for an entire landscape, producing a predictive model map for the whole area.

An example was developed by the Illinois State Museum for the Shawnee National Forest in southern Illinois. It predicts the likelihood of finding a prehistoric site anywhere within the 91 sq. km (35 sq. miles) of the forest by using the observed characteristics of the 68 sites that are known from the 12 sq. km (4.6 sq. miles) that have been surveyed. A GIS database was constructed for the entire area and the characteristics of the known sites were compared with the characteristics of the locations known not to contain sites. This resulted in a model that can be used to predict the likelihood that any location with known environmental characteristics will contain a prehistoric site.

Survey and Excavation on the Giza Plateau

For more than two decades American Egyptologist Mark Lehner has been systematically exploring Egypt's Giza Plateau in an effort to find the settlements that housed the workforce that built the pyramids. To the south of the Great Sphinx, 4500-year-old paved streets have been uncovered, as well as various buildings, from barracks to bakeries. The Giza Plateau Mapping Project (GPMP) has so far exposed about 10.5 ha (26 acres) of what seems to be a vast urban center attached to the pyramids, sometimes known as "The Lost City of the Pyramid Builders."

Directed by Camilla Mazzucato and Rebekah Miracle, GIS is being used to integrate all the project's drawings, thousands of digital photographs, notebooks, forms, and artifacts into a single organized data store. This enables the team to map patterns of architecture, burials, artifacts, and other materials, such as foodstuffs: for example, it has been found that the people in the bigger houses ate the best meat (beef) and fish (perch), while the others ate more pig and goat. Color-coded graphs and charts can be produced, representing the densities and distributions of various artifact types in different areas, buildings, rooms or even features.

The Giza Plateau Mapping Project (left) began with an extremely accurate survey of the cultural and natural features of the entire area. The survey grid is centered on the Great Pyramid.

Using digitized 1-meter contours of the plateau and CAD data depicting the architectural components of the pyramid complex, the GPMP GIS team created a nearly three-dimensional surface called a TIN, or triangulated irregular network, over which they can lay other data layers, such as maps. Here (left), the GPMP survey grid is draped over the surface of the plateau. The Lost City of the Pyramid Builders is clearly visible in the foreground.

Data collected over 15 years all being incorporated in the GIS:

- more than 5000 field drawings
- more than 11,900 digital photographs
- more than 16,500 non-burial features
- more than 1100 burial features
- survey and remote sensing data
- artifact/ecofact content and distribution information for every feature

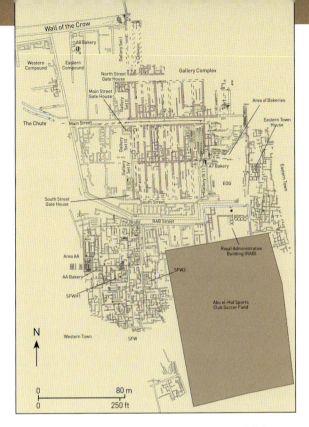

Since 1988 survey and excavations have been concentrated on the area known as "The Lost City of the Pyramid Builders," some 400 m (1300 ft) south of the Sphinx. This detailed plan (left) of the settlement, which was abandoned at the end of the 4th Dynasty (2575–2465 BC), the period of Giza pyramid building, now forms part of the GIS.

0 mL	3.4-4.4 mL	18.4-31 mL
0.1-1.4 mL	4.5-10.4 mL	Unexcavated features
1.5-3.3 mL	10.5-18.4 mL	

GIS presentation (below) of the features that have been digitally recorded in the Royal Administrative Building (RAB), one of the GPMP's largest and most complex excavation areas.

The spatial distribution of finds is easy to represent within the GIS (above). The total volumes of charcoal recovered in different areas of the first occupation phase of the RAB is shown here.

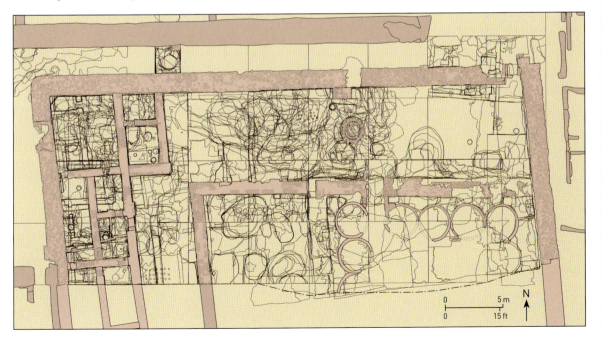

Assessing the Layout of Sites and Features

Finding and recording sites and features is the first stage in fieldwork, but the next stage is to make some assessment of site size, type, and layout. These are crucial factors for archaeologists, not only for those who are trying to decide whether, where, and how to excavate, but also for those whose main focus may be site management, the study of settlement patterns, site systems, and **landscape archaeology** without planning to carry out any excavation.

We have already seen how aerial images may be used to plot the layout of sites as well as helping to locate them in the first place. What are the other main methods for investigating sites without excavating them?

Site Surface Survey

The simplest way to gain some idea of a site's extent and layout is through a site surface survey – by studying the distribution of surviving features, and recording and possibly collecting artifacts from the surface.

The Teotihuacan Mapping Project, for instance, used site surface survey to investigate the layout and orientation of the city, which had been the largest and most powerful urban center in Mesoamerica in its heyday from AD 200 to 650. The layout and orientation of the city had intrigued scholars for decades; however, they considered the grandiose pyramid-temples, plazas, and the major avenue – an area now known as the ceremonial center – to be the entire extent of the metropolis. It was not until the survey conducted by the Teotihuacan Mapping Project that the outer limits, the great east–west axis, and the grid plan of the city were discovered and defined.

Fortunately, structural remains lay just beneath the surface, so that the team were able to undertake the mapping from a combination of aerial and surface survey, with only small-scale excavation to test the survey results. Millions of potsherds were collected, and more than 5000 structures and activity areas recorded. Teotihuacan had been laid out on a regular plan, with four quadrants orientated on the great north–south "Street of the Dead" and another major avenue running east–west across it. Construction had occurred over several centuries, but always following the master plan.

For artifacts and other objects collected or observed during site surface survey, it may not be worth mapping their individual locations if they appear to come from badly disturbed secondary **contexts**. Or there may simply be too many artifacts to record all their individual **proveniences**. In this latter instance the archaeologist will probably use sampling procedures for the selective recording of finds. However, where time and funds are sufficient and the site is small enough, collection and recording of artifacts from the total site area may prove possible.

For example, a site surface survey was conducted at the Bronze Age city of Mohenjodaro in Pakistan. Here, a team of archaeologists from Pakistan, Germany, and Italy investigated the distribution of craft-working debris and

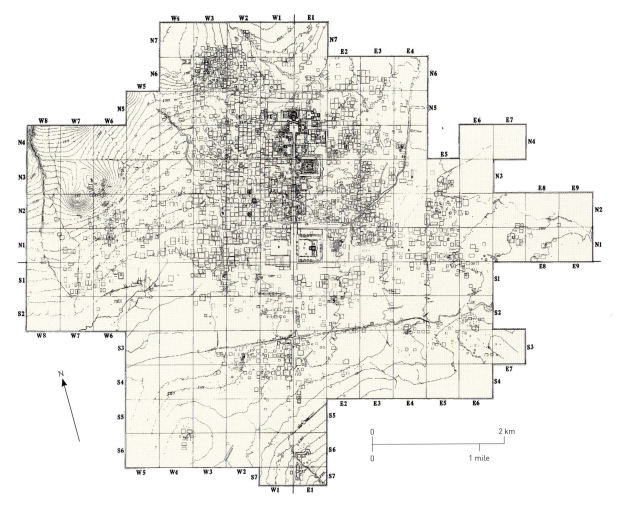

MEXICO

Teotihuacan

Archaeological and topographic map of Teotihuacan (above) produced by the Teotihuacan Mapping Project. The survey grid system of 500-m squares is oriented to the north–south axis of the city, in particular the central "Street of the Dead" (dividing W1 and E1 on the map).

(Right) View south along the Street of the Dead, with the Pyramid of the Sun prominent on the left, echoing the shape of the mountain behind.

found, to their surprise, that craft activities were not confined to a specific manufacturing zone within the city, but were scattered throughout the site, representing assorted small-scale workshops.

Reliability of Surface Finds. Archaeologists have always used limited surface collection of artifacts as one way of trying to assess the date and layout of a site prior to excavation. However, now that surface survey has become not merely a preliminary to excavation but also in some instances a substitute for it – for cost and time reasons – a vigorous debate is taking place in archaeology about how far surface traces do in fact reflect distributions below ground.

We would logically expect single-period or shallow sites to show the most reliable surface evidence of what lies beneath. Equally one might predict that multi-period, deep sites, such as Near Eastern village mounds, would show few if any traces on the surface of the earliest and deepest levels. This is by no means always true, however – for example, at Tell Halula in northern Syria, a survey

(Left) The survey and collecting team at Tell Halula, using a theodolite.

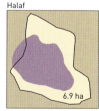

(Below left) CORONA satellite image of the Halula district, showing the location of the tell and the boundary of the sampling area.

(Below) Plan of Tell Halula showing the layout of collection squares, plus outline plans of the tell showing the changing location and size of settlement during 5 of the 10 occupation phases.

satellite image © USGS

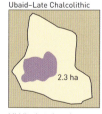

Topography and Collection Areas
200m
N

Pre-Pottery Neolithic B
8.0 ha

Halaf
6.9 ha

Ubaid–Late Chalcolithic
2.3 ha

Uruk–Early Bronze Age
1.9 ha

Middle–Late Iron Age
1.2 ha

was carried out by an Australian team in 1986, involving the collection of such artifacts as potsherds and stone tools from the surface, using stratified random sampling procedures based on a grid system. Forty-six squares in this grid were sampled, amounting to 4 percent of the 12.5-ha (31-acre) site area. Typological analysis of the artifacts made it possible to identify 10 major occupation phases, representing 15 different cultural periods.

Those who support the validity of surface survey, while agreeing that there is bound to be a quantitative bias in favor of the most recent periods on the surface, nevertheless point out that one of the surprises for most survey archaeologists is how many of their sites, if collected with care, are truly multi-period, reflecting many phases of a site's use, not just the latest one. The reasons for this are not yet entirely clear, but they certainly have something to do with the kind of **formation processes** discussed in Chapter 2 – from erosion and animal disturbance to such human activity as plowing.

The relationship between surface and subsurface evidence is undoubtedly complex and varies from site to site. It is therefore wise wherever possible to try to determine what really does lie beneath the ground, perhaps by digging test pits (usually meter squares) to assess a site's horizontal extent, or ultimately by more thorough excavation (see below). There are, however, a whole battery of **subsurface detection** devices that can be used before – or indeed sometimes instead of – excavation, which of course is destructive as well as expensive.

Subsurface Detection

Probes. The most traditional technique is that of probing the soil with rods or augers, and noting the positions where they strike solids or hollows. Metal rods with a T-shaped handle are the most common, but augers – large corkscrews with a similar handle – are also used, and have the advantage of bringing samples of soil to the surface, clinging to the screw. Many archaeologists routinely use hand-held probes that yield small, solid cores. Probing of this type was used, for example, by Chinese archaeologists to plot the 300 pits remaining to be investigated near the first emperor's famous buried terracotta army. However, there is always a risk of damaging fragile artifacts or features.

One notable advance in this technique was developed by Carlo Lerici in Italy in the 1950s as part of the search for Etruscan tombs of the 6th century BC. Having detected the precise location of a tomb through aerial photography and **soil resistivity** (see p. 90), he would bore down into it a hole 8 cm (3 in) in diameter, and insert a long tube with a periscope head and a light, and also a tiny camera attached if needed. Lerici examined some 3500 Etruscan tombs in this way, and found that almost all were completely empty, thus saving future excavators a great deal of wasted effort. He also discovered more than 20 with painted walls, thus doubling the known heritage of Etruscan painted tombs at a stroke.

Shovel-Test Pits (STPs). To gain a preliminary idea of what lies beneath the surface, small pits may often be dug into the ground at consistent distances from each other; in Europe these are usually in the form of meter-squares, but in some parts of North America small round holes are dug, about the diameter of a dinner-plate and less than a meter deep. These pits help show what an area has to offer, and help identify the extent of a possible site, while analysis and plotting of the material retrieved from them by sieving of the soil can produce maps showing areas with high concentrations of different kinds of artifacts. This method is commonly employed as part of site surveys for CRM projects in areas of the USA with poor surface visibility, such as forested areas of the east coast.

Probing the Pyramids. Modern technology has taken this kind of work even further, with the development of the endoscope and miniature TV cameras. In a project reminiscent of Lerici's, a probe was carried out in 1987 of a boat pit beside the Great Pyramid of Cheops (Khufu), in Egypt. This lies adjacent to another pit, excavated in 1954, that contained the perfectly preserved and disassembled parts of a 43-m (141-ft) long royal cedarwood boat of the 3rd millennium BC. The 1987 probe revealed that the unopened pit did indeed contain all the dismantled timbers of a second boat. In 2008 a team from Waseda University inserted a second miniature camera to reexamine the boat's condition and ascertain whether it could be safely lifted. The covering stone blocks and boat's timbers were duly removed in 2011. Robot probes with miniature cameras have been sent up two of the so-called "airshafts" of the Great Pyramid to discover whether or not they link up to hidden chambers – tantalizingly, stone blocking part-way up hinders further investigation.

Projects of this kind are beyond the resources of most archaeologists. But in future, funds permitting, probes of this type could equally well be applied to other Egyptian sites, to cavities in Maya structures, or to the many unexcavated tombs in China. The Great Pyramid itself has been the subject of further probes by French and Japanese teams, who believe it may contain as yet undiscovered chambers or corridors. Using ultrasensitive microgravimetric equipment – which is normally employed to search for deficiencies in dam walls, and can tell if a stone has a hollow behind it – they detected what they think is a cavity some 3 m (10 ft) beyond one of the passage walls. However, test drilling to support this claim has not been completed, and all tests are carefully monitored by the Egyptian authorities until their potential contribution to Egyptology has been established.

Ground-Based Remote Sensing

Probing techniques are useful, but inevitably involve some disturbance of the site. There are, however, a wide range of non-destructive techniques ideal for the archaeologist seeking to learn more about a site before – or increasingly often without – excavation. These are geophysical sensing devices, which can be either active (i.e. they pass energy of various kinds through the soil and measure the response in order to "read" what lies below the surface); or passive (i.e. they measure such physical properties as magnetism and gravity without the need to inject energy to obtain a response).

Electromagnetic Methods.   A method that employs radio pulses is called ground-penetrating (or probing) radar (GPR). An emitter sends short pulses through the soil, and the echoes not only reflect back any changes in the soil and sediment conditions encountered, such as filled ditches, graves, walls, etc., but also measure the depth at which the changes occur on the basis of the travel time of the pulses. Three-dimensional maps of buried archaeological remains can then be produced from data processing and image-generation programs.

In archaeological exploration and mapping, the radar antenna is generally dragged along the ground with the aid of a low trolley at walking speed in transects, sending out and receiving many pulses per second. The reflection data are stored digitally, which enables sophisticated data processing and analysis to be carried out, producing records that are relatively easy to interpret. Powerful computers and software programs make it possible to store and process very large three-dimensional sets of GPR data, and computer advances now permit automated data and image processing that can help to interpret complicated reflection profiles.

One such advance is the use of "time-slices" or "slice-maps." Thousands of individual reflections are combined into a single three-dimensional dataset that can then be "sliced" horizontally, each slice corresponding to a specific estimated depth in the ground, and revealing the general shape and location of buried features at successive depths. A variety of colors (or shades of gray) are used to make a visual image that the brain can interpret more easily – e.g. areas with little or no subsurface reflection may be colored blue, those with high reflection

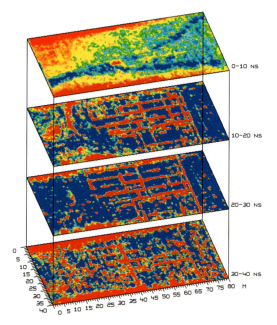

Amplitude slice-maps from the Forum Novum site, Italy. The top slice, at 0–10 ns (nanosecond, equivalent to 0–50 cm) reveals a Y-shaped anomaly, reflecting two gravel roads. As the slices go deeper, the Roman walls begin to emerge very clearly, showing a well-organized plan of rooms, doors, and corridors. The deepest slice shows the actual floor levels of the rooms and the objects preserved on them.

may be red. Each slice therefore becomes like a horizontal surface, and can illustrate the buried components of the site.

For example, in the Forum Novum, an ancient Roman marketplace about 100 km (60 miles) north of Rome, British archaeologists from the University of Birmingham and the British School of Archaeology in Rome needed a fuller picture of an unexcavated area than they had been able to obtain from aerial photographs and other techniques, such as resistivity (see below). A series of GPR slices of the area revealed a whole series of walls, rooms, doorways, courtyards – in short, producing an architectural layout of the site that means that future excavation can be concentrated on a representative sample of the structures, thus avoiding a costly and time-consuming uncovering of the whole area.

Earth Resistance Survey. A commonly used method that has been employed on archaeological sites for several decades, particularly in Europe, is **electrical resistivity**. The technique derives from the principle that the damper the soil the more easily it will conduct electricity, i.e. the less resistance it will show to an electric current. A resistivity meter attached to electrodes in the ground can thus measure varying degrees of subsurface resistance to a current passed between the electrodes. Silted-up ditches or filled-in pits retain more moisture than stone walls or roads, and will therefore display lower resistivity than stone structures.

The technique works particularly well for ditches and pits in chalk and gravel, and masonry in clay. It usually involves first placing two "remote" probes, which remain stationary, in the ground. Two "mobile" probes, fixed to a frame that also supports the meter, are then inserted into the earth for each reading. A variation of the method is "resistivity profiling," which involves the measurement of

Measuring Magnetism

Most terrestrial magnetometer surveys are undertaken either with fluxgate or with alkali-metal vapor magnetometers.

Fluxgate instruments usually comprise two sensors fixed rigidly at either end of a vertically held tube, and measure only the vertical component of the local magnetic field strength. The magnetometer is carried along a succession of traverses, usually 0.5–1.0 m apart, tied in to an overall pre-surveyed grid, until the entire site is covered. The signal is logged automatically and stored in the instrument's memory, to be downloaded and processed later. To speed up the coverage of large areas, two or more fluxgate instruments can be moved across the site at once – either on a frame carried by the operator, or sometimes on a wheeled cart. In this way, many hectares of ground can be covered quite quickly, revealing such features as pits, ditches, hearths, kilns, or entire settlement complexes and their associated roads, trackways, and cemeteries.

An alternative and sometimes more effective magnetometer is the alkali-metal vapor type, typically a caesium magnetometer. Although more expensive and quite difficult to operate, an advantage these magnetometers have over fluxgate types is that they are more sensitive and can therefore detect features that are only very weakly magnetic, or more deeply buried than usual. Such instruments have been used for many years with great success in continental Europe and are finding favor elsewhere. Unlike a fluxgate gradiometer they measure the total magnetic field (but can be operated as a total-field gradiometer if configured with two vertically mounted sensors). It is also usual for two or more of these sensors to be used at once

The Bartington Grad601-2 single-axis, vertical-component, high-stability fluxgate gradiometer system.

– often mounted on a non-magnetic wheeled cart. Surveys with such systems can cover up to about 5 ha (12 acres) each day at a high resolution sampling interval (0.5 m × 0.25 m). Arrays of fluxgate sensors are now also being introduced, but many surveys are conducted with a dual sensor system (as in the photograph above) with a sample interval of c. 0.1 m × 0.25 m. Fluxgates are often favored for their lower cost, versatility, and ability to detect a similar range of features to caesium systems.

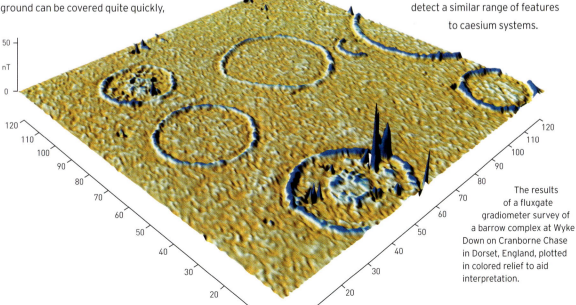

The results of a fluxgate gradiometer survey of a barrow complex at Wyke Down on Cranborne Chase in Dorset, England, plotted in colored relief to aid interpretation.

earth resistance at increasing depths by widening the probe spacings and thus building up a vertical "pseudosection" across a site.

Magnetic Survey Methods.   These are among the most widely used methods of survey, particularly helpful in locating such fired-clay structures as hearths and pottery kilns; iron objects; and pits and ditches. Such buried features all produce slight but measurable distortions in the earth's magnetic field. The reasons for this vary according to the type of feature, but are based on the presence of minute amounts of iron. For example, grains of iron oxide in clay, their magnetism randomly orientated if the clay is unbaked, will line up and become permanently fixed in the direction of the earth's magnetic field when heated to about 700°C (1292°F) or more. The baked clay thus becomes a weak permanent magnet, creating an anomaly in the surrounding magnetic field. Anomalies caused by pits and ditches, on the other hand, occur because the so-called magnetic susceptibility of their contents is greater than that of the surrounding subsoil.

All the magnetic instruments (see box on p. 91) can produce informative site plans that help to delimit archaeological potential. Today, multiple types of sensors – both electromagnetic and magnetic – are often integrated on moving platforms or "mobile arrays," which allows for simultaneous measurements. The most common means of presentation are color and grayscale maps that, along with contour maps, are used to display **earth resistance survey** results. In the case of magnetic survey, the contour map has contour lines that join all points of the same value of the magnetic field intensity – this successfully reveals separate anomalies, such as tombs in a cemetery.

Metal Detectors.   These electromagnetic devices are also helpful in detecting buried remains. An alternating magnetic field is generated by passing an electrical current through a transmitter coil. Buried metal objects distort this field and are detected as a result of an electrical signal picked up by a receiver coil. Metal detectors can be of great value to archaeologists, particularly as they can provide general results and are able to locate modern metal objects that may lie near the surface. They are also very widely used by non-archaeologists, most of whom are responsible enthusiasts. Some, however, vandalize sites mindlessly and often illegally dig holes without recording or reporting the finds they make, which are therefore without context.

So far, we have discovered sites and mapped as many of their surface and subsurface features as possible. But, despite the growing importance of survey, the only way to check the reliability of surface data, confirm the accuracy of the remote sensing techniques, and actually see what remains of these sites is to excavate them. Furthermore, survey can tell us a little about a large area, but only excavation can tell us a great deal about a relatively small area.

Excavation

Excavation retains its central role in fieldwork because it yields the most reliable evidence for the two main kinds of information archaeologists are interested in: (1) human activities at a particular period in the past; and (2) changes in those activities from period to period. Very broadly we can say that contemporary activities take place horizontally in space, whereas changes in those activities occur vertically through time. It is this distinction between horizontal "slices of time" and vertical sequences through time that forms the basis of most excavation methodology.

In the horizontal dimension archaeologists demonstrate that activities occurred at the same time by proving through excavation that artifacts and features are found in association in an undisturbed context. Of course, as we saw in Chapter 2, there are many formation processes that may disturb this primary context. One of the main purposes of the survey and remote sensing procedures outlined in the earlier sections is to select for excavation sites, or areas within sites, that are reasonably undisturbed. On a single-period site, such as an East African early human camp site, this is vital if human behavior at the camp is to be reconstructed at all accurately. But on a multi-period site, such as a long-lived European town or Near Eastern village mound, finding large areas of undisturbed deposits will be almost impossible. Here archaeologists have to try to reconstruct during and after excavation just what disturbance there has been, and then decide how to interpret it. Clearly, adequate records must be made as excavation progresses if the task of interpretation is to be undertaken with any chance of success. In the vertical dimension archaeologists analyze changes through time by the study of **stratigraphy**.

Key Concepts
Excavation

- Excavation yields evidence of contemporary activities (which are found horizontally through space) and changes through time (which are found vertically in sequences)

- Stratigraphy is the study of archaeological layers found during excavations. The law of superposition states that where one layer overlies another, the lower was deposited first. This forms the basis of the way archaeologists investigate changes through time

- Excavation methods should be adapted to the site and particular questions that need to be answered. The two main strategies are the Wheeler box-grid and open-area excavation; a combination of both is often used. A sampling strategy of some kind can be required to save time and money

Stratigraphy

As we saw in Chapter 1, one of the first steps in understanding the great antiquity of humankind was the recognition by geologists of the process of **stratification** – that layers or strata are laid down, one on top of the other, according to processes that still continue. Archaeological strata (the layers of cultural or natural debris visible in the side of any excavation) accumulate over much shorter periods of time than geological ones, but nevertheless conform to the same law of superposition. Put simply, this states that where one layer overlies another, the lower was deposited first. Hence, an excavated vertical profile showing a series of layers constitutes a sequence that has accumulated through time.

Chapter 4 explores the significance of this for dating purposes. Here we should note that the law of superposition refers only to the sequence of deposition, not to the age of the material in the different strata. The contents of lower layers are indeed usually older than those of upper layers, but the archaeologist must not simply assume this. Pits dug down from a higher layer or burrowing animals (even earthworms) may introduce later materials into lower levels. Moreover, occasionally strata can become inverted, as when they are eroded all the way from the top of a bank to the bottom of a ditch.

The complexity of stratification varies with the type of site. This hypothetical section through an urban deposit indicates the kind of complicated stratigraphy, in both vertical and horizontal dimensions, that the archaeologist can encounter. There may be few undisturbed stratified layers. The chances of finding preserved organic material increase as one approaches the water table, near which deposits may be waterlogged.

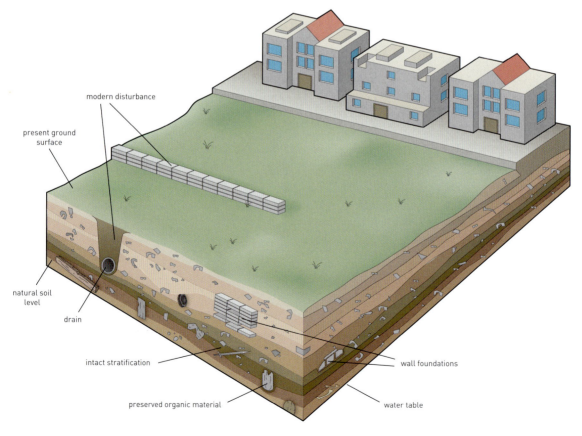

modern disturbance

present ground surface

natural soil level

drain

intact stratification

preserved organic material

wall foundations

water table

Archaeologists have developed an ingenious and effective method of checking that artifacts – so far mostly of stone or bone – discovered in a particular deposit are contemporaneous and not intrusive. They have found that in a surprising number of cases flakes of stone or bone can be fitted back together again: reassembled in the shape of the original stone block or pieces of bone from which they came. At the British **Mesolithic** (Middle Stone Age) site of Hengistbury Head, for example, reanalysis of an old excavation showed that two groups of flint flakes, found in two different layers, could be **refitted**. This cast doubt on the stratigraphic separation of the two layers, and demolished the original excavator's argument that the flints had been made by two different groups of people. As well as clarifying questions of stratification, these refitting or conjoining exercises are transforming archaeological studies of early technology (Chapter 7).

Stratigraphy, then, is the study and validating of stratification – the analysis in the vertical, time dimension of a series of layers in the horizontal, space dimension (although in practice few layers are precisely horizontal).

What are the best excavation methods for retrieving this information?

Methods of Excavation

Excavation is both costly and destructive, and therefore never to be undertaken lightly. Wherever possible, non-destructive approaches (outlined earlier) should be used to meet research objectives in preference to excavation. But assuming excavation is to proceed, and the necessary funding and permission to dig have been obtained, what are the best methods to adopt?

This book is not an excavation or field manual, but although such things do exist, a few days or weeks spent on a well-run dig are worth far more than reading any book on the subject. Nevertheless, some brief guidance as to the main methods is given here. In addition, we look at the excavation of one site, the Jamestown settlement in Virginia, in a little more detail (see box overleaf).

It goes without saying that all excavation methods need to be adapted to the research question in hand and the nature of the site. It is no good digging a deeply stratified urban site, with hundreds of complex structures, thousands of intercutting pits, and tens of thousands of artifacts, as if it were the same as a shallow **Paleolithic** open site, where only one or two structures and a few hundred artifacts may survive. On the Paleolithic site, for example, it may be possible to uncover all the structures and record the exact position or provenience, vertically and horizontally, of each and every artifact. On the urban site there is no chance of doing this, given time and funding constraints. Instead, we have to adopt a sampling strategy, and only key artifacts, such as coins (important for dating purposes: see Chapter 4), will have their provenience recorded with three-dimensional precision, the remainder being allocated simply to the layer and perhaps the grid-square in which they were found

Jamestown Rediscovery: The Excavation Process

On 13 May 1607, a hundred Englishmen established a settlement on Jamestown Island in Virginia. Soon under attack from Native Americans, they quickly built a wooden fort. Periodic resupply of settlers and stores, investment by the sponsoring Virginia Company of London, and the discovery of a cash crop, tobacco, kept the venture alive. Ultimately, Jamestown proved to be the first permanent English colony and so the birthplace of modern America and the British Empire. For centuries the site of the fort was thought to have been eroded away by the adjacent James River, but archaeological excavations from 1994 onward by the Jamestown Rediscovery project have proved that the "lost" site has actually escaped erosion. Most of the archaeological footprint of the fort and more than one million artifacts have been recovered, at least half of these dating to the first three struggling years of settlement.

The Jamestown Rediscovery research design is straightforward: uncover, record, and interpret the remnants of the James Fort; determine the original and evolving fort plan; learn as much as possible about the daily lives of the settlers and the Native Americans; and record prehistoric and post-James Fort occupations. From the outset, it was clear that the best way to record and recover all this required a hybridized excavation process combining the traditional grid-based control system with open-area excavation. A thorough documentary search was also essential, both to pinpoint areas to investigate, and to reassess the records continually in light of new and more complex questions raised by the digging.

The Ongoing Field Process

Initially, a grid of 3-m (10-ft) squares is employed in each area to be excavated, facilitating the recording of artifacts

Delicate field recovery of arms and armor in a backfilled metalworking shop/bakery cellar after full feature definition by open-area excavation.

deposited in post-fort layers. Once the 17th-century level is exposed, the grid is replaced with a feature-based open-area recording method. At this stage, both physical remains and variations in soil color and texture together delineate features: building foundations, fireplaces, postholes, cellars, wells, pits, ditches, and graves. These defined contexts are assigned ascending "JR" numbers, which are then entered into a GIS site map.

The decision to excavate partially or fully (or leave unexcavated) features or related components of features is dependent upon whether or not they can be associated with other known James Fort/Jamestown period (1607–24) remains, such as wall lines. More recent features are usually mapped but left unexcavated. Once it is decided that a given feature is likely to be a remnant of the fort occupation, excavation determines the cultural deposition sequence, indicated by changes in the soil color, texture, or inclusions of strata. Each layer is then sequentially assigned a letter

The grid-based (foreground) and open-area (background) excavations at James Fort.

of the alphabet. In this manner, the JR number and letter permanently label each individual feature, and layers within them, as distinct contexts. Most contexts are then drawn, photographed, systematically archived, and eventually linked to the GIS site map.

The artifacts are recovered in two stages: as the feature layers are excavated and then as the loose spoil is wet or dry screened (the latter either by hand or mechanically). The specific screening process employed depends on the age and integrity of the context. The resulting artifact collections are washed, conserved, and catalogued in a laboratory on site, permanently carrying their JR number and letter.

Soil samples of individual layers are collected and archived for future flotation and/or chemical analysis. Once selected features in an area have been excavated and/or recorded, that area is covered with a geotextile fabric and backfilled, usually with 50 cm (20 in) of soil. As of 2011, about 15 percent of features in the fort have been partially or fully excavated, with the remainder preserved for future investigation.

Collections Management

After initial cleaning, artifacts are sorted according to conservation requirements, balancing the need for rescue and long-term preservation with interpretive potential. A number of techniques, including X-ray recording and mechanical/chemical treatments, are applied to metallic objects and organic materials.

The computer cataloguing program is straightforward and searchable, utilizing minimal attribute fields (number, material, form, and

GIS site map of the James Fort open-area excavations, 1994–2010.

design), but with the ability to enter other useful data in a separate field. To facilitate analysis and publication, the digital catalogue is linked to the GIS site map so that plans, photos, and artifacts can be interpreted at a single computer station. Descriptive reports are generated for each year of the excavation, but interpretation is limited because of the ongoing nature of the project.

Reconstruction of James Fort based on excavated evidence and historical records.

97

(sites are usually divided up into grid-squares, just like maps are, in order to aid in accurate recording; naturally, the size and number of the grid squares will depend on the type, size, and likely depth of the site).

It should be noted, however, that we have already reintroduced the idea of the vertical and horizontal dimensions. These are as crucial to the methods of excavation as they are to the principles behind excavation. Broadly speaking we can divide excavation techniques into:

1 those that emphasize the vertical dimension, by cutting into deep deposits to reveal stratification;
2 those that emphasize the horizontal dimension, by opening up large areas of a particular layer to reveal the spatial relationships between artifacts and features in that layer.

Most excavators employ a combination of both strategies, but there are different ways of achieving this. All presuppose that the site has first been surveyed and a grid of squares laid down over it. A site grid is laid out from a datum, which is simply a selected location that serves as a reference point for all horizontal and vertical measurements taken, so that the site can be accurately mapped and the exact location of any artifact or feature can be recorded in three dimensions if that is necessary or feasible.

The **Wheeler box-grid** – developed from the work of Pitt-Rivers, as noted in Chapter 1 – seeks to satisfy both vertical and horizontal requirements by retaining intact balks of earth between the squares of the grid, as can be clearly seen in the picture to the right, so that different layers can be traced and correlated across the site in vertical profiles. Once the general extent and layout of the site have been ascertained, some of the balks can be removed and the squares joined into an open excavation to expose any features (such as a mosaic floor) that are of special interest.

Advocates of **open-area excavation** criticize this method, arguing that the balks are invariably in the wrong place or wrongly orientated to illustrate the relationships required from sections, and that they prevent the distinguishing of spatial patterning over large areas. It is far better, these critics say, not to have such permanent or semi-permanent balks, but to open up large areas and only to cut vertical sections (at whatever angle is necessary to the main site grid) where they are needed to elucidate particularly complex stratigraphic relationships. Apart from these "running sections," the vertical dimension is recorded by accurate three-dimensional measurements as the dig proceeds and reconstructed on paper after the end of the excavation. The introduction since Wheeler's day of more advanced recording methods, including field computers, makes this more demanding open-area method feasible, and it has become the norm, for instance, in much of British archaeology. The open-area method

(Above) Box-grid excavation trenches at Anuradhapura's Abhayagiri Buddhist monastery, Sri Lanka.

(Above right) The Native American site of Koster, in the Illinois River Valley: large horizontal areas were uncovered to locate living floors and activity zones. However, in order for the vertical dimension to be analyzed at this deep site, vertical sections were cut as steps as the excavation descended. At this complex site 14 occupation levels were identified, dating from c. 7500 BC to AD 1200.

is particularly effective where single-period deposits lie near the surface, as for instance with remains of Native American or European **Neolithic** long houses. Here the time dimension may be represented by lateral movement (a settlement rebuilt adjacent to, not on top of, an earlier one) and it is essential to expose large horizontal areas in order to understand the complex pattern of rebuilding. Large open-area excavations are often undertaken in "applied archaeology" when land is going to be destroyed – otherwise farmers are naturally opposed to stripping large areas of plow-disturbed soil. The box-grid method is still widely used in parts of South Asia, where it was introduced by Wheeler in the 1940s. It remains popular as it enables large numbers of untrained workers in individual boxes to be easily supervised by small numbers of staff.

No single method, however, is ever going to be universally applicable. The rigid box-grid, for instance, has rarely been employed to excavate very deep sites, such as Near Eastern **tells**, because the trench squares rapidly become uncomfortable and dangerous as the dig proceeds downward. One solution commonly adopted is **step-trenching**, with a large area opened at the top that gradually narrows as the dig descends in a series of large steps. This technique was used effectively at the Koster site, Illinois.

Each site is different and one needs to adapt to its conditions – for example, in some cases by following the natural geological strata or the cultural layers instead of using arbitrary spits or imposing a false regularity where it does not exist. Whatever the method of excavation, a dig is only as good as its methods of recovery and recording. Since excavation involves destruction of much of the evidence, it is an unrepeatable exercise. Well-thought-out recovery methods are essential, and careful records must be kept of every stage of the dig.

Underwater Archaeology

One special category of both survey and excavation is constituted by underwater archaeology, which is generally considered to have been given its first major impetus during the winter of 1853–54, when a particularly low water level in the Swiss lakes laid bare enormous quantities of wooden posts, pottery, and other artifacts. From the earliest investigations, using crude diving-bells, it has developed into a valuable complement to work on land. It encompasses a wide variety of sites, including wells, sink holes, and springs (e.g. the great sacrificial well at Chichen ltza, Mexico); submerged lakeside settlements; and marine sites ranging from shipwrecks to sunken harbors and drowned cities.

The invention in recent times of miniature submarines, other submersible craft, and above all of scuba diving gear has been of enormous value, enabling divers to stay underwater for much longer, and to reach sites at previously impossible depths. As a result, the pace and scale of discovery have greatly increased. More than 1000 shipwrecks are known in shallow Mediterranean waters, but recent explorations using deep-sea submersibles, such as miniature unmanned submarines (remotely operated vehicles – ROV) with sonar, high-powered lighting, and video cameras, have begun to find Roman wrecks at depths of up to 850 m (2790 ft): and two Phoenician wrecks packed with amphorae discovered off the coast of Israel are the oldest vessels ever found in the deep sea.

Underwater Reconnaissance. Geophysical methods are as useful for finding sites underwater as they are for locating land sites. For example, in 1979 it was magnetometry combined with side-scan sonar that discovered the *Hamilton* and the *Scourge*, two armed schooners sunk during the War of 1812 at a depth of 90 m (295 ft) in Lake Ontario, Canada. The latest multibeam side-scan sonar gives brilliantly clear images and allows accurate measurements to be taken of shipwrecks on the seabed. Nevertheless, in such regions as the Mediterranean the majority of finds have resulted from methods as simple as talking to local sponge-divers, who collectively have spent thousands of hours scouring the seabed.

Underwater Excavation. Excavation underwater is complex and expensive (not to mention the highly demanding post-excavation conservation and analytical work that is also required). Once under way, the excavation may involve shifting vast quantities of sediment, and recording and removing bulky objects as diverse as storage jars (amphorae), metal ingots, and cannons. George Bass, founder of the Institute of Nautical Archaeology in Texas, and others have developed many helpful devices, such as baskets attached to balloons to raise objects, and air lifts (suction hoses) to remove sediment. If the vessel's hull survives at all, a 3D plan must be made so that specialists can later reconstruct the overall form and lines, either on paper or in three dimensions as a model or full-size replica. In some rare cases, for example that of England's *Mary Rose*

Three methods of geophysical underwater survey. (1) The proton magnetometer is towed well behind the survey boat, detecting iron and steel objects (e.g. cannons, steel hulls) that distort the earth's magnetic field. (2) Side-scan sonar transmits sound waves in a fan-shaped beam to produce a graphic image of surface (but not sub-surface) features on the seafloor. (3) The sub-bottom profiler emits sound pulses that bounce back from features and objects buried beneath the seafloor.

(a 16th-century AD warship that sank off Portsmouth), preservation is sufficiently good for the remains of the hull to be raised – funds permitting.

Nautical archaeologists have now excavated more than 100 sunken vessels, revealing not only how they were constructed but also many insights into shipboard life, cargoes, trade routes, early metallurgy, and glassmaking. For example, a Basque whaling ship, the *San Juan*, which had sunk in Red Bay, Labrador, in 1565, was excavated in the 1980s from a specially equipped barge, anchored above the site, that contained a workshop, storage baths for artifacts, a crane for lifting timbers, and a compressor able to run 12 air lifts for removing silt. Salt water was heated on board and pumped down through hoses direct to the divers' suits to maintain body warmth in the near-freezing conditions. An important technique devised during the project was the use of latex rubber to mold large sections of the ship's timbers in position underwater, thereby reproducing accurately the hull shape and such details as toolmarks and wood grain. The remains of the vessel were also raised in pieces to the surface for precise recording, but the latex molds eliminated the need for costly conservation of the original timbers, which were reburied on-site.

Underwater excavation techniques: at left, the lift bag for raising objects; center, measuring and recording finds in situ; right, the air lift for removing sediment.

Recovery and Recording of the Evidence

As we saw above, different sites have different requirements. We should aim to recover and plot the three-dimensional provenience of every artifact from a shallow single-period Paleolithic or Neolithic site, an objective that is simply not feasible for the urban archaeologist. On both types of site, a decision may be made to save time by using mechanical diggers to remove topsoil, but thereafter the Paleolithic or Neolithic specialist will usually want to screen or sieve as much excavated soil as possible in order to recover tiny artifacts, animal bones, and plant remains. The urban archaeologist on the other hand will only be able to

(Below) Structural plan of the wreck on the harbor bottom (2-m grid squares).

(Below right) Model, at a scale of 1:10, to show how the *San Juan*'s surviving timbers may have fitted together.

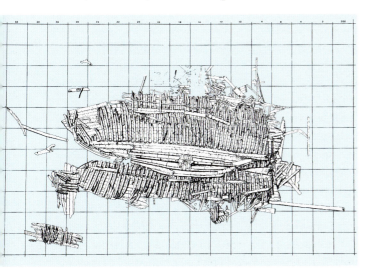

adopt sieving much more selectively, as part of a sampling strategy, for instance where plant remains can be expected to survive, as in a latrine or garbage pit. Decisions need to be made about the type of sieving to be undertaken, the size of the screen and its mesh, and whether dry or wet sieving will yield the best results. Naturally all these factors will depend on the resources of the excavation project, the period and scale of the site, whether it is dry or waterlogged, and what kind of material can be expected to have survived and to be retrievable.

Once an artifact has been recovered, and its provenience recorded, it must be given a number that is entered in a catalog book or field computer and on the bag in which it is to be stored. Day-to-day progress of the dig is recorded in site notebooks, or on data sheets preprinted with specific questions to be answered (which helps produce uniform data suitable for later analysis by computer).

Unlike artifacts, which can be removed for later analysis, features and structures usually have to be left where they were found (or in situ), or destroyed as the excavation proceeds to another layer. It is thus imperative to record them, not simply by written description in site notebooks, but by accurately scaled drawings and photography. The same applies to vertical profiles (sections), and for each horizontally exposed layer, good overhead photographs taken from a stand or tethered balloon are also essential.

It is the site notebooks, scaled drawings, photographs and digital media – in addition to recovered artifacts, animal bones, and plant remains – that form the total record of the excavation, on the basis of which all interpretations of the site will be made. This post-excavation analysis will take many months, perhaps years, often much longer than the excavation itself. However, some preliminary analysis, particularly sorting and **classification** of the artifacts, will be made in the field during the course of the excavation.

Processing and Classification

Like excavation itself, the processing of excavated materials in the field laboratory is a specialized activity that demands careful planning and organization. For example, an archaeologist excavating a wet site will need experts in the conservation of waterlogged wood, and facilities for coping with such material.

Two important aspects of field laboratory procedure are cleaning of artifacts and sorting and classifying them. In both cases the archaeologist always needs to consider in advance what kinds of questions the newly excavated material might be able to answer. Thorough cleaning of artifacts, for example, is a traditional part of excavations worldwide. But many of the new scientific techniques discussed later in this book make it quite evident that artifacts should not necessarily be cleaned thoroughly before a specialist has had a chance to study them. For instance, we now know that food residues are often preserved in pots, and possible blood residues on stone tools. The chances of such preservation need to be assessed before evidence is destroyed.

Nevertheless most artifacts eventually have to be cleaned to some degree if they are to be sorted and classified. Initial sorting is into such broad categories as stone tools, pottery, and metal objects. These categories are then subdivided or classified, so as to create more manageable groups that can later be analyzed. Classification is commonly done on the basis of three kinds of characteristics or **attributes**: surface attributes (including decoration and color); shape attributes (dimensions as well as shape itself); and technological attributes (primarily raw material). Artifacts with similar attributes are grouped together into artifact types – hence the term **typology**, which simply refers to the creation of such types.

Typology dominated archaeological thinking until the 1950s, and still plays an important role. The reason for this is straightforward. Artifacts make up a large part of the archaeological record, and typology helps archaeologists create order in this mass of evidence. As we saw in Chapter 1, C. J. Thomsen demonstrated early on that artifacts could be ordered in a **Three Age System** or sequence of

Terms used in archaeological classification, from attributes (shape, decoration) of a pot to the complete archaeological culture: a diagram developed by the American archaeologist James Deetz. The columns at left and right give the inferred human meaning of the terms.

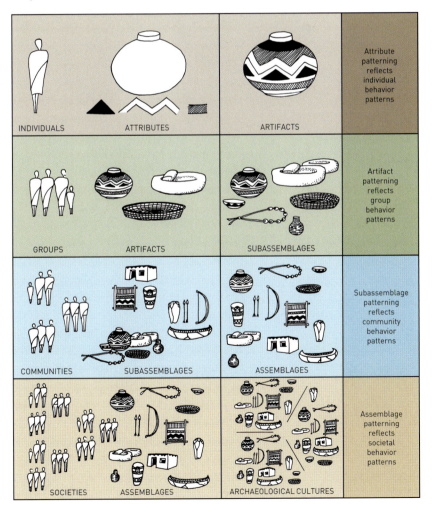

INDIVIDUALS   ATTRIBUTES   ARTIFACTS

Attribute patterning reflects individual behavior patterns

GROUPS   ARTIFACTS   SUBASSEMBLAGES

Artifact patterning reflects group behavior patterns

COMMUNITIES   SUBASSEMBLAGES   ASSEMBLAGES

Subassemblage patterning reflects community behavior patterns

SOCIETIES   ASSEMBLAGES   ARCHAEOLOGICAL CULTURES

Assemblage patterning reflects societal behavior patterns

stone, bronze, and iron. This discovery underlies the continuing use of typology as a method of dating (Chapter 4). Typology has also been used as a means of defining archaeological entities at a particular moment in time: groups of artifact (and building) types at a particular time and place are termed **assemblages**, and groups of assemblages have been taken to define **archaeological cultures**. These definitions are also long established, but, as we shall see later, the difficulty comes when one tries to translate this terminology into human terms and to relate an archaeological "culture" with an actual group of people in the past.

This brings us back to the purpose of classification. Types, assemblages, and **cultures** are all concepts designed to put order into disordered evidence – they are artificial. The trap that former generations of scholars fell into was to allow these concepts to determine the way they thought about the past, rather than using them merely as one means of giving shape to the evidence. We now recognize more clearly that different classifications are needed for the different kinds of questions we want to ask. A student of ceramic technology would base a classification on variations in raw material and methods of manufacture, whereas a scholar studying the various functions of pottery for storage, cooking, and so forth might classify the vessels according to shape and size. Our ability to construct and make good use of new classifications has been immeasurably enhanced by computers, which allow archaeologists to compare the association of different attributes of thousands of objects at once.

Post-excavation work in the laboratory or store does not cease with cleaning, labeling and classification. Curation is also of immense importance, and the conservation of objects and materials plays a major role, not only for the arrangement of long-term storage but also for collections management in general. The material needs to be preserved and readily available for future research, re-interpretation and, in some cases, display to the public, whether permanently or in temporary exhibitions.

In conclusion, it cannot be stressed too strongly that all the effort put into survey, excavation, and post-excavation analysis will have been largely wasted unless the results are published.

Study Questions

- What are the pros and cons of unsystematic and systematic survey methods?
- What types of archaeological sites can be identified through aerial photography?
- What is GIS and how can archaeologists use it?
- How is archaeological excavation different from archaeological survey?
- What are the benefits and drawbacks of the Wheeler box-grid method of excavation?
- What are some of the ways in which artifacts can be classified?

Summary

- Although many sites are found either by accident or during modern development, the archaeologist has a barrage of ground and aerial reconnaissance techniques available with which to find new sites.

- Until the present century, individual sites were the main focus of archaeological attention, but today archaeologists study whole regions, often employing sampling techniques to bring ground reconnaissance survey within the scope of individual research teams. Having located sites within those regions, and mapped them (usually using GIS), archaeologists can then turn to a whole battery of remote sensing site survey devices able to detect buried features without excavation.

- Remote sensing methods almost all involve either passing energy into the ground and locating buried features from their effect on that energy or measuring the intensity of the earth's magnetic field. In either case, they depend on contrast between the buried features and their surroundings. Many of the techniques are costly in both equipment and time, but they are often cheaper and certainly less destructive than random trial trenches. They allow archaeologists to be more selective in deciding which parts of a site, if any, should be fully excavated.

- Excavation itself relies on methods designed to elucidate the horizontal extent of a site in space, and the vertical stratification representing changes through time. Good recording methods are essential, together with a well-equipped field laboratory for processing and classifying the finds. Classification based on selected attributes (decoration, shape, material) of each artifact is the fundamental means of organizing the excavated material, usually into types – hence typology. But classification is only a means to an end, and different schemes are needed for the different questions archaeologists want to address.

- However, little of the material retrieved during survey and excavation will be of much use unless it can be dated in some way. In the next chapter we turn to this crucial aspect of archaeology.

Further Reading

Useful introductions to methods of survey and excavation can be found in the following:

Collis, J. 2004. *Digging up the Past: An Introduction to Archaeological Excavation*. Sutton: Stroud.

Conyers, L. B. 2012. *Interpreting Ground-Penetrating Radar for Archaeology*. Left Coast Press: Walnut Creek, CA.

English Heritage 2008. *Geophysical Survey in Archaeological Field Evaluation* (2nd ed.). English Heritage: London.

Gaffney, V. & Gater, J. 2003. *Revealing the Buried Past. Geophysics for Archaeologists*. Tempus: Stroud.

Hester, T.N., Shafer, H.J., & Feder, K.L. 2008. *Field Methods in Archaeology* (7th ed.). Left Coast Press: Walnut Creek.

Oswin, J. 2009. *A Field Guide to Geophysics in Archaeology*. Springer: Berlin.

Wheatley, D. & Gillings, M. 2002. *Spatial Technology and Archaeology. The Archaeological Applications of GIS*. Routledge: London.

Wiseman, J.R. & El-Baz, F. (eds). 2007. *Remote sensing in Archaeology* (with CD-Rom). Springer: Berlin.

Zimmerman, L.J. & Green, W. (eds). 2003. *The Archaeologist's Toolkit* (7 vols). AltaMira Press: Walnut Creek.

[See p. 345 for a list of useful websites]

When?
Dating methods and chronology

RELATIVE DATING

Stratigraphy: Ordering Archaeological Layers

Typological Sequences: Comparing Objects

- Seriation: Comparing Assemblages of Objects

Environmental Sequences

ABSOLUTE DATING

Calendars and Historical Chronologies

- Using a Historical Chronology

Annual Cycles

- Tree-Ring Dating

Radioactive Clocks

- Radiocarbon Dating
- Other Radiometric Methods

Other Absolute Dating Methods

World Chronology

Study Questions
Summary
Further Reading

All human beings experience time. An individual experiences a lifetime of perhaps 70 years or so. That person, through the memories of his or her parents and grandparents, may also indirectly experience earlier periods of time, back over more than 100 years. The study of history gives us access to hundreds more years of recorded time. But it is only **archaeology** that opens up the almost unimaginable vistas of thousands and even a few millions of years of past human existence. This chapter will examine the various ways in which we, as archaeologists, date past events within this great expanse of time.

Relative and Absolute Dating.　It might seem surprising that in order to study the past it is not always essential to know precisely how long ago (in years) a particular period or event occurred. It is often very helpful simply to know whether one event happened before or after another. By ordering **artifacts**, deposits, societies, and events into sequences, earlier before later, we can study developments in the past without knowing how long each stage lasted or how many years ago such changes took place. This idea that something is older (or younger) relative to something else is the basis of **relative dating**.

Ultimately, however, we want to know the full or absolute age in years before the present of different events or parts of a sequence – we need methods of **absolute dating**. Absolute dates help us find out how quickly such changes as the introduction of agriculture occurred, and whether they occurred simultaneously or at different times in different regions of the world. Only in the last 60 years or so have independent means of absolute dating become available, transforming archaeology in the process. Before then, virtually the only reliable absolute dates were historical ones, such as the date of the reign of the ancient Egyptian pharaoh Tutankhamun.

Measuring Time.　How do we detect the passage of time? We can all observe its passing through the alternating darkness and light of nights and days, and then through the annual cycle of the seasons. In fact, for most of human history these were the only ways of measuring time, other than by the human lifespan. As we shall see, some dating methods still rely on the annual passage of the seasons. Increasingly, however, dating methods in archaeology have come to rely on other physical processes, many of them not observable to the human eye. The most significant of these is the use of radioactive clocks.

Some degree of error, usually expressed as an age-bracket that can stretch over several centuries or even millennia, is inevitable when using any dating technique. But while the science behind dating methods is being ever more refined, the main source of errors remains the archaeologist – by poor choice of samples to be dated, by contaminating those samples, or by misinterpreting results.

Dating Conventions. To be meaningful, our timescale in years must relate to a fixed point in time. In the Christian world, this is by convention taken as the birth of Christ, supposedly in the year AD 1 (there is no year 0), with years counted back before Christ (BC) and forward after Christ (AD or *Anno Domini*, which is Latin for "In the Year of Our Lord"). However, this is by no means the only system. In the Muslim world, for example, the basic fixed point is the date of the Prophet's departure from Mecca (AD 622 in the Christian calendar). As a result of these differences some scholars prefer to use the terms "Before the Common Era" (BCE) and "in the Common Era" (CE) instead of BC and AD.

Scientists who derive dates from radioactive methods want a neutral international system, and have chosen to count years back from the present (BP). But since scientists too require a firm fixed point to count from, they take BP to mean "before 1950" (the approximate year of the establishment of the first radioactive method, radiocarbon). This may be convenient for scientists, but can be confusing for everyone else (a date of 400 BP is not 400 years ago but AD 1550, currently more than 460 years ago). It is therefore clearest to convert any BP date for the last few thousand years into the BC/AD system.

For the **Paleolithic** period, however (stretching back two or three million years before 10,000 BC), archaeologists use the terms "BP" and "years ago" interchangeably, since a difference of 50 years or so between them is irrelevant. For this remote epoch we are dating **sites** or events at best only to within several thousand years of their "true" date. If even the most precise dates for the Paleolithic give us glimpses of that epoch only at intervals of several thousand years, clearly archaeologists can never hope to reconstruct a conventional history of Paleolithic events. On the other hand, Paleolithic archaeologists can gain insights into some of the broad long-term changes that shaped the way modern humans evolved – insights that are denied archaeologists working with shorter periods of time, where in any case there may be too much "detail" for the broader pattern to be apparent.

The way in which archaeologists carry out their research therefore depends very much on the precision of dating obtainable for the period of time in question. In what follows we deal first with relative dating, whereby principles of sequence – what comes before, what comes after – are established. That is what stratigraphy is all about. Then we deal with absolute dating, establishing dates in years. There radiocarbon dating and its calibration are crucial. Other methods of absolute dating are then briefly discussed.

RELATIVE DATING

The first, and in some ways the most important, step in much archaeological research involves ordering things into sequences. The things to be put into sequence can be archaeological deposits in a stratigraphic **excavation**. Or they can be artifacts, as in a typological sequence. Changes in the Earth's climate also give rise to local, regional, and global environmental sequences – the most notable being the sequence of global fluctuations during the Ice Age. All these sequences can be used for relative dating.

Stratigraphy: Ordering Archaeological Layers

Stratigraphy, as we saw in Chapter 3, is the study of **stratification** – the laying down or depositing of strata or layers (also called deposits) one above the other. From the point of view of relative dating, the important principle is that the underlying layer was deposited first and therefore earlier than the overlying layer. A succession of layers provides a relative chronological sequence, from earliest (bottom) to latest (top).

Good stratigraphic excavation at an archaeological site is designed to obtain such a sequence. Part of this work involves detecting whether there has been any human or natural disturbance of the layers since they were originally deposited (such as garbage pits dug down by later occupants of a site into earlier layers, or animals burrowing holes). Armed with carefully observed stratigraphic information, the archaeologist can hope to construct a reliable relative chronological sequence for the deposition of the different layers.

Key Concepts
Relative Dating Methods

- *Stratigraphy:* in a succession of layers the bottom layer is the earliest and the top layer the latest

- *Association:* objects found in the same stratigraphic layer were buried at the same time

- *Typological Sequences:* artifacts with similar characteristics were produced at the same time. "Like goes with like"

- *Seriation:* assemblages of objects can be arranged in serial order to create a relative chronology

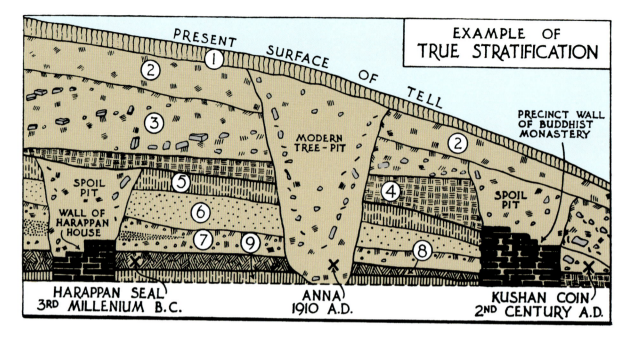

EXAMPLE OF
TRUE STRATIFICATION

PRESENT SURFACE OF TELL

① ② ③ ④ ⑤ ⑥ ⑦ ⑧ ⑨

MODERN TREE-PIT

PRECINCT WALL OF BUDDHIST MONASTERY

SPOIL PIT

WALL OF HARAPPAN HOUSE

SPOIL PIT

HARAPPAN SEAL 3RD MILLENIUM B.C.

ANNA 1910 A.D.

KUSHAN COIN 2ND CENTURY A.D.

Stratigraphy in action: a section across a mound or tell in the Indus Valley. Attention to stratigraphy is crucial because, as with the coins and the seal here, not everything found at the same level is always equally old.

But of course what we mostly want to date are not so much the layers or deposits themselves as the materials that humans have left within them – artifacts, structures, organic remains – that ultimately reveal past human activities at the site. Here the idea of **association** is important. When we say that two objects were found in association within the same archaeological deposit, we generally mean that they became buried at the same time. Provided that the deposit is a sealed one, without stratigraphic intrusions from another deposit, the associated objects can be said to be no more recent than the deposit itself. A sequence of sealed deposits thus gives a sequence – and relative chronology – for the time of burial of the objects found associated in those deposits.

This is a crucial concept to grasp, because if one of those objects can later be given an absolute date – say a datable coin or a piece of charcoal that can be dated by radiocarbon in the laboratory – then it is possible to assign that absolute date not only to the charcoal but to the sealed deposit and the other objects associated with it as well. A series of such dates from different deposits will give an absolute chronology for the whole sequence. It is this interconnecting of stratigraphic sequences with absolute dating methods that provides the most reliable basis for dating archaeological sites and their contents. The example shown above is Sir Mortimer Wheeler's drawing of a section across an ancient mound in the Indus Valley (modern Pakistan). The site has been disturbed by more recent pits, but the sequence of layers is still visible, and the Harappan seal, of known age and found in an undisturbed **context** in layer 8, helps to date that layer and the wall next to it.

But there is another important point to consider. So far we have dated, relatively and, with luck, absolutely, the time of burial of the deposits and their associated material. As we have observed, however, what we want ultimately to reconstruct and date are the past human activities and behavior that those deposits and materials represent. If a deposit is a garbage pit with pottery in it, the deposit itself is of interest as an example of human activity, and the date for it is the date of human use of the pit. This will also be the date of final burial of the pottery – but it will *not* be the date of human use of that pottery, which could have been in circulation tens or hundreds of years earlier, before being discarded with other garbage in the pit. It is necessary therefore always to be clear about which activity we are trying to date, or can reliably date in the circumstances.

Typological Sequences: Comparing Objects

When we look at the artifacts, buildings, or any of the human creations around us, most of us can mentally arrange them into a rough chronological sequence. One kind of aircraft looks older than another, one set of clothes looks more "old-fashioned" than the next. How do archaeologists exploit this ability for relative dating?

Archaeologists define the form of such an artifact as a pot by its specific **attributes** of material, shape, and decoration. Several pots with the same attributes constitute a pot **type**, and **typology** groups artifacts into such types. Underlying the notion of relative dating through typology are two other ideas.

The first is that the products of a given period and place have a recognizable **style**: through their distinctive shape and decoration they are in some sense characteristic of the society that produced them. The archaeologist or anthropologist can often recognize and classify individual artifacts by their style, and hence assign them to a particular place in a typological sequence.

The second idea is that the change in style (shape and decoration) of artifacts is often quite gradual, or evolutionary. This idea came from the Darwinian theory of the **evolution** of species, and was used by 19th-century archaeologists who applied a very convenient rule, that "like goes with like." In other words, particular artifacts (e.g. bronze daggers) produced at about the same time are often alike, but those produced several centuries apart will be different as a result of centuries of change. It follows, then, that when studying a series of daggers of unknown date, it is logical first to arrange them in a sequence in such a way that the most closely similar are located beside each other. This is then likely to be the true chronological sequence, because it best reflects the principle that "like goes with like." In the diagram to the left, designs of automobiles and prehistoric European axes have been arranged in a relative chronological sequence; however, the rate of change (a century for the automobile, millennia for the axe) has to be deduced from absolute dating methods.

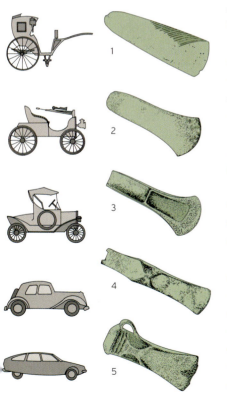

Gradual changes in design are evident in the history of the automobile and of the prehistoric European axe – (1) stone; (2–5) bronze.

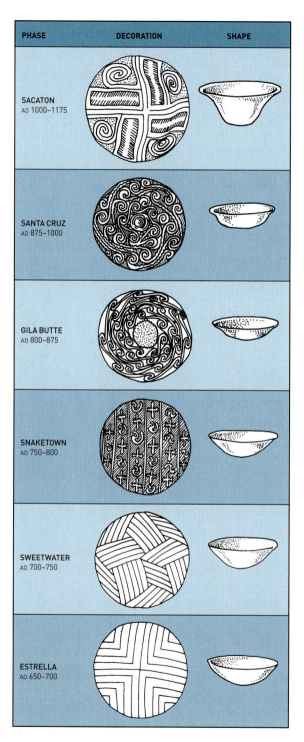

PHASE	DECORATION	SHAPE

SACATON
AD 1000–1175

SANTA CRUZ
AD 875–1000

GILA BUTTE
AD 800–875

SNAKETOWN
AD 750–800

SWEETWATER
AD 700–750

ESTRELLA
AD 650–700

Pottery typology, as exemplified by this 500-year sequence of Hohokam bowl styles from the American Southwest.

For many purposes, the best way to assign a relative date to an artifact is to match it with an artifact already recognized within a well-established typological system. Pottery typologies usually form the backbone of the chronological system, and nearly every area has its own well-established ceramic sequence. One example is the very extensive ceramic sequence for the ancient societies of the American Southwest, a part of which is shown in the diagram, left. If such a typology is tied into a stratigraphic sequence of deposits that can be dated by radiocarbon or other absolute means, then the artifacts in the typological sequence can themselves be assigned absolute dates in years.

Different types of artifact change in style (decoration and shape) at different rates, and therefore vary in the chronological distinctions that they indicate. Usually, with pottery, surface decoration changes most rapidly (often over periods of just a few decades) and is therefore the best attribute to use for a typological sequence. On the other hand, the shape of a vessel or container may be most strongly influenced by a practical requirement, such as water storage, which need not alter for hundreds of years.

Other artifacts, such as metal weapons or tools, can change in style quite rapidly, and so may be useful chronological indicators. By contrast, stone tools, such as **hand-axes**, are often very slow to change in form and therefore rarely make useful indicators of the passage of time (and are more useful in making general distinctions between much longer periods).

Seriation: Comparing Assemblages of Objects

The insights of the principle that "like goes with like" have been developed further to deal with associations of finds (**assemblages**) rather than with the forms of single objects taken in isolation. The technique of **seriation** allows assemblages of artifacts to be arranged in a succession or serial order, which is then taken to indicate their ordering in time, or their relative chronology.

The great pioneer of Egyptian archaeology, Sir William Flinders Petrie, was one of the first to develop a technique for arranging the graves of a cemetery in

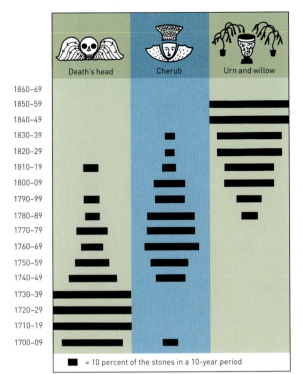

	Death's head	Cherub	Urn and willow

= 10 percent of the stones in a 10-year period

Seriation: changes in the popularity of central Connecticut tombstone designs. (Above right) The Death's head design.

relative order by considering carefully and systematically the associations of the various pottery forms found within them. His lead in the late 19th century was taken up half a century later by American scholars who realized that the frequency of a particular ceramic style, as documented in the successive layers of a settlement, is usually small to start with, rises to a peak as the style gains popularity, and then declines again (which diagrammatically produces a shape like a battleship viewed from above, known as a "battleship curve"). Using this insight they were able to compare the pottery assemblages from different sites in the same area, each with a limited stratigraphic sequence, and arrange these sites into chronological order so that the ceramic frequencies would conform to the pattern of rising to a maximum and then declining.

The diagram above shows how this technique has been applied to changes in the popularity of three tombstone designs found in central Connecticut cemeteries dating from 1700 to 1860. The fluctuating fortunes of each design produce characteristic and successive battleship curves – as elsewhere in New England, the Death's head design (peak popularity 1710–1739) was gradually replaced by the Cherub (peak 1760–1789), which in turn was replaced by the Urn and willow tree (peak 1840–1859).

Seriation has been used in an archaeological context by the American archaeologist Frank Hole in his excavations in the Deh Luran Plain in Iran. The **Neolithic** ceramic assemblages he was studying were derived from stratigraphic excavations, so it was possible to compare the sequences obtained through **frequency seriation** with the true stratigraphic sequences discovered in their excavations. There were no serious contradictions, again proving the validity of the method.

Environmental Sequences

So far in this chapter we have been discussing sequences that can be established either stratigraphically for individual sites, or typologically for artifacts. In addition, there is a major class of sequences, based on changes in the earth's climate, that has proved useful for relative dating on a local, regional, and even global scale. Some of these environmental sequences can also be dated by various absolute methods.

The Ice Age (or Pleistocene epoch, dating from 2.6 million years ago to 11,700 years ago), when world temperatures were usually much lower and ice covered large parts of the earth's surface, was not one long unbroken spell of cold. A complex sequence of cold periods (called glacials) were separated by warmer interludes (called interglacials). The interglacial period we now live in, known as the Holocene, covers the last 11,700 years. These climatic fluctuations are recorded in **deep-sea cores**, **ice cores**, and sediments containing pollen.

Foraminifera. These tiny (up to 1 mm) shells form the deep-sea sediments of the ocean floor. Analysis of shells in successive sediment layers gives a record of world sea temperature change.

Deep-Sea Cores and Ice Cores. The most coherent record of climatic changes on a worldwide scale is provided by deep-sea cores. These cores contain shells of microscopic marine organisms known as foraminifera, laid down on the ocean floor through the slow continuous process of sedimentation. Variations in the chemical structure of these shells are a good indicator of the sea temperature at the time the organisms were alive. Cold episodes in the deep-sea cores relate to glacial periods of ice advance, and the warm episodes to interglacial periods of ice retreat. Radiocarbon and uranium-series dating (see pp. 122–30) can also be applied to the foraminiferan shells to provide absolute dates for the sequence, which now stretches back 2.3 million years.

As with deep-sea cores, cores extracted from the polar ice of the Arctic and Antarctic have yielded impressive sequences revealing past climatic changes. The layers of compacted ice represent annual deposits for the last 2000–3000 years that can be counted – thus giving an absolute chronology for this part of the sequence. For earlier time periods – at greater depths – the annual stratification is no longer visible, and dating of the ice cores is much less certain. Good correlations have been made with climatic variations deduced from the study of the deep-sea cores.

Evidence of major volcanic eruptions can also be preserved in the ice cores, theoretically meaning that particular eruptions, such as the huge Thera eruption in the Aegean roughly 3500 years ago (associated by some scholars with the destruction of Minoan palaces on Crete), can be given a precise absolute date.

Key Concepts
Environmental Dating Methods

- *Deep-sea cores*: analysis of the chemical structure of microscopic marine organisms in datable layers of sediment can be used to reconstruct climate and provide a relative chronology

- *Ice cores*: similarly, layers of annual ice deposits can produce a chronology of world climate

- *Pollen dating*: pollen produced by past vegetation in a given area can reveal the climate of particular pollen zones and help to produce a relative chronology

In practice, though, it is hard to be certain that a volcanic event preserved in the ice actually relates to a particular historically documented eruption – it could relate to an unknown eruption that happened somewhere else in the world.

Pollen Dating.   All flowering plants produce grains called pollen, and these are almost indestructible, surviving for many thousands (and even millions) of years in all types of conditions. The preservation of pollen in bogs and lake sediments has allowed pollen experts (palynologists) to construct detailed sequences of past vegetation and climate. These sequences are an immense help in understanding ancient environments, but they have also been – and to some extent still are – important as a method of relative dating.

The best-known pollen sequences are those developed for the Holocene of northern Europe, where an elaborate succession of so-called pollen zones covers the last 10,000 years. By studying pollen samples from a particular site, that site can often be fitted into a broader pollen zone sequence and thus assigned a relative date. Isolated artifacts and such finds as bog bodies discovered in contexts where pollen is preserved can also be dated in the same way. It is important to remember, however, that the pollen zones are not uniform across large areas. Regional pollen zone sequences must first be established, and then the sites and finds in the area can be linked to them. If tree-ring or radiocarbon dates are available for all or part of the sequence, we can work out an absolute chronology for the region.

Thanks to the durability of pollen grains, they can yield environmental evidence even as far back as 3 million years ago for sites in East Africa. Different interglacial periods in such areas as northern Europe have also been shown to have characteristic pollen sequences, which means that the pollen evidence at an individual site in the area can sometimes be matched to a particular interglacial – a useful dating mechanism since radiocarbon cannot be used for these early time periods.

ABSOLUTE DATING

Although relative dating methods can be extremely useful, archaeologists ultimately want to know how old sequences, sites, and artifacts are in calendar years. To achieve this they need to use the methods of absolute dating described in the following sections. The three most commonly used and most important to the archaeologist are calendars and historical chronologies, **tree-ring dating**, and **radiocarbon dating**. For the Paleolithic period, potassium-argon dating and uranium-series dating are vital. Genetic dating is also now beginning to be used to date population events.

Calendars and Historical Chronologies

Until the development of the first scientific dating techniques around the beginning of the 20th century, dating in archaeology depended almost entirely on historical methods. That is to say, it relied on archaeological connections with chronologies and calendars that people in ancient times had themselves established. Such dating methods are still of immense value today. In the ancient world, literate societies recorded their own history in written documents. In Egypt, the Near East, and ancient China, for example, history was recorded in

Chronological table summarizing the spans of time for which different absolute dating methods are applicable.

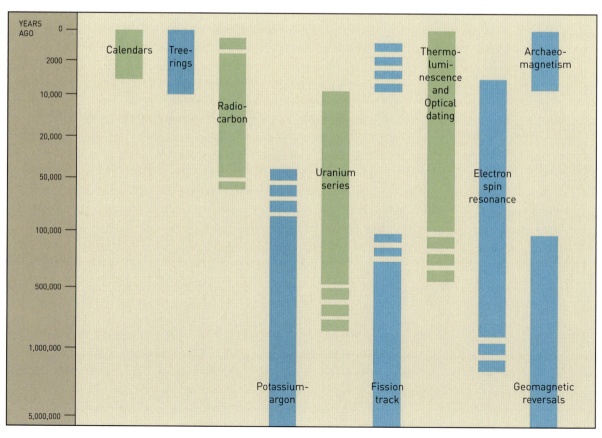

A Maya Long Count date in a tomb at the city of Río Azul, Guatemala. In modern terms the date given equates to 27 September AD 417.

terms of the successive kings, who were organized in groups of "dynasties." As we shall see, there were also very precise calendrical systems in Mesoamerica.

Archaeologists have to bear in mind three main points when working with early historical chronologies. First, the chronological system requires careful reconstruction, and any list of rulers or kings needs to be reasonably complete. Second, the list, although it may reliably record the number of years in each reign, has still to be linked with our own calendar. Third, the artifacts, **features**, or structures to be dated at a particular site have somehow to be related to the historical chronology, for example by their association with an inscription referring to the ruler of the time.

These points can be well illustrated by the Egyptian and Maya chronologies. Egyptian history is arranged in terms of 31 dynasties, themselves organized into the Old, Middle, and New Kingdoms. The modern view is a synthesis based on several documents including the so-called Turin Royal Canon. This synthesis gives an estimate of the number of years in each reign, right down to the conquest of Egypt by Alexander the Great in the year 332 BC (a date recorded by Greek historians). So the Egyptian dynasties can be dated by working backward from there, although the exact length of every reign is not known. This system can be confirmed and refined using astronomy: Egyptian historical records describe observations of certain astronomical events that can be independently dated using current astronomical knowledge and knowledge of where in Egypt the ancient observations were carried out. Egyptian dates are generally considered to be quite reliable after about 1500 BC, with a margin of error of perhaps one or two decades at most, but by the time we go back to the beginning of the dynastic period, around 3100 BC, the accumulated errors might amount to some 200 years or so.

Of the calendrical systems of Mesoamerica, the Maya calendar was the most elaborate and precise. It was used for recording exact dates of historical (and mythical) events in inscriptions on stone columns or **stelae** erected at Maya sites during the so-called Classic period (AD 300–900). The Maya had glyphs or signs for the days and the months, and a straightforward system of numerals, with a stylized shell representing zero, a dot "one," and a bar "five." The Maya actually had two concurrent calendrical systems, the first of which, the Calendar Round, was used for everyday purposes. Any day in the Calendar Round was identified by the conjunction of two different cycles: a Sacred Round of 260 named days, and a solar year of 365 named days. A specific day would only recur once every 52 years.

The second system, the Long Count, recorded days past since a mythical zero or starting point – 13 August 3113 BC in terms of our own calendar – and was used to refer to historical (or future) dates. The understanding of the Maya calendar, and the more recent decipherment of the Maya glyphs, mean that a well-dated Maya history is now emerging in a way that seemed impossible a few decades ago.

Using a Historical Chronology

It is relatively easy for the archaeologist to use a historical chronology when abundant artifacts are found that can be related closely to it. Thus, at major Maya sites, such as Tikal or Copan, there are numerous stelae with calendrical inscriptions that can often be used to date the buildings with which they are associated. The artifacts associated with the buildings can in turn be dated: for instance, if a pottery typology has been worked out, the finding of known types of pottery in such historically dated contexts allows the pottery typology itself to be dated. Contexts and buildings on other sites lacking inscriptions can be dated approximately through the occurrence of similar pot types.

Sometimes artifacts themselves carry dates, or the names of rulers that can be dated. This is the case with many Maya ceramics that bear hieroglyphic inscriptions. For the Roman and medieval periods of Europe, coins normally carry the name of the issuing ruler, and inscriptions or records elsewhere usually allow the ruler to be dated. But it is crucial to remember that to date a coin or an artifact is not the same thing as to date the context in which it is found. The date of the coin indicates the year in which it was made. Its inclusion within a sealed archaeological deposit establishes simply a *terminus post quem* (Latin for "date after which"): in other words, the deposit can be no earlier than the date on the coin – but it could be later (perhaps much later) than that date.

A well-established historical chronology in one country may be used to date events in neighboring and more far-flung lands that lack their own historical records but are mentioned in the histories of the literate homeland. Similarly, archaeologists can use exports and imports of objects to extend chronological linkages by means of cross-dating with other regions. For instance, the presence of foreign pottery in well-dated ancient Egyptian contexts establishes a *terminus ante quem* ("date before which") for the manufacture of that pottery: it cannot be more recent than the Egyptian context. In addition, Egyptian objects, some with inscriptions allowing them to be accurately dated in Egyptian terms, occur at various sites outside Egypt, thereby helping to date the contexts in which they are found.

Dating by historical methods remains the most important procedure for the archaeologist in countries with a reliable calendar supported by a significant degree of literacy. Where there are serious uncertainties over the calendar, or over its correlation with the modern calendrical system, the correlations can often be checked using other absolute dating methods, to be described below.

Outside the historic and literate lands, however, cross-dating and broad typological comparisons have been almost entirely superseded by the various scientifically based dating methods described below. Now, all the world's **cultures** can be assigned absolute dates.

Annual Cycles

Any absolute dating method depends on the existence of a regular, time-dependent process. The most obvious of these is the system by which we order our modern calendar: the rotation of the earth around the sun once each year. Because this yearly cycle produces regular annual fluctuations in climate, it has an impact on features of the environment that can in certain cases be measured to create a chronology. For absolute dating purposes the sequence needs to be a long one (with no gaps), linked somehow to the present day, and capable of being related to the structures or artifacts we actually want to date.

Evidence of these annual fluctuations in climate is widespread. For example, the changes in temperature in polar regions result in annual variations in the thickness of polar ice, which scientists can study from cores drilled through the ice (see p. 114). Similarly, in lands bordering the polar regions, the melting of the ice sheets each year when temperatures rise leads to the formation of annual deposits of sediment in lake beds, called **varves**, which can be counted. Considerable deposits of varves were found in Scandinavia, representing thousands of years, stretching (when linked together) from the present back to the beginning of the retreat of the glacial ice sheets in that region some 13,000 years ago. The method allowed, for the first time, a fairly reliable estimate for the date of the end of the last Ice Age, and hence made a contribution to archaeological chronology not only in Scandinavia but also in many other parts of the world.

But today, while varves remain of restricted use, another annual cycle, that of tree-rings, has come to rival radiocarbon as the main method of dating for the last few thousand years in many parts of Europe, North America, and Japan.

Tree-Ring Dating

The modern technique of tree-ring dating (**dendrochronology**) was developed by an American astronomer, A.E. Douglass, in the early decades of the last century – although many of the principles had been understood long before that. Working on well-preserved timbers in the arid American Southwest, by 1930 Douglass could assign absolute dates to many of the major sites there, such as Mesa Verde and Pueblo Bonito. But it was not until the end of the 1930s that the technique was introduced to Europe, and only in the 1960s that the use of statistical procedures and computers laid the foundations for the establishment of the long tree-ring chronologies now so fundamental to modern archaeology. Today dendrochronology has two distinct archaeological uses: (1) as a successful means of calibrating or correcting radiocarbon dates (see below); and (2) as an independent method of absolute dating in its own right.

Basis of Method. Most trees produce a ring of new wood each year, and these circles of growth can easily be seen in a cross-section of the trunk of a felled tree. These rings are not of uniform thickness. In an individual tree, they will vary for

Section of an oak beam from the wall of a log cabin in Hanover, Pennsylvania, USA: the annual growth rings are clearly visible, and since this sample contains complete sapwood (top of image), a precise felling date of 1850/1 can be established.

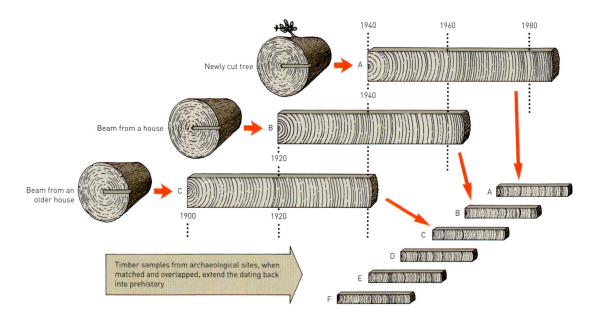

Tree-ring dating: annual growth rings can be counted, matched, and overlapped, to build up a master sequence for a particular region.

two reasons. First, the rings become narrower with the increasing age of the tree. Second, the amount a tree grows each year is affected by fluctuations in climate. In arid regions, rainfall above the average one year will produce a particularly thick annual ring. In more temperate regions, sunlight and temperature may be more critical than rainfall in affecting a tree's growth. Here, a sharp cold spell in spring may produce a narrow growth ring.

Dendrochronologists measure and plot these rings and produce a diagram indicating the thickness of successive rings in an individual tree. Trees of the same species growing in the same area will generally show the same pattern of rings so that the growth sequence can be matched between successively older timbers to build up a chronology for an area. (It is not necessary to fell trees in order to study

Key Concepts
Tree-Ring Dating

- *Method*: based on the annual cycle of tree-ring growth

- *Range*: up to 5300 BC (Ireland); 8500 BC (Germany); 6700 BC (US)

- *Precision*: 1 year

- *Applications*: direct dating of wood; calibration of radiocarbon dates

- *Limitations*: restricted to regions outside the tropics and to certain species of tree (although calibration is thought to work on a worldwide scale); care must be taken interpreting results

the ring sequence: a usable sample can be extracted by boring without harming the tree.) By matching sequences of rings from living trees of different ages as well as from old timber, dendrochronologists can produce a long, continuous sequence, such as that in the diagram opposite, extending back hundreds, even thousands, of years from the present. Thus, when an ancient timber of the same species (e.g. Douglas fir in the American Southwest or oak in Europe) is found, it should be possible to match its tree-ring sequence of, say, 100 years with the appropriate 100-year length of the master sequence or chronology. In this way, the felling date for that piece of timber can usually be dated to within a year.

Applications. One of the most important uses of tree-ring dating has been the development of long tree-ring sequences, against which it is possible to check radiocarbon dates. The pioneering research was done in Arizona on a remarkable species, the Californian bristlecone pine, which can live up to 4900 years. By matching samples from dead trees also, an unbroken sequence was built up back from the present as far as 6700 BC. The importance of this for the calibration of radiocarbon dates is discussed below. The research in the American Southwest has been complemented by studies in Europe of tree-rings of oak, often well preserved in waterlogged deposits. The oak sequence in Northern Ireland stretches back unbroken to c. 5300 BC, and the master sequence in western Germany to c. 8500 BC.

Direct tree-ring dating of preserved timber found in archaeological contexts has itself been important in several areas, but results are particularly impressive in the American Southwest, where the technique is longest established and wood is well preserved in the arid conditions. For instance, Betatakin, a cliff dwelling in Arizona, has been precision dated using dendrochronology so that not only do we know that the settlement was founded in AD 1267, but we also can track the expansion of the site room by room, year by year, until it reached a peak in the mid-1280s, before being abandoned shortly thereafter.

Limiting Factors. Unlike radiocarbon, dendrochronology is not a worldwide dating method because of two basic limitations:

1 it applies only to trees in regions outside the tropics where pronounced differences between the seasons produce clearly defined annual rings;
2 a direct tree-ring date is restricted to wood from those species that (a) have yielded a master sequence back from the present and (b) people actually used in the past, and where (c) the sample affords a sufficiently long record to give a unique match.

In addition, there are important questions of interpretation to consider. A tree-ring date refers to the date of felling of the tree. This is determined by matching the tree-ring sample ending with the outermost rings (the sapwood) to a regional sequence. Where most or all of the sapwood is missing, the felling date cannot be identified. But even with an accurate felling date, the archaeologist has to make a judgment – based on context and **formation processes** – about how soon after felling the timber entered the archaeological deposit. Timbers may be older or younger than the structures into which they were finally incorporated, depending on whether they were reused from somewhere else, or used to make a repair in a long-established structure. The best solution is to take multiple samples, and to check the evidence carefully on-site. Despite these qualifications, dendrochronology looks set to become the major dating technique, alongside radiocarbon, for the last 8000 years in temperate and arid lands.

Radioactive Clocks

Many of the most important developments in absolute dating have come from the use of what might be called "radioactive clocks," based on that widespread and regular feature in the natural world, **radioactive decay**. The best known of these methods is radiocarbon, today the main dating tool for the last 50,000 years or so.

Radiocarbon Dating

Radiocarbon is the single most useful method of dating for the archaeologist. As we shall see, it has its limitations, both in terms of accuracy, and for the time range where it is useful. Archaeologists themselves are also the cause of major errors, thanks to poor sampling procedures and careless interpretation. Nevertheless, radiocarbon has transformed our understanding of the past, helping archaeologists to establish for the first time a reliable chronology of world cultures.

History and Basis of Method.   In 1949, the American chemist Willard Libby published the first radiocarbon dates. During World War II he had been studying cosmic radiation, the sub-atomic particles that constantly bombard the earth. These produce high-energy neutrons, which in turn react with nitrogen atoms in the atmosphere to produce atoms of carbon-14 (^{14}C), or radiocarbon, which are unstable because they have eight neutrons in the nucleus instead of the usual six as for ordinary carbon (see box opposite). This instability leads to radioactive decay of ^{14}C at a regular rate. Libby estimated that it took 5568 years for half the ^{14}C in any sample to decay – its **half-life** (see diagram opposite) – although modern research indicates that the more accurate figure is 5730 years.

Libby realized that the decay of radiocarbon at a constant rate should be balanced by its constant production through cosmic radiation, and that therefore the proportion of ^{14}C in the atmosphere should remain the same throughout time. Furthermore, this steady atmospheric concentration of radiocarbon is passed on uniformly to all living things through carbon dioxide,

The Principles of Radioactive Decay

Like most elements occurring in nature, carbon exists in more than one isotopic form. It has three isotopes: ^{12}C, ^{13}C, and ^{14}C – the numbers correspond to the atomic weights of these isotopes. In any sample of carbon, 98.9 percent of atoms are of ^{12}C type and have six protons and six neutrons in the nucleus, and 1.1 percent are of the ^{13}C type with six protons and seven neutrons. Only one atom in a million millions of atoms of carbon will be that of the isotope ^{14}C, with eight neutrons in the nucleus. This isotope of carbon is produced in the upper atmosphere by cosmic rays bombarding nitrogen (^{14}N) and it contains an excess of neutrons,

making it unstable. It decays by the emission of weak beta radiation back to its precursor isotope of nitrogen – ^{14}N – with seven protons and seven neutrons in a nucleus. Like all types of radioactive decay the process takes place at a constant rate, independent of all environmental conditions.

The time taken for half of the atoms of a radioactive isotope to decay is called its half-life. In other words, after one half-life, there will be half of the atoms left; after two half-lives, one-quarter of the original quantity of isotope remains, and so on. In the case of ^{14}C, the half-life is now agreed to be 5730 years.

Half-lives of radioactive isotopes of other elements can range from thousands of millions of years to a minute fraction of a second. But in every case, there is a regular pattern to the decay.

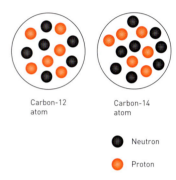

Carbon-12 atom Carbon-14 atom

● Neutron
● Proton

(Below left) Radiocarbon is produced in the atmosphere and absorbed by plants through carbon dioxide, and by animals through feeding off plants or other animals. Uptake of ^{14}C ceases when the plant or animal dies. (Below) After death, the amount of ^{14}C decays at a known rate (50 percent after 5730 years, etc.). Measurement of the amount left in a sample gives the date.

NEUTRON + NITROGEN-14
CARBON-14
CARBON DIOXIDE

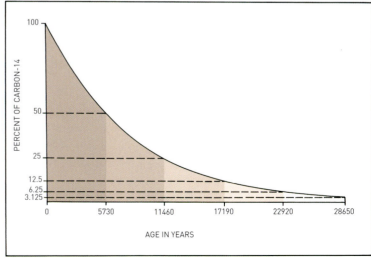

as part of what is known as the "carbon cycle." Plants take up carbon dioxide during photosynthesis, they are eaten by herbivorous animals, which in turn are eaten by carnivores. When a plant or animal dies the uptake of ^{14}C ceases, and the steady concentration of ^{14}C begins to decline through radioactive decay. Thus, knowing the decay rate or half-life of ^{14}C, Libby recognized that the age of dead plant or animal tissue could be calculated by measuring the amount of radiocarbon left in a sample. Samples usually consist of organic materials found on archaeological sites, such as charcoal, wood, seeds, and other plant remains, and human or animal bone. Inorganic materials, for example stone, are not part of the carbon cycle and so cannot be radiocarbon dated.

Libby's great practical achievement was to devise an accurate means of measurement. He discovered that each atom of ^{14}C decays by releasing a beta particle, and he succeeded in counting these emissions using a Geiger counter, still the basis of the conventional method employed by many radiocarbon laboratories today. Advances were made in the late 1970s and early 1980s with the introduction of special gas counters capable of taking measurements from very small samples.

In the conventional method some 5 g of pure carbon after purification was needed, which means an original sample of some 10–20 g of wood or charcoal, or 100–200 g of bone. The special gas-counting equipment required only a few hundred milligrams (mg) of charcoal.

Increasingly, the accelerator mass spectrometry (AMS) method is becoming the dominant technique used in radiocarbon dating. This requires smaller samples still. Disregarding their radioactivity, AMS counts the atoms of ^{14}C directly. The minimum sample size is reduced to as little as 5–10 mg – thus enabling precious organic materials, such as the Turin Shroud (see p. 128), to be sampled and directly dated, and making feasible the direct dating of pollen.

Key Concepts
Radiocarbon Dating

- *Method*: based on the regular decay of a radioactive isotope of carbon

- *Range*: 400–50,000 years ago (AMS)

- *Precision*: Many complicating factors, but often within c. 50–100 years

- *Applications*: dating of any organic matter (containing carbon); new techniques allow very small sample sizes, meaning grain, seeds, and precious objects can be dated

- *Calibration*: radiocarbon dates must be calibrated to arrive at a calendar date

- *Limitations*: samples must be carefully chosen; samples can easily be contaminated; results can be difficult to interpret correctly and require statistical treatment

Initially it was hoped that the datable timespan for radiocarbon using AMS could be pushed back from 50,000 to 80,000 years, although this is proving difficult to achieve, in part because of sample contamination.

Radiocarbon dates are usually quoted in years BP (before the present, currently taken to be AD 1950), but because the accurate measurement of the ^{14}C activity of a sample is affected by counting errors, background cosmic radiation, and other intrinsic factors, there is always an element of uncertainty to the measurements. Thus there is always a statistical error or "standard deviation" attached to a radiocarbon date, expressed as a plus/minus term. Radiocarbon dates are quoted with an error of one standard deviation. For a date of 3700 ±100 BP, for example, this means that there is a 68.2 percent probability, or roughly two chances in three, that the correct estimate in radiocarbon years lies between 3800 and 3600 BP (of course this also means that there is a one in three chance that it doesn't). Double to two standard deviations, and there is a 95.4 percent chance (19 chances in 20) that the radiocarbon age of the sample lies between 3900 and 3500 BP, or in other words 3700 ±200 BP.

But there is a complication: these dates still do not, unfortunately, equate with true calendar years. To convert radiocarbon years into calendar years requires calibration.

Calibration of Radiocarbon Dates.   One of the basic assumptions of the radiocarbon method has turned out to be not quite correct. Libby assumed that the concentration of ^{14}C in the atmosphere has been constant through time, but we now know that it has varied. The method that demonstrated the inaccuracy – tree-ring dating – has also provided the means of correcting or calibrating radiocarbon dates.

Radiocarbon dates obtained from tree-rings show that before about 1000 BC dates expressed in radiocarbon years are increasingly too young in relation to true calendar years. In other words, before 1000 BC trees (and all other living things) were exposed to greater concentrations of atmospheric ^{14}C than they are today. By obtaining radiocarbon dates systematically from the long tree-ring master sequences of bristlecone pine and oak (see p. 121), scientists have been able to plot radiocarbon ages against tree-ring ages (in calendar years) to produce calibration curves, such as the one shown on p. 127. Very broadly, these curves show that radiocarbon ages diverge increasingly from true ages before 1000 BC, so that by 5000 BC in calendar years the radiocarbon age is 900 years too young. Thus an age estimate in radiocarbon years of 6050 BP might well in fact when calibrated be somewhere near 5000 BC. For dates beyond 12,600 years ago, the current scope of tree-ring dating, scientists have been able to use data from uranium-thorium dated corals and varve-counted marine sediments to produce a calibration curve going back some 50,000 years. The box overleaf gives a more detailed explanation of the calibration process.

How to Calibrate Radiocarbon Dates

Radiocarbon laboratories will generally supply calibrated dates of their samples, but archaeologists may need to calibrate raw radiocarbon dates themselves.

The calibration curve, part of which is shown in the diagram on p. 127, illustrates the relationship between radiocarbon years (BP) and samples dated in actual calendar years (Calibrated or "Cal" BP or BC/AD). In order to find the calibrated age range of a radiocarbon sample, a computer program is most often used. There are several that are freely available on the Internet (OxCal, BCal, CALIB, etc). With OxCal (http://c14.arch.ox.ac.uk/oxcal) a simple plot is generated of a single calibrated result, such as in the

diagram below. In this example one can see the radiocarbon date of 470 ±35 BP is represented in the form of a probability distribution on the y-axis. This distribution is transformed, using the calibration curve, into a probability distribution on the x-axis, representing calendar years. The calibrated date at one standard deviation is thus 530–503 Cal BP, or 1420–1447 Cal AD. The parts of the radiocarbon distribution that have higher levels of probability also have a higher probability on the calendar scale.

The calibration curve is full of steep and sometimes wiggly sections, including sections with plateaux where the amount of radiocarbon in the atmosphere remains the same

over long periods of time. Here the calibration precision is always wide (the problem is particularly irksome for dating in the period 800–400 BC). Even dating single samples at high levels of precision (some laboratories are able to produce dates with a ± of 15–20 years), or dating multiple samples (which can then be averaged), cannot substantially improve the situation.

This diagram shows the calibration of a single radiocarbon date using OxCal. The y-axis shows the probability distribution of the radiocarbon age 470 ±35 BP (in pink). The measured age is calibrated using the INTCAL09 calibration curve (in blue), forming the new probability distribution (in gray), which is the calibrated age. Age ranges at 68.2 and 95.4 percent probability are given.

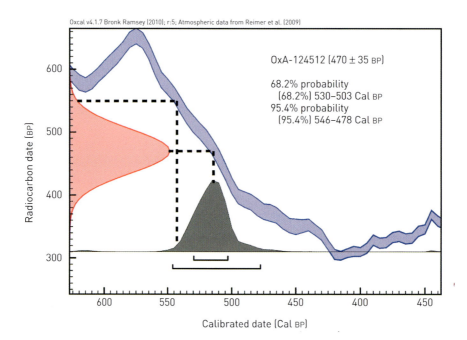

Oxcal v4.1.7 Bronk Ramsey (2010); r:5; Atmospheric data from Reimer et al. (2009)

OxA-124512 (470 ± 35 BP)

68.2% probability
(68.2%) 530–503 Cal BP
95.4% probability
(95.4%) 546–478 Cal BP

Radiocarbon date (BP)

Calibrated date (Cal BP)

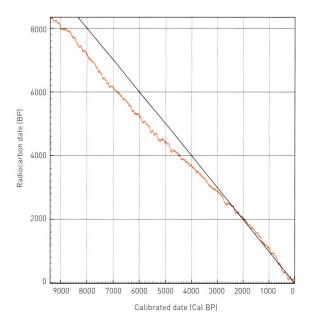

The wiggles of the INTCAL09 calibration curve over the last 9000 years. The straight line indicates the ideal 1:1 timescale.

Contamination and Interpretation of Radiocarbon Samples. Although radiocarbon dates have certain inescapable levels of error associated with them, inaccurate results are as likely to derive from poor sampling and incorrect interpretation by the archaeologist as from inadequate laboratory procedures. The major sources of error in the field are summed up below:

- *Contamination before sampling.* Problems of contamination of the sample within the ground can be serious. For instance, groundwater on waterlogged sites can dissolve organic materials and also deposit them, thus changing the amount of ^{14}C in a sample. These matters can usually be tackled in the laboratory.
- *Contamination during or after sampling.* Any modern organic material coming into contact with a sample can contaminate it, but some, such as roots and earth, cannot always be prevented. However, such sources of contamination can be eliminated in the laboratory.
- *Context of deposition.* Many errors arise because the excavator has not fully understood the formation processes of the context in question. Unless it is appreciated how the dated material found its way to its find spot, and how and when it came to be buried, then precise interpretation is impossible.
- *Date of context.* Too often, it is assumed that a radiocarbon determination, e.g. on charcoal, will simply date the charcoal's burial. However, if that charcoal derives from roof timbers that might themselves have been several centuries old when destroyed by fire, then some early construction is being dated, not the fire. For this reason, samples with a short life are often preferred, such as twigs or charred cereal grains, which are not likely to be old at the time of burial.

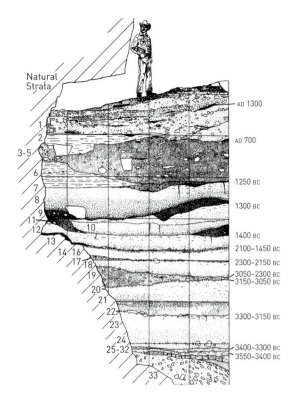

Natural Strata

AD 1300
AD 700
1250 BC
1300 BC
1400 BC
2100–1450 BC
2300–2150 BC
3050–2300 BC
3150–3050 BC
3300–3150 BC
3400–3300 BC
3550–3400 BC

A strategy for sampling should be based on the wise saying that "one date is no date": several are needed. The best procedure is to work toward an internal relative sequence of dates – for instance, in the stratigraphic succession on a well-stratified site, such as the Gatecliff Shelter, Monitor Valley, Nevada, shown left. If the samples can be arranged in relative sequence in this way, with the lowest unit having the earliest date and so on, then there is an internal check on the coherence of the laboratory determinations and on the quality of field sampling. Some of the dates from such a sequence may come out older than expected. This is quite reasonable as some of the material may have been "old" at the time of burial. But if they come out younger (i.e. more recent) than expected, then there is something wrong. Either some contamination has affected the samples, or the laboratory has made a serious error, or the stratigraphic interpretation is wrong.

(Above) Master profile for Gatecliff Shelter, Nevada, showing how dates derived from radiocarbon determinations are consistent with the stratigraphic succession.

(Below) Part of the Turin Shroud. Radiocarbon AMS dating has given a calibrated age range for the cloth of AD 1260–1390.

The Impact of Radiocarbon Dating. Radiocarbon has undoubtedly offered the most generally useful way of answering the question "When?" in archaeology. The greatest advantage is that the method can be used anywhere, whatever the climate, as long as there is material of organic (i.e. living) origin. Thus the method works as well in South America or Polynesia as it does in Egypt or Mesopotamia. And it can take us back 50,000 years – although at the other end of the timescale it is too imprecise to be of much use for the 400 years of the most recent past. Radiocarbon has been incredibly important in establishing for the first time broad chronologies for the world's cultures that previously lacked timescales (such as calendars) of their own. Calibration of radiocarbon has increased, not diminished, this success.

Radiocarbon dating by the AMS technique is opening up new possibilities. Precious objects and works of art can now be dated because minute samples are all that is required. In 1988 AMS dating was used on the Turin Shroud, a piece of cloth with the image of a man's body on it that many genuinely believed to be the actual imprint of the body of Christ. Laboratories at Tucson, Oxford, and Zurich all placed it in the 14th century AD, not from the time of Christ at all, although this remains a matter of controversy.

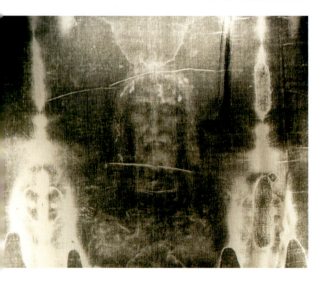

Other Radiometric Methods

Radiocarbon is likely to maintain its position as the main dating tool back to 50,000 years ago for organic materials, but the half-life of radiocarbon is such that, for particularly old samples, there is hardly any radioactivity left to measure. So, for inorganic or very ancient materials, other methods have to be used.

The most important of them are also radiometric – they depend upon the measurement of natural radioactivity. But they use elements the radioactive isotopes of which have very much longer half-lives than the 5730 years of carbon-14. They have two drawbacks. In the first place, they depend upon elements less frequently found in archaeological contexts than is carbon. And secondly, the long half-lives generally mean that the datings are less precise.

Potassium-Argon Dating   The **potassium-argon** (K-Ar) method is used by geologists to date volcanic rocks hundreds or even thousands of millions of years old, but no more recent than around 80,000 years old.

K-Ar dating is based on the steady but very slow decay of the radioactive isotope potassium-40 (^{40}K) to the inert gas argon-40 (^{40}Ar) in volcanic rock. Knowing the decay rate of ^{40}K – its half life is around 1.3 billion years – a measure of the quantity of ^{40}Ar trapped within a 10g rock sample gives an estimate of the date of the rock's formation. The principal limitation of the technique is that it can only be used to date sites buried by volcanic rock.

The results are effectively geological dates for the eruption leading to the formation of volcanic strata. Fortunately, some of the most important areas for the study of the Lower Paleolithic, notably the Rift Valley in East Africa, are volcanic areas. The chronology of Olduvai Gorge, for example, which has provided important fossil remains of **Australopithecus**, *Homo habilis*, and *Homo erectus*, has been well established by K-Ar dating. At this and other similar sites, archaeological remains frequently lie on volcanic strata, and moreover they are often overlain by comparable volcanic rock, so that K-Ar dates for these two geological strata provide a time range for the material we are trying to date. The K-Ar method, in conjunction with a variety of other techniques, has also been used to date the important early human site at Atapuerca in Spain (see box overleaf).

Uranium-Series Dating   This dating method is based on the radioactive decay of isotopes of uranium. It has proved particularly useful for the period 500,000 to 50,000 years ago, which again lies outside the time range of radiocarbon dating. In Europe, where there are relatively few volcanic rocks suitable for dating by the potassium-argon technique, **uranium series** (U-series) **dating** may be the method of first choice for early human sites – it has been used effectively, for example, on the skulls and other skeletal remains of very early *Homo sapiens* found at Qafzeh and Skhul caves in Israel. It has also been used successfully at Atapuerca in Spain.

The method dates the time of formation of travertine (calcium carbonate), which is often deposited on cave walls and floors, and hence can be used to date any material, such as an artifact or bone, embedded in a layer of travertine or in another type of sediment between two layers of it. The method is also applicable to teeth, since these absorb water-soluble uranium when buried. High-precision measurement can give an error margin of fewer than 1000 years for a 100,000 year-old sample, and the method can also be cross-checked with **electron spin resonance** dates using the same materials (see p. 133).

Fission-Track Dating Fission-track dating depends upon the spontaneous fission (or division) of radioactive uranium atoms (^{238}U), present in a wide range of rocks and minerals, which causes damage to the structures of the minerals involved. In materials where ^{238}U is present, including volcanic and manufactured glasses, and such minerals as zircon and apatite, found within rock formations, the damage is recorded in pathways called fission tracks. The tracks can be counted in the laboratory under an optical microscope. Since we know the rate of fission of ^{238}U, this allows the date of formation of the rock or glass to be determined.

In this case, the radioactive clock is set at zero by the formation of the mineral or glass, either in nature (as with **obsidian**) or at the time of manufacture (as with manufactured glass). The method produces useful dates from suitable rocks that contain or are adjacent to those containing archaeological evidence, and has been used with success at early Paleolithic sites, such as Olduvai Gorge, Tanzania, providing independent confirmation of potassium-argon and other results.

Examples of fission tracks, after etching.

Dating Early Europeans at Atapuerca, Spain

The Sierra de Atapuerca, near Burgos in northern Spain, is a veritable treasure house of sites – mostly infilled caves – that are rewriting the early prehistory of western Europe, where human occupation before 500,000 years ago had been doubtful. Excavations there have been continuing for decades, but still only a tiny fraction of the Sierra's contents have been investigated. Atapuerca ranks as one the world's most important archaeological areas.

A variety of dating techniques has been used, from faunal analysis (making comparisons between animal remains found at the site and others of known date) to radiocarbon, potassium-argon, and uranium-series. They have combined to present evidence of human occupation stretching back more than 1 million years. Of particular importance are levels at the Gran Dolina site, dating from c. 800,000 to 1 million years ago. In 1994 human remains and stone tools found in them provided the first undeniable evidence for hominins in Europe during the Lower Pleistocene – the hominins were given a new species name, *Homo antecessor*. Electron spin resonance and uranium-series dating of teeth confirmed the Lower Pleistocene dates.

In the Galeria site, the lowest layers have been dated to more than 780,000 years ago by means of archaeomagnetism (which indicated a period of reversed polarity known as the Matuyama epoch), while younger layers have been dated by electron spin resonance and uranium-series to 350,000–300,000 and 200,000.

The Sima del Elefante has a deep stratigraphy; faunal, microfaunal,

and archaeomagnetic analyses here have shown that the lowest section – which has yielded stone flakes made by humans – dates to the Lower Pleistocene, more than 1 million years ago. In 1998 it was announced that a human jaw together with stone tools had been recovered from a layer that a number of methods has combined to place at 1.1–1.2 million years ago, making it the oldest and most securely dated record of human occupation in Europe.

Microfaunal analysis, electron spin resonance, and uranium-series methods in the Sima de los Huesos have established that a speleothem (mineral deposit) that covers the layer containing human bones dates to at least 350,000 years ago, while high-resolution uranium-series dates have shown that the bodies were placed here about 600,000 years ago.

(Top) Some of the 5500 human fossils from the Sima de los Huesos, dating to more than 350,000 years ago. (Center) The skull of *Homo antecessor*, found at Gran Dolina. (Below) Excavation at Gran Dolina

Other Absolute Dating Methods

There are several more dating methods that can be used in special circumstances, but none is as important in practice to archaeologists as those already described. Some are of relevance to the solution of specific problems, such as the dating of Paleolithic rock art. Several of the most significant are mentioned below, so that the overview given in this chapter is reasonably complete. But the discussion here is deliberately kept brief, to give a flavour of a field that can easily become rather complicated, and that is not directly relevant to much mainstream archaeology. The rather special case of DNA dating is of particular interest.

Thermoluminescence Dating **Thermoluminescence** (TL) dating can be used to date crystalline materials (minerals) buried in the ground, which have been fired – usually pottery, but also baked clay, burnt stone, and in some circumstances burnt soil. But unfortunately it is a method that is difficult to make precise, and so it is generally used when other methods, such as radiocarbon dating, are not available.

Like many other methods it depends upon radioactive decay, but in this case it is the amount of radioactivity received by the specimen since the start date that is of interest, not the radiation emitted by the specimen itself. When atoms located within the structure of a mineral are exposed to radiation from the decay of radioactive elements in the nearby environment, some of that energy is "trapped." If the amount of radiation remains constant over time, then this energy will accumulate at a uniform rate and the total amount of energy will depend upon the total time of exposure. When a sample is heated to 500°C or more, the trapped energy is released as thermoluminescence, and the "radioactive clock" is set back to zero.

This means that archaeological artifacts, such as pottery, will have had their clocks reset when they were originally fired, and that by reheating samples from these objects, we can measure the thermoluminescence released and hence date the material. The main complication of the method is that the level of background radiation that a sample might have been exposed to is not

Key Concepts
Thermoluminescence Dating

- *Range*: Up to 100,000 years ago

- *Precision*: ±5–10 percent on site; 25 percent otherwise

- *Applications*: Dates minerals that have been sufficiently heated and then buried. Can be applied to pottery, other baked clay, and burnt stone

uniform – it must be measured for every sample by burying a small capsule containing a radiation-sensitive material, or by using a radiation counter at the exact spot the sample was found. In general, the difficulties of making these measurements mean that TL dates rarely have a precision of better than ±10 percent of the age of the sample.

A good example of the archaeological application of TL is the dating of the terracotta head known as the Jemaa head, from the alluvium of a tin mine near the Jos Plateau of Nigeria. The head and similar examples belong to the Nok culture, but such sculptures could not be dated reliably at the site of Nok itself because of the lack of any plausible radiocarbon dates. A TL reading on the head gave an age of 1520 ±260 BC, allowing this and similar heads from the Nok region to be given a firm chronological position for the first time.

Optical Dating   This method is similar in principle to TL, but it is used to date minerals that have been exposed to light, rather than heat. Most minerals contain some trapped energy that will be released by several minutes' exposure to sunlight. Such exposure is in effect the start point. Once buried they begin to accumulate electrons once more, as a result of radioactive radiation experienced in the soil. In the laboratory, optically stimulated luminescence (OSL) is produced by directing light of a visible wavelength onto the sample, and the resultant luminescence is measured. And once again the background radiation at the place of burial has to be measured, so optical dating suffers from many of the same complications as TL.

Electron Spin Resonance Dating   Electron spin resonance (ESR) is a technique similar to but less sensitive than TL, but it can be used for materials that decompose when heated and thus where TL is not applicable. Its most successful application so far has been for the dating of tooth enamel. Newly formed tooth enamel contains no trapped energy, but it begins to accumulate once the tooth is buried and exposed to natural background radiation. The precision of the method when used to date tooth enamel is in the order of 10–20 percent, but it is still very useful for the study of early humans and the cross-checking of other dating methods.

Archaeomagnetic Dating and Geomagnetic Reversals   **Archaeomagnetic** (or paleomagnetic) **dating** has so far been of limited use in archaeology. It is based on the constant change, both in direction and intensity, of the earth's magnetic field. The direction of that magnetic field at a particular time is recorded in any baked-clay structure (oven, kiln, hearth etc.) that has been heated to a temperature of 650 to 700°C. At that temperature the iron particles in the clay permanently take up the earth's magnetic direction and intensity at the time of firing. This principle is called thermoremanent magnetism (TRM).

This 2-million-year-old skull was discovered in South Africa in 2008. It has been tentatively assigned to a new species, *Australopithecus sediba*, possibly representing a transitional phase between the australopithecines and hominins.

Charts can be built up of the variation through time that can be used to date baked-clay structures of unknown age, the TRM of which is measured and then matched to a particular point on the master sequence.

Another aspect of archaeomagnetism, relevant for the dating of the Lower Paleolithic, is the phenomenon of complete reversals in the earth's magnetic field (magnetic north becomes magnetic south, and vice versa). The most recent major reversal occurred about 780,000 years ago, and a sequence of such reversals stretching back several millions of years has been built up with the aid of potassium-argon and other dating techniques.

Genetic Dating The methods now being used by molecular geneticists present rather a special case. They use DNA samples from living human populations to date population events, notably migrations. Genetic dating is now well established as one of the principal dating methods available in human population studies. Using assumptions about genetic mutation rates, they can date approximately the appearance of new genetic categories and thus give a date to such important processes as the "Out of Africa" dispersal of our species (around 60,000–50,000 years ago; see following section on world chronology). It is the information within living humans that provides the data, not ancient excavated samples: our past within us! Recently, however, techniques of analysis have improved, so that it is now sometimes also possible to analyse the DNA from human bones found in secure archaeological contexts. But in such cases the date of the bones derives from the context, not from the DNA.

World Chronology

As a result of the application of the various dating techniques discussed above, it is possible to summarize the world archaeological chronology, from the evolution of human ancestors millions of years ago in Africa, to the spread of our own species around the world, and the eventual development of agriculture and complex societies.

The human story as understood at present begins in East Africa, with the emergence there of the earliest **hominins** of the genus *Australopithecus*, such as *A. afarensis*, around 4 million years ago, and the possibly earlier *Ardipithecus*. By around 2 million years ago, there is clear fossil evidence for the first known representative of our own genus, *Homo habilis*, from such sites as Koobi Fora (Kenya) and Olduvai Gorge (Tanzania). The earliest stone tools (from Hadar, Ethiopia) date from about 2.5 million years ago, but it is not known which hominin made them because *Homo* fossils of this age have not yet been found. It is possible that australopithecines also had a tool culture before or during *Homo*'s time. The early toolkits, comprising flake and pebble tools, are called the **Oldowan industry** – after Olduvai Gorge, where they are particularly well represented.

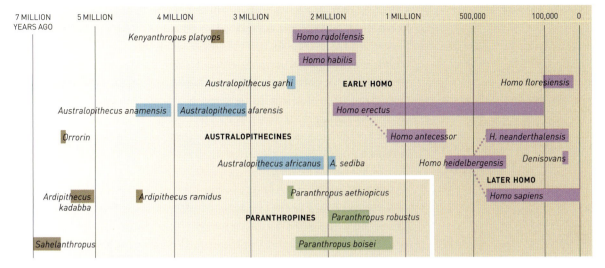

| 7 MILLION YEARS AGO | 5 MILLION | 4 MILLION | 3 MILLION | 2 MILLION | 1 MILLION | 500,000 | 100,000 | 0 |

Kenyanthropus platyops

Homo rudolfensis

Homo habilis

Australopithecus garhi   **EARLY HOMO**   *Homo floresiensis*

Australopithecus anamensis *Australopithecus afarensis* *Homo erectus*

Orrorin   **AUSTRALOPITHECINES**   *Homo antecessor*   *H. neanderthalensis*

Australopithecus africanus *A. sediba* *Homo heidelbergensis* *Denisovans*

LATER HOMO

Ardipithecus kadabba *Ardipithecus ramidus* *Paranthropus aethiopicus* *Homo sapiens*

PARANTHROPINES *Paranthropus robustus*

Sahelanthropus *Paranthropus boisei*

By more than 1.6 million years ago, the next stage in human evolution, *Homo erectus*, had emerged in East Africa. These hominins had larger brains than *Homo habilis*, their probable ancestor, and were makers of the characteristic teardrop-shaped stone tools flaked on both sides called Acheulian hand-axes. These artifacts are the dominant tool form of the Lower Paleolithic. By the time *Homo erectus* became extinct (around 100,000 years ago, or possibly even as recently as 50,000 years ago), the species had colonized the rest of Africa, southern, eastern, and western Asia, and central and western Europe. Their remote descendants (now designated *Homo floresiensis*) seem to have survived in Indonesia to the remarkably recent date of 17,000 years ago, as new discoveries on the island of Flores suggest.

The Middle Paleolithic period – from about 200,000 to 40,000 years ago – saw the emergence of modern *Homo sapiens*. Neanderthals, who used to be classified as a subspecies of *Homo sapiens* (*H. sapiens neanderthalensis*) lived in Europe and western and central Asia from about 400,000 to 30,000 years ago. But as a result of analysis of ancient Neanderthal DNA they are now seen as more distant cousins, and again regarded as a different species, *Homo neanderthalensis*, although they may have made some contribution to *Homo sapiens* DNA through contact. As a result of DNA work it seems clear that *Homo sapiens* evolved in Africa, and that there was a major "Out of Africa" expansion between 60,000 and 50,000 years ago of humans ancestral to all present-day humans. Australia was colonized by humans some 50,000 years ago (the dates are still debated), and Europe and Asia by at least 40,000 years ago. There may have been an earlier dispersal of archaic modern humans who reached the eastern Mediterranean some 100,000 to 90,000 years ago, but they probably have no surviving descendants.

(Opposite) Monuments and sites constructed by state societies around the world (clockwise from top left): the ziggurat of Ur, in modern Iraq, *c*. 2000 BC; a giant Olmec head, possibly a portrait of a ruler, Mexico, *c*. 1200–600 BC; elaborate reliefs at Persepolis, Iran, *c*. 515 BC; the Inca site of Machu Picchu, 15th century AD; the temple of Ramesses II (*c*. 1279–1213 BC) at Abu Simbel, Egypt, with statues of the pharaoh.

It is uncertain when humans initially crossed from northeastern Asia into North America across the Bering Strait, and south to Central and South America. The earliest secure dates for the first Americans are around 14,000 years ago, but there is controversial evidence that the continent was populated before then.

By 10,000 BC, most of the land areas of the world, except the deserts and Antarctica, were populated. The most conspicuous exception is the Pacific, where Western Polynesia does not seem to have been colonized until the 1st millennium BC, and Eastern Polynesia progressively from *c*. AD 300. By around AD 1000 the colonization of Oceania was complete. The spread of humans around the world is summarized in the map overleaf.

Nearly all the groups of humans so far mentioned may be regarded as **hunter-gatherer** societies, made up of relatively small groups of people.

One of the most significant occurrences in world history at a global level is the development of food production, based on domesticated plant species and also (although in some areas to a lesser extent) of domesticated animal species. One of the most striking facts of world **prehistory** is that the transition from hunting and gathering to food production seems to have occurred independently in several areas, in each case after the end of the Ice Age, i.e. after *c*. 10,000 years ago.

In the Near East, we can recognize the origins of this transition even before this time, for the process may have been gradual, the consequence (as well as the cause) of restructuring of the social organization of human societies. At any rate, well-established farming, dependent on wheat and barley as well as sheep and goats (and later cattle), was underway there by about 8000 BC. Farming had spread to Europe by 6500 BC, and is documented in South Asia at Mehrgarh in Baluchistan, Pakistan, at about the same time.

A separate development, based at first on the cultivation of millet, seems to have taken place in China, in the valley of the Huang Ho, by 5000 BC or even earlier. Rice cultivation began at about the same time in the Yangzi Valley in China and spread to Southeast Asia. The position in Africa south of the Sahara is more complicated due to the diversity of environments, but millet and sorghum wheat were cultivated by the 3rd millennium BC. The Western Pacific (Melanesian) complex of root and tree crops had certainly developed by that time: indeed, there are indications of field drainage for root crops very much earlier.

World Chronology
Key Events

• Earliest stone tools	2.5 million years ago
• Acheulian hand-axes	1.6 million years ago
• *Homo sapiens*	at least 100,000 years ago
• First Australians	50,000 years ago
• First Americans	14,000 years ago or more
• First farmers	at least 10,000 years ago in the Near East
	9000 years ago in China
	9000 years ago in the Americas
	8500 years ago in Europe
• First state societies	5500 years ago in the Near East
	3500 years ago in China
	3500 years ago in the Americas

In the Americas, a different range of crops was available. Cultivation of beans, squash, peppers, and some grasses may have begun by 7000 or even 8000 BC in Peru, and was certainly underway there and in Mesoamerica by the 7th millennium BC. Other South American species, including manioc and potato, were soon added, but the plant with the greatest impact on American agriculture was maize, believed to have been brought into cultivation in Mexico by 5600 years ago, though possibly earlier in northwest Argentina.

These agricultural innovations were rapidly adopted in some areas (e.g. in Europe), but in others, such as North America, their impact was less immediate. Certainly, by the time of Christ, hunter-gatherer economies were very much in the minority.

The urban revolution, the next major transformation that we recognize widely, is not simply a change in settlement type: it reflects profound social changes. Foremost among these is the development of **state** societies displaying more clearly differentiated institutions of government than do **chiefdoms**. Many state societies had writing. We see the first state societies in the Near East by about

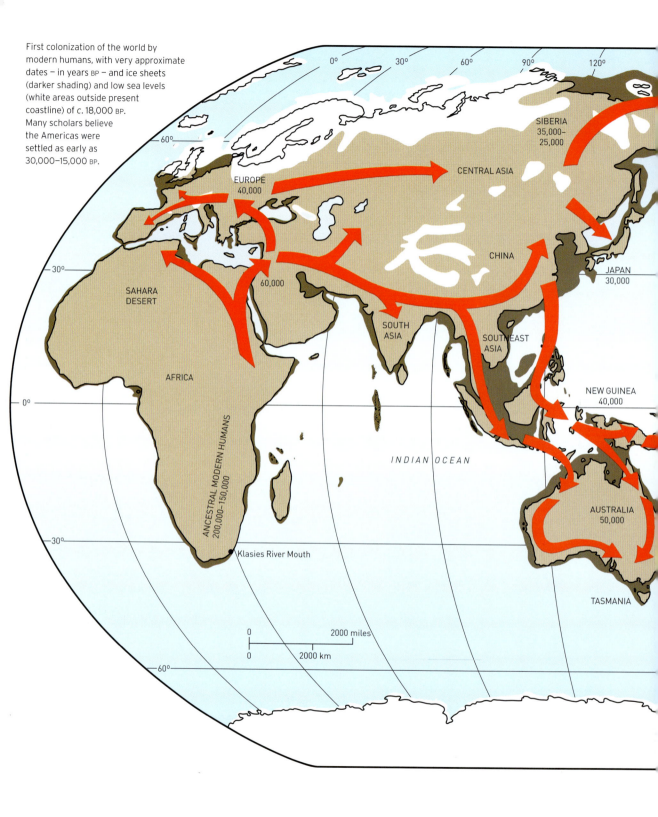

First colonization of the world by modern humans, with very approximate dates – in years BP – and ice sheets (darker shading) and low sea levels (white areas outside present coastline) of c. 18,000 BP. Many scholars believe the Americas were settled as early as 30,000–15,000 BP.

EUROPE
40,000

CENTRAL ASIA

SIBERIA
35,000–
25,000

CHINA

JAPAN
30,000

SAHARA
DESERT

60,000

SOUTH
ASIA

SOUTHEAST
ASIA

NEW GUINEA
40,000

AFRICA

ANCESTRAL MODERN HUMANS
200,000–150,000

INDIAN OCEAN

AUSTRALIA
50,000

Klasies River Mouth

TASMANIA

0   2000 miles

0   2000 km

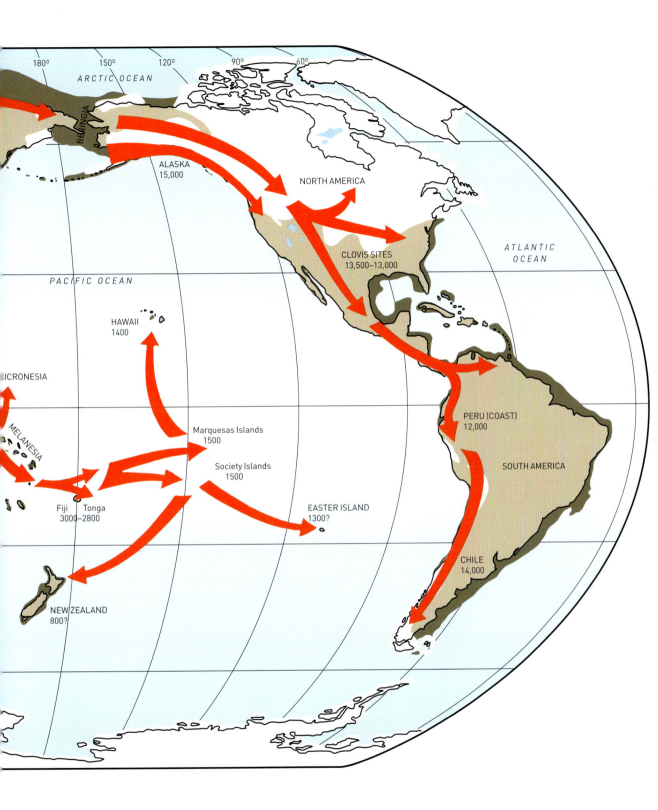

3500 BC, in Egypt only a little later, and in the Indus Valley by 2500 BC. In the Near East, the period of the early Mesopotamian city-states was marked by the rise of such famous sites as Ur, Uruk, and later Babylon, and was followed in the 1st millennium BC by an age of great empires, notably those of Assyria and Achaemenid Persia. In Egypt, it is possible to trace the continuous development of cultural and political traditions over more than 2000 years, through the pyramid age of the Old Kingdom and the imperial power of New Kingdom Egypt.

On the western edge of the Near East, further civilizations developed: Minoans and Mycenaeans in Greece and the Aegean during the 2nd millennium BC, Etruscans and Romans in the 1st millennium BC. At the opposite end of Asia, state societies with urban centers appear in China before 1500 BC, marking the beginnings of the Shang civilization. At about the same time, Mesoamerica saw the rise of the Olmec, the first in a long sequence of Central American civilizations including Maya, Zapotec, Toltec, and Aztec. On the Pacific coast of South America, the Chavín (from 900 BC), Moche, and Chimú civilizations laid the foundations for the rise of the vast and powerful Inca empire that flourished in the 15th century AD.

The remaining story is the more familiar one of literate history, with the rise of the Classical world of Greece and Rome as well as of China, and then of the world of Islam, the Renaissance of Europe, and the development of the colonial powers. From the 18th century to the present there followed the independence of the former colonies, first in the Americas, then in Asia and in Africa. We are talking now not simply of state societies but of nation states and, especially in colonial times, of empires.

Study Questions

- How are absolute dating methods different from relative dating methods?
- Why is an understanding of stratigraphy vital to most relative dating methods?
- Why is tree-ring dating considered to be an absolute dating method?
- Why is it necessary to calibrate radiocarbon dates?
- What types of artifacts cannot be radiocarbon dated? Why?
- What are some of the main sources of errors in the field of radiocarbon dating?

Summary

- The answer to the question "When?" in archaeology has two main components. Relative dating methods allow us to determine that something is *relatively* older or younger than something else. Absolute methods make it possible to give a date in years. Archaeological dating is at its most reliable when the two methods are used together, e.g. when the relative order assigned to layers in an excavation can be confirmed by absolute dates for each layer. Wherever possible, results from one absolute method should be cross-checked by those from another.

- In areas where ancient calendars and historical chronologies are available, such as Mesoamerica, these remain one of the most important methods of dating. Elsewhere, the two methods most useful to the archaeologist are radiocarbon dating and tree-ring dating. Although many other absolute dating techniques exist, these tend to be reserved either for very specific applications or for sites that are beyond the range of radiocarbon, back in the Paleolithic period.

- Ultimately, the precision of dating attainable for each period helps determine the kinds of questions we ask about the past – for the Paleolithic, questions are about long-term change; for later periods, the questions are more usually concerned with the shorter-term variations in worldwide human development.

Further Reading

The following provide a good introduction to the principal dating techniques used by archaeologists:

Aitken, M.J. 1990. *Science-based Dating in Archaeology*. Longman: London & New York.

Biers, W.R. 1992. *Art, Artefacts and Chronology in Classical Archaeology*. Routledge: London.

Brothwell, D.R. & Pollard, A.M. (eds). 2005. *Handbook of Archaeological Sciences*. Wiley: Chichester & New York.

Pollard, A.M., Batt, C.M., Stern, B., & Young S.M.M. 2007. *Analytical Chemistry in Archaeology*. Cambridge University Press: Cambridge.

Speer, J.H. 2010. *Fundamentals of Tree-Ring Research*. University of Arizona Press: Tucson.

Taylor, R.E. & Aitken, M.J. (eds). 1997. *Chronometric Dating in Archaeology*. Plenum: New York.

Taylor R.E. & Bar-Yosef, O. 2013. *Radiocarbon Dating: An Archaeological Perspective* (2nd ed.). Left Coast Press: Walnut Creek.

Wintle, A.G. 1996. "Archaeologically relevant dating techniques for the next century." *Journal of Archaeological Science* 23, 123–38.

[See p. 345 for a list of useful websites]

How Were Societies Organized?
Social archaeology

Establishing the Nature and Scale of the Society

- Classification of Societies

Methods of Social Analysis

- Settlement Analysis and Site Hierarchy
- Burial Analysis: The Study of Ranking from Individual Burials
- Monuments and Public Works
- Written Records
- Ethnoarchaeology

The Archaeology of the Individual and of Identity

- Social Inequality
- Ethnicity and Conflict
- Investigating Gender

Study Questions
Summary
Further Reading

Some of the most interesting questions we can ask about early societies are social. They are about people and about relations between people, about the exercise of power, and about the nature and scale of organization. But the answers are not directly visible in the archaeological record: we have to ask the right questions of the data, and devise the means of answering them.

In this respect **archaeology** is very different from cultural or social **anthropology**, where the observer can actually visit the living society and rapidly form conclusions about its social and power structures before moving on to other more complex matters, such as the details of the kinship system or the minutiae of ritual behavior. The archaeologist has to work hard to gain even basic details of these kinds, but the prize is a rich one: an understanding of the social organization not just of societies in the present or very recent past (like **cultural anthropology**) but also of societies at many different points in time, with all the scope that that offers for studying change. Only the archaeologist can obtain that perspective, and hence seek some understanding of the processes of long-term change.

Different kinds of society need different kinds of questions, and the techniques of investigation will need to vary radically with the nature of the evidence. We cannot tackle a **Paleolithic hunter-gatherer** camp in the same way as the capital city of an early **state**. Thus, the questions we put, and the methods for answering them, must be tailored to the community we are dealing with. So it is all the more necessary to be clear at the outset about the general nature of that community, which is why the most basic social questions are always the first ones to ask.

We must first address the size or scale of the society. The archaeologist will often be excavating a single **site**. But was that an independent political unit, for example a Maya or Greek city-state, or a simpler unit, such as the base camp of a hunter-gatherer group? Or was it, on the other hand, a small cog in a very big wheel, a subordinate settlement in some far-flung empire, such as that of the Incas of Peru? Any site we consider will have its own hinterland, or catchment area, for the feeding of its population. But one of our interests is to go beyond that local area, and to understand how that site interacts with others. From the standpoint of the individual site – which is often a convenient perspective to adopt – that raises questions of dominance. Was the site politically independent, autonomous? Or, if it was part of a larger social system, did it take a dominant part (like the capital city of a kingdom) or a subordinate one?

If the scale of the society is a natural first question, the next is certainly its internal organization. What kind of society was it? Were the people forming it on a more-or-less equal social footing? Or were there instead prominent differences in status, rank, and prestige within the society – perhaps different social classes? And what of the professions: were there people who specialized in particular crafts? And if so, were they controlled within a centralized system, as in some of the palace economies of the Near East and Egypt? Or was this a freer economy, with a flourishing free exchange, where merchants could operate at will in their own interest?

These questions, however, may all be seen as "top-down," looking at the society from above and investigating its organization. But increasingly an alternative perspective is being followed, looking first at the individual, and at the way the identity of the individual in the society in question is defined – a "bottom-up" perspective. Archaeologists have come to realize that the way such important social constructs as gender, status, and even age are constituted in a society are not "givens," but are specific to each different society. These insights have led to new fields: the archaeology of the individual and the archaeology of identity.

Establishing the Nature and Scale of the Society

The first step in social archaeology is so obvious that it is often overlooked. It is to ask, what was the scale of the largest social unit, and what kind of society, in a very broad sense, was it? The largest social unit could be anything from a small and completely independent hunter-gatherer **band** to a great empire. In the case of a complex society it can comprise many lesser units.

In terms of research in the field, the question is often best answered from a study of settlement: both in terms of the scale and nature of individual sites and in relationships between them, through the analysis of settlement pattern. But we should not forget that written records, where a society is literate and uses writing, oral tradition, and **ethnoarchaeology** – the study from an archaeological point of view of present-day societies – can be equally valuable in assessing the nature and scale of the society under review.

First, however, we need a frame of reference, a hypothetical **classification** of societies against which to test our ideas.

Classification of Societies

The American anthropologist Elman Service developed a four-fold classification of societies that many archaeologists have found useful, though his terminology has since been amended. Particular kinds of site and settlement

Key Concepts
The Classification of Societies

	MOBILE HUNTER-GATHERER GROUPS	SEGMENTARY SOCIETY	CHIEFDOM	STATE
	San hunters, South Africa	*Man plowing, Valcamonica, Italy*	*Horseman, Gundestrup caldron*	*Terracotta army, tomb of first emperor of China*
TOTAL NUMBERS	Less than 100	Up to a few 1000	5000–20,000+	Generally 20,000+
SOCIAL ORGANIZATION	Egalitarian Informal leadership	Segmentary society Pan-tribal associations Raids by small groups	Kinship-based ranking under hereditary leader High-ranking warriors	Class-based hierarchy under king or emperor Armies
ECONOMIC ORGANIZATION	Mobile hunter-gatherers	Settled farmers Pastoralist herders	Central accumulation and redistribution Some craft specialization	Centralized bureaucracy Tribute-based Taxation Laws
SETTLEMENT PATTERN	Temporary camps	Permanent villages	Fortified centers Ritual centers	Urban: cities, towns Frontier defenses Roads
RELIGIOUS ORGANIZATION	Shamans	Religious elders Calendrical rituals	Hereditary chief with religious duties	Priestly class Pantheistic or monotheistic religion
ARCHITECTURE	Temporary shelters *Paleolithic skin tents, Siberia*	Permanent huts Burial mounds Shrines *Neolithic shrine, Çatalhöyük, Turkey*	Large-scale monuments *Stonehenge, England – final form*	Palaces, temples, and other public buildings *Pyramids at Giza* *Castillo, Chichen Itza, Mexico*
ARCHAEOLOGICAL EXAMPLES	All Paleolithic societies, including Paleo-Indians	All early farmers (Neolithic/Archaic)	Many early metalworking and Formative societies	All ancient civilizations, e.g. in Mesoamerica, Peru, Near East, India, and China; Greece and Rome
MODERN EXAMPLES	Inuit San, southern Africa Australian Aborigines	Pueblos, Southwest USA New Guinea Highlanders Nuer and Dinka, E. Africa	Northwest Coast Native Americans, USA 18th-century Polynesian chiefdoms in Pacific	All modern states

pattern are associated with each of the societies. Some archaeologists question the value of such broad classifications as "**chiefdom**," but at a preliminary stage of analysis they are useful, especially if they are not taken too seriously. The classification is summarized in the box on p. 145.

Mobile hunter-gatherer groups.   These are small-scale societies of hunters and gatherers (sometimes called "bands"), generally of fewer than 100 people, who move seasonally to exploit wild food resources. Most surviving hunter-gatherer groups today are of this kind, such as the San of southern Africa. Band members are generally kinsfolk, related by descent or marriage, and bands do not have formal leaders, so there are no marked economic differences or disparities in status among their members.

Because bands are mobile groups, their sites consist mainly of seasonally occupied camps, and other smaller and more specialized sites. These include kill or butchery sites – locations where large mammals are killed and sometimes butchered – and work sites, where tools are made or other specific activities carried out. Camps may show evidence of insubstantial dwellings or temporary shelters, along with the debris of residential occupation.

During the Paleolithic period (before 12,000 years ago) most archaeological sites seem to conform to one or other of these categories – camp sites, kill sites, work sites – and archaeologists usually operate on the assumption that most Paleolithic societies were organized into bands.

Segmentary societies.   These are generally larger than mobile hunter-gatherer groups, but their population rarely numbers more than a few thousand, and their diet or subsistence is based largely on cultivated plants and domesticated animals. They are sometimes referred to as "**tribes**." Typically, they are settled farmers, but they may be nomad pastoralists with a mobile economy based on the intensive exploitation of livestock. **Segmentary societies** generally consist of many individual communities integrated into the larger society through kinship ties. Although some have officials and even a "capital" or seat of government, such officials lack the economic base necessary for effective use of power.

The typical settlement pattern for segmentary societies is one of settled agricultural homesteads or villages. Characteristically, no one settlement dominates any of the others in the region. Instead, the archaeologist finds evidence for isolated, permanently occupied houses (a dispersed settlement pattern) or for permanent villages (a nucleated pattern). Such villages may be made up of a collection of free-standing houses, for example those of the first farmers of the Danube valley in Europe, c. 4500 BC. Or they may be clusters of buildings grouped together – so-called "agglomerate structures" – for example, the pueblos of the American Southwest.

Chiefdoms.   These societies are characterized by ranking – differences in social status between people. Different **lineages** (a lineage is a group claiming descent from a common ancestor) are graded on a scale of prestige, and the senior lineage, and hence the society as a whole, is governed by a chief. Prestige and rank are determined by closeness of relationship to the chief. There is no true stratification into classes, and the role of the chief is crucial. Chiefdoms vary greatly in size, but the range is generally between about 5000 and 20,000 persons.

Often, there is local specialization in craft production, and surpluses of these and of foodstuffs are periodically paid as obligations to the chief. He uses these to maintain his close personal followers, and may use them for **redistribution** to his subjects.

The chiefdom generally has a center of power, often with temples, residences of the chief and his retainers, and craft specialists. It is a permanent ritual and ceremonial center that acts as a central focus for the entire group. However, this is not a permanent urban center (such as a city) with an established bureaucracy, as we find in state societies. But chiefdoms do give indications that some sites were more important than others (or in other words, that there was a site hierarchy). An example is Moundville in Alabama, USA, which flourished c. AD 1000–1500 (see box on pp. 156–57).

The personal ranking characteristic of chiefdom societies is also visible in the very rich grave-goods that often accompany the burials of deceased chiefs.

Early States.   These share many of the features of chiefdoms, but the ruler (perhaps a king or sometimes a queen) has explicit authority to establish laws and also to enforce them by the use of a standing army. Society no longer depends totally upon kin relationships: it is now stratified into different classes. Agricultural workers or serfs and the poorer urban dwellers form the lowest classes, with the craft specialists above, and the priests and kinsfolk of the ruler higher still. The functions of the ruler are often separated from those of the priest: palace is distinguished from temple. The territory is "owned" by the ruling lineage and populated by tenants who have an obligation to pay taxes. Taxes and other revenues are collected by officials based in the central capital, and then distributed to government, army, and craft specialists. Many early states developed complex redistributive systems to support these essential services.

Early state societies generally show a characteristic urban settlement pattern in which cities play a prominent part. The city is typically a large population center (often of more than 5000 inhabitants) with major public buildings, including temples and work places for the administrative bureaucracy. Often, there is a pronounced settlement hierarchy, with the capital city as the major center, and with subsidiary or regional centers as well as local villages.

This rather simple social typology should not be used unthinkingly. For instance, there is some difference between the rather vague idea of the "tribe" and the more modern concept of the "segmentary society." The term "tribe," implying a larger grouping of smaller units, carries with it the assumption that these communities share a common ethnic identity and self-awareness, which is now known not generally to be the case. The term "segmentary society" refers to a relatively small and autonomous group, usually of agriculturalists, who regulate their own affairs: in some cases, they may join together with other comparable segmentary societies to form a larger ethnic unit or "tribe"; in other cases, they do not. For the remainder of this chapter, we shall therefore refer to segmentary societies in preference to the term "tribe." And what in Service's typology were called "bands" are now more generally referred to as "mobile hunter-gatherer groups."

Certainly, it would be wrong to overemphasize the importance of the four types of society given above, or to spend too long trying to decide whether a specific group should be classed in one category rather than another. It would also be wrong to assume that somehow societies inevitably evolve from hunter-gatherer groups to segmentary societies, or from chiefdoms to states. One of the challenges of archaeology is to attempt to explain why some societies become more complex and others do not.

Nevertheless, Service's categories provide a good framework to help organize our thoughts. They should not, however, deflect us from focusing on what we are really looking for: changes over time in the different institutions of a society – whether in the social sphere, the organization of the food quest, technology, contact and exchange, or spiritual life. Archaeology has the unique advantage of being able to study processes of change over thousands of years, and it is these processes we are seeking to isolate. Fortunately there are sufficiently marked differences between simple and more complex societies for us to find ways of doing this.

As we saw above, in the description of Service's four types of society, complex societies show in particular an increased specialization in, or separation between, different aspects of their **culture**. In complex societies people no longer combine, say, the tasks of obtaining food, making tools, or performing religious rites, but become specialists at one or other of these tasks, either as full-time farmers, craftspeople, or priests. As technology develops, for example, groups of individuals may acquire particular expertise in pottery-making or metallurgy, and will become full-time craft specialists, occupying distinct areas of a town or city and thus leaving traces for the archaeologist to discover. Likewise, as farming develops and population grows, more food will be obtained from a given piece of land (food production will intensify) through the introduction of the plow or irrigation. As this specialization and intensification take place, so too does the tendency for some people to become wealthier and wield more authority than others – differences in social status and ranking develop.

It is the methods for looking at these processes of increasing specialization, intensification, and social ranking that help us identify the presence of more complex societies in the archaeological record. For simpler groups like hunter-gatherers, other methods are needed if we are to identify them archaeologically, as will become apparent.

Methods of Social Analysis

Different methods are suitable for investigating the social interactions and social structures of different kinds of societies. The principal source of data about early societies comes from settlement analysis and **excavation**. The study of burials with their associated **artifacts** is often a very good way of assessing the dress, possessions, and status of deceased individuals in a society. For some societies, the study of the monuments that they have built can also be very informative.

The data available from a hunter-gatherer camp are naturally very different from those from a city. For one thing, state societies are often literate societies, and written records may be available. For societies for which no written testimony is available, archaeologists have often relied upon ethnographic analogy, drawing upon what anthropologists have observed in more recent non-urban societies so as to suggest interpretations for what is found in the archaeological record. Ethnoarchaeology, as this field is known, seeks to use the experience derived from living societies to suggest interpretive and explanatory approaches to archaeological data.

Key Concepts
Methods of Social Analysis

- *Settlement Analysis*: the main method of investigating past social organization. Data are collected by survey and excavation, but the specific methods used can vary greatly depending on the society in question

- *Burial Analysis*: rank and social status are best revealed by the analysis of grave-goods within individual burials

- *Monuments and Public Works*: the scale of monuments and public works, as well as their distribution, can be a good indicator of social organization

- *Written Records*: an excellent source of information about the organization of early state societies

- *Ethnoarchaeology*: the study of living societies in order to help interpret the past, with a specific emphasis on the use and significance of artifacts, buildings and structures, and how these material things might become incorporated into the archaeological record

Settlement Analysis and Site Hierarchy

One of the principal ways of answering the basic question "what is the scale of the society" is through an understanding of settlement pattern, and this can come only from survey. Whatever the period in question, we should be interested in finding the major center or centers of settlement along with any smaller sites. We can use many of the survey, sampling, and **remote sensing** techniques described in Chapter 3 to do this, but the exact nature of the work will depend on the society in question – it is much harder to find the scanty traces that are left by mobile hunter-gatherers than it is to find an ancient city, so more intensive survey is needed.

Any survey will result in a map and a catalog of the sites discovered, together with details of each site including size, chronological range (as may be determined from such surface remains as pottery), architectural features, and possibly an approximate estimate of population. The aim is then to reach some classification of the sites on the basis of their relative importance – a site hierarchy. Possible categories for the different types of site encountered might include, for instance, Regional Center, Local Center, Nucleated Village, Dispersed Village, and Hamlet.

Various techniques can be used to establish the site hierarchy of a region, but the simplest is based solely on site size. Sites are arranged in rank order by size and then displayed as a histogram, which will usually show that the small sites are the most frequent. Such histograms allow comparisons to be made between the site hierarchies of different regions, different periods, and different types of society. In band societies, for example, there will usually be only a narrow range of variation in site size and all the sites will be relatively small. State societies, on the other hand, will have both hamlets and farmsteads and large towns and cities. The degree to which a single site is dominant within a settlement system will also be evident from this type of analysis, and the organization of the settlement system will often be a direct reflection of the organization of the society that created it. In a general way, the more hierarchical the settlement pattern, the more hierarchical the society.

Work by Gregory Johnson on the Early Dynastic (*c.* 2800 BC) settlement sites in a region of Mesopotamia showed this very clearly, as can be seen in the graph to the left. The sites ranged in size from 25 ha (60 acres) to just over one tenth of a hectare (0.25 acres), and could be divided into five categories based on their size: Johnson called these large towns, towns, large villages, small villages, and hamlets. The existence of a settlement hierarchy of this kind has been used by some archaeologists as an indicator of a state society.

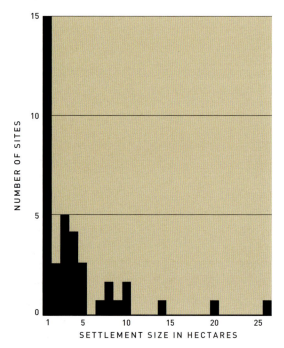

Site hierarchy for Early Dynastic settlements in a region of Mesopotamia.

The excavation of settlement remains, however, is the major source of information about social relations within a society. This applies for any level of complexity, but the methods used can vary greatly, the main distinction being between mobile and sedentary societies.

Mobile Hunter-Gatherer Societies.   In mobile hunter-gatherer societies organization is exclusively at a local level, with no permanent administrative centers. So having identified various sites, the first approach is to concentrate on the sites themselves, with the aim being to understand the nature of the activities that took place there, and of the social group that used them.

Among mobile communities of hunter-gatherers archaeologists draw a distinction between cave sites and open sites. Occupation deposits in cave sites tend to be deep, usually indicating intermittent human activity over thousands or tens of thousands of years, and meticulous excavation and recording are required to interpret the **stratigraphy** of the site accurately. Open sites may have been occupied for shorter periods of time, but the deposits, without the protection provided by a cave, may have suffered greater erosion.

If it proves possible to distinguish single short phases of human occupation at a hunter-gatherer site, we can then look at the distribution of artifacts and bone fragments within and around **features** and structures (hut foundations, remains of hearths) to see whether any coherent patterns can be observed. However, it is not always clear whether the distribution is the result of human activity on the spot (or *in situ*) or whether the materials have been transported by flowing water and redeposited. In some cases, too, especially with bone debris, distribution may be the result of the action of predatory animals, not of humans.

The study of such questions requires sophisticated sampling strategies and very thorough analysis. The work of Glynn Isaac's team at the early Paleolithic site of Koobi Fora on the eastern shore of Lake Turkana, Kenya, gives an indication of the recovery and analytical techniques involved. The excavation procedure was highly controlled, with exact recording of the coordinates of every piece of bone or stone recovered, and careful analysis of the degree of post-depositional disturbance. Isaac's team was able to fit some fragments of bone and stone back together again. The team interpreted the network of joins (see diagram overleaf) as showing areas where **hominins** broke open bones to extract marrow, and where stone tools were made – so-called activity areas.

For a wider perspective, we need to consider the entire territory in which the group or band operated, and the relationship between sites. Ethnoarchaeology (see pp. 165–67) has helped to establish a framework of analysis, so that we may think in terms of an annual home range (i.e. the whole territory covered by the group in the course of a year) and specific types of site within it, such as a home base camp (for a particular season), transitory camps, hunting blinds, butchery or kill sites, storage caches, and so on. These issues are basic to hunter-gatherer

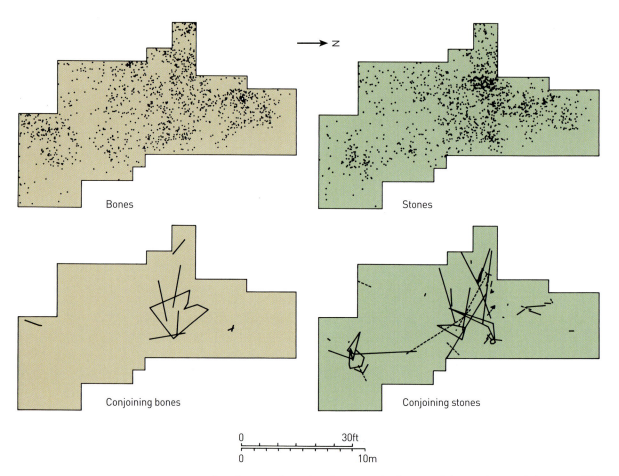

Bones

Stones

Conjoining bones

Conjoining stones

0   30ft

0   10m

Glynn Isaac's research at the Early Paleolithic site of Koobi Fora, Kenya, East Africa. (Top row) Location of bones and stone artifacts. (Second row) Lines joining bones and stones that could be fitted back together, perhaps indicating activity areas.

archaeology, and a regional perspective is essential to understand the annual life cycle of the group and its behavior. This means that, in addition to conventional sites (with a high concentration of artifacts), we need to look for sparse scatters of artifacts, consisting of perhaps just one or two objects in every 10-m survey square. We must also study the whole regional environment and the likely human use of it by hunter-gatherers.

A good example is provided by the work of the British anthropologist Robert Foley in the Amboseli region of southern Kenya. He collected and recorded some 8531 stone tools from 257 sample locations within a study area covering 600 sq. km (232 sq. miles). From this evidence he was able to calculate the rate of discard of stone tools within different environmental and vegetation zones, and interpret the distribution patterns in terms of the strategies and movements of hunter-gatherer groups. In a later study, he developed a general model of stone tool distribution based on a number of studies of hunter-gatherer bands in different parts of the world. One conclusion was that a single band of some 25 people might be expected to discard as many as 163,000 artifacts within their annual territory in the course of a single year. These artifacts would be scattered, but with significant

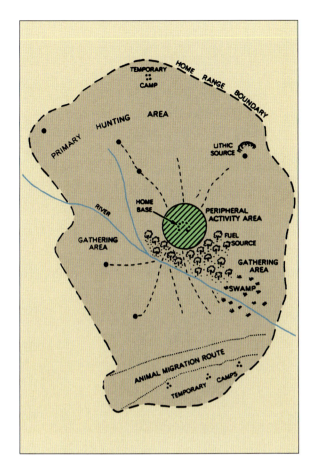

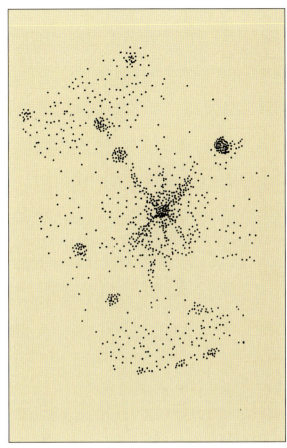

Robert Foley's model (above left) of activities within the annual home range of a hunter-gatherer band, and the artifact scatters (above right) resulting from such activities.

concentrations at home base camps and temporary camps. According to Foley's study, however, only a very small proportion of the artifacts discarded would be found by archaeologists working at a single site, and it is vitally important that individual site **assemblages** are interpreted as parts of a broader pattern.

Sedentary Societies. Investigation of the social organization of sedentary communities, which include segmentary societies, chiefdoms, and states, is best approached with an investigation of settlement (although, as we shall see below, cemeteries and public monuments evident in these societies also form useful areas of study).

Although much can be learned from survey, for effective analysis of the community as a whole some structures need to be excavated completely and the remainder sampled intensively enough to obtain an idea of the variety of different structures. The careful excavation of individual houses and of complete villages is a standard procedure when dealing with smaller sedentary communities. This opens the way to the study of households, and of community structure, as well as to well-founded estimates of population.

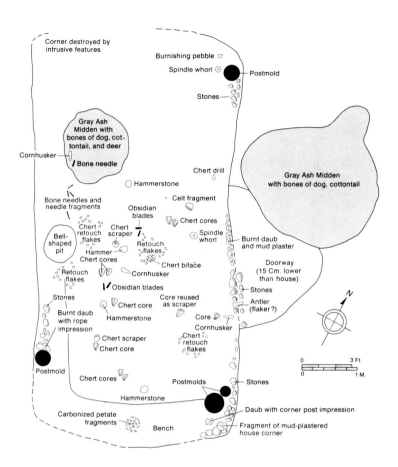

Plan of a house at Tierras Largas, c. 900 BC, with certain artifacts plotted in position.

Kent Flannery's excavation of Early Formative houses at Tierras Largas in Oaxaca, Mexico, offers a useful example. He was able to establish the first map showing the layout of a Formative village in Oaxaca. Evidence for differences in social status emerged. Residences, deduced to be of relatively high status, had not only a house platform built of higher-quality adobe and stone, but also a greater quantity of animal bone, imported **obsidian**, and imported marine shell than the area of wattle-and-daub houses deduced to be of lower status. Significantly, locally available (and therefore less prestigious) chert formed a higher proportion of the tools in the lower-status area.

Most of the techniques of analysis appropriate to less developed societies remain valid for the study of centralized chiefdoms and states, which incorporate within themselves most of the social forms and patterns of interaction seen in the simpler societies. Additional techniques are needed because of the centralization of society, the hierarchy of sites, and the organizational and communicational devices that characterize chiefdom and state societies. A wide-ranging example is provided by the work at the Mississippian site of Moundville, described in the box overleaf.

One of the first steps when looking at a complex society is to identify one or more primary centers, and this is done by considering the size of a site, either in absolute terms, or in terms of the distances between major centers, so as to determine which are dominant and which subordinate. With this information a map can be created identifying the principal independent centers and the approximate extent of the territories surrounding them.

The reliance on size alone, however, can be misleading, and it is necessary to seek other indications of which are the primary centers. The best way is to try to find out how the society in question viewed itself and its territories. This might seem an impossible task until one remembers that, for most state societies at any rate, written records exist. These may name various sites, identifying their place within the hierarchy. The archaeologist's task is then to find those named sites, usually by the discovery of an actual inscription including the name of the relevant site – one might for example hope to find such an inscription in any substantial town of the Roman empire. The decipherment of Maya hieroglyphs in the second half of the 20th century has opened up a whole new source of evidence of this sort.

Usually, however, site hierarchy must be deduced by more directly archaeological means, without relying on the written word. A "highest-order" center, such as the capital city of an independent state, can best be identified from direct indications of central organization, on a scale not exceeded elsewhere, and comparable with that of other highest-order centers of equivalent states.

One indication is the existence of an archive (even without understanding anything of what it says) or of other symbolic indications of centralized organization. For instance, many controlled economies used seals to make impressions in clay as indications of ownership, source, or destination. The finding of a quantity of such materials can indicate organizational activity. Indeed, the whole practice of literacy and of symbolic expression is so central to organization that such indications are valuable evidence.

A further indication of central status is the presence of buildings of standardized form known to be associated with central functions of high order. Examples of such buildings include palaces, such as those found in Minoan Crete; buildings of ritual function (since in most early societies the control of administration and control of religious practice were closely linked), for example a Maya temple complex; fortifications; and mints for producing coinage.

In a hierarchically organized society, it always makes sense to study closely the functions of the center, considering such possible factors as kinship, bureaucratic organization, redistribution and storage of goods, organization of ritual, craft specialization, and external trade. All of these offer insights into how the society worked.

Social Analysis at Moundville

During its heyday from the 13th into the 15th centuries AD, Moundville was one of the greatest ceremonial centers of the Mississippian culture in North America. The site takes its name from an impressive group of 20 mounds constructed within a palisaded area, 150 ha (370 acres) in extent, on the banks of the Black Warrior river in west-central Alabama. Moundville was first dug into as long ago as 1840, but major excavations did not take place until the 20th century. Recently, Christopher Peebles and his colleagues have combined systematic survey with limited excavation and reanalysis of earlier work to produce a convincing social study of the site.

Peebles and his team first needed a reliable chronology. This was achieved through an analysis of the pottery. The resultant relative chronology was then cross-checked with excavated ceramics from radiocarbon-dated contexts to produce an absolute chronology.

This chronology enabled the team to study the development of the site through several phases. Preliminary survey of neighboring sites also established the regional settlement pattern for each phase, summarized in the maps below. More than 3000 burials have been excavated at Moundville, and Peebles used statistical techniques to group 2053 of them according to social rank. Peebles observed that the small number of people of highest rank (Segment A: classes IA, IB and II in the pyramid diagram opposite) were buried in or near the mounds with artifacts exclusive to them, such as copper axes and earspools. Lower-ranking individuals of Segment B (Classes III and IV) had non-mound burials with some grave-goods but no copper artifacts, while those of Segment C, buried on the periphery, had few or no grave-goods.

Peebles found interesting differences according to age and sex. The seven individuals in Class IA, the top of the social pyramid, were all adults, probably males. Those of Class IB were adult males and children, while Class II comprised individuals of all ages and both sexes. It seems

Changing settlement patterns in the Moundville region. In Phase I (AD 1050–1250) Moundville was simply a site with a single mound, like other similar sites in the area. By Phase II, however, it had grown larger, establishing itself as the major regional center. After its heyday in Phase III, Moundville disappeared as a significant site in Phase IV (after 1550), when the region no longer had a dominant center.

Multiple mound center
Single mound center
Settlement

I

N

5 miles
8 km

Moundville

II

Moundville

III

Moundville

IV

? Moundville

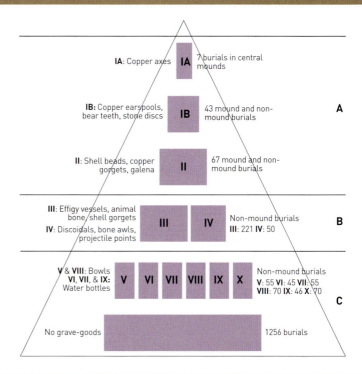

clear that adult males had the highest status. The presence of children in Class IB suggests that their high status was inherited at birth.

Peebles's study suggests a regional organization with a well-marked hierarchy of sites, controlled by a highly ranked community at Moundville itself – what Peebles terms a chiefdom society.

Pyramid-shaped social hierarchy at Moundville, based on the analysis of 2053 burials. Artifacts listed against each rank (Classes I–X) are grave-goods.

Within the pyramid figure:

IA: Copper axes — **IA** — 7 burials in central mounds

IB: Copper earspools, bear teeth, stone discs — **IB** — 43 mound and non-mound burials — **A**

II: Shell beads, copper gorgets, galena — **II** — 67 mound and non-mound burials

III: Effigy vessels, animal bone/shell gorgets — **III** **IV** — Non-mound burials III: 221 IV: 50 — **B**
IV: Discoidals, bone awls, projectile points

V & VIII: Bowls / VI, VII, & IX: Water bottles — **V VI VII VIII IX X** — Non-mound burials V: 55 VI: 45 VII: 55 VIII: 70 IX: 46 X: 70 — **C**

No grave-goods — 1256 burials

Burial Analysis: The Study of Ranking from Individual Burials

In archaeology, the individual is seen all too rarely. One of the most informative insights into the individual and his or her social status is offered by the discovery of human physical remains – the skeleton or the ashes – accompanied by artifacts deposited in the grave. Examination of the skeletal remains will often reveal the sex and age at death of each individual, and possibly any dietary deficiency or other pathological condition (see Chapter 8). Communal or collective burials (burials of more than one individual) may be difficult to interpret, because it will not always be clear which grave-goods go with which deceased person. It is, therefore, from single burials that we can hope to learn most.

In segmentary societies, and others with relatively limited differentiation in terms of rank, a close analysis of grave-goods can reveal much about disparities in social status. It is important to remember, however, that what is buried with a deceased person is not simply the exact equivalent either of status or of material goods owned or used during life. Burials are made by living individuals, and are used by them to express and influence their relationships with others still alive as much as to symbolize or serve the dead. But there is nevertheless often a relationship between the role and rank of the deceased during life and the manner in which the remains are disposed of and accompanied by artifacts.

The analysis will seek to determine differences between male and female burials, and to assess whether these differences carry with them distinctions in terms of wealth or higher status. The other common factor involved with rank or status is age, and age differences may be systematically reflected in the treatment of the deceased. In relatively egalitarian societies, high status won through the individual's own achievements (e.g. in hunting) in his or her own lifetime is something commonly encountered, and often reflected in funerary practice.

But the archaeologist must ask, from the evidence available, whether such a burial really reflects status achieved by the individual or instead hereditary status through birth. To distinguish between the two is not easy. One useful criterion is to investigate whether children are in some cases given rich burial goods and other indications of preferential attention. If so, there may have been a system of hereditary ranking, because at so early an age the child is unlikely to have reached such a status through personal distinction alone.

Once the graves in the cemetery have been dated, the first step in most cases is simply to produce a frequency distribution (a histogram) of the number of different artifact **types** in each grave. For further analysis, however, it is more interesting to seek some better indication of wealth and status so that greater weight can be given to valuable objects, and less weight to commonplace ones. This at once raises the problem of the recognition of value (for we cannot assume that past societies had the same ideas of value as we do). One answer might be to assume that valuable objects were those that took a long time to make, or were made of materials brought from a distance or difficult to obtain. We must also remember that ranking is not expressed solely in the grave-goods, but in the entire manner of burial.

A good example of the analysis of an entire cemetery is offered by the excavations of Charles Higham and Rachanie Thosarat at the site of Khok Phanom Di, a large mound inland from the Gulf of Siam in central Thailand. The settlement had been occupied for about 500 years from *c.* 2000 BC, and left a cemetery containing 154 human burials with bone and shell ornaments intact. The graves occurred in clusters with spaces between them. A very detailed burial sequence was worked out that provided insights into the community's kinship system over about 20 generations. The ability to trace families down the generations in this way is extremely rare in **prehistory**. In the later phases there was a predominance of women, some of them, such as the so-called "Princess," buried with considerable wealth. Also there was a clear link between the wealth of children and the adults with whom they were buried – poor children accompanied poor adults. The analysis of a complete cemetery in this way can yield many insights that are not available even from the very careful examination of a single grave.

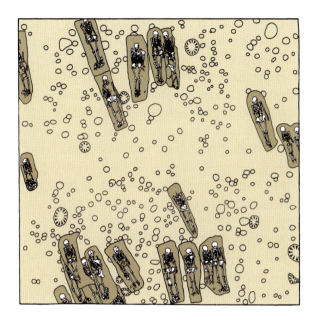

Khok Phanom Di. (Above left) The dead were buried individually, in neat, clustered rows. (Above right) The "Princess," who was accompanied by a set of shell jewelry, with more than 120,000 beads, a headdress, and a bracelet, as well as fine pottery vessels.

View south across the central plaza at Monte Albán, with the restored ruins of several temples visible. The site was founded on a mountain top in 500 BC.

Monuments and Public Works

Some societies invest a great deal of labor and considerable resources in the construction of monuments and public works. Such monuments were generally built with the intention of being conspicuous, and in some cases – such as the pyramids of Egypt – they remain conspicuous today. Many early state societies had at their center a major ceremonial site, and the monuments at such sites are informative not only about the religious beliefs of the society in question but also about aspects of their social organization.

The great plazas at the ceremonial centers of Mesoamerica are an excellent example. Monte Albán in Oaxaca, Mexico, became the principal center of the Zapotec state around 200 BC. Its wonderfully situated central plaza, shown below, dominated the surrounding areas. From this time on, Monte Albán was the home

of some 10,000 to 20,000 people, and the primary center of Oaxaca. Its monuments celebrate and reflect the power of the state and the city's central authority.

In some segmentary societies the surviving monuments were much more conspicuous than the settlements. In some cases the settlements are rarely recovered, while clear traces of the monuments remain. This is the case for the **Neolithic** period in the Wessex area of southern England, where earthen burial mounds, called "long barrows," are the most evident trace of the farmers who lived there from *c.* 4000 BC. With each cluster of mounds is associated a larger, circular monument with concentric ditches, termed a "causewayed camp."

Despite the sparse remains of settlements, the analysis of the scale and distribution of the Wessex monuments does allow the reconstruction of important aspects of social organization. In the early phase of monument construction (*c.* 4000–3000 BC), the spatial distribution and size of the long barrows suggests a possible interpretation: lines drawn between them divide the landscape into many possible territories, which are roughly equivalent in size. Each monument seems to have been the focal point for social activities and the burial place of the farming community inhabiting the local territory. A group of 20 people would have needed about 50 working days to construct a long barrow.

(Right) In Neolithic southern England, in the earlier long barrow/causewayed camp phase, clusters of burial mounds establish a social landscape, each cluster with its causewayed enclosure. Analysis indicates that each mound was the territorial focus for a small group of farmers. This was a segmentary society, where no one group was dominant. (Far right) In the later phase, the causewayed enclosures were replaced by major henge monuments (see key on p. 161). Their scale indicates centralized organization, and hence perhaps a chiefdom society. At this time the two great monuments Stonehenge and Silbury Hill were built.

West Kennet long barrow is one of the largest known monuments of its type.

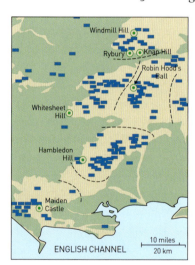

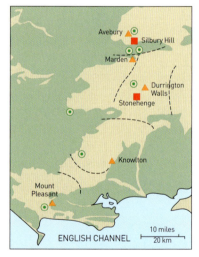

5 How Were Societies Organized?

In this early phase there is little suggestion of the ranking of sites or individuals: this was an egalitarian society. The causewayed enclosures may have served as a ritual focus and periodic meeting place for the larger group of people represented by one whole cluster of long barrows. (The 100,000 hours' labor required to construct one could be achieved in 40 working days by 250 people.) This would have been a segmentary, or tribal, society.

In the later phase (*c.* 3000–2000 BC), the long barrows and causewayed camps went out of use. In place of the latter, major ritual enclosures are seen. These were large circular monuments delimited by a ditch with a bank usually outside it: they are termed "henges." Each would have required something in the order of 1 million hours of labor for its construction. The labor input suggests the mobilization of the resources of a whole territory. About 300 people working full time for at least a year would be needed: their food would have to be provided for them unless the process was spread over a very long period. At this time (*c.* 2800 BC) the great earth mound at Silbury Hill was built. According to its excavator, it required 18 million hours of work, and was completed within 2 years. A few centuries later (*c.* 2500 BC) the great monument at Stonehenge took final shape, with its circle of stones, representing an even greater labor investment –

Analysis of the scale of the Wessex monuments in terms of labor hours needed for their construction suggests the emergence of a hierarchy in the later phase that may mirror a development in social relations and the emergence of a ranked society. Stonehenge, built at this time, is the greatest of the Wessex monuments. In the earlier Neolithic the scale of monuments is commensurate with an egalitarian, segmentary society.

Stonehenge, formed of huge sarsen stones and smaller bluestones, and the greatest of the Wessex monuments, had largely reached its current form by around 2500 BC.

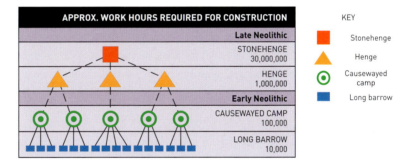

APPROX. WORK HOURS REQUIRED FOR CONSTRUCTION	KEY	
Late Neolithic	🟧	Stonehenge
STONEHENGE 30,000,000	🔺	Henge
HENGE 1,000,000	◉	Causewayed camp
Early Neolithic	🟦	Long barrow
CAUSEWAYED CAMP 100,000		
LONG BARROW 10,000		

30 million hours if the transport of the stones is taken into account, amounting to a massive corporate endeavor. Although such labor calculations are very approximate they do show how some notion of the changing social organization can be formed through the study of the monuments, even at a time when the traces of domestic life are scanty.

The structures built at this early time can be very impressive. Stonehenge is certainly one of the largest, but it is not the oldest. Indeed over much of northwestern Europe there are stone monuments of the Neolithic period, mainly collective tombs, which are often termed "megalithic" (from the Greek *megas* (great) and *lithos* (stone)). Some of these go back as far as 4000 BC, a millennium before the pyramids of Egypt. In the Orkney Islands, beyond the northern tip of Scotland, the local sandstone could readily be worked, even before the use of metal tools, and the remaining monuments, some of them well preserved, are sophisticated works of stone architecture. For instance, in the chambered tomb at Quanterness, dating to *c.* 3300 BC, remains of a large number of individuals were found, perhaps as many as 390. Males and females were about equally represented, and the age distribution could represent the pattern of deaths in the population at large; that is to say, that the age at death of the people buried in the tomb (46 percent below 20 years, 47 percent aged 20–30 years, and only 7 percent over the age of 30 years) could in proportional terms be the same as that of the whole population. The excavators concluded that this was a tomb equally available to most sectors of the community, and representative of a segmentary society rather than a hierarchical one, which the sophistication of its architecture might at first have suggested.

Some of the 5000 clay tablets discovered in the royal palace at Ebla (Tell Mardikh in modern Syria), dating from the late 3rd millennium BC. The tablets formed part of the state archives, recording more than 140 years of Ebla's history. Originally they were stored on wooden shelving, which collapsed when the palace was sacked.

Written Records

For literate societies – those that use writing, for instance all the great civilizations in Mesoamerica, China, Egypt, and the Near East – historical records can answer many of the social questions set out at the beginning of this chapter. One of the main goals of the archaeologist dealing with these societies is therefore to find appropriate texts. Many of the early excavations of the great sites of the Near East, for example, concentrated on the recovery of archives of clay writing tablets. Major finds of this kind are still made today – for example, at the ancient city of Ebla (Tell Mardikh) in Syria in the 1970s, where an archive of 5000 clay tablets written in an early, probably provincial, dialect of Akkadian (Babylonian) was discovered.

In each early literate society, writing had its own functions and purposes. For instance, the clay tablets of Mycenaean Greece, dating from *c.* 1200 BC, are almost without exception records of commercial transactions (goods coming in or going out) at the Mycenaean palaces. This gives us an impression of many aspects of the Mycenaean economy, and a glimpse into craft organization (through the names for the different kinds of craftspeople), as well as introducing the names of the offices of state. But here, as in other cases, accidents of preservation may be important. It could be that the Mycenaeans wrote on clay only for their commercial records, and used other, perishable materials for literary or historical texts now lost to us. It is certainly true that for the Classical Greek and Roman civilizations, it is mainly official decrees inscribed on marble that have survived. Fragile rolls of papyrus – the predecessor of modern paper – with literary texts on them, have usually only remained intact in the dry air of Egypt, or, for example, buried in the volcanic ash covering Pompeii. Coinage is also an important written source. The findspots of coins give interesting economic evidence about trade. But the inscriptions themselves are informative about the issuing authority – whether city-state (as in ancient Greece) or sole ruler (as in Imperial Rome, or the kings of medieval Europe).

The decipherment of an ancient language transforms our knowledge of the society that used it. In recent times one of the most significant advances has been the decipherment of Maya glyphs. It had been widely assumed that Maya inscriptions were exclusively of a calendrical nature, or that they dealt with purely religious matters, notably the deeds of deities. But the inscriptions can now in many cases be interpreted as relating to real historical events, mainly the

The Inca had no writing system as such, but kept records of accounts and other transactions using knotted ropes called quipu.

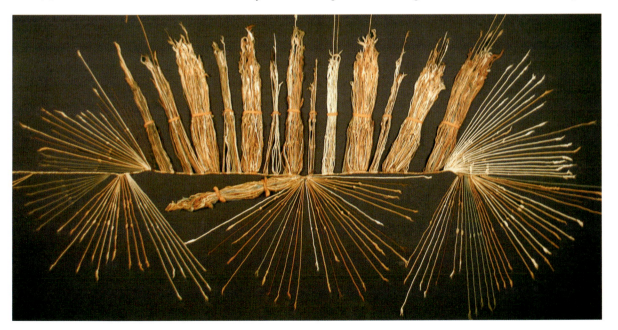

deeds of the Maya kings. We can also now begin to deduce the likely territories belonging to individual Maya centers. Maya history has thus taken on a new dimension.

A more detailed example of the value of written sources for reconstructing social archaeology is Mesopotamia, where a huge number of records of Sumer and Babylon (c. 3000–1600 BC), mainly in the form of clay tablets, have been preserved. The uses of writing in Mesopotamia may be summarized as follows:

Recording information for future use	- Administrative purposes
	- Codification of law
	- Formulation of a sacred tradition
	- Annals
	- Scholarly purposes
Communicating current information	- Letters
	- Royal edicts
	- Public announcements
	- Texts for training scribes
Communicating with the gods	- Sacred texts, amulets, etc.

Perhaps most evocative of all are the law codes, of which the most impressive example is the law code of Hammurabi of Babylon, written in the Akkadian language (and in cuneiform script) around 1750 BC. The ruler is seen at the top of the stone, standing before Shamash, the god of justice. The laws were promulgated, as Hammurabi states, "so that the strong may not oppress the weak, and to protect the rights of the orphan and widow." These laws cover many aspects of life – agriculture, business transactions, family law, inheritance, terms of employment for different craftspeople, and penalties for such crimes as adultery and homicide.

The famous law code of the Babylonian king Hammurabi, c. 1750 BC.

Akkadian cylinder seal of c. 2400 BC and its rollout impression, showing armed men, possibly hunters. The inscription, written in the cuneiform script like Hammurabi's law code (above), reveals that the owner of the seal was Kalki, a servant of Ubilishtar, the brother of the king (who is not named, but was probably Sargon of Akkad). Such seals were used to mark ownership or authenticity. Many thousands have been recovered from Mesopotamian sites.

Impressive and informative as it is, Hammurabi's law code is not straightforward to interpret, and emphasizes the need for the archaeologist to reconstruct the full social context that led to the drafting of a text. As the British scholar Nicholas Postgate has pointed out, the code is by no means complete, and seems to cover only those areas of the law that had proved troublesome. Moreover, Hammurabi had recently conquered several rival city states, and the law code was therefore probably designed to help integrate the new territories within his empire.

Ethnoarchaeology

Ethnoarchaeology is a fundamental method of approach for the social archaeologist. It involves the study of both the present-day use and significance of artifacts, buildings, and structures within living societies, and the way these material things become incorporated into the archaeological record – what happens to them when they are thrown away or (in the case of buildings and structures) torn down or abandoned. It is therefore an *indirect* approach to the understanding of any past society.

There is nothing new in the idea of looking at living societies to help interpret the past. In the 19th and early 20th centuries European archaeologists frequently turned for inspiration to researches done by ethnographers among societies in Africa or Australia. But the so-called "ethnographic parallels" that resulted often simply and crudely likened past societies to present ones, stifling new thought rather than promoting it. In the United States archaeologists were confronted from the beginning with the living reality of complex Native American societies, which taught them to think rather more deeply about how **ethnography** might be used to aid archaeological interpretation. Nevertheless, fully fledged ethnoarchaeology is a development really of only the last 40 years. The key difference is that now it is archaeologists themselves, rather than ethnographers or anthropologists, who carry out the research among living societies.

A good example is the work of Lewis Binford among the Nunamiut, a hunter-gatherer group of Alaska. In the 1960s Binford was attempting to interpret archaeological sites of the Middle Paleolithic of France (the Mousterian period, 180,000–40,000 years ago). He realized that only by studying how *modern* hunter-gatherers used and discarded bones and tools, or moved from site to site, could he begin to understand the mechanisms that had created the Mousterian archaeological record – itself almost certainly the product of a mobile hunter-gatherer economy. Between 1969 and 1973 he lived intermittently among the Nunamiut and observed their behavior. For instance, he studied the way bone debris was produced and discarded by men at a seasonal hunting camp (the Mask site, Anaktuvuk Pass, Alaska). He saw that, when sitting round a hearth and processing bone for marrow, there was a "drop

Ethnoarchaeology: the work of Lewis Binford. (Right) The "drop zone" and "toss zones" model derived from observations of the Nunamiut. (Center) At the site of Pincevent, France, the excavator Leroi-Gourhan interpreted three hearths as being evidence for a complex skin tent (plan and reconstruction shown). (Below left) Binford applied his "outside hearth model" to the three Pincevent hearths, and deduced from the distribution of bones that his model fitted the evidence better than that of Leroi-Gourhan: i.e. that the hearths lay outside, and not within a tent. (Below right) Classic semicircular arrangement around an outside hearth, as demonstrated by Gwi Bushmen at Ghanzi, Botswana, in the 1980s.

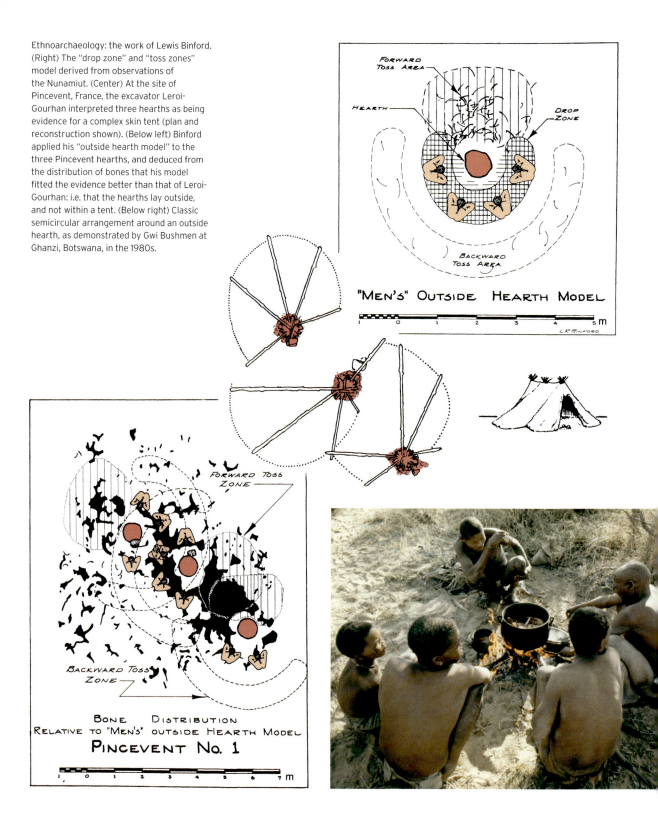

FORWARD TOSS AREA

HEARTH

DROP ZONE

BACKWARD TOSS AREA

"MEN'S" OUTSIDE HEARTH MODEL

L R BINFORD

5 m

FORWARD TOSS ZONE

BACKWARD TOSS ZONE

BONE DISTRIBUTION RELATIVE TO "MEN'S" OUTSIDE HEARTH MODEL
PINCEVENT No. 1

7 m

In the Lake Baringo area of Kenya, East Africa, Hodder studied the female ear decorations worn by the Tugen, Njemps, and Pokot (shown here) tribes, and showed how these ornaments were used to assert tribal distinctiveness.

zone" where small fragments of bone fell as they were broken. The larger pieces, which were thrown away by the men, formed a "toss zone," both in front and behind them.

The Nunamiut might not provide an exact "ethnographic parallel" for Mousterian societies, but Binford recognized that there are certain actions or functions likely to be common to all hunter-gatherers because – as in the case of the processing of bone – the actions are dictated by the most convenient procedure when seated round a camp fire. The discarded fragments of bone then leave a characteristic pattern round the hearth for the archaeologist to find and interpret – indeed, Binford went on to use his model to reinterpret data from a Paleolithic camp site. From such analysis, it also proved possible to infer roughly how many people were in the group, and over what period of time the camp site was used. These are questions very relevant to our understanding of the social organization (including the size) of hunter-gatherer groups.

Ethnoarchaeology is not restricted to observations at the local scale. The British archaeologist Ian Hodder, in his study of the female ear decorations used by different tribes in the Lake Baringo area of Kenya, undertook a regional study to investigate the extent to which **material culture** (in this case personal decoration) was being used to express differences between the tribes. Partly as a result of such work, archaeologists no longer assume that it is an easy task to take archaeological assemblages and group them into regional "cultures," and then to assume that each "culture" so formed represents a social unit. Such a procedure might, in fact, work quite well for the ear decorations Hodder studied, because the people in question chose to use this feature to assert their tribal distinctiveness. But, as Hodder showed, if we were to take other features of the material culture, such as pots or tools, the same pattern would not necessarily be followed. His example documents the important lesson that material culture cannot be used by the archaeologist in a simple or unthinking manner in the reconstruction of supposed ethnic groups.

The Archaeology of the Individual and of Identity

The discussion so far in this chapter has as its starting point the concept of the society and its organization. This is a deliberate feature of the structure of this book: before questions are asked about the variety of human experience it is necessary first to form some view about the scale of a society and its complexity. But at the same time this might be criticized as a "top-down" approach, beginning with questions of organization and of hierarchy, of power and of centralization, and only then turning to the individual who actually lives in society, to that person's role, gender, and status and to what it was really *like* to live there at that time and in that social context.

It would be equally valid to start with the individual and with social relationships, including kinship relations, and to work outward from there:

what one might term a "bottom-up" approach. This involves the consideration of such issues as social inequality, **ethnicity**, and gender.

One important aspect of the individual to remember is that most sides of our "humanness" and many of the concepts that we enshrine as "human," including our schemes of perception, thought, gender, and sense of morals, our ways of moving our bodies around and communicating (such as standing, sitting, looking, speaking, and walking), and even the way we respond to our senses (such as our sense of smell and taste), are not natural "givens" but are in fact culturally specific: they are developed and adopted by humans within a society and vary through time and space. If we are really to know what it was like to live in a past society, we must be careful not to make assumptions based on our own experience of what it is to be "human."

Social Inequality

The theme of the archaeology of social inequality has perhaps not been very comprehensively addressed yet, but in the field of historical archaeology there have been systematic studies of the material culture of some underprivileged groups, including some interesting studies of town areas known from documentary accounts to be considered poor.

The infamous Five Points slum area of lower Manhattan, New York, described by early 19th-century writers including Charles Dickens, has been investigated through salvage excavations at the site of a new federal courthouse at Foley Square. The excavated area included the site of a cellar brothel at 12 Baxter Street, historically documented (in the 1843 indictment of its keeper) as a "disorderly house – a nest for prostitutes and others of ill fame and name, where great numbers of characters are in the nightly practice of revelling until late and

Key Concepts
Finding the Individual

- Many aspects of individual human behavior are not a cross-cultural "given" but are learned, and differ widely across both ancient and modern cultures

- The existence of ethnic groups is difficult to recognize from the archaeological record: an affiliation to a particular style of material culture, for example, does not necessarily equate to ethnicity

- It is important to recognize gender in the archaeological record (particularly the roles of women, which have traditionally been overlooked). There is also a distinction between sex and gender: sex is biologically determined, whereas gender roles in different societies vary greatly

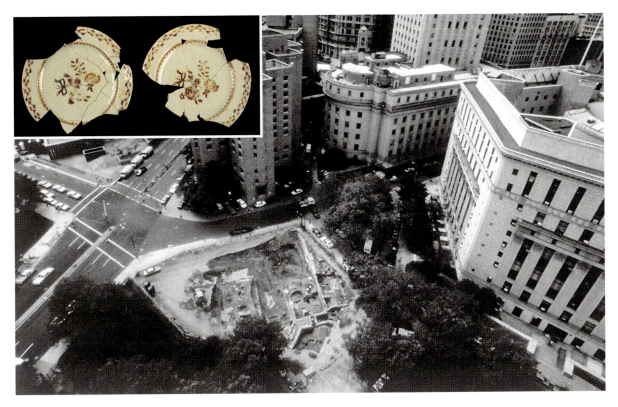

(Above) A view of the rescue excavation of the 19th-century slum area of Five Points in lower Manhattan, New York. The cellar of a brothel was investigated and yielded much information concerning the daily lives of the inhabitants. While of a low social rank, the prostitutes at least enjoyed the use of Chinese porcelain (inset).

improper hours of the night." The excavations revealed insights based upon the material culture:

> The quality of the household goods found in the privy behind 12 Baxter far exceeded that of goods found anywhere else on the block. The prostitutes lived well, at least when they were at work. One attraction was the opportunity to live in a style that seamstresses, laundresses, and maids could not afford. Afternoon tea at the brothel was served on a set of Chinese porcelain that included matching teacups and coffee cups, saucers and plates, a slop bowl and a tea caddie. Meals consisted of steak, veal, ham, soft-shell clams and many kinds of fish. There was a greater variety of artifacts from the brothel than from other excavated areas of the courthouse block.

Not far from Foley Square another excavation, that of the African Burial Ground, formerly known as the Negros Burial Ground, which was recorded on a plan of 1755, has proved highly informative and has had wide repercussions.

The rescue excavation of skeletons there in 1991 provoked outrage in the African-American community of today, which felt it had not been adequately consulted, and ultimately led to the establishment of a Museum of African and

A Yoruba priestess and a Khamite priest perform a libation ceremony for the ancestors over the grave of a person buried in the African Burial Ground in lower Manhattan, New York.

African-American History in New York City. There were no grave markers, and other than wood, coffin nails, and shroud pins, few artifacts were found. Studies of the skeletons have combined **DNA** analysis with cranial metrics, morphology, and historical data, to discover where the people came from. The large size of the sample will allow study of nutrition and pathology. The remains of 419 individuals disinterred during the excavations were ceremonially reburied in October 2003, after being taken in a procession up Broadway.

Certainly the controversy and the excavation have proved a stimulus toward the development of African-American archaeology, already well-defined through the investigation of plantation sites.

Ethnicity and Conflict

Ethnicity (i.e. the existence of ethnic groups) is difficult to recognize from the archaeological record. For example, the idea that such features as pottery decoration are automatically a sign of ethnic affiliation has been questioned. This is a field where ethnoarchaeology is only now beginning to make progress.

The theme of ethnicity is a difficult one to approach archaeologically, unless with the help of written records, since ethnicity is based largely upon self-awareness. There is frequently a correlation between ethnic groups and language groups, which can offer further avenues for study. Questions of group self-identity, which is often much the same as ethnicity, often underlie conflict and warfare.

The role of warfare in early societies is one topic that merits further investigation. It has long been agreed that warfare is a recurrent feature of early

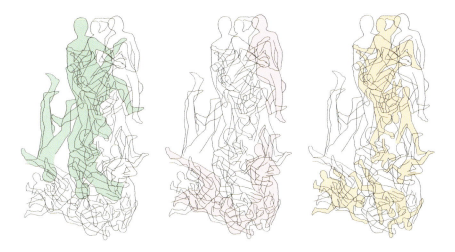

Skeletons found in a pit at Talheim, Germany, dating to c. 5000 BC, indicative of mass killing, contradict the notion of peaceful early farming society (left to right, males, females, and children).

state societies, but for prehistoric times it has been more common to think in terms of peace-loving "noble savages." There is, however, an increasing amount of evidence to suggest that warfare in prehistory was not so much the exception as the norm. A good example is provided by the Neolithic ditched enclosures (c. 5000 to 2000 BC) of Talheim, Germany. Fieldwork suggested that they were not simply of symbolic significance, as many archaeologists had thought, but genuine fortifications. One pit contained the bodies of 18 adults and 16 children, all killed by blows from at least six different axes, contradicting the notion of a peaceful early farming society.

War need not be undertaken with the objective of permanently occupying the lands of the vanquished in a process of territorial expansion. The American archaeologist David Freidel made this point in his study of Maya warfare, based on the wall paintings at the site of Bonampak and also early written sources. According to his analysis, the function of Maya warfare was not to conquer, and thus enlarge the frontiers of the state in question, but instead to give Maya rulers the opportunity to capture kings and princes from neighboring states, many of whom were then later offered as sacrifices to the gods. Warfare thus allowed the Maya rulers to reaffirm their royal status: it had a central role in upholding the system of government, but that role was not one of territorial expansion.

Investigating Gender

An important aspect of the study of social archaeology is the investigation of gender. Initially this was felt to overlap with feminist archaeology, which often had the explicit objective of exposing and correcting the male bias (androcentrism) of archaeology. There is no doubt that in the modern world the role of women professionals, including archaeologists, has often been a difficult one. For instance, Dorothy Garrod, the first female professor of archaeology in Britain, was appointed in 1937, at a time when women at her university

(Cambridge) were not allowed to take a degree at the end of their course, as male undergraduates did, but only a diploma. There was – and still is – an imbalance to be rectified in the academic world, and that was one of the early objectives of feminist archaeology. A second was to illuminate the roles of women in the past more clearly, where frequently they had been overlooked.

But the study of gender is much more than simply the study of women. An important central idea soon became the distinction between sex and gender. It was argued that sex – female or male – may be regarded as biologically determined and can be established archaeologically from skeletal remains. But gender – at its simplest woman or man – is a social construct, involving the sex-related roles of individuals in society. Gender roles in different societies vary greatly both from place to place and through time. Systems of kinship, of marriage, inheritance, and the division of labor are all related to biological sex but not determined by it. These perspectives permitted a good deal of profitable work in this second phase of gender studies in archaeology, but they have now in their turn been criticized by a new "third wave" feminism, as emphasizing supposedly "inherent" differences between women and men, and emphasizing women's links to the natural world through reproduction.

The work of Marija Gimbutas on the prehistory of southeast Europe, for example, is now criticized. She argued that the predominantly female figurines seen in the Neolithic and Copper Age of southeast Europe and in Anatolia demonstrate the important status of women at that time. She had a vision of an Old Europe influenced by feminine values, which was to disappear in the succeeding Bronze Age with the dominance of a warlike male hierarchy, supposedly introduced by Indo-European warrior nomads from the east.

Marija Gimbutas became something of a cult figure in her own right, and her support for the concept of a great "Mother Goddess" representing a fertility principle has been embraced by modern "ecofeminist" and New Age enthusiasts. The current excavations by Ian Hodder at the early Neolithic site of Çatalhöyük in Turkey, where female figurines of baked clay have been found, are now visited regularly by devotees of the "Goddess" whose views are treated respectfully by the excavators, even though they do not share them. Hodder has argued instead that the figurines may represent the subordination of women as objects of ownership and male desires. Comparable figurines from the Aegean can often be shown to lack definite features diagnostic of sex or gender, and studies of rather similar baked clay figurines from Oaxaca, Mexico, have suggested that they were made by women for use in rituals relating to ancestors rather than deities. The notion that they represented a "Mother Goddess" lacks supporting evidence.

The third phase in the development of gender archaeology, in tune with the "third wave" of feminists of the 1990s, takes a different view of gender in two senses. First, in the narrower sense, and, as Lynn Meskell puts it, "led by women of color, lesbian feminists, queer theorists and postcolonial feminists," it recognizes

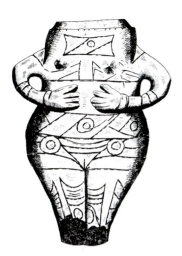

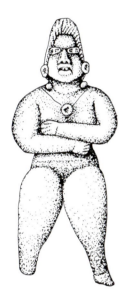

Different images symbolizing female power? (Clockwise, from top) A Neolithic vase from Romania; a late Neolithic seated stone figure from Hagar Qim, Malta, originally with a removable head that could be manipulated with strings; and a Zapotec figurine from Oaxaca, Mexico.

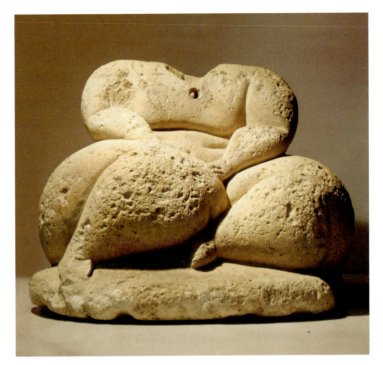

that the field of gender and gender difference is more complex than a simple polarity between male and female, and that other kinds of difference have to be recognized. Indeed the very recognition of a simple structural opposition between male and female is itself, even in our own society, an over-simplification. In many societies children are not regarded as socially male or female until they reach the age of puberty – in the modern Greek language, for instance, while men and women are grammatically male and female in gender, the words for children generally belong to the third, neuter gender.

This leads on to the second point, that gender is part of a broader social framework, part of the social process – in Margaret Conkey's words "a way in which social categories, roles, ideologies and practices are defined and played out." While gender is, in any society, a system of classification, it is part of a larger system of social differences, including age, wealth, **religion**, ethnicity, and so forth. Moreover these are not static constructs but fluid and flexible, constructed and re-constructed in the practice of daily life.

The complexities in analyzing burial data with respect to gender are indicated by the study by Bettina Arnold of the so-called "Princess of Vix" burial from east-central France. The grave contained skeletal remains that analysis indicated were female, but the grave-goods consisted of various prestige items normally thought to be indicative of males. This exceptionally rich 5th-century BC burial was initially interpreted as a transvestite priest because it was considered inconceivable that a woman could be honored in such a way. Arnold's careful

(Left) Reconstruction of part of the "Princess of Vix" burial. A woman's body adorned with jewelry lay on a cart, the wheels of which had been stacked against the wall of a timber chamber. (Right) This huge bronze krater, 1.64 m (5 ft 4 in.) high, was among the grave-goods.

reanalysis of the grave-goods supported the interpretation of the burial as an elite female. This may lead to a fresh assessment of the potentially powerful, occasionally paramount role that women played in Iron Age Europe. But this work may yet lead on to a wider consideration of gender distinctions in the Iron Age in a context that may reassess whether in individuals of very high status the traditional bipolar concept of gender is appropriate.

Study Questions

- Societies are typically classified into what four main groups?
- Why is the analysis of burials important to the study of segmentary societies?
- How can the ethnoarchaeology of modern societies inform us about the past?
- What are the key methods through which the structure of societies is analyzed?
- Why is it hard to study ethnicity in the archaeological record?
- What is the difference between sex and gender? Why is this difference important to archaeologists?

Summary

- This chapter has shown that a formidable battery of techniques is now available to archaeologists who wish to investigate the social organization of early societies. Only the main themes have been touched on, but these will have made it clear that the potential for understanding the more complex and highly organized societies represented by states and chiefdoms is especially great.

- We can investigate ranked societies through their site hierarchies and, in the case of state societies, through their urban centers. It should in this way be possible to identify the ruling center using archaeological methods alone, and the extent of the area over which it held jurisdiction.

- For ranked or stratified societies (chiefdoms and states), the study of the buildings and other evidence of administration at the center gives valuable information about the social, political, and economic organization of society, as well as a picture of the life of the ruling elite. We can identify and analyze their palaces and tombs, and studies of lower-order administrative centers give further information about the social and political structure. The study of the differences in the treatment accorded to different individuals at death, in both the size and wealth of grave offerings, can reveal the complete range of status distinctions in a society.

- Similar approaches may be applied to segmentary societies: the study of individual settlements, the evidence for social ranking revealed by burials, and the existence of cooperative communal mechanisms for the construction of major monuments.

- On a smaller scale (and particularly important for the Paleolithic period), the camps of mobile hunter-gatherer societies and the seasonal movement between different sites may also be studied using the methods outlined in this chapter, especially when the insights provided by ethnoarchaeological research on living societies are used in conjunction with direct study of the archaeological record.

- In recent studies a "bottom-up" perspective in social archaeologies has become important: the archaeology of individuals and of identity. Gender studies in particular are now adding new insight into the structure of society.

Further Reading

The following works illustrate some of the ways in which social organization can be reconstructed:

Binford, L.R. 2002. *In Pursuit of the Past*. University of California Press: Berkeley & London.

Hodder, I. 2009. *Symbols in Action*. Cambridge University Press: Cambridge & New York.

Janusek, J.W. 2004. *Identity and Power in the Ancient Andes*. Routledge: London & New York.

Journal of Social Archaeology (since 2001).

Meskell, L. 2006. *A Companion to Social Archaeology*. Wiley-Blackwell: Oxford.

Pyburn, K.A. (ed.). 2004. *Ungendering Civilization*. Routledge: London & New York.

[See p. 345 for a list of useful websites]

What Was the Environment and What Did They Eat?
Environment, subsistence, and diet

Environment and diet constitute two of the most fundamental and crucial factors of human life that the archaeologist needs to assess. The environment governs human life: latitude, altitude, landforms, and climate determine the vegetation, which in turn determines animal life, and both of these determine diet. And all these things taken together determine how and where humans have lived – or at least they did until very recently.

The reconstruction of the environment first requires an answer to very general questions of global climate change. What was the global climate like when the human activities under study took place? Does a **context** belong to a glacial or interglacial phase? These broad questions can be answered by relating the date of a context to evidence of long-term climatic fluctuations obtained from sea and **ice cores**, as well as from tree-rings.

More specific questions about past environments will follow, and these are particularly relevant for all postglacial contexts, after about 10,000 years ago. There are two main sources of evidence: plant and animal remains. Analysis of these will not only reveal the range of flora and fauna that people would have encountered at a particular time and place, but since many plants and animals are quite sensitive to climate change, we can also find out what the regional and local environment would have been like.

Unfortunately, owing to the poor preservation of many forms of organic evidence, and to the distorted samples we recover, we can never be certain about our conclusions. We simply have to aim for the best approximation available. No single method will give a full and accurate picture – all are problematic in one way or another – and so as many methods as data and funds will allow need to be applied to build up a composite image.

Once we know what the environment might have been like, as well as the kinds of plants and animals present, we can try to find out how people exploited those conditions and resources and what they might have been eating. Subsistence, the quest for food, is one of the most basic of all necessities, and there is a variety of evidence for it to be found in the archaeological record.

Plant and animal remains and the residues found on **artifacts**, such as pots or stone tools, can give indirect clues to what peoples' diet might have consisted of, but the only direct evidence we have is from the study of actual human remains: stomach contents, fecal material, teeth, and bones.

Investigating Environments on a Global Scale

The first step in assessing previous environmental conditions is to look at them globally. Local changes make little sense unless seen against this broader climatic background. Tree-rings are a good source of information for the last 10,000 years or so, but since water covers almost three-quarters of the Earth, we should begin by examining evidence about past climates that can be obtained from this area, including data within glaciers and ice caps. We will then go on to look at what can be learned about past environments at a more local level, from plant and animal remains.

Evidence from Water and Ice

The sediments of the ocean floor accumulate very slowly, just a few centimeters every thousand years, but they can contain evidence of thousands or even millions of years of climate history. In some areas ocean sediments consist primarily of an ooze made up of microfossils, such as the shells of foraminifera – tiny one-celled marine organisms that live in the surface water of the oceans and sink to the bottom when they die. As in an archaeological **stratigraphy**, we can trace changes in environmental conditions through time by studying cores extracted from the seabed and fluctuations in the species represented and the physical form of single species through the sequence. Oxygen isotope analysis of foraminifera can also reveal changes in the environment (see box opposite).

Thousands of **deep-sea cores** have now been extracted and studied, but cores can also be obtained from stratified ice sheets (some containing hundreds of thousands of annual growth layers), and here the oxygen isotopic composition also gives some guide to climatic oscillations. Results from cores in Greenland and the Antarctic, as well as Andean and Tibetan glaciers, are consistent with, and add detail to, those from deep-sea cores. It is also possible to analyze bubbles of ancient methane gas trapped in the ice (resulting from plant decomposition, which is sensitive to temperature and moisture variations).

Ancient Winds. Isotopes can be used not merely for temperature studies but also for data on precipitation. And since it is the temperature differences between the equatorial and polar regions that largely determine the storminess of our weather, isotope studies can even tell us something about winds in different periods.

As air moves from low latitudes to colder regions, the water it loses as rain or snow is enriched in the stable isotope oxygen 18, while the remaining vapour

Sea and Ice Cores and Global Warming

The stratigraphy of sediment on the ocean floor is obtained from cores taken out of the seabed. Ships use a "piston-corer" to extract a thin column of sediment, usually about 10–30 m (30–100 ft) in length. The core can then be analyzed in the laboratory.

Dates for the different layers in the core are obtained by radiocarbon, archaeomagnetism, or the uranium-series method (Chapter 4). Changing environmental conditions in the past are then deduced by two kinds of tests on microscopic fossils of tiny one-celled organisms, called foraminifera, found in the sediment. First, scientists study the simple presence, absence, and fluctuations of different foraminiferan species. Second, they analyze, by mass spectrometer, fluctuations in the ratio of the stable oxygen isotopes 18 and 16 in the calcium carbonate of the foraminiferan shells. Variations discernible by these two tests reflect not simply changes in temperature, but also oscillations in the continental glaciers. For example, as the glaciers grew, water was drawn up into them, reducing sea levels and increasing the density and salinity of the oceans, and thus causing changes in the depths at which certain foraminiferan

Three climate records compared. Left to right: proportions of different shell species in a deep-sea core; ratio of oxygen 18 to 16 in shells from a deep-sea core; and oxygen ratios from an ice core. The resemblance of the three records is good evidence that long-term climatic variation has been worldwide.

Microscopic fossils of the foraminiferan species *Globorotalia truncatulinoides*, which coils to the left during cold periods, and to the right during warm ones.

species lived. At the same time the proportion of oxygen 18 in seawater increased. When the glaciers melted during periods of warmer climate, the proportion of oxygen 18 decreased.

Cores can also be extracted from present-day ice sheets in Greenland and Antarctica. Here too, variations in oxygen and also hydrogen isotopic composition at different depths reveal the temperature when the ice formed, and thus provide an indication of past

climate; results coincide well with those from deep-sea cores. In addition, high carbon and methane levels (the so-called "greenhouse gases") indicate periods of global warming.

The ice cores suggest that the next ice age is about 15,000 years away; however, the stability of our climate has been overturned by human activity, and the ice shows that today's greenhouse gas concentrations in the atmosphere are the highest for at least 440,000 years. In the cores, even much smaller rises in the gas level have been followed by significant rises in global temperatures, but the current rate of increase in greenhouse gases is more than 100 times faster than anything recorded in the last half a million years. During that period, levels of carbon dioxide varied between 200 parts per million (ppm) in ice ages, and 280 ppm in interglacials – but since the industrial revolution, the levels have risen to 375 ppm, which alarms scientists.

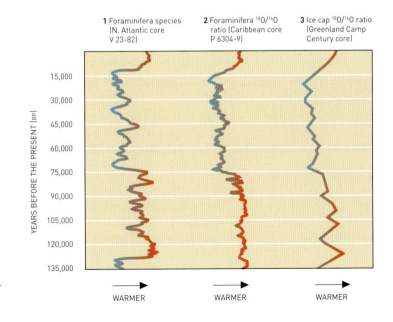

1 Foraminifera species (N. Atlantic core V 23-82)

2 Foraminifera $^{18}O/^{16}O$ ratio (Caribbean core P 6304-9)

3 Ice cap $^{18}O/^{16}O$ ratio (Greenland Camp Century core)

YEARS BEFORE THE PRESENT (BP)

15,000
30,000
45,000
60,000
75,000
90,000
105,000
120,000
135,000

WARMER   WARMER   WARMER

- *Evidence from sea and ice cores*: analysis of isotopic ratios within dateable layers of ocean sediment and ice can give an accurate idea of climate. Studies from all over the world are all in broad agreement about what global climate was like over the past few million years

- *Evidence from tree-rings*: Similar analysis of tree-rings gives a finer-scale idea of what the environment was like in different areas up to about 10,000 years ago

becomes correspondingly richer in the other stable isotope of oxygen, oxygen 16. Thus from the ratio between the two isotopes in precipitation at a particular place, we can calculate the temperature difference between that place and the equatorial region.

Using this technique, the changing ratios found over the last 100,000 years in ice cores from Greenland and the Antarctic have been studied. The results show that during glacial periods the temperature difference between equatorial and polar regions increased by 20–25 percent, and thus wind circulation must have been far more violent. Confirmation has come from a deep-sea core off the coast of West Africa, analysis of which led to estimates of wind strength over the last 700,000 years. Apparently wind "vigor" was greater by a factor of two during each glacial episode than at the present; and wind speeds were 50 percent greater during glacial than interglacial phases. In future, analysis of the minute plant debris in these cores may also add to the history of wind patterns.

It has also been found that raindrops in hurricanes have more oxygen 16 than normal rain, and this leaves traces in layers of stalagmites – for example in caves in Belize – as well as in tree-rings. This method has pinpointed hurricane events of the past 200 years, and so it should also be possible to use older stalagmites to establish a record of hurricanes stretching back tens of thousands of years, thus revealing any changes in their patterns, locations, and intensity. So data from the past may clarify the possible linkage of modern global warming with such extreme weather.

Why should archaeologists be interested in ancient winds? The answer is that winds can have a great impact on human activity. For example, it is thought that increased storminess may have caused the Vikings to abandon their North Atlantic sea route at the onset of a cold period. Similarly, some of the great Polynesian migrations in the southwestern Pacific during the 12th and 13th centuries AD seem to have coincided with the onset of a short period of slightly warmer weather, when violent storms would have been rare. These migrations were brought to an end a few centuries later by the Little Ice Age, which may have caused a sharp increase in the frequency of storms. Had the Polynesians been able to continue, they might conceivably have gone on from New Zealand to reach Tasmania and Australia.

Tree-Rings and Climate

Tree-rings have a growth that varies with the climate, being strong in the spring and then declining to nothing in the winter; the more moisture available, the wider the annual ring. As we saw in Chapter 4, these variations in ring width have formed the basis of a major dating technique. Study of a particular set of rings, however, can also reveal important environmental data, for example whether growth was slow (implying dense local forest cover) or fast (implying light forest). Tree growth is complex, and many other factors may affect it, but temperature and soil moisture do tend to be dominant.

Annual and decade-to-decade variations show up far more clearly in tree-rings than in ice cores, and tree-rings can also record sudden and dramatic shocks to the climate. For example, data from Virginia indicate that the alarming mortality and near abandonment of Jamestown, Virginia, the first permanent white settlement in the United States, occurred during an extraordinary drought, the driest 7-year episode in 770 years (AD 1606–12; see pp. 96–97).

The study of tree-rings and climate (dendroclimatology) has also progressed by using X-ray measurements of cell-size and density as an indication of environmental productivity. More recently, ancient temperatures have been derived from tree-rings by means of the carbon isotope ratios preserved in their cellulose. Isotopic evidence preserved in the cellulose of timbers of the tamarisk tree, contained in the ramp that the Romans used to overcome the besieged Jewish citadel of Masada in AD 73, have revealed to Israeli archaeologists that the climate at that time was wetter and more amenable to agriculture than it is today.

The role of tree-rings makes it clear that it is organic remains above all that provide the richest source of evidence for environmental reconstruction. We now take a look at the surviving traces of plants and animals and what these can tell us about ancient environments.

Reconstructing the Plant Environment

The prime goal in archaeological plant studies is to try to reconstruct what the vegetation was like in the past at any particular time or place. But we should not forget that plants lie at the base of the food chain. The plant communities of a given area and period will therefore provide clues to local animal and human life, and will also reflect soil conditions and climate. Some types of vegetation react relatively quickly to changes in climate (though less quickly than insects, for instance), and the shifts of plant communities in both latitude and altitude are the most direct link between climatic change and the terrestrial human environment, for example in the Ice Age.

Pollen Analysis

All hay fever sufferers will be aware of the pollen "rain" that can afflict them in the spring and summer. Pollen grains – the tiny male reproductive bodies of flowering plants – have an almost indestructible outer shell (exine) that can survive in certain sediments for tens of thousands of years. In pollen analysis the exines are extracted from the soil, studied under the microscope, and identified according to the distinctive exine shape and surface ornamentation of different families and genera of plants. Once quantified, these identifications are plotted as curves on a pollen diagram. Fluctuations in the curve for each plant category may then be studied for signs of climatic fluctuation, or forest clearance and crop-planting by humans.

Preservation

The most favorable sediments for preservation of pollen are acidic and poorly aerated peat bogs and lake beds, where biological decay is impeded and grains undergo rapid burial. Cave sediments are also usually suitable because of their humidity and constant temperature. Other contexts, such as sandy sediments or open sites exposed to weathering, preserve pollen poorly.

In wet sites, or unexcavated areas, samples are extracted in long cores, but in dry sites a series of separate samples can be removed from the sections. On an archaeological excavation, small samples are usually extracted at regular stratified intervals. Great care must be taken to avoid contamination from the tools used or from the atmosphere. Pollen can also be found in mud bricks, vessels, tombs, mummy wrappings,

A selection of pollen grains, as seen under the microscope.

Alnus (*alder*)

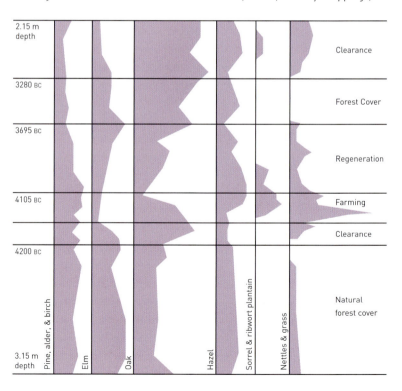

Betula (*birch*)

Quercus (*oak*)

Salix (*willow*)

Corylus (*hazel*)

Hedera helix (*ivy*)

Tilia (*lime*)

Ulmus (*elm*)

Pollen data from Northern Ireland reveal the impact of the first farmers in the region.

the guts of preserved bodies, ancient feces, and many other contexts.

Examination and Counting

The sealed tubes containing the samples are examined in the laboratory, where a small portion of each sample is studied under the microscope in an attempt to identify a few hundred grains in that sample. Each family and almost every genus of plant produce pollen grains distinctive in shape and surface ornamentation, but it is difficult to go further and pinpoint the species. This imposes certain limits on environmental reconstruction, since different species within the same genus can have markedly different requirements in terms of soil, climate, etc.

After identification, the quantity of pollen for each plant-type is calculated for each layer – usually as a percentage of the total number of grains in that layer – and then plotted as a curve. The curves can be seen as a reflection of climatic fluctuations through the sequence, using the present-day tolerances of these plants as a guide.

The curves can also show the human impact on past vegetation. The diagram shown here is based on a pollen core from Northern Ireland, and reveals the impact of the first farmers in the region. Forest clearance is indicated c. 4150 BC with a fall in tree pollen (especially elm and oak) and a marked increase in open-country and field species, such as grass and sorrel. The subsequent regeneration of forest cover, followed by a second period of clearance, shows the non-intensive nature of early farming in the area.

Plant studies in **archaeology** have always been overshadowed by faunal analysis, simply because bones are more conspicuous than plant remains in **excavation**. Bones may sometimes survive better, but usually plant remains are present in greater numbers than bones. Thanks to the discovery that some of the constituent parts of a plant are much more resistant to decomposition than was previously believed, and that a huge amount of data survives that can tell us something about long-dead vegetation, plant studies have become very important. As with so many of the specializations on which archaeology can call, these analyses require a great deal of time and funds.

Some of the most informative techniques for making an overall assessment of plant communities in a particular period involve analysis not of the biggest remains but of the tiniest, microbotanical remains, especially pollen.

Microbotanical Remains

Pollen Analysis. **Palynology**, or the study of pollen grains (see box), was developed by a Norwegian geologist, Lennart von Post, at the beginning of the 20th century. It has proved invaluable to archaeology, since it can be applied to a wide range of **sites** and provides information on chronology as well as environment and forest clearance.

While palynology cannot produce an exact picture of past environments, it does give some idea of fluctuations in vegetation through time, whatever their causes may be (whether climatic or human), which can be compared with results from other methods. Pollen studies can also supply much-needed information for environments as ancient as those of the Hadar sediments and the Omo valley in Ethiopia around 3 million years ago. It is usually assumed that these regions were always as dry as they are now, but pollen analysis has shown that they were much wetter and greener between 3.5 and 2.5 million years ago, with even some tropical plants present. The Hadar, which is now semi-desert with scattered trees and shrubs, was rich, open grassland, with dense woodland by lakes and along rivers. The change to drier conditions, around 2.5 million years ago, can be seen in the reduction of tree pollen in favor of more grasses.

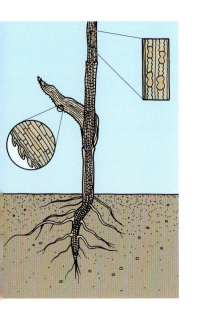

Phytoliths are minute particles of silica in plant cells that survive after the rest of the plant has decomposed. Some are specific to certain parts of the plant (e.g. stem or leaf).

Phytoliths.   A better-known and fast-developing branch of microbotanical studies concerns phytoliths, which were first recognized as components in archaeological contexts as long ago as 1908, but have only been studied systematically in the last few decades. These are minute particles of silica (plant opal) derived from the cells of plants, and they survive after the rest of the organism has decomposed or been burned. They are common in hearths and ash layers, but are also found inside pottery, plaster, and even on stone tools and the teeth of animals: grass phytoliths have been found adhering to herbivorous animal teeth from Bronze Age, Iron Age, and medieval sites in Europe.

These crystals are useful because, like pollen grains, they are produced in large numbers, they survive well in ancient sediments, and they have myriad distinctive shapes and sizes that vary according to type. They inform us primarily about the use people made of particular plants, but their simple presence adds to the picture of the environment built up from other sources.

In particular, a combination of phytolith and pollen analysis can be a powerful tool for environmental reconstruction, since the two methods have complementary strengths and weaknesses. The American scholar Dolores Piperno has studied cores from the Gatun Basin, Panama, the pollen content of which had already revealed a sequence of vegetation change from 11,300 years ago to the present. She found that the phytoliths in the cores confirmed the pollen sequence, with the exception that evidence for agriculture and forest clearance (i.e. the appearance of maize, and an increase in grass at the expense of trees) appeared around 4850 years ago in the phytoliths, about 1000 years earlier than in the pollen. This early evidence is probably attributable to small clearings that do not show up in pollen diagrams because grains from the surrounding forest overwhelm the samples.

Moreover, phytoliths often survive in sediments that are hostile to the preservation of fossil pollen (because of oxidation or microbial activity), and may thus provide the only available evidence for paleoenvironment or vegetational change. Another advantage is that, while all grass pollen looks the same, grass phytoliths can be assigned to ecologically different groups. It has recently been discovered that aluminium ions in phytoliths can be used to distinguish between forested and herbaceous vegetations, while oxygen and hydrogen isotope signatures in phytoliths will also provide important environmental data.

Diatom Analysis.   Another method of environmental reconstruction using plant microfossils is **diatom analysis**. Diatoms are single-cell algae that have cell walls of silica instead of cellulose, and these silica cell walls survive after the algae die. They accumulate in great numbers at the bottom of any body of water in which the algae live; a few are found in peat, but most come from lake and shore sediments.

Diatoms have been recorded, identified, and classified for more than 200 years. The process of identifying and counting them is much like that used in palynology, as is the collection of samples in the field. Their well-defined shapes and ornamentations permit identification to a high level, and their assemblages directly reflect the types of algae present and their diatom productivity, and, indirectly, the water's salinity, alkalinity, and nutrient content. From the environmental requirements of different species (in terms of habitat, salinity, and nutrients), one can determine what their immediate environment was at different periods.

Since diatom assemblages can indicate whether water was fresh, brackish, or salt, they have been used to identify, for example, the period when lakes became isolated from the sea in areas of tectonic uplift, to locate the past shorelines, and to reveal water pollution. For instance, the diatom sequence in sediments at the site of the former Lake Wevershoof, Medemblick (the Netherlands) suggests that in around AD 800 seawater entered and overcame what had been a freshwater lake, causing a hiatus in human occupation of the immediate area.

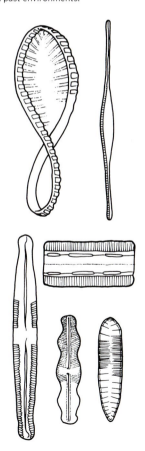

A variety of diatoms, the microscopic single-cell algae, the silica cell walls of which survive in many sediments after death. Study of the changing species in a deposit can help scientists reconstruct fluctuations in past environments.

All these microbotanical techniques mentioned – studies of pollen, phytoliths, and diatoms – can only be carried out by specialists. For archaeologists, however, a far more direct contact with environmental evidence comes from the larger, macrobotanical plant remains that they can actually see and conserve themselves in the course of excavation.

Macrobotanical Remains

A variety of bigger types of plant remains are potentially retrievable, and provide important information about which plants grew near sites, which were used or consumed by people, and so on. Here we shall focus on the valuable clues that macrobotanical remains provide regarding local environmental conditions.

Retrieval of vegetation from sediments has been made easier by the development of screening (sieving) and **flotation** techniques able to separate organic material from soil. In flotation, samples of soil from an excavation are poured into an overflowing tank, the lighter organic material floating to the top and spilling over the lip to be caught in sieves of different grades. This material is then dried and identified.

Sediments are by no means the only source of plant remains, which have also been found in the stomachs of frozen mammoths and preserved bog bodies; in ancient feces; on teeth; on stone tools; and in residues inside vessels. The remains themselves are varied:

Seeds and Fruits.   Ancient seeds and fruits can usually be identified to species, despite changes in their shape caused by charring or waterlogging. In some cases, the remains have disintegrated but have left their imprint behind – grain impressions are fairly common on pottery, leaf impressions are also known, and imprints exist on materials ranging from plaster to leather and corroded bronze. Identification, of course, depends on type and quality of the traces. Not all such finds necessarily mean that a plant grew locally: grape pips, for example, may come from imported fruit, while impressions on potsherds may mislead since pottery can travel far from its place of manufacture.

Plant Residues.   Chemical analysis of plant residues in vessels will be dealt with below in the context of human diet, but the results can give some idea of what species were available. Pottery vessels themselves may incorporate plant fibers (not to mention shell, feathers, or blood) as a tempering material, and microscopic analysis can sometimes identify these remains – for example, study of early pots from South Carolina and Georgia in the United States revealed the presence of shredded stems of Spanish Moss, a member of the pineapple family.

Remains of Wood.   Study of charcoal (burnt wood) is making a growing contribution to archaeological reconstruction of environments and of human use of timber. A very durable material, charcoal is commonly found by the archaeologist during excavation. Fragments can be examined by the specialist under the microscope, and identified (thanks to the anatomy of the wood) normally at the genus level, and sometimes to species. Charcoal and charred seeds have also proved the most reliable material from which to take samples for **radiocarbon dating** (Chapter 4).

Many charcoal samples are the remains of firewood, but others may come from wooden structures, furniture, and implements burnt at some point in a site's history. Samples therefore inevitably tend to reflect human selection of wood rather than the full range of species growing around the site. Nevertheless, the totals for each species provide some idea of one part of the vegetation at a given time.

Occasionally, charcoal analysis can be combined with other evidence to reveal something not only of local environment but also of human adaptation to it. At Boomplaas Cave, in southern Cape Province (South Africa), excavation has uncovered traces of human occupation stretching back 70,000 years. There is a clear difference between Ice Age and post-Ice Age charcoals: at times of extreme cold when conditions were also drier, between 22,000 and c. 14,000 years ago, the species diversity both in the charcoals and the pollen was low, whereas at times of higher rainfall and/or temperature the species diversity increased. A similar pattern of species diversity is seen also in the small mammals.

The vegetation around Boomplaas Cave at the time of maximum cold and drought was composed mainly of shrubs and grass with few plant resources that could be used by people; the larger mammal fauna was dominated by grazers that included "giant" species of buffalo, horse, and hartebeest, which became extinct by about 10,000 years ago.

The Boomplaas charcoal directly reflects the gradual change in climate and vegetation that led to the disappearance of the large grazers, and to a corresponding shift in subsistence practices by the cave's occupants. The charcoal analysis also highlights more subtle changes that reflect a shift in the season of maximum rainfall. The woody vegetation in the Cango Valley today is dominated by the thorn tree, *Acacia karroo*, characteristic of large areas in southern Africa where it is relatively dry and rain falls mostly in summer. Thorn tree charcoal is absent in the Ice Age samples at Boomplaas, but it appears from about 5000 years ago and by 2000 years ago is the dominant species, indicating a shift to hot, relatively moist summers. As the number of species that enjoy summer rainfall increased, the inhabitants of the cave were able to make more use of a new range of fruits, the seeds of which can be found preserved at the site.

By no means all wood subjected to this kind of analysis is charred. Increasing quantities of waterlogged wood are recovered from wet sites in many parts of the world. And in some conditions, such as extreme cold or dryness, desiccated wood may survive without either burning or waterlogging.

Scanning electron microscope photograph of charcoal from the thorn tree *Acacia karroo* found at Boomplaas Cave.

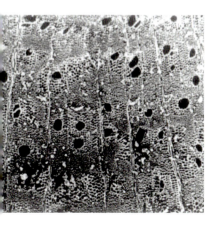

Other Sources of Evidence. A great deal of information on vegetation in the less remote periods studied by archaeologists can be obtained from art, from texts (e.g. the writings of Pliny the Elder, Roman farming texts, accounts and illustrations by early explorers, such as Captain Cook), and even from early photographs.

No single category of evidence can provide us with a total picture of local or regional vegetation, of small-scale trends or long-term changes: each produces a partial version of past realities. Input is needed from every source available, and, as will be seen below, these must be combined with results from the other forms of data studied in this chapter in order to reconstruct the best approximation of a past environment.

In this section we have seen how we can use a variety of archaeological data to try to reconstruct the plant environment at any particular place or time in the past. But what evidence of animal life is there and what can this tell us about past environments?

Reconstructing the Animal Environment

Animal remains were the first evidence used by 19th-century archaeologists to characterize the climate of the prehistoric periods that they encountered in their excavations. It was realized that different species were absent, present, or particularly abundant in certain layers, and hence also in certain periods, and the assumption was that this reflected changing climatic conditions.

Today, in order to use faunal remains as a guide to environment, we need to look more critically at the evidence than did those 19th-century pioneers. For instance, we need to understand the complex relationship that exists between modern animals and their environment. We also need to investigate how the animal remains we are studying arrived at a site – either naturally, or through the activities of carnivores or people, and thus how representative they may be of the variety of animals in their period.

Microfauna

Small animals (microfauna) tend to be better indicators of climate and environmental change than are large species, because they are much more sensitive to small variations in climate and adapt to them relatively quickly. In addition, since microfauna tend to accumulate naturally on a site, they reflect the immediate environment more accurately than the larger animals, whose remains are often accumulated through human or animal predation. As with pollen, small animals, and especially insects, are also usually found in far greater numbers than larger ones, which improves the statistical significance of their analysis.

The remains of a wide variety of insectivores, rodents, and bats are found on archaeological sites, but it is necessary to ensure as far as possible that

Key Concepts
Reconstructing the Animal Environment

- Microfauna are better indicators of climate and environmental change than macrofauna because they are much more sensitive to small variations in climate and adapt to them relatively quickly

- Microfauna tend to accumulate naturally on a site and reflect the immediate environment more accurately than the larger animals, whose remains are often accumulated through human or animal predation

the bones were deposited at the same time as the layer in question, and that burrowing has not occurred. Certain small species can be indicative of fairly specific environmental conditions, but it should be remembered that, even if the remains are not intrusive, they will not always indicate the immediate environment – if they come from owl pellets, for example, they may have been caught up to a few kilometers from the site (the contents of bird pellets can nevertheless be of great value in assessing local environments).

Bones of birds and fish are particularly fragile, but are well worth studying. They can for example be used to determine the seasons in which particular sites were occupied. Birds are sensitive to climatic change, and the alternation of "cold" and "warm" species in the last Ice Age has been of great help in assessing environment. One problem is that it is sometimes difficult to decide whether a bird is present naturally or has been brought in by a human or animal predator.

The calcium carbonate shells of land molluscs (such as snails) are preserved in many types of sediment. They reflect local conditions, and can be responsive to changes in microclimate, particularly to changes in temperature and rainfall. But we need to take into account that many species have a very broad tolerance, and their reaction to change is relatively slow, so that they "hang on" in adverse areas, and disperse slowly into newly acceptable areas. The changing percentages of marine mollusc species through time can reveal something of the nature of the coastal micro-environment – such as whether it was sandy or rocky – through study of the modern preferences of the species represented. The climatic change suggested by these alterations in the presence or abundance of different species can be matched with the results of oxygen isotope analysis of the shells.

A wide range of insects may also be found, in the form of adults, larvae, and (in the case of flies) puparia. The study of insects (**paleoentomology**) was rather neglected in archaeology until about 30 years ago, since when a great deal of pioneering work has been done. Insect exoskeletons can be quite resistant to decomposition,

Grasshopper engraved on a bone fragment from the late Ice Age (Magdalenian) site of Enlène, Ariège, France. Insects respond rapidly to climatic change, and are sensitive indicators of the timing and scale of environmental variations.

and some assemblages comprise thousands of individuals. Since we know the distribution and environmental requirements of their modern descendants, it is often possible to use insect remains as accurate indicators of the likely climatic conditions (and to some extent of the vegetation) prevailing in particular periods and local areas. Some species have very precise requirements in terms of where they like to breed and the kinds of food their larvae need. Rather than use single "indicator species" to reconstruct a micro-environment, however, it is safer to consider a number of species (the ancient climate lying within the area of overlap of their tolerance ranges).

Macrofauna

Remains of large animals found on archaeological sites mainly help us build up a picture of past human diet (see below). As environmental indicators they have proved less reliable than was once assumed, primarily because they are not so sensitive to environmental changes as small animals, but also because their remains will very likely have been deposited in an archaeological context through human or animal action. Bones from animals killed by people or by carnivores have been selected, and so cannot accurately reflect the full range of fauna present in the environment. The ideal is therefore to find accumulations of animal remains brought about by natural accident or catastrophe – animals caught in a flash flood perhaps, or buried by volcanic eruption, or that became frozen in permafrost. But such discoveries are rare – very different from the usual accumulations of animal bones encountered by archaeologists.

Assuming a suitable bone assemblage has been found and identified to species, what can the results tell us about the ancient environment?

The anatomy and especially the teeth of large animals tell us something about their diet and hence, in the case of herbivores, of the type of vegetation they prefer. Most information about range and habitat comes from studies of modern species, however, on the assumption that behavior has not changed substantially since the period in question. These studies also show that large animals will tolerate – that is, have the potential to withstand or exploit – a much wider range of temperatures and environments than was once thought. So the presence of such species as woolly rhinoceros in an Ice Age deposit should be regarded merely as proof of the ability of that species to tolerate low temperatures, rather than as evidence of a cold climate.

Large mammals are also not generally good indicators of vegetation, since herbivores can thrive in a wide range of environments and eat a variety of plants. Thus, individual species cannot usually be regarded as characteristic of one particular habitat, but there are exceptions. For example, reindeer reached northern Spain in the last Ice Age, as is shown not only by discoveries of their bones but also by cave art. Such major shifts clearly reflect environmental change. In the rock art of the Sahara, too, one can see clear evidence for the presence of species, such as giraffe and elephant, that could not survive in the area today, and thus for dramatic environmental modification.

As will be seen below, fauna can also be used to determine in which seasons of the year a site was occupied. In coastal sites, marine resources and herbivore remains may come and go through the archaeological sequence as changes in sea level extended or drowned the coastal plain, thus changing the sites' proximity to the shore and the availability of grazing.

We always have to bear in mind that faunal fluctuations can have causes other than climate or people; additional factors may include competition, epidemics, or fluctuations in numbers of predators. Moreover, small-scale local variations in climate and weather can have enormous effects on the numbers and distribution of wild animals, so that despite its high powers of resistance a species may decline from extreme abundance to virtual extinction within a few years.

Subsistence and Diet

Having discussed methods for reconstructing the environment, we now turn to how we find out about what people extracted from it, in other words, how they subsisted. When reconstructing early subsistence, it is useful to make a distinction between meals, direct evidence of various kinds as to what people were eating at a particular time, and diet, which implies the pattern of consumption over a long period of time.

So far as meals are concerned, the sources of information are varied. Written records, when they survive, indicate some of the things people were eating, and so do representations in art. Even modern **ethnoarchaeology** helps indicate what they *might* have been eating by broadening our understanding of the range of options. And the actual remains of the foodstuffs eaten can be highly informative.

For the much more difficult question of diet, there are several helpful techniques of investigation. Some methods focus on human bones. Isotopic analyses of the skeletal remains of a human population can indicate, for example, the balance of marine and terrestrial foods in the diet, and even show differences in nutrition between the more and less advantaged members of the same society.

Most of our information about early subsistence, however, comes directly from the remains of what was eaten. Zooarchaeology (or **archaeozoology**), the study of past human use of animals, is now big business in archaeology. There can be few excavations anywhere that do not have a specialist to study the animal bones found. The Paleo-Indian rockshelter of Meadowcroft, Pennsylvania, for example, yielded about a million animal bones (and almost 1.5 million plant specimens). On medieval and recent sites, the quantities of material recovered can be even more formidable. **Paleo-ethnobotany** (or archaeobotany), the study of past human use of plants, is likewise a growing

These millet noodles, the earliest known (dating from around 4000 years ago) were found preserved in an overturned bowl at the Lajia site in northwestern China. Discovered in 2005, the remains indicate that routine millet-milling, including the repeated stretching of dough by hand to form a strand and its cooking in boiling water, was practiced in Late Neolithic China.

discipline. In both areas, a detailed understanding of the conditions of preservation on a site is a first prerequisite to ensure that the most efficient extraction technique is adopted. In both areas, too, the focus of interest has developed to include not just the species eaten, but also the way these were managed. The process of domestication for both plants and animals is now a major research topic.

Interpretation of food remains can be problematic, and requires quite sophisticated procedures. We can initially reconstruct the range of food available in the surrounding environment (see above), but the only incontrovertible proof that a particular plant or animal species was actually consumed is the presence of its traces in stomach contents or in desiccated ancient fecal matter. If such evidence is not available, the archaeologist must try to determine whether a foodstuff was actually eaten from the context or condition of the finds. For instance, if bones are cut or burned they may have been butchered and cooked.

Plants that were staples in the diet may be under-represented thanks to the generally poor preservation of vegetable remains; fish bones likewise may not survive well. The archaeologist therefore has to consider how far a site's food remains are representative of total diet. Here we need to assess a site's function, and whether it was inhabited once or frequently, for short or long periods, irregularly or seasonally (season of occupation can sometimes be deduced from plant and animal evidence as well). A long-term settlement is likely to provide more representative food remains than a specialized camp or kill site. Ideally, however, archaeologists should sample remains from a variety of contexts or sites before making judgments about diet.

We will now look at some of the main forms of evidence for human subsistence, as well as some of the different types of interpretations that can be made.

6 **What Was the Environment and What Did They Eat?**

What Can Plant Foods Tell Us About Diet?

We can learn something of diet from the study of microbotanical remains, particularly through the study of phytoliths, which can, for example, help in differentiating between wild and domestic species of plant. But the vast majority of plant evidence that reaches the archaeologist is in the form of macrobotanical remains, and these are much more useful when trying to reconstruct diet.

Macrobotanical Remains

Macrobotanical remains may be desiccated (only in absolutely dry environments, such as deserts or high mountains), waterlogged (only in environments that have been permanently wet since the date of deposition), or preserved by charring. In exceptional circumstances, volcanic eruption can preserve botanical remains, such as at Cerén in El Salvador, where a wide variety have been found carbonized, or as impressions, in numerous vessels. Plant remains preserved in several different ways can sometimes be encountered within the same site, but in most parts of the world charring is the principal or only cause of preservation on habitation sites.

Occasionally, a single sample on a site will yield very large amounts of material. More than 27 kg (60 lb) of charred barley, wheat, and other plants came from one storage pit on a Bronze Age farm at Black Patch, southern England, for example. This can sometimes give clues to the relative importance of different cereals and legumes and weed flora, but the sample nevertheless simply reflects a moment in time. What the archaeologist really needs is a larger number of samples (each of preferably more than 100 grains) from a single period on the site, and, if possible, from a range of types of deposit, in order to obtain reliable information about what species were exploited, their importance, and their uses during the period of time in question.

Key Concepts
What Can Plant Foods Tell Us About Diet?

- *Macrobotanical Remains*: these can give us a good idea of what plants were present at a site, but there are problems of quantification and interpretation. It's important to understand how a plant might have been processed and used

- *Plant Residues on Artifacts*: chemical traces of plants can be found on some artifacts (often pots and tools) and these can be tested and compared against a reference collection in order to identify a species

- *Domestication of Wild Plant Species*: various techniques can help to answer the crucial question of whether plant remains found in the archaeological record are from wild or domesticated species

When we have obtained enough samples we need to quantify the plant remains: for example by weight or by number of remains. Some archaeologists simply arrange samples in order of abundance. But this can be misleading, as was shown by the British archaeobotanist Jane Renfrew in her study of the material from the **Neolithic** settlement of Sitagroi, Greece. She noted that the most abundant plants may have been preserved by chance (such as an accident in the course of baking). Similarly, species that produce large quantities of seeds or grains may appear more important in the archaeological record than they actually were: at Sitagroi 19,000 seeds of knotgrass barely filled a thimble.

Interpreting the Context and the Remains. It is crucial for the archaeologist or specialist to try to understand the archaeological context of a plant sample, as this can reveal more about exactly how the plant was being used. In the past, attention used to be focused primarily on the botanical history of the plants themselves, their morphology, place of origin, and **evolution**. Now, however, archaeologists also want to know more about the human use of plants in hunting-and-gathering economies, and in agriculture – which plants were important in the diet, and how they were gathered or grown, processed, stored, and cooked. This means understanding the different stages of traditional plant processing; recognizing the effect different processes have on the remains; and identifying the different contexts in the archaeological record. In many cases it is the plant remains that reveal the function of the location where they are found, and thus the nature of the context, rather than vice versa.

In a farming economy, for instance, there are many different stages of plant processing, summed up in the illustration opposite: cereals have to be threshed, winnowed, and cleaned before consumption, in order to separate the grain from the chaff, straw, and weeds; but seed corn also has to be stored for the next year's crop; and food grain might also be stored unthreshed in order to get the harvested crop out of the rain, and would then be threshed only when needed. From ethnoarchaeological and experimental observations it is known that certain of these activities leave characteristic residues with which archaeological samples can be compared, whether they are from ovens, living floors, latrines, or storage pits.

Chemical Residues in Plant Remains. Various chemicals survive in plant remains themselves, which provide an alternative basis for their identification. These compounds include proteins, fatty lipids, and even **DNA**. The analysis of lipids has so far proved the most useful method for distinguishing different cereal and legume species, but always in combination with other non-chemical identification techniques. DNA offers the prospect of eventually resolving identification at an even more detailed level and of perhaps tracing family trees of the plants and patterns of trade in plant products.

1 THRESHING
straw flooring, etc.

2 RAKING to remove straw

3 WINNOWING

4 COURSE SCREENING

WELLS AND PITS

5 ROASTING (& MALTING)
accidental charring

6 POUNDING

WINNOWING

8 SCREENING

9 FINE SCREENING

HEARTHS

10 OVEN DRYING

11 STORAGE
infested grain burnt, granary fire

12 HAND SORTING

13 GRINDING

LATRINES

waterlogged sewage

Cereal crop processing: waste products from many of these stages may survive as charred or waterlogged remains.

Plant Impressions. Impressions of plant remains are quite common in fired clay, and do at least prove that the species in question was present at the spot where the clay was worked. Such impressions, however, do not necessarily prove that the plant was important in the economy or diet, since they constitute a very skewed sample and only seeds or grains of medium size tend to leave imprints. One has to be particularly careful with impressions on potsherds, because pottery can be discarded far from its point of manufacture, and in any case many pots were deliberately decorated with grain impressions, thus perhaps overemphasizing the importance of a species.

Analysis of Plant Residues on Artifacts

As we shall see in Chapter 7, **microwear analysis** of a tool edge can identify broadly whether the tool was used to cut meat, wood, or some other material. Discovery of phytoliths can show what type of grasses were cut by a tool. Microscopic study can also reveal and identify plant fibers. Another method is chemical analysis of residues on tool edges: certain chemical reagents can provide a means of proving whether plant residues are present on tools or in vessels – thus, potassium iodide turns blue if starch grains are present, and yellow-brown for other plant materials.

Starch grains can also be detected by microscope and, for example, have been extracted with a needle from crevices in the surfaces of prehistoric grinding stones from Aguadulce Shelter in the humid tropics of Panama. The species of the grains can be identified, and show that such tubers as manioc and arrowroot – which do not usually leave recoverable fossilized remains – were being cultivated here c. 5000 BC, the earliest recorded occurrence of manioc in the Americas.

The site also yielded maize starch, and this technique is thus important for proving the presence of maize in structures or sites without charred remains: for example, at the Early Formative village of Real Alto (Ecuador), maize starch grains and phytoliths from maize cobs have been retrieved from stone tools and sediments dating to 2800–2400 BC. Starch grains have even been recovered from a large flat piece of basalt in a hut at Ohalo II, Israel, dating to about 23,000 years ago. This was clearly a grindstone, and the grains from barley, and perhaps wheat, show that wild cereals were already being processed at this early date. Recently, in Mozambique, starch grains retrieved from the surfaces of Middle Stone Age stone tools showed that early *Homo sapiens* was consuming grass seeds at least 105,000 years ago.

Chemical investigation of fats preserved in vessels is also making progress, because it has been found that fatty acids, amino acids (the constituents of protein), and similar substances are very stable and preserve well. Samples are extracted from residues, purified, concentrated in a centrifuge, dried, and then analyzed by means of a spectrometer, and by a technique known as chromatography, which separates the major constituent components of the fats. Interpretation of the results is made by comparison with a reference collection of "chromatograms" (read-outs) from different substances.

For example, the German chemist Rolf Rottländer has identified mustard, olive oil, seed oils, butter, and other substances on potsherds, including specimens from Neolithic lake dwellings. In work on sherds from the German Iron Age hillfort of the Heuneburg, he was able to prove that some amphorae – storage vessels usually associated with liquids – did indeed contain olive oil and wine, whereas in the case of a Roman amphora the charcoal-like black residue proved to be not liquid but wheat flour. This important technique not only provides dietary evidence, but also helps to define the function of the vessels with which the fats are associated. Ever more refined techniques are currently being developed for identifying food species from protein, lipid, and DNA biochemical analysis of small fragments of plant material. Indeed, DNA extracted from two 2400-year-old amphorae from a shipwreck off the Greek island of Chios has revealed that they probably contained olive oil flavoured with herbs.

The Domestication of Wild Plant Species

One of the major areas of debate in modern archaeology concerns the question of human management of plants, and particularly whether some species that we

Wild and domestic cereals. Left to right: wild and domestic einkorn, domestic maize, extinct wild maize. The wild einkorn sheds its grain easily. But the tougher domestic form does so only when threshed: a real advantage for the early farmer, since if grains fall off before threshing, they are lost.

find were wild or domesticated, since this sheds light on one of the most crucial aspects of human history: the transition from a mobile (**hunter-gatherer**) to a settled (agricultural) way of life. It can often be difficult, impossible, or irrelevant to try to distinguish between wild and domesticated varieties, since many types of cultivation do not change the form of the plant, and even in cases where such change occurs we do not know how long it took to appear. Experimental evidence suggests that the transition from wild to domestic could have been complete within only 20 to 200 years – without conscious intervention on the farmers' part – but in practice it seems to have taken about a millennium. Any line drawn between wild and domestic plants does not necessarily correspond to a distinction between gathering and agriculture.

There are nevertheless cases where a clear distinction can be made between wild and fully domestic forms. Macrobotanical remains are of most use here. For example, the American archaeologist Bruce Smith found that 50,000 charred seeds of *Chenopodium* (goosefoot), nearly 2000 years old from Russell Cave, Alabama, exhibited a set of interrelated characteristics reflecting domestication. He was thus able to add this starchy-seed species to the brief list of cultivated plants – including bottle gourd, squash, marsh elder, sunflower, and tobacco – available in the garden plots of the Eastern Woodlands before the introduction of maize by about AD 200.

There has been some debate in recent years about whether wild and domestic legumes can be differentiated by their structure, but archaeobotanical work by the British scholar Ann Butler suggests that there is no foolproof way to do this, even in a scanning electron microscope. Cereals, on the other hand, where well preserved, are more straightforward, and domestication can be identified by clues, for example the loss of anatomical features, such as the brittle rachis, which facilitate the dispersal of seed by natural agents. In other words, once people began to cultivate cereals, they gradually developed varieties that retained their seeds until they could be harvested.

Plant Evidence from Literate Societies

Archaeologists studying the beginnings of plant cultivation, or plant use among hunter-gatherers, have to rely on the kind of scientific evidence outlined above, coupled with the judicious use of ethnoarchaeological research and modern experiments. For the student of diet among literate societies, however, particularly the great civilizations, there is a wealth of evidence for domestication of plants, as well as for farming practices, cookery, and many other aspects of diet to be found written in documents and in art.

The Greek writer Herodotus, for example, gives us plenty of information about eating habits in the 5th century BC, notably in Egypt, a civilization for which there is extensive evidence about food and diet. Much of the evidence for the pharaonic period comes from paintings and foodstuffs in tombs, so it

Harvesting and processing a cereal crop: scenes depicted on the walls of a New Kingdom tomb at Thebes in Egypt.

has a certain upper-class bias, but there is also information to be found about the diet of humbler folk, from plant remains in workers' villages, such as that at Tell el-Amarna, and from hieroglyphic texts. In the later Ptolemaic period there are records of corn allowances for workers, such as the 3rd-century BC accounts concerning grain allotted to workers on a Faiyum agricultural estate. Models are also instructive about food preparation: the tomb of Meketre, a nobleman of the 12th dynasty (2000–1790 BC), contained a set of wooden models, including women kneading flour into loaves, and others brewing beer. Three newly deciphered Babylonian clay tablets from Iraq, 3750 years old, present cuneiform texts containing 35 recipes for a wide variety of rich meat stews, and thus constitute the world's oldest cookbook.

In the New World, we owe much of our knowledge of Aztec food crops, fishing practices, and natural history to the invaluable writings of the 16th-century Franciscan scholar Bernardino de Sahagún, based on his own observations and on the testimony of his Native American informants.

It should be remembered, however, that written evidence and art tend to give a very short-term view of subsistence. Only archaeology can look at human diet with a long-term perspective.

Investigating Diet, Seasonality, and Domestication From Animal Remains

Although plant foods may always have constituted the greater part of the diet – except in special circumstances or high latitudes such as the Arctic – meat may well have been considered more important, either as food or as a reflection of the prowess of the hunter or the status of the herder. Animal remains are usually better preserved on archaeological sites too so that, unlike plant remains, they have been studied since the very beginnings of archaeology.

The first question the archaeologist must face when interpreting animal remains is to decide whether they are present through human actions rather than through natural causes or other predators (as in the case of carnivore debris, owl pellets, burrowing animals, etc.). Animals may also have been exploited at a site for non-dietary purposes (skins for clothing, bone and antler for tools).

As with plant remains, therefore, one must be particularly careful to examine the context and content of faunal samples. This is usually straightforward in sites of recent periods, but in the **Paleolithic**, especially the Lower Paleolithic, the question is crucial.

Proving Human Exploitation of Animals in the Paleolithic.   In the past, association of animal bones and stone tools was often taken as proof that humans were responsible for the presence of the faunal remains, or at least exploited them. We now know, however, that this is not always a fair assumption, and since in any case many used bones are not associated with tools, archaeologists have sought more definite proof from the marks of stone tools on the bones themselves. A great deal of work is currently aimed at proving the existence of such marks, and finding ways of differentiating them from other traces, such as scratches and punctures made by animal teeth, etching by plant

Key Concepts
Information From Animal Resources

- Animal remains are often well-preserved on archaeological sites

- It's important to establish whether animal remains are present on a site through human agency or through other causes

- We can sex and age animal bones, study their seasonality, and deduce whether the animals were wild or domesticated, all of which helps us to understand how humans were exploiting the animal environment

roots, abrasion by sedimentary particles or post-depositional weathering, and damage by excavation tools. This is also part of the search for reliable evidence in the current major debate in Paleolithic studies as to whether early humans were genuine hunters, or merely scavenged meat from carcasses of animals killed by other predators.

Much attention has been directed to bones from the famous Lower Paleolithic sites of Olduvai Gorge and Koobi Fora, in East Africa, that are more than 1.5 million years old. Archaeologists used a scanning electron microscope to examine suspected toolmarks on the bones, comparing their results with marks produced by known processes on modern bones. The diagnostic feature of a toolmark produced by a slicing action, for example, was a V-shaped groove with a series of longitudinal parallel lines at the bottom; marks made by carnivores were much more rounded (see illustration opposite). They found that many bones had both toolmarks and carnivore scratches, suggesting some competition for the carcass. In some cases, the carnivore marks were clearly superimposed on the toolmarks, but in most cases the carnivores seem to have got there first!

Recent work, however, suggests that very similar marks can be produced by other causes, such as when bones are damaged by trampling. Thus microscopic features alone are not sufficient evidence to prove human intervention. The context of the find and the position of the marks need to be studied too.

More work still needs to be done before we can be sure of proving early human activity in this way, and also of identifying episodes where our early ancestors were hunters rather than scavengers. There are other types of evidence, however, that can provide proof of human processing of bones. These include artificial concentrations of bones in particular places, such as the use of mammoth bones for the construction of huts in the Paleolithic of Central and Eastern Europe. Burning of bones is another clear indication of human processing.

Having demonstrated so far as possible that animal remains were indeed produced by human action, the archaeologist then can move on to try to answer the interesting questions, such as what did people eat, in which seasons did they eat particular foods, how did they hunt and butcher the animals, and were the animals domesticated?

The most abundant and informative residues of animals are the macroremains – bones, teeth, antlers, shells, etc. Numerous techniques are now available to help extract information from data of this type. In analyzing an assemblage of bones, we have first to identify them and then quantify them, both in terms of numbers of animals and of meat weight. The amount of meat represented by a bone will depend on the sex and age of the animal, the season of death, and geographical variation in body size and in nutrition. But if factors of age, sex, and season of death need to be allowed for, how are they established?

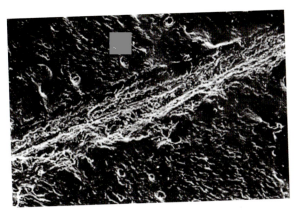

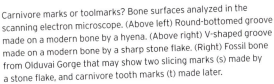

Carnivore marks or toolmarks? Bone surfaces analyzed in the scanning electron microscope. (Above left) Round-bottomed groove made on a modern bone by a hyena. (Above right) V-shaped groove made on a modern bone by a sharp stone flake. (Right) Fossil bone from Olduvai Gorge that may show two slicing marks (s) made by a stone flake, and carnivore tooth marks (t) made later.

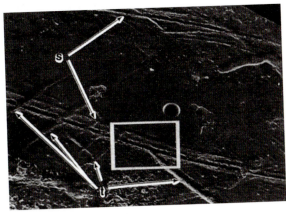

Bones of contention: marks on two animal bones from Dikika, Ethiopia, are thought by some specialists to have been made by australopithecines with stone tools – at 3.4 million years ago, this is almost a million years older than the earliest recognized stone tools (see pp. 212–15) and also pushes back the date for butchery and meat eating. The marks were examined by microscopy and chemical analysis, and were clearly made before the bones fossilized; their morphology fits tools far better than teeth.

Strategies of Use:
Deducing Age, Sex, and Seasonality From Large Fauna

Sexing is easy in cases where only the male has antlers (most deer), or large canines (pig), or where a penis bone is present (e.g. dog), or where the female has a different pelvic structure. Measurements of certain bones, such as the foot bones of some animals, can sometimes provide two distinct clusters of results, interpreted as male (large) and female (small).

The Question of Animal Domestication

An entirely different set of methods is required to assess the status of the animals – i.e. whether they were wild or domesticated. Like the study of plant domestication described on pp. 196–97, this is a crucial question about one of the most important developments in human history: the transition from a mobile to a settled, agricultural way of life. In some cases the answer can be obvious, such as where non-indigenous animals have been introduced on to islands by humans – for example, the appearance of cattle, sheep, goat, dog, and cat on Cyprus.

One criterion of animal domestication is human interference with the natural breeding habits of certain species, which has led to changes in the physical characteristics of those species from the wild state. But there are other definitions, and specialists disagree about which physical changes in animals are diagnostic of domestication. Too much emphasis on the wild/domestic dichotomy may also mask a whole spectrum of human-animal relationships, such as herd management without selective breeding. Nevertheless, domestication, by any definition, clearly occurred separately in many parts of the world, and archaeologists therefore need to differentiate fully wild from fully domestic animals, and to investigate the process of domestication.

Amongst a number of other possible lines of evidence, certain tools may indicate the presence of domesticated animals – for example, plows, yokes, and horse trappings. Deformities and disease can also provide convincing evidence for domestication. When used for traction, horses, cattle, and camels all sometimes suffer osteoarthritis or strain-deformities on their lower limbs. Work is also progressing on tracing the history of domestication through DNA.

Remains of Individual Meals

One of the most direct kinds of evidence of what people ate comes from occasional finds of actual meals. At Pompeii, for example, meals of fish, eggs, bread, and nuts were found intact on tables, as well as food in shops. Food is often preserved in funerary contexts, as in the desiccated corncobs and other items in Peruvian graves, or at Saqqara, Egypt, where the 2nd-dynasty tomb of a noblewoman contained a huge variety of foodstuffs, constituting a rich and elaborate meal – cereals, fish, fowl, beef, fruit, cakes, honey, cheese, and wine – which, to judge by the tomb paintings, was not unusual. The Han period in China (206 BC–AD 220) has tombs stocked with food: that of the wife of the Marquis of Dai has a unique collection of provisions, herbal medicines, and prepared dishes in containers of lacquer, ceramic, and bamboo, with labels attached, and even inventory slips giving the composition of the dishes! It is unlikely, however, that such magnificent remains are representative of everyday diet. Even the meals found so wonderfully preserved at Pompeii are merely a tiny sample from a single day.

A meal as a funerary offering: elaborate food remains, more than 3000 years old, found in Egyptian New Kingdom tombs at Thebes, including (front left) unleavened bread on a woven palm leaf dish; (front center) a bowl of figs; (front right) a bowl containing sun-dried fish. The wicker stand holds cooked duck and loaves of bread.

The only way in which we can really study what people ate habitually is to examine actual human remains.

Assessing Diet From Human Remains

The only incontrovertible evidence that something was actually consumed by humans is its presence in either stomachs or feces. Both kinds of evidence give us invaluable information about individual meals and short-term diet. The study of human teeth also helps us to reconstruct diet, but the real breakthrough in recent years in understanding long-term diet has come from the analysis of bone collagen. What human bones can reveal about general health will be examined in Chapter 8.

Individual Meals

Stomach Contents.   Stomachs survive only rarely in archaeological contexts, except in bog bodies. Some mummies also provide dietary evidence: the overweight wife of the Marquis of Dai from 2nd-century BC China, mentioned above, seems to have died of a heart attack caused by acute pain from her gallstones an hour or so after enjoying a generous helping of watermelon (138 melon seeds were discovered in her stomach and intestines).

When stomachs survive in bog bodies, the dietary evidence they provide can be of the greatest interest. Pioneering studies of the stomach contents of Danish Iron Age bogmen showed that Grauballe Man, for instance, had consumed more than 60 species of wild seeds, together with one or two cereals and a little meat (as shown by some small bone splinters), while Tollund Man had eaten only plants. But we should keep in mind that these results, while fascinating, do not necessarily indicate everyday diet, since these victims were possibly executed or sacrificed, and thus their last meal may have been out of the ordinary.

Fecal Material.   Experiments have been done to assess the survival properties of different foodstuffs relevant to the study of ancient diet, and it has been found that many organic remains can survive surprisingly well after their journey through the human digestive tract. Feces themselves survive only rarely, in very dry sites, such as caves in the western United States and Mexico, or very wet sites (these feces are often wrongly called "**coprolites**," which means fossilized/petrified excrement). But, where they are preserved, they have proved to be a highly important source of information about what individuals ate in the past.

Macroremains can be extremely varied in human excrement, in fact this variety is an indication of human origin. Bone fragments, plant fibers, bits of charcoal, seeds, and the remains of fish, birds, and even insects are known. Shell fragments – from molluscs, eggs, and nuts – can also be identified. Hair can be assigned to certain classes of animals by means of its scale pattern, visible under the microscope, and it can thus help us to know which animals were eaten.

Exceptional conditions in Lovelock Cave, Nevada, have preserved 5000 feces dating from 2500 to 150 years ago, and Robert Heizer's study of their contents yielded remarkable evidence about diet, which seems to have comprised seeds, fish, and birds. Feather fragments were identified from waterfowl, such as the heron and grebe; fish and reptile scales, which pass through the alimentary canal unaltered, also led to identification of several species. Fish remains were abundant in some of the feces; one, for example, from 1000 years ago, contained 5.8 g (0.2 oz) of fish bone, which, it was calculated, came from 101 small chubs, representing a total live weight of 208 g (7.3 oz) – the fish component of a meal for a single person.

Excrement and fecal residues represent single meals, and therefore provide short-term data on diet, unless they are found in great quantities, as at Lovelock Cave, and even there the feces represent only a couple of meals a year. For human diet over whole lifetimes, we need to turn to the human skeleton itself.

Human Teeth as Evidence for Diet

Teeth survive in extremely good condition, made as they are of the two hardest tissues in the body, and microscopic examination of the abrasions on certain dental surfaces can provide evidence for the sort of food that their owners enjoyed. Abrasive particles in food leave striations on the enamel, the orientation and length of which are directly related to the meat or vegetation in the diet and its process of cooking. Modern meat-eating Greenland Inuit,

Key Concepts
Assessing Diet From Human Remains

- *Individual Meals*: we can find direct evidence of what humans in the past ate from the examination of preserved stomach contents and fecal material

- *Teeth*: evidence of wear on human teeth, which survive well in many archaeological sediments, can tell us about the relative importance of meat and plants in past diets

- *Isotopic Evidence*: can be used as evidence for long-term human diet, but needs to be combined with other evidence for a finer picture

for instance, have almost exclusively vertical striations on their lateral tooth surfaces, while largely vegetarian Melanesians have both vertical and horizontal striations, with a shorter average length.

When these results are compared with data from fossil teeth hundreds of thousands of years old, it has been found that there is an increase in horizontal and a decrease in vertical striations, and a decrease in average striation length over time. In other words, less and less effort was needed to chew food, and meat may have decreased in importance as the diet became more mixed: early people crushed and broke down their food with their teeth, but less chewing was required as cooking techniques developed and improved.

Tooth decay as well as wear will sometimes provide us with dietary information. Remains of the California Native Americans display very marked tooth decay, attributed to their habit of leaching the tannin out of acorns, their staple food, through a bed of sand, which caused excessive tooth abrasion. Decay and loss of teeth can also set in thanks to starchy and sugary foods. Dental caries became abundant on the coast of Georgia (USA) in the 12th century AD, particularly among the female population. It was in this period that the transition occurred from hunting, fishing, and gathering to maize agriculture. Anthropologist Clark Larsen believes that the rise in tooth decay over this period, revealed by a study of hundreds of skeletons, was caused by the carbohydrates in maize. Since the women of the group were more subject to the caries than were the men, it is probable that they were growing, harvesting, preparing, and cooking the corn, while the men ate more protein and less carbohydrate.

Isotopic Methods: Diet Over a Lifetime

A revolution has been taking place in dietary studies through the realization that **isotopic analysis** of human tooth enamel and bone collagen can reveal a great deal about long-term food intake. The method relies on reading the chemical signatures left in the body by different foods – we are what we eat.

Plants can be divided into three – temperate and tropical land plants and marine plants – groups based on their differing ratios of two carbon isotopes. As animals eat plants, these different chemical signatures are passed along the food chain and are eventually fixed in human and animal bone tissue. They can show whether diet was based on land or marine plants. Only archaeological evidence, however, can provide more detail about precisely which species of plants or animals contributed to the diet. Recently, for example, isotopic analysis of tooth enamel from four *Australopithecus africanus* individuals from Makapansgat, South Africa, revealed that they ate not only fruits and leaves, as had been thought, but also large quantities of grasses or sedges, or the animals that ate those plants, or both. In other words, they regularly exploited fairly open environments (woodlands or grasslands) for food; and since their tooth wear lacks the characteristic scratches of grass-eaters, it is possible that they were indeed already consuming meat, by hunting small animals or scavenging larger ones.

Study Questions

- What techniques do scientists use to study the environment on a global scale?
- How are plant remains used to reconstruct past environments?
- Why is the question of plant and animal domestication important to archaeologists?
- What is the difference between meals and diet?
- What are some of the complications in determining if humans have processed animal bones?
- How can human teeth aid in the study of diet?

6 What Was the Environment and What Did They Eat?

Summary

- Humankind has developed from being an inconsequential species at the mercy of the environment and the food resources it provided to one with a huge influence over its surroundings. The environment is of crucial importance to archaeology. During every period of the past it has played a vital role in determining where and how people could live, and on what. Archaeologists now have a battery of techniques, largely based on the analysis of plant and animal remains, to help reconstruct such past environments.

- Where food is concerned, the evidence available varies from botanical and animal remains, large and microscopic, to tools and vessels, plant and animal residues, and art and texts. We can discover what was eaten, in which seasons, and sometimes how it was prepared. We need to assess whether the evidence arrived in the archaeological record naturally or through human actions, and whether the resources were wild or under human control. Occasionally we encounter the remains of individual meals left as funerary offerings or the contents of stomachs or feces. Finally, the human body itself contains a record of diet in its tooth wear and in the chemical signatures left in bones by different foods.

- Many of the techniques must be carried out by the specialist, particularly the biochemist, but archaeologists should know how to interpret the results, because the rewards are enormous for our knowledge of what the environment was like, what people ate, how they exploited their resources, and in what proportions.

Further Reading

General introductions to environmental archaeology and the subject of diet can be found in the following:

Barker, G. 2006. *The Agricultural Revolution in Prehistory*. Oxford University Press: Oxford.

Bellwood, P. 2004. *First Farmers: The Origins of Agricultural Societies*. Blackwell: Oxford.

Brothwell, D. & P. 1997. *Food in Antiquity: A Survey of the Diet of Early Peoples*. Johns Hopkins Univ. Press: Baltimore, MD.

Dincauze, D.F. 2000. *Environmental Archaeology*. Cambridge University Press: Cambridge.

Gilbert, R.I. & Mielke, J.H. (eds). 1985. *The Analysis of Prehistoric Diets*. Academic Press: New York & London.

O'Connor, T. 2000. *The Archaeology of Animal Bones*. Sutton: Stroud.

O'Connor, T. & Evans, J.G. 2005. *Environmental Archaeology. Principles and Methods* (2nd ed.). Tempus: Stroud.

Pearsall, D.M. 2009. *Paleoethnobotany: A Handbook of Procedures* (2nd ed.). Left Coast Press: Walnut Creek.

Reitz, E.J. & Wing, E.S. 2008. *Zooarchaeology* (2nd ed.). Cambridge University Press: Cambridge.

Smith, B.D. 1998. *The Emergence of Agriculture* (2nd ed.). Scientific American Library: New York.

[See p. 345 for a list of useful websites]

How Were Artifacts Made, Used, and Distributed?
Technology, trade, and exchange

7

It is the physical remains of humanly made **artifacts** that form the bulk of the archaeological record. We have seen how archaeologists can find and date artifacts, but in this chapter we will start by addressing two questions of fundamental importance: how were artifacts made, and what were they used for? There are several approaches to these two questions – the purely archaeological, the scientific analysis of objects, the ethnographic, and the experimental.

When assessing ancient technologies, the archaeologist always needs to bear in mind that the sample preserved may well be biased. During the long **Paleolithic** period, for instance, wood and bone artifacts must surely have rivaled those of stone in importance – as they do in hunting-and-gathering societies today – but stone tools dominate the archaeological record.

Once made, artifacts usually move around as they are acquired or passed on between individuals or groups – a phenomenon that can tell us a great deal about the frequency and extent of contacts between different groups, as well as about transportation, economics, and so forth. By analyzing where the materials used to make an artifact came from, as well as the distribution of artifacts as found by archaeologists, we can reconstruct something of these trading relationships: who was exchanging goods with whom, and by what method?

When an archaeologist investigates an object, it must first be decided whether it was actually made or used by people in the past. For most periods the answer will be obvious (although we have to beware of fakes and forgeries), but for the Paleolithic, and especially the Lower Paleolithic, judgment can be more difficult. Where the very earliest tools are concerned, on which we would expect the traces of human work to be minimal, the question is not easy to resolve, since the crudest human working may be indistinguishable from damage caused by nature.

We will make a convenient distinction in the next section on ancient technology between two classes of raw material used in creating objects – between those that are largely unaltered, such as flint, and those that are synthetic, the product of human activities, such as pottery or metal. Of course, even supposedly unaltered materials have often been treated by heat or by chemical reactions in order to assist the manufacturing process. But synthetic materials have undergone an actual change in state, usually through heat treatment. The human use of fire – **pyrotechnology** – is a crucial factor here.

Unaltered Materials

Stone

From the first recognizable tools, dating back about 2.6 million years, up to the adoption of pottery-making, dated to 16,000 BC in China, the archaeological record is dominated by stone. How were stone artifacts, from the smallest stone tools to the greatest stone monuments, extracted, manufactured, and used?

Much of the stone used for making early tools was probably picked up from streambeds or other parts of the landscape, but the sources most visible archaeologically are the mines and quarries. The best-known mines are the **Neolithic** and later flint mines in various parts of northern Europe, such as Grimes Graves in England, where multiple 15-m (50-ft) deep shafts were sunk into the chalk to reach the best quality flint layers; rough estimates suggest that the **site** could have produced 28 million flint axes. Quarries were a common source of larger stones for building or monuments. The job of the archaeologist is sometimes made easier by the discovery of unfinished or abandoned stones within or near to ancient quarry sites. One of the most impressive examples is the statue-quarry on Easter Island, where many statues lie in various stages of manufacture.

A combination of archaeological investigation and modern experimentation can give us valuable insights into how stones were worked. Here we will concentrate on stone tool manufacture, although much archaeological and experimental work is also done on larger stones and how they were moved, dressed, and fitted.

Stone quarry on Easter Island: a giant statue lies flat on its back, unfinished and still attached to the rock face, but at an advanced stage of manufacture – yielding clues as to how it was made.

Stone Tool Manufacture and Function.
Most stone tools are made by removing material from a pebble or "**core**" until the desired shape has been attained. The first flakes struck off (primary flakes) bear traces of the outer surface (cortex). Trimming flakes are then struck off to achieve the final shape, and certain edges may then be "retouched" by further removal of tiny secondary flakes. Although the core is the main implement thus produced, the flakes themselves may well be used as knives, scrapers, etc. The toolmaker's work will have varied in accordance with the type and amount of raw material available.

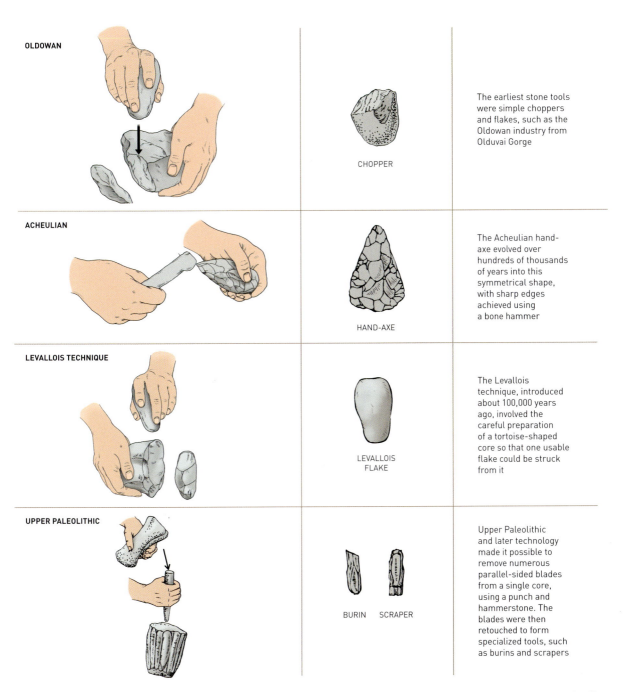

OLDOWAN

CHOPPER

The earliest stone tools were simple choppers and flakes, such as the Oldowan industry from Olduvai Gorge

ACHEULIAN

HAND-AXE

The Acheulian hand-axe evolved over hundreds of thousands of years into this symmetrical shape, with sharp edges achieved using a bone hammer

LEVALLOIS TECHNIQUE

LEVALLOIS FLAKE

The Levallois technique, introduced about 100,000 years ago, involved the careful preparation of a tortoise-shaped core so that one usable flake could be struck from it

UPPER PALEOLITHIC

BURIN   SCRAPER

Upper Paleolithic and later technology made it possible to remove numerous parallel-sided blades from a single core, using a punch and hammerstone. The blades were then retouched to form specialized tools, such as burins and scrapers

The evolution of stone tools, from the earliest, Oldowan technology to the refined methods of the Upper Paleolithic onwards.

The history of stone tool technology (illustrated above) shows a sporadically increasing degree of refinement. The first recognizable tools are simple choppers and flakes made by knocking pieces off pebbles to obtain sharp edges. The best-known examples are the so-called Oldowan tools from Olduvai Gorge, Tanzania, the earliest of which date back some 2.6 million years. After hundreds of thousands of years, people progressed to flaking both surfaces of the tool, eventually producing the symmetrical Acheulian **hand-axe** shape. The next improvement, dating to around 100,000 years ago, came with the introduction of the "Levallois technique" – named after a site in a Paris suburb where it was first identified – where the core was knapped in such a way that large flakes of predetermined size and shape could be removed.

Around 35,000 years ago, with the Upper Paleolithic period, blade technology became dominant in some parts of the world. Long, parallel-sided blades were systematically removed with a punch and hammerstone from a cylindrical core. This was a great advance, not only because it produced large numbers of blanks that could be further trimmed and retouched into a wide range of specialized tools (scrapers, burins, borers), but also because it was far less wasteful of the raw material, obtaining a much greater total length of working edges than ever before from a given amount of stone. This trend toward greater economy reached its peak around 10,000 years ago, with the rise to dominance of microliths, tiny stone tools many of which were probably used as barbs on composite implements.

To find out how a stone tool was made we must try to reconstruct the sequence of manufacturing steps, and there are two principal approaches to doing this: replication and **refitting**. Stone tool replication is a type of **experimental archaeology** that involves making exact copies of different types of stone tool – using only the technology available to the original makers – in order to assess the processes entailed, and the amount of time and effort required. Many years of patient practice are required to become proficient at tool replication.

One specific problem that expert knapper Donald Crabtree was able to solve through trial and error was how the Paleo-Indians of North America had made their fluted stone tools known as Folsom points, dating to some 11,000–10,000 years ago. In particular, how had they removed the "flute" or channel flake? This had remained a mystery and experiments with a variety of techniques met with disappointing results, until the decisive clue was found in a 17th-century text by a Spanish priest who had seen Aztecs make long knife-blades from **obsidian**. The method, as experiments proved, involves pressing the flake out, downward, by means of a T-shaped crutch placed against the chest; the crutch's tip is forced down against a precise point on the core, which is clamped firm.

Replication cannot usually prove conclusively which techniques were used in the past, but it does narrow the possibilities and often points to the most likely method, as in the Folsom example above. Refitting, on the other hand, involves working with the original tools and demonstrates clearly the precise chain of actions of the knapper. This entails attempting to put tools and flakes back together again, like a 3-D jigsaw puzzle. The work is tedious and time-consuming, but when successful can allow us to follow the stages of the knapper's craft.

How were Paleo-Indian Folsom points made? Experiments by Donald Crabtree showed that the flakes were pressed from the core using a T-shaped crutch (above). Flintknappers have produced almost perfect replica points (below).

Key Concepts
Artifacts Made From Unaltered Materials

- *Stone*: the archaeological record is dominated by stone artifacts. A combination of archaeological investigation, modern experimentation, and ethnographic observation can tell us a great deal about how stone artifacts were made and used

- *Wood*: wood does not survive well, apart from in very dry or waterlogged conditions, but was almost certainly as important a resource as stone

- *Plant and animal fibers*: containers, fabrics, and cords made from plant and animal fibers would also have been common objects in the past, but, again, they rarely survive in the archaeological record

- *Other materials*: bone, antler, shell, and leather are also often found by archaeologists, but, along with most other artifacts made from unaltered materials, we must be careful to establish whether an object is actually humanly made, or whether it has been created by natural processes

But how can we discover the function of a stone tool? Ethnographic observation of the use of similar tools in living societies often gives valuable clues, as do the minute traces of organic residues that can sometimes be found on tool surfaces; and experimentation can determine which uses are feasible or most probable. A single tool, however, can be used for many different purposes – an Acheulian hand-axe could be used for hacking wood from a tree, for butchering, smashing, scraping, and cutting – and conversely the same task can be done by many different tools. The only direct proof of function is to study the minute traces, or microwear patterns, that remain on the original tools. These minute polishes and marks, only properly visible using a scanning electron microscope, can be compared against evidence from modern experiments, and we can deduce the type of material a tool was used to work (such as wood, bone, hide, or meat) and the type of action used (such as piercing, cutting, or scraping).

Wood

Wood is one of the most important organic materials, and must have been used to make tools for as long as stone and bone. Indeed, many prehistoric stone tools were employed to obtain and work timber. If wood survives in good condition, it may preserve toolmarks to show how it was worked. A wide range of wooden tools can survive under special conditions. In the dry environment of ancient Egypt, for instance, numerous wooden implements for farming (rakes, hoes, grain-scoops, sickles), furniture, weapons and toys, such carpentry tools as mallets and chisels, and even whole ships have come

down to us. Egyptian paintings, such as those in the tomb of the nobleman Rekhmire at Thebes, sometimes depict carpenters using drills and saws. But it has been waterlogged wood (including the remains of ships and boats) that has yielded the richest information about woodworking skills.

Plant and Animal Fibers

The making of containers, fabrics, and cords from skins, bark, and woven fibers probably dates back to the very earliest archaeological periods, but these fragile materials rarely survive. As we saw in Chapter 2, however, they do survive in very dry or wet conditions. In arid regions, such as Egypt or parts of the New World, such perishables have come down to us in some quantity, and the study of basketry and cordage there reveals complex and sophisticated designs and techniques that display complete mastery of these organic materials. Waterlogged conditions can also yield a great deal of fragile evidence.

Where textiles are concerned, the most crucial question is how they were made, and of what. In the New World, information on pre-Columbian weaving methods is available from ethnographic observation, as well as from Colonial accounts and illustrations, from depictions on Moche pottery, and from actual finds of ancient looms and other objects found preserved in the Peruvian desert. The richest New World evidence, however, comes from Peruvian textiles themselves, which have survived well in the dry conditions. The Andean **cultures** mastered almost every method of textile weaving or decoration now known, and their products were often finer than those of today – indeed, were some of the best ever made.

In 1954 the dismantled parts of a cedarwood boat were found buried in a pit on the south side of the Great Pyramid of Cheops (Khufu) at Giza, Egypt. One important clue to the reconstruction proved to be the four classifying signs, marked on most of the timbers, that indicated to which of the four quarters of the ship the timbers belonged. After 14 years of work, the 1244 pieces of the ship were finally reassembled.

Other Unaltered Materials

Artifacts made from bone, antler, shell, and leather are also commonly found on archaeological sites. **Microwear analysis** combined with experimental archaeology are the most successful means of determining firstly whether the find really is humanly made (sharp bone points or pierced shells, for instance, can easily be created by natural processes), as well as reconstructing manufacturing techniques and deducing function.

Synthetic Materials

It is possible to consider the whole development of technology, as far as it relates to synthetic materials, in terms of the control of fire: pyrotechnology. Until very recent times, nearly all synthetic materials depended upon the control of heat; and the development of new technologies has often been largely dependent upon achieving higher and higher temperatures under controlled conditions.

Clearly the first step along this path was the mastery of fire, possible evidence for which already occurs in the Swartkrans Cave, South Africa, in layers dating to 1.5 million years ago. Cooked food and preserved meat then became a possibility, as did the use of heat in working flint, and in hardening wooden implements, such as the yew spear from the Middle Paleolithic site of Lehringen, Germany.

A significant development of the Early Neolithic period in the Near East, around 8000 BC, was the construction of special ovens used both to parch cereal grains (to facilitate the threshing process) and to bake bread. These ovens consisted of a single chamber in which the fuel was burnt. When the oven was hot the fuel was raked out and the grain or unbaked bread placed inside. This represents the first construction of a deliberate facility to control the conditions under which the temperature was raised. We may hypothesize that it was through these early experiences in pyrotechnology that the possibility of making pottery by firing clay was discovered. Initially pottery was made by firing in an open fire, but the introduction of the potter's kiln meant higher temperatures could be achieved, which also spurred on the development of metallurgy.

Pottery

Throughout the earlier periods of **prehistory**, containers made of light, organic materials were probably used. This does not mean, as has often been assumed, that Paleolithic people did not know how to make pottery: every fire lit on a cave floor will have hardened the clay around it, and terracotta figurines were sometimes produced. The lack of pottery vessels before the Neolithic period is mainly a consequence of the mobile way of life of Paleolithic **hunter-gatherers**, for whom heavy containers of fired clay would have been of limited usefulness.

Key Concepts
Artifacts Made From Synthetic Materials

- Many of the developments in pottery and metalworking technology can be linked to developments in pyrotechnology – the ability to control fire and attain and maintain ever higher temperatures

- *Pottery*: pottery is very hard-wearing and potsherds are a common find on archaeological sites. We can learn through simple observation how pottery was made (either by hand or on a wheel) and through experiment and ethnographic studies how it was fired

- *Metals*: we can identify what metal or combination of metals an artifact is made from with simple laboratory techniques. The examination of the microscopic structure of the metal can give clues as to how an artifact was manufactured

The introduction of pottery generally seems to coincide with the adoption of a more sedentary way of life, for which vessels and containers that are durable and strong are a necessity. The almost indestructible potsherd is as common in later periods as the stone tool is in earlier ones – and just as some sites yield thousands of stone tools, others contain literally tons of pottery fragments.

How Were Pots Made? The making or "throwing" of pots on a wheel or turntable was only introduced after 3400 BC at the earliest (in Mesopotamia), but in the New World only after European contact. The previous method, still used in some parts of the world, was to build the vessel up by hand in a series of coils or slabs of clay. A simple examination of the interior and exterior surfaces of a pot usually allows us to identify the method of manufacture. Wheelthrown pots generally have a telltale spiral of ridges and marks that is absent from handmade wares. These marks are left by the fingertips as the potter draws the vessel up on the turntable.

Evidence for pot-making using a wheel. An Egyptian potter shapes a vessel on the turntable type of wheel in this limestone portrait of c. 2400 BC.

The firing technique can be inferred from certain characteristics of the finished product. For example, if the surfaces are vitrified or glazed (i.e. have a glassy appearance), the pot was fired at more than 900°C (1652°F) and probably in an enclosed kiln. The extent of oxidization in a pot (the process by which organic substances in the clay are burnt off) is also indicative of firing methods. Complete oxidization produces a uniform color throughout the paste. If the core of a sherd is dark (gray or black), the firing temperature was too low to oxidize the clay fully, or the duration of the firing was insufficient, factors that often point to the use of an open kiln. Experimental firing of different pastes at different temperatures and in various types of kiln provides a guide to the colors and effects that can be expected.

Unlike the making of stone tools, the production of pottery by traditional methods is still widespread in the world, so a good deal can be learned from ethnoarchaeological studies not only about the technological aspects but also about the use and trade of pottery.

Metals

The study of ancient metal artifacts and manufacturing processes is known as archaeometallurgy. Many of the advances in metalworking techniques made in the past were dependent on the ability to achieve and control ever higher temperatures.

Non-Ferrous Metals. The most important non-ferrous metal – that is, one not containing iron – used in early times was copper. In due course people learned that a harder, tougher product could be made by **alloying** the copper with tin to produce bronze. Other elements, notably arsenic and antimony, were sometimes used in the alloying process; and in the later Bronze Age of Europe it was realized that a small amount of lead would improve the casting qualities. Gold and silver were also important, as was lead itself.

The techniques of manufacture of artifacts made from these materials can be investigated in several ways. The first point to establish is composition. Traditional laboratory methods readily allow the identification of major constituents. For instance, the alloys present in bronze may be identified in this way. In practice, however, it is now more usual to utilize the techniques of **trace-element analysis** (see p. 224). The other essential approach is that of **metallographic examination**, when the structure of the material is examined microscopically. This will determine whether an artifact has been formed by cold-hammering, **annealing**, casting, or a combination of these methods.

Iron. Iron was not used in the New World during pre-Columbian times, and makes its appearance in quantity in the Old World with the beginning in the Near East of the Iron Age around 1000 BC. Once the technique of smelting iron was well understood, it became very important, since iron is more widely found in nature than is copper. But it is much more difficult to reduce – i.e. to separate from oxygen, with which it is found combined in nature in the form of iron oxides – requiring temperatures of about 800°C (1472°F).

It is clearly important and interesting to identify what an artifact is made of, how it was made, and what it was used for. But once an artifact has been created, it takes on a life of its own – not only in terms of being used, broken, or discarded, but also in terms of being transported, bought, or exchanged. The study of these processes teaches us a great deal about past human societies and how they operated. In the next section we will discuss what can be learned from the study of trade and exchange, and examine some methods for investigating the movements of different kinds of materials.

Trade and Exchange

Societies and economies depend upon exchanges – of information and of actual goods – between individuals and between organizations. Every social transaction implies some interaction between people, and the study of the movement and flow of goods in the course of exchange transactions is often the most direct way for the archaeologist to monitor such interactions.

In many exchanges the relationship is more important than what is exchanged. In the Christian tradition, for instance, when presents are exchanged within a family at Christmas, the giving of presents between relatives is generally more important than the actual objects: "it's the thought that counts." There are also different kinds of exchange relationship: some where generosity is the order of the day (as in the family Christmas); others where the aim is profit, and the personal relationship is not emphasized. Moreover, there are different kinds of goods: everyday commodities that are bought and sold, and special goods, valuables (see box overleaf), that are suitable for gifts.

Fifty years ago, when "diffusionist" explanations were popular in archaeology, the presence of objects of foreign type or material at an archaeological site was often thought to indicate significant "influence" from other, perhaps more advanced, cultures. Today, however, we are more interested in finding out what those objects can tell us about social and economic interactions between distant groups. But the mere resemblance in the form of an artifact with those found elsewhere is not usually enough to be sure an exchange has occurred or that there is a definite link between two groups. We must show that the actual material the artifact is made from *must* have come from a distant source, and we can do this by **characterization**.

Discovering the Sources of Traded Goods: Characterization

The discovery of an artifact at a particular location does not mean that it originated in that place: it may, in fact, have been brought over hundreds or even thousands of miles. The study of where artifacts originated is not simple: artifact forms can be imitated, or can resemble each other by chance. So it is not always safe to recognize an import in an archaeological **context** just because it resembles objects that are known to have been made elsewhere. Much more reliable evidence for trade can be provided if the raw material from which the object is made can be reliably shown to have originated elsewhere. Characterization, or sourcing, refers to those techniques of examination by which characteristic properties of the constituent material may be identified, and so allow the source of that material to be determined. Some of the main methods for sourcing of materials by characterization are described below.

For characterization to work, there must obviously be something about the source of the material that distinguishes its products from those coming from other sources. Of course, sometimes a material is so unusual and distinctive in itself that it can at once be recognized as deriving from a given source. But in practice, there are very few materials for which the different sources can be distinguished by eye. Usually, it is necessary to use scientific techniques that allow a much more precise description of the material. During the past 40 years there have been striking advances in the ability to analyze very small samples with accuracy. A successful characterization, however, does not just depend on analytical precision: sources of some materials (e.g. flint, or some metals) are often very similar and so cannot be distinguished whatever the precision

- Characterization allows archaeologists to discover the source of the material from which an artifact was made

- Successful characterization depends on all the sources of a material being sufficiently different so as to be distinguishable through scientific analysis

- The main methods for sourcing materials by characterization are microscopic thin-section analysis, trace-element analysis, and isotopic analysis

of the testing. For other materials (e.g. obsidian), the sources are all quite different and can be distinguished relatively easily.

An important point to note is that the sourcing of materials by characterization studies depends crucially on our knowledge of the distribution of the raw materials in nature. This comes mainly from the fieldwork of such specialists as geologists. For example, we might have a good knowledge of the exact kinds of rock a whole range of stone axes were made from, but this would not help us unless we could match those particular kinds of rock with their specific occurrences in nature (i.e. the quarries). Thus, good geological mapping is a necessary basis for a sound sourcing study.

Microscopic Examination of Thin Section.   Since the middle of the 19th century techniques have existed for cutting a thin section of a sample taken from a stone object or a potsherd to determine the source of the material. It is made thin enough to transmit light, and then, by means of petrological examination (studying the rock or mineral structure) with a light microscope, it is usually possible to recognize specific minerals that may be characteristic of a specific source. This part of the work has to be done by someone with petrological training.

This method has been applied to stone objects in different parts of the world – to pinpoint the sources of building stones (e.g. the special colored stones used by the ancient Greeks and Romans), monuments (e.g. Olmec heads, Stonehenge), and portable artifacts, such as stone axes (e.g. in Australia and New Guinea). One of the success stories of characterization studies is the analysis of the patterns of trade in stone axes in Neolithic times in Britain, which started before 3000 BC.

With pottery, the clay itself may be distinctive, but more often it is the inclusions – particles of minerals or rock fragments – that are characteristic. Sometimes the inclusions are naturally present in the clay. In other cases, the inclusions are deliberately added as "**temper**" to improve drying and firing qualities, and this can complicate characterization studies, since the pottery

Materials of Prestige Value

Nearly all cultures have valuables. Although some of these are useful (e.g. pigs in Melanesia, which can be eaten) most of them have no use at all, other than display. They are simply prestige objects.

Valuables tend to be in a limited range of materials to which a particular society ascribes a high value. For instance, in our own society gold is so highly valued as to be a standard against which all other values are measured.

We tend to forget that this valuation is entirely arbitrary, speaking of gold's intrinsic value, as if in some way it were inherent. But gold is not a very useful material (although it is bright, and does not tarnish), nor is it the product of any special skills of the craftsperson. Intrinsic value is a misnomer: the Aztecs valued feathers more highly, unlike the Conquistadors, who craved gold; both were following subjective systems of value. When we survey the range of materials to which different societies have ascribed intrinsic value we can see that many of them had the qualities of rarity, of durability, and of being visually conspicuous:

- The bright *feathers* favored by the Aztecs and by tribes of New Guinea fulfill two of these qualities.

- *Ivory*: elephant and walrus tusks have been valued since Upper Paleolithic times.

- *Shell*, especially of large marine molluscs, has been highly prized in many cultures for millennia.

- That very special organic material *amber* was valued in Upper Paleolithic times in northern Europe.

- *Jade* is a favored material in many cultures, from China to Mesoamerica, and was valued as long ago as 4000 BC in Neolithic Europe.

- Other naturally hard and *colorful stones* (e.g. rock crystal, lapis lazuli, obsidian, quartz, and onyx) have always been valued.

- *Gemstones* have taken on a special value in recent centuries, when the technique of cutting them to a faceted, light-catching shape was developed.

- *Gold* has perhaps pride of place (certainly in European eyes) among "intrinsically" valuable commodities, followed by silver.

- *Copper* and other metals have taken a comparable role: in North America copper objects had a special value.

- With the development of pyrotechnology, artificial materials such as *faience* and *glass* came into full prominence.

- The finest *textiles* and other clothing materials (e.g. tapa, bark-cloth, in Polynesia) have also always been highly valued, for prestige often means personal display.

A jade mask from Palenque, Mexico, found in Lord Pakal's tomb.

Woven silk robe (left) from the reign of the Chinese Qianlong Emperor (1735–96), bearing the Imperial dragon.

Feathered headdress (above) of the Aztec emperor Motecuhzoma II (Moctezuma).

The Portland vase (left), a superb example of 1st-century AD Roman glassworking.

Gold mask (right) thought by Schliemann to represent King Agamemnon, from a shaft grave at Mycenae, late 16th century BC.

Prestige objects of North America's Mississippian culture (c. AD 900–1450). (Left) Embossed copper face, with typical forked eye motif. (Right) Shell pendant (c. 14 cm) from Texas, showing a panther and bird of prey.

Mammoth ivory carving (above) of a lion-human figure from Hohlenstein-Stadel in southern Germany, c. 30,000 years old.

fabric may then consist of material from two or more separate sources. Fossil constituents, such as diatoms (see Chapter 6) can also be an aid to identification of the source of the raw materials.

The picture of the prehistoric trade in pottery in Britain that such analyses have documented is quite surprising. Until the **thin-section** work of David Peacock and his associates it was simply not realized that pottery bowls and other vessels might be traded over quite long distances (of the order of 100 km (62 miles)) in Neolithic times, before 3000 BC. Now that we know the extent of this exchange of pottery, and that of stone axes discussed above, it is clear that many individuals and settlements were linked by quite far-flung exchange systems.

Trace-Element Analysis. The basic composition of many materials is very consistent. Obsidian, a volcanic glass used in the manufacture of chipped stone tools in the same manner as flint, is a good example of this. The concentration of the main elements of which obsidian is formed (silicon, oxygen, calcium, etc.) is broadly similar whatever the source of the material. The trace elements (elements present only in very small quantities, measured in just a few parts per million) do vary according to the source, however, and there are a variety of useful methods for measuring their concentration.

When obsidian from New Britain and the Admiralty Islands in the Pacific was examined using trace-element analysis, it was found that obsidian from one source in New Britain (Talasea) was being traded as far as Fiji to the east and Sabah (northern Borneo) to the west, a distance of 6500 km (4000 miles), at about 3000 years ago. This is surely the widest distribution of any commodity in the global Neolithic record.

Isotopic Analysis. Atoms of the same element, but with different numbers of neutrons in the nucleus, are called isotopes. Most elements occurring in nature consist of a number of isotopes. Particularly when we are investigating metal sources, we can analyze the sources (as well as the artifacts we are investigating) for the presence of different proportions of lead isotopes in order to characterize them. Sometimes more than one source can have the same isotope ratios, but this can usually be resolved by consideration of trace-element data.

Lead isotope analysis is of direct use not only for lead artifacts, but also for those of silver, in which lead is usually present as an impurity. Copper sources also contain at least a trace of lead, and it has been shown by experimentation that a large proportion of that lead passes into the copper metal produced during smelting. Here, then, is a characterization method applicable to lead, silver, and copper artifacts. It has been used successfully for the determination of mineral sources of Classical and medieval silver coins, Bronze Age copper and bronze tools, lead weights, as well as lead in pigments of glasses and glazes, and lead-based white paint.

Oxygen isotope ratios have also proved useful for the characterization of marine shell. The shell of *Spondylus gaederopus* was widely traded in the form of bracelets and decorations during the Neolithic in southeast Europe. Archaeologists needed to know whether it came from the Aegean, or possibly from the Black Sea. As discussed in the section on **deep-sea cores** in Chapter 6, the oxygen isotopic composition of marine shell is dependent on the local temperature of the sea. The Black Sea is much colder than the Mediterranean, and analysis confirmed that the shells in question came from the Aegean.

The Study of Distribution

The study of the traded goods themselves, and the identification of their sources by means of characterization, are the most important procedures in the investigation of exchange. But it is the study of distribution, or the movement of goods, that allows us to get to the heart of the matter – how societies operated and how they interrelated socially and economically.

In the absence of written records it is not easy to determine what were the mechanisms of distribution, or what was the nature of the exchange relationship. Where such records exist they can be most informative. Earlier evidence from pre-literate societies – societies without written records – can, however, give some clear idea of ownership and of the managed distribution of goods. For example, clay sealings, used to stopper jars, to secure boxes, and to seal the doors of storehouses, and distinguished by the impression of a carved seal, are widely found in the pre-literate phases in the Near East, and in the Aegean Bronze Age.

In some cases, however, the traded goods themselves were marked by their owner or producer. For instance, the potters who produced storage containers (amphorae) in Roman times used to stamp their name on the rim. The general pattern of export can be made clear by the production of a distribution map.

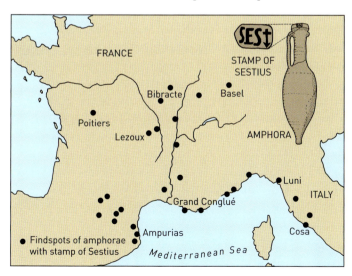

A distribution study. Roman storage containers (amphorae) bearing the stamp of the potter Sestius (above) have been found in northern Italy and widely throughout central and southern France. They and their contents (probably wine) were probably made on an estate near Cosa. The distribution map thus indicates the general pattern of the export from the Cosa area of this commodity.

- Analysis of the spatial distribution of finds can help us to understand the exchange mechanisms that were operating in the past

- The main different exchange mechanisms can be summarized as: direct access; down-the-line; freelance; and emissary trading

- Quantitative studies, for example fall-off analysis, can give a statistical indication of which method was in use

But a distribution map must be interpreted if we are to understand the processes that lay behind it: and at this point it is useful to consider how the spatial distribution of finds may depend on the exchange mechanism – or in other words, what can the pattern of distribution of finds tell us about the type of exchange that was occurring? The different mechanisms can be summarized as follows:

- "Direct access": the user goes directly to the source of the material, without the intervention of any exchange mechanism
- "Down-the-line" exchange: repeated exchanges of a **reciprocal** nature, so that a commodity travels across successive territories through successive exchanges
- "Freelance (middleman)" trading: traders operate independently and for gain: usually the traders work by bargaining, but instead of a fixed marketplace they are travelers who take the goods to the consumer
- "Emissary" trading: the "trader" is a representative of a central organization based in the home country

Not all of these types of transaction can be expected to leave clear and unmistakable indications in the archaeological record, although, as we shall see, down-the-line trading apparently does. And a former port of trade ought to be recognizable if the materials found there come from a wide range of sources, and it is clear that the site was not principally an administrative center, but was specialized in trading activities.

Spatial Analysis of Distribution

Several formal techniques are available for the study of distribution. The first and most obvious technique is naturally that of plotting the distribution map for finds, as in the case of the stamped Roman amphorae mentioned on the previous page. Quantitative studies of distributions are also helpful; the size of the dot or some other feature can be used as a simple device to indicate the number of finds on the map. This kind of map can give a good indication

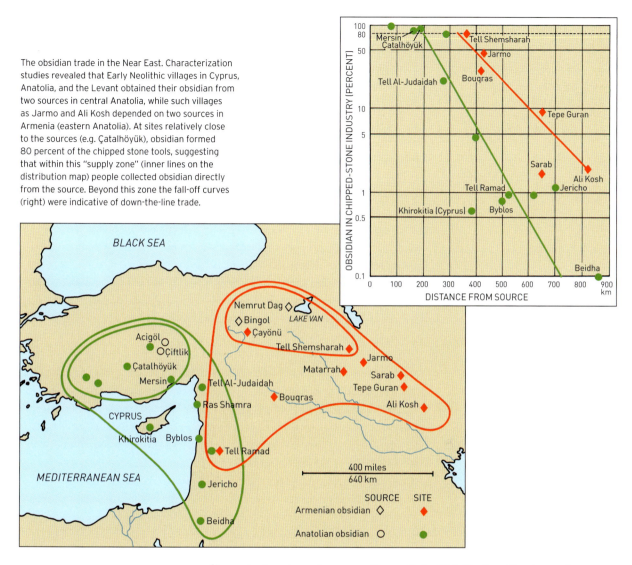

The obsidian trade in the Near East. Characterization studies revealed that Early Neolithic villages in Cyprus, Anatolia, and the Levant obtained their obsidian from two sources in central Anatolia, while such villages as Jarmo and Ali Kosh depended on two sources in Armenia (eastern Anatolia). At sites relatively close to the sources (e.g. Çatalhöyük), obsidian formed 80 percent of the chipped stone tools, suggesting that within this "supply zone" (inner lines on the distribution map) people collected obsidian directly from the source. Beyond this zone the fall-off curves (right) were indicative of down-the-line trade.

of important centers of consumption and of **redistribution**. Direct use of distribution maps, even when aided by quantitative plotting, may not, however, be the best way of studying the data, and more thorough analysis may be useful.

Recently, there has been a considerable focus of interest in "**fall-off analysis**." The quantity of a traded material usually declines as the distance from the source increases. This is not really very surprising, but in some cases (such as when a particular type of trade is happening) there are regularities in the way in which the decrease occurs. If the quantities of material are plotted against the distance from source on a graph, a fall-off curve is created. Although different mechanisms of distribution sometimes produce comparable end results, down-the-line trading, for instance, produces a quite distinctive exponential curve (which on a logarithmic scale is represented by a straight line, as in the example above).

Distribution Studies of Obsidian.   A good example is the obsidian found at Early Neolithic sites in the Near East (see illustration on p. 227). Characterization studies pinpointed two sources in central Anatolia and two in eastern Anatolia. Samples were obtained from most of the known Early Neolithic sites in the Near East, dating from the 7th and 6th millennia BC. A rather clear picture emerged with the central Anatolian obsidians being traded in the Levant area (down to Palestine), while those of eastern Anatolia were mostly traded down the Zagros Mountain range to sites in Iran, such as Ali Kosh.

A quantitative distributional study revealed a pattern of fall-off that indicated down-the-line trade. It could therefore be concluded that obsidian was being handed on down from village settlement to village settlement. Only in the area close to the sources (within 320 km (200 miles) of the sources) – termed the supply zone – was there evidence that people were going direct to the source to collect their own obsidian. Outside that area – within what has been termed the contact zone – the exponential fall-off indicates a down-the-line system. There is no indication of specialist middleman traders at this time, nor does it seem that there were central places that had a dominant role in the supply of obsidian.

Shipwrecks and Hoards: Trade by Sea and Land.   A different approach to distribution questions is provided by the study of transport. Travel by water was often much safer, quicker, and less expensive than travel by land. The best source of information, both for questions of transport and for the crucial question of what commodity was traded against what, and on which scale, is offered by shipwrecks. From earlier times, for instance, complete cargoes of the Roman amphorae referred to on p. 255 have been recovered. Our knowledge of marine trade has been greatly extended by George Bass's investigations of two important Bronze Age shipwrecks off the south coast of Turkey, at Cape Gelidonya and Uluburun (see box overleaf).

The terrestrial equivalent of the shipwreck is the trader's cache or **hoard**. When substantial **assemblages** of goods are found in archaeological deposits, it is not easy to be clear about the intentions of those who left them there: some hoards evidently had a votive character, left perhaps as offerings to deities, but those with materials for recycling, such as scrap metal, may well have been buried by itinerant smiths who intended to return and retrieve them.

In such cases, particularly with a well-preserved shipwreck, we come as close as we shall ever do to understanding the nature of distribution.

Exchange and Interaction: The Complete System

The archaeological evidence is rarely sufficient to permit the reconstruction of a complete exchange system. It is extremely difficult, for example, to establish without written records what was traded against what, and which particular values were ascribed to each commodity. Furthermore, exchange in perishable materials will have left little or no trace in the archaeological record. In most cases, all we can hope to do is to fit together the evidence about sources and distribution that can be established archaeologically. A good example of such a project is the work of Jane Pires-Ferreira in Oaxaca, Mexico.

An Exchange System in Ancient Mexico.   Pires-Ferreira studied five materials used in Oaxaca during the Early and Middle Formative periods (1450–500 BC). The first was obsidian, of which some nine sources were identified. These were characterized and the relevant networks were established. Pires-Ferreira then proceeded to consider exchange networks for another material, mother-of-pearl shell, and concluded that two different networks were in operation here, one bringing marine material from the Pacific Coast, the other material from freshwater sources in the rivers draining into the Atlantic.

For her next study she considered the iron ore (magnetite) used to manufacture mirrors in the Formative period. Finally, she was able to bring into consideration two classes of pottery, the area of manufacture of which (in Oaxaca and in Veracruz, respectively) could be determined stylistically. These results were then fitted together onto a single map, showing some of the commodities that linked regions of Mesoamerica in the Early Formative period into several exchange networks. The picture is evidently incomplete, and it does not offer any notion of the relative values of the traded goods. But it does make excellent use of the available characterization data, and undertakes a preliminary synthesis of the area's exchange networks that is securely based on the archaeological evidence.

The complete system: Jane Pires-Ferreira's map, which shows some of the commodities that linked regions of Early Formative Mesoamerica from the study of five different materials.

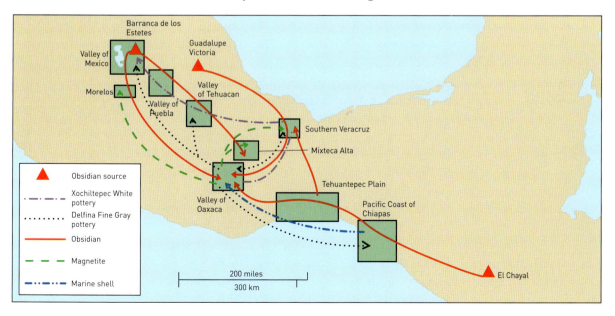

Distribution: The Uluburun Wreck

It is difficult for the archaeologist to learn what commodity was traded against what other commodity, and to understand the mechanics of trade. The discovery of the shipwreck of a trading vessel, complete with cargo, is thus of particular value.

In 1982, just such a wreck, dating from close to 1300 BC, was found at Uluburun, near Kaş, off the south Turkish coast in 43 m (141 ft) to 60 m (198 ft) of water. It was excavated between 1984 and 1994 by George Bass and Cemal Pulak of the Institute of Nautical Archaeology in Texas.

The ship's cargo contained about 10 tons of copper in the form of more than 350 of the four-handled ingots already known from wall paintings in Egypt and from finds in Cyprus, Crete, and elsewhere. The copper for these ingots was almost certainly mined on the island of Cyprus (as suggested by lead-isotope analysis, and trace-element analysis). Also of particular importance are nearly a ton of ingots and other objects of tin found on the seafloor in the remains of the cargo. The source of the tin used in the Mediterranean at this time is not yet clear. It seems evident that at the time of the shipwreck, the vessel was sailing westwards from the east Mediterranean coast, and taking with it tin, from some eastern source, as well as copper from Cyprus.

The pottery included Canaanite amphorae, so called because they were made in Palestine or Syria (the Land of Canaan). Most held turpentine-like resin from the terebinth tree, but several contained olives, and another

glass beads. Similar jars have been found in Greece, Egypt, and especially along the Levantine coast.

The exotic goods included lengths of a wood resembling ebony, which grew in Africa south of Egypt. Then there were Baltic amber beads, which came originally from northern Europe (and that probably reached the Mediterranean overland). There was also ivory in the form of elephant and

Three striking objects from the wreck (above, clockwise from left): a bronze statuette of a female diety, partly clad in gold foil, that may have been the ship's protective goddess; a boxwood diptych (object with folding plates) with ivory hinges, and with recesses to hold beeswax writing surfaces; and a gold pendant showing an unknown goddess with a gazelle in each upraised hand.

(Left) The map shows the probable route of the ill-fated ship found at Uluburun. Also indicated are likely sources of materials for the various artifacts found on board the wreck.

hippopotamus tusks, possibly from the eastern Mediterranean, and ostrich eggshells that probably came from North Africa or Syria. Bronze tools and weapons from the wreck show a mixture of types that include Egyptian, Levantine, and Mycenaean forms. Among other important finds were several cylinder seals of Syrian and Mesopotamian types, ingots of glass (at that time a special and costly material), and a chalice of gold.

This staggering treasure gives a glimpse into Bronze Age trade in the Mediterranean. Bass and Pulak consider it likely that the ship started its final voyage on the Levantine coast. Its usual circuit probably involved sailing across to Cyprus, then along the Turkish coast, past Kaş and west to Crete, or, more likely, to one of the major Mycenaean sites on the Greek mainland, or even further north, as hinted by the discovery on the wreck of spears and a ceremonial scepter/mace from the Danube region of the Black Sea. Then, profiting from seasonal winds, it would head south across the open sea to the coast of North Africa, east to the mouth of the Nile and Egypt, and, finally, home again to Phoenicia. On this occasion, however, the crew lost their ship, their cargo, and possibly their lives at Uluburun.

Divers working on the four-handled ingots.

Symbolic Exchange and Interaction. Interaction involves the exchange not only of material goods but also of information, which includes ideas, **symbols**, inventions, aspirations, and values. Modern archaeology has been able to learn quite a lot about material exchanges, using characterization studies and spatial analyses, but it has been more difficult to identify and explain the more symbolic aspects of interaction.

While similar innovations separated by long distances should not be used as indicators of contact in the absence of other evidence, the development of a striking new technology, making its appearance at a number of locations over a limited area, usually indicates the flow of information and hence contact.

In the past archaeologists talked of "diffusion" when they discussed interactions between neighboring areas. The term implied that one area was dominant over the other, and that new technologies passed down to the subordinate area. The opposite approach would be to consider different areas as completely autonomous and independent. But it seems unrealistic to exclude the possibility of significant interactions between different groups.

The solution is to seek ways of analyzing interactions, including their symbolic components, that do not make assumptions about dominance and subordination, core and periphery, but consider different areas as on a more or less equal footing. When discussing such interactions between independent societies of equal status, it has been found useful to speak of **interaction spheres**.

Potlatch ceremony at Sitka, Alaska, on 9 December 1904, with Tlingit chiefs dressed in their ceremonial finery. Such occasions involved the elaborate display of wealth and the public destruction of valuable items to manifest the high status of their owners.

One major interaction sphere is competition. Neighboring areas compete with one another in various ways, judging their own success against that of their neighbors. This often takes a symbolic form in periodic meetings at some major ceremonial centers where representatives of the various areas meet, celebrate ritual, and sometimes compete in games and other enterprises.

Such behavior is seen among hunter-gatherer **bands**, which meet periodically in larger units (at what in Australia are called corroborees). It is seen also in the pilgrimages and rituals of **state** societies, most conspicuously in ancient Greece at the Olympic Games and at other Panhellenic assemblies, when representatives of all the city states would meet.

At such gatherings there is a tendency for one society to try to outdo its neighbors in conspicuous consumption, such as in the expensive public feasts of the Northwest Coast Native Americans, the institution of the potlatch. Very similar in some ways is the erection of magnificent monuments at regional ceremonial centers, each outdoing its neighbor in scale and grandeur. Something similar may have occurred in the ceremonial centers of Maya cities, and the same phenomenon is seen in the magnificent cathedrals in the capital cities of medieval Europe.

Warfare is, of course, an obvious form of competition. But the object of the competition is not necessarily to gain territory – for example, it might also be used to capture prisoners for sacrifice. It operated under well-understood rules, and was as much a form of interaction as the others listed here.

Innovations can also be transmitted – naturally a technical advance made in one area will soon spread to other areas. And there may also be a ceremonial exchange of valuables: although we have emphasized non-material (i.e. symbolic) interactions here, it is certainly the case that between the elites of different societies there may also be a series of material exchanges – the transfer of marriage partners and of valuable gifts. At the same time, large-scale exchanges between participating societies of everyday commodities should not, of course, be overlooked. Economies in some cases became linked together.

Such concepts, where as much emphasis is laid on symbolic aspects as on the physical exchange of material goods, can profitably be used to analyze interactions in most early societies and cultures. Systematic analysis of this kind has, however, so far been rare in archaeology.

Study Questions

- What are some of the differences between unaltered and synthetic materials?
- How is experimental archaeology used in the study of stone tools?
- What is characterization and how does it aid in the study of ancient trade?
- What are the four main types of exchange mechanisms and how do they differ?
- What are some of the common qualities of valuables?
- What is fall-off analysis and how does it relate to the study of distribution?

Summary

- In this chapter we have highlighted some basic questions about early technology, and considered how to find answers to them. First, one must assess whether an object is indeed an artifact, and then of what material – unaltered (primarily stone, wood, fibers) or synthetic (pottery, metals). Ethnography and archaeological context may suggest the function of a tool; but only analysis of its microwear or residues can demonstrate its likely use. Nevertheless, ethnoarchaeology is proving extremely valuable.

- Studies of characterization – i.e. the sources of the raw materials that make up artifacts – have been of enormous importance in archaeology, by shedding light on technological processes, and contact and trade between different regions and cultures. Thin-sections, as well as trace-element analysis and isotopic analysis, have played a major role in these investigations.

- Once an understanding of the whole process of making and using the artifacts has been attained, we can turn to their distribution – the spatial analysis of their places of manufacture and discovery, and hence the exchange and transportation systems that have caused these distribution patterns to come about.

Further Reading

Broad surveys of ancient technology, trade, and exchange include:

Cuomo, S. 2007. *Technology and Culture in Greek and Roman Antiquity*. Cambridge University Press: Cambridge.

Earle, T.K. & Ericson, J.E. (eds). 1977. *Exchange Systems in Prehistory*. Academic Press: New York & London.

Ericson, J.E. & Earle, T.K. (eds). 1982. *Contexts for Prehistoric Exchange*. Academic Press: New York & London.

Fagan, B.M. (ed.). 2004. *The Seventy Great Inventions of the Ancient World*. Thames & Hudson: London & New York.

Forbes, R.J. (series). *Studies in Ancient Technology*. E.J. Brill: Leiden.

Lambert, J.B. 1997. *Traces of the Past: Unraveling the Secrets of Archaeology through Chemistry*. Helix Books/Addison-Wesley Longman: Reading, Mass.

Nicholson, P. & Shaw, I. (eds). 2009. *Ancient Egyptian Materials and Technology*. Cambridge University Press: Cambridge.

Scarre, C. & Healy, F. (eds). 1993. *Trade and Exchange in Prehistoric Europe*. Oxbow Monograph 33: Oxford.

Torrence, R. 2009. *Production and Exchange of Stone Tools: Prehistoric Obsidian in the Aegean*. Cambridge University Press: Cambridge.

[See p. 345 for a list of useful websites]

What Were They Like?
The bioarchaeology of people

- The Variety of Human Remains

Identifying Physical Attributes

- Which Sex?
- How Long Did They Live?
- What Did They Look Like?
- How Were They Related?

Disease, Deformity, and Death

- Evidence in Soft Tissue
- Skeletal Evidence for Deformity
  and Disease

Diet and Nutrition

- Malnutrition
- Cannibalism

Study Questions
Summary
Further Reading

One of archaeology's principal aims is to re-create the lives of the people who produced the archaeological record, and what more direct evidence can there be than the physical remains of past humanity? In the next chapter we will see how **archaeology** can help us to understand the ways in which ancient people thought, but we have much more tangible evidence – complete skeletons, bones, and bone fragments, and sometimes corpses that have been preserved in special circumstances – that enables us to reconstruct the physical attributes of past individuals and groups. If sufficient remains have survived, archaeologists can determine, for example, the sex and age of an individual, perhaps how that person died, and even his or her physical appearance. The study of such human remains is known as "**bioarchaeology**"; the topic also raises ethical issues, and these are examined in Chapter 11.

The Variety of Human Remains

How does the archaeologist know that human remains are present? This is relatively easy where intact bodies, complete skeletons, or skulls are found. Archaeologists can usually reliably identify individual bones and large fragments as human. In cases of fragmentary multiple burials or cremations, the minimum number of individuals can be assessed from the part of the body that is most abundant. Even small fragments may include diagnostic features by which human beings can be recognized. In some recent, careful **excavations**, individual hairs have been recovered that can be identified under the microscope as human.

Even where the physical remains of a body have disappeared, evidence may sometimes survive. The best-known examples are the hollows left by the bodies of the people of Pompeii as they disintegrated inside their hardened casing of volcanic ash. Modern plaster casts of these bodies show not only the general physical appearance, hairstyles, clothing, and posture, but also even such fine and moving detail as the facial expression at the moment of death.

Nevertheless the vast majority of human remains are in the form of actual skeletons and bone fragments, which yield a wide range of information, as we

Plaster, poured into the cavity left by the body, recreates the shape of a Pompeian struck down in flight.

shall see. Indirect physical evidence about people also comes from ancient art, and provides important clues about what people looked like.

Identifying Physical Attributes

Once the presence and abundance of human remains have been established, how can we attempt to reconstruct physical characteristics – sex, age at death, build, appearance, and relationships? A good example of what we can learn

Bones of the human skeleton, with salient differences between the sexes.

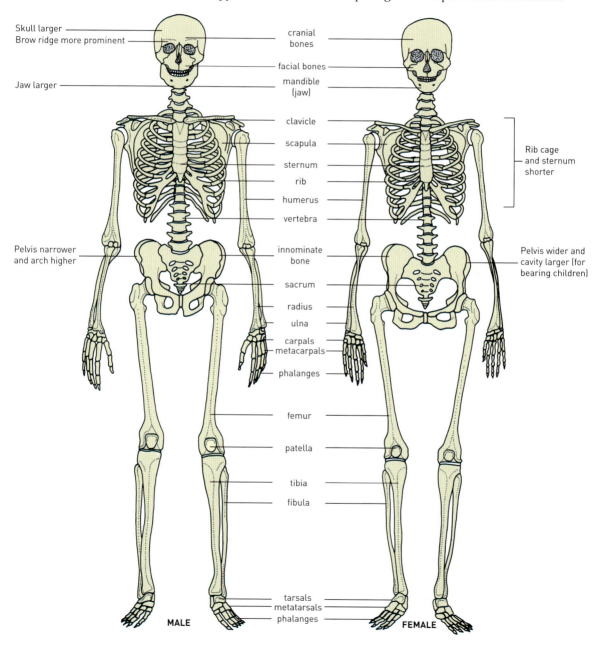

Skull larger
Brow ridge more prominent

cranial bones

facial bones

Jaw larger

mandible (jaw)

clavicle

scapula

sternum

rib

humerus

vertebra

Rib cage and sternum shorter

Pelvis narrower and arch higher

innominate bone

sacrum

Pelvis wider and cavity larger (for bearing children)

radius

ulna

carpals
metacarpals

phalanges

femur

patella

tibia

fibula

tarsals
metatarsals
phalanges

MALE

FEMALE

The variety of human remains. (Above) The well-preserved 2000-year-old, blindfolded body of a girl, drowned in a bog at Windeby, north Germany. (Left) Early medieval burials at Sutton Hoo, eastern England, could be recovered only as outlines in the acid sandy soil. (Right) The 8500-year-old skeleton of a child from Çatalhöyük in Turkey.

from human remains is provided by the Lindow Man bog body (see box overleaf). The techniques for assessing each different physical characteristic are described below.

Which Sex?

Where intact bodies and artistic depictions are concerned, sexing is usually straightforward from the genitalia. If these are not present, secondary characteristics, such as breasts and facial hair, provide fairly reliable indicators. Where human skeletons and bone remains without soft tissue are concerned, however, there are lots more sources of evidence, owing to differences between the sexes in the size and shape of various bones, known as sexual dimorphism.

The best indicator of sex is the shape of the pelvis, since this is visibly different in males and females (see diagram, opposite). Other parts of the skeleton can also be used in sex differentiation: male bones are generally bigger, longer, more robust, and have more developed muscle markings than those of females, which are slighter.

Lindow Man:
The Body in the Bog

In 1984, part of a human leg was found by workers at a peat-shredding mill in northwest England. Subsequent investigation of the site at Lindow Moss, Cheshire, where the peat had been cut, revealed the top half of a human body still embedded in the ground. This complete section of peat was removed and later "excavated" in the laboratory by a multidisciplinary team of scientists. The various studies made of the body have yielded remarkable insights into the life and death of this ancient individual, now dated to the late Iron Age or Roman period – perhaps the 1st century AD.

Despite the missing lower half, it was obvious from the beard, sideburns, and moustache that this was the body of a male. The age of Lindow Man (as he is now called) has been estimated at around the mid-20s. He appears to have been well-built, and probably weighed around 60 kg (132 lb). His height, calculated from the length of his humerus (upper arm bone), was estimated to be between 1.68 and 1.73 m (5 ft 6 in to 5 ft 8 in) – average today, but fairly tall for the period.

Lindow Man wore no clothing apart from an armband of fox fur. His brown/ginger hair and whiskers were cut, and analysis by scanning electron microscopy indicated that their ends had a stepped surface, implying that they had probably been cut by scissors or shears. His manicured fingernails indicate that he did not do any heavy or rough work – he was clearly not a laborer.

The bog acid had removed the enamel from his teeth, but what survived seemed normal and quite healthy – there were no visible cavities.

Lindow Man appears to have had very slight osteoarthritis; and a CT scan revealed changes in some vertebrae caused by stresses and strains. Parasite eggs show that he had a relatively high infestation of whipworm and maw worm, but these would have caused him little inconvenience. Overall, therefore, he was fairly healthy.

His blood group was found to be O, like the majority of modern Britons. The food residues in the part of his

Cleaning the back of Lindow Man in the laboratory. Distilled water is being sprayed to keep the skin moist.

upper alimentary tract that survived revealed that his last meal had consisted of a griddle cake.

X-rays confirmed that his head had been fractured from behind – they revealed splinters of bone in the vault of the skull. A forensic scientist deduced from the two lacerated wounds joined together that the skull had been driven in twice by a narrow-bladed weapon. There may also have

been a blow (from a knee?) to his back, because X-rays showed a broken rib.

The blows to the head would have rendered him unconscious, if not killed him outright, so that he cannot have felt the subsequent garotting or the knife in his throat. A knotted thong of sinew, 1.5 mm thick, around his throat had broken his neck and strangled him, and his throat had been slit with a short, deep cut at the side of the neck

The fully conserved remains of Lindow Man, now on display at the British Museum.

that severed the jugular. Once he had been bled in this way, he was dropped face-down into a pool in the bog.

We do not know why he died – perhaps as a sacrifice, or as an executed criminal – but we have been able to learn a great deal about the life and death of Lindow Man.

239

For children it is worth noting that, with the exception of preserved bodies and artistic depictions showing genitalia, their remains cannot be sexed with the same degree of reliability as adults, although analysis of teeth can provide some evidence. When we examine subadult skeletal remains we can often only guess – though the odds of being right are 50:50. Recently, a new technique has been developed for determining the sex of fragmentary or infant skeletal remains from **DNA** analysis.

How Long Did They Live?

Some scholars feel able to assign exact age at death to particular deceased human beings, but it should be stressed that what we can usually establish with any certainty is biological age at death – young, adult, old – rather than any accurate measurement in years and months. The best indicators of age, as with animals, are the teeth. We can study the eruption and replacement of the milk teeth; the sequence of eruption of the permanent dentition; and finally the degree of wear, allowing as best one can for the effects of diet and method of food preparation.

A timescale for age at death derived from this kind of dental information in modern people works reasonably well for recent periods, despite much individual variation. But can it be applied to the dentition of our remote ancestors? New work on the microstructure of teeth suggests that old assumptions may not be correct. Tooth enamel grows at a regular, measurable rate, and its microscopic growth lines form ridges that can be counted from epoxy resin replicas of the tooth placed in a scanning electron microscope. In modern populations a new ridge grows approximately each week, and analysis of molar structure in Neanderthals has shown that they had a very similar rate of growth to that of modern humans. By measuring tooth growth ridges in fossil specimens, Tim Bromage and Christopher Dean have concluded that previous investigators overestimated the age at death of many early **hominins**. The famous 1–2 million-year-old australopithecine skull from Taung, South Africa, for example, belonged to a child who probably died at just over 3 years of age, not at 5 or 6 as had been believed. This suggests that our earliest ancestors grew up more quickly than we do, and that their development into maturity was more like that of the modern great apes.

Bones are also used in assessing age. The sequence in which the articulating ends of bones become fused to the shafts gives a timescale that can be applied to the remains of young people. One of the last bones to fuse is the inner end of the clavicle (collar bone) at about 26; after that age, different criteria are needed to age bones. Skull thickness in immature individuals also bears a rough relationship to age – the thicker the skull the older the person – and in old age all bones usually get thinner and lighter, although skull bones actually get thicker in about 10 percent of elderly people.

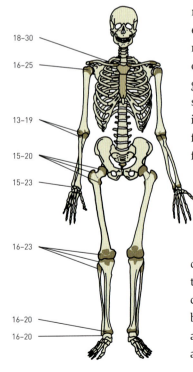

Assessing age: the years at which bone ends fuse.

18–30

16–25

13–19

15–20

15–23

16–23

16–20
16–20

8 What Were They Like?

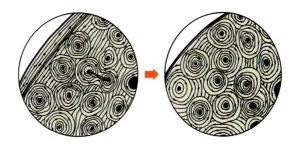

Assessing age: changes in bone structure are visible under the microscope as humans grow older. The circular osteons become more numerous and extend to the edge of the bone.

But what if the bone remains are small fragments? The answer lies under the microscope, in bone microstructure. As we get older, the architecture of our bones changes in a distinct and measurable way. A young longbone, at about 20, has rings around its circumference, and a relatively small number of circular structures called osteons. With age the rings disappear, and more and smaller osteons appear. By this method, even a fragment can provide an age. Putting a thin section of a femur (thigh bone) under the microscope and studying the stage of development is a technique that, in tests with documented known skeletons, has achieved accuracy to within 5 years.

Interpreting Age at Death. It must be stressed that we can only calculate average age at death for the bodies and skeletons that have survived and been discovered. Many scholars used erroneously to believe that to dig up a cemetery, and assess the age and sex of its occupants, provided an accurate guide to the life expectancy and mortality pattern of a particular culture. This entails the considerable assumption that the cemetery contains all members of the community who died during the period of its use – that everyone was buried there regardless of age, sex, or status; that nobody died elsewhere; and that the cemetery was not reused at another time. This assumption cannot realistically be made. A cemetery provides a sample of the living population, but we do not know how representative that sample might be. Figures on life expectancy and average age should therefore be looked at critically before they are accepted and used by archaeologists.

What Did They Look Like?

Once again, it is preserved bodies that provide us with our clearest glimpses of faces. Tollund Man, one of the remarkable Iron Age bog bodies from Denmark, is the best-known prehistoric example. Discoveries at Thebes in Egypt in 1881 and 1898 of two royal burial caches have given us a veritable gallery of mummified pharaohs, their faces still vivid, even if some shrinkage and distortion has taken place.

Thanks to artists from the Upper **Paleolithic** onward, we also have a huge array of portraits. Some of them, such as images painted on mummy cases, are directly associated with the remains of their subject. Others, such as Greek and

Roman busts, are accurate likenesses of well-known figures whose remains may be lost for ever. The extraordinary life-size terracotta army found near Xi'an, China, is made up of thousands of different models of soldiers of the 3rd century BC. Even though only the general features of each are represented, they constitute an unprecedented "library" of individuals, as well as providing invaluable information on hairstyles, armor, and weaponry. From later periods we have many life- or death-masks, sometimes used as the basis for life-size funerary effigies or tomb-figures, such as those of European royalty and other notables from medieval times onward.

Attempts to reconstruct faces were already being carried out in the 19th century by German anatomists in order to produce likenesses from the skulls of such celebrities as Schiller, Kant, and Bach. But the best-known exponent of the technique in the 20th century was the Russian Mikhail Gerasimov, who worked on remains ranging from fossil humans to Ivan the Terrible. It is now felt that much of his work represented "inspired interpretation," rather than factual reconstruction. Currently, the process has reached a higher degree of accuracy.

One of the most intriguing recent facial reconstructions has been of the best-preserved Etruscan skeleton known today, that of a noblewoman called Seianti Hanunia Tlesnasa, who died about 2200 years ago in central Italy. Since 1887 her remains have been housed in the British Museum inside a splendid painted terracotta sarcophagus that bears her name engraved on it (illustrated overleaf). The lid of this sarcophagus features a life-size image of the dead woman, reclining on a soft pillow, with a bronze mirror in her jeweled hand. This is perhaps the earliest identifiable portrait in western art, but is it really Seianti?

Anthropologists deduced from the skeleton that the woman was about 1.5 m (4 ft 11 in) tall, and middle-aged at death. Damage and wear on her bones, and the fact that she was almost toothless, had at first suggested old age, but in fact she had incurred severe injuries, most likely a riding accident that had crushed her right hip and knocked out the teeth of her right lower jaw. The bone was damaged where the jaw joins the skull, and opening her mouth wide would have been painful. This prevented her from eating anything but soups and gruels, and from keeping her remaining teeth clean – most of them subsequently fell out. Seianti would also have had painful arthritis and increasing disabilities.

Two of the surviving teeth confirmed, from analysis of the dentine, that she was about 50 when she died. And **radiocarbon dating** of the bones produced a result of 250–150 BC, which proved that the skeleton was genuinely ancient and of the right period. The facial reconstruction showed a middle-aged woman who had grown rather obese. How did it compare with the coffin image?

From the side, there were differences, since the artist had given Seianti a prettier nose, but from the front the resemblances were clearer. The final confirmation came from a computerized technique for matching facial proportions and features – the computer photocomparison of the

Faces from the past. (Above) Tollund Man, the Iron Age bog body from Denmark. (Right) Bronze head of the Roman emperor Hadrian (reigned AD 117–138), from the Thames river. (Far right and below center) Tutankhamun's mummy was unwrapped in 1923, revealing within the bandages a shrunken body. The young king's original height was estimated by measuring the longbones. Tutankhamun's facial features have recently been reconstructed using CT scans of his skull as a base – three teams separately produced very similar reconstructions, one of which is shown here. (Below) An old man with a wrinkled face is portrayed (with an accompanying duck) on this 1000-year-old Tiwanaku-period (AD 500–1100) vase from the island of Pariti in Lake Titicaca, Bolivia.

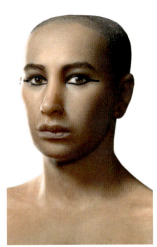

(Right) The terracotta sarcophagus of Seianti Hanunia Tlesnasa, which contained her bones; the lid takes the form of a life-size image of the dead woman – but how accurately did it represent her appearance? (Above) The reconstruction made from the skull found in the sarcophagus.

reconstruction and the portrait left no doubt that this was the same person. The sarcophagus image showed her as some years younger, with fewer chins, and a smaller, more girlish mouth. In other words, the sculptor had made flattering improvements to the portrait of this short, portly, middle-aged woman, but also captured Seianti's likeness extremely well.

How Were They Related?

In certain cases it is possible to assess the relationship between two individuals by comparing skull shape or analyzing the hair. There are other methods of achieving the same result, primarily by study of dental morphology. Some dental anomalies (such as enlarged or extra teeth, and especially missing wisdom teeth) run in families.

Blood groups can be determined from soft tissue, bone, and even from tooth dentine up to more than 30,000 years old. Since blood groups are inherited in a simple fashion from parents, different systems – of which the best-known is the A-B-O system, in which people are divided into those with blood types A, B, O, AB etc. – can sometimes help clarify physical relationships between different bodies. For example, it was suspected that Tutankhamun was somehow related to the unidentified body discovered in Tomb 55 at Thebes in 1907. The shape and diameter of the skulls were very similar, and when X-rays of the two crania were superimposed there was almost complete conformity. Robert Connolly and his colleagues therefore analyzed tissue from the two mummies, which showed that both had blood of group A, subgroup 2 with antigens M and N, a type relatively rare in ancient Egypt. This fact, together with the skeletal similarities, made it almost certain that the two were closely related. This has now perhaps been resolved through DNA analysis that, it has been claimed, confirms that the Tomb 55 body is indeed Tutankhamun's father, Akhenaten, and has also identified his mother, grandparents, wife, and children, although these results have not been accepted by all specialists.

Over long time periods, DNA molecules are broken up by chemical action, so there is no question of reconstituting functioning genes, far less a living body. But studies have shown that family relationships can be worked out through DNA analysis. In 2005, at Eulau in Germany, archaeologists discovered four closely grouped and well-preserved multiple burials dating to the Neolithic period, about 4600 years ago. Each contained a group of adults and children, buried facing each other. Their simultaneous interment and signs of conflict showed that they must have been the victims of some kind of violent event. One particular grave ("Tomb 99") produced the clearest results. Anatomical analysis showed that it contained a man aged between 40 and 60, a woman between 35 and 50, and two boys aged 4 to 5 and 8 to 9. Each adult was buried facing one of the boys, their arms and hands linked. This constitutes the earliest known genetic evidence for a nuclear family unit. Perhaps they were slaughtered in a raid, and later buried by the survivors.

(Below) Photo and X-ray of a flint arrowhead embedded in a woman's vertebra; she may have been one of the victims of a violent raid. (Below right) The skeletons in Tomb 99 at Eulau, and a reconstruction painting of how the bodies were arranged.

A highly significant breakthrough was also achieved in 1997 by Matthias Krings, Svante Pääbo, and their colleagues, with the extraction of DNA from 40,000-year-old hominin fossil remains. Even more remarkable was the analysis in 2010 of effectively the entire Neanderthal genome. The recent advances in genetic engineering thus open up fascinating possibilities for future work in human evolution and past human relationships.

Disease, Deformity, and Death

In addition to the basic physical attributes described above, it is also necessary to look at the other, often more negative aspects of the picture: What was people's quality of life? What was their state of health? We may know how long they lived, but how did they die?

Where we have intact bodies, the precise cause of death can sometimes be deduced – indeed, in some cases, such as the asphyxiated people of Pompeii and Herculaneum, it is obvious from the circumstances (the effect of the eruption of the volcano Vesuvius). For the more numerous skeletal remains that come down to us, however, cause of death can be ascertained only rarely, since most afflictions leading to death leave no trace on bone. Paleopathology (the study of ancient disease) tells us far more about life than about death, a fact of great benefit to the archaeologist.

In parallel, biological and forensic anthropologists are increasingly using techniques developed within archaeology to assist them with the recovery and study of human remains. Indeed, a new sub-discipline has now developed – forensic archaeology – which helps in the recovery and interpretation of murder victims, as well as trying to identify individuals within mass burials, as encountered in Rwanda and the former Yugoslavia.

Evidence in Soft Tissue

Since most infectious diseases rarely leave detectable traces in bones, a proper analysis of ancient diseases can only be carried out on surviving soft tissue, which rarely survives except in specific environments. The surface tissue sometimes reveals evidence of illness, such as eczema. It can also reveal some causes of violent death, such as the slit throats of several bog bodies.

Where inner tissue is involved, a number of methods are at the analyst's disposal. X-rays can provide much information, and have been used on Egyptian mummies, but newer, more powerful methods, such as Computed Tomography (CT scans) and Magnetic Resonance Imaging (MRI), are also now available.

Skeletal Evidence for Deformity and Disease

Skeletal material is far more abundant than preserved soft tissue, and can reveal a great deal of paleopathological information. Effects on the outer surface of bone can be divided into those caused by violence or accident, and those caused by disease or congenital deformity. Where violence or accidents resulting in skeletal

The coffin of Meresamun, an ancient Egyptian singer-priestess of c. 800 BC in the temple at Karnak, was acquired by the Oriental Institute in Chicago in 1920 and has remained unopened. It has been CT-scanned three times as technology improved – most recently in 2008 when a state-of-the-art 256-slice scanner was used. The data can be rendered in 3D and manipulated in different ways, effectively allowing one to strip away successive layers, and to isolate particular bones or features of interest for analysis; movie sequences can also be created. Many details missed in the previous scans were uncovered, from items of jewelry and dental features to degenerate spinal changes and minor post-mortem fractures.

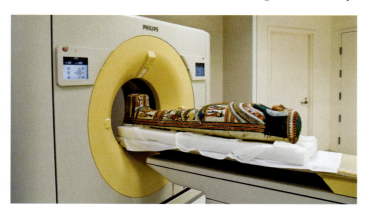

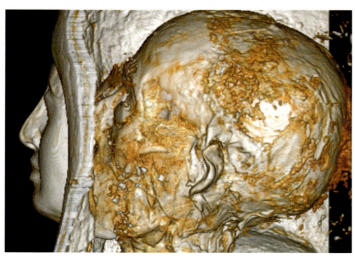

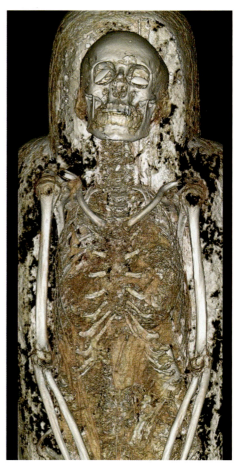

trauma are concerned, observations by experts can often reveal how the damage was caused, and how serious its consequences were for the victim. The small number of diseases that affect bone do so in three basic ways – they can bring about erosion, growths, or an altered structure. Furthermore, the bony lesions associated with various illnesses can differ in terms of their number and location in the skeleton. Some afflictions leave quite clear signs, whereas others do not. The former include several infections, nutritional deficiencies, and cancers. It is also possible to detect growth disorders by the overall size and shape of bones.

Diet and Nutrition

Nutrition can be described as the measure of a diet's ability to maintain the human body in its physical and social environment. We are of course interested to be able to learn whether a particular group of people in the past enjoyed good nutrition. Furthermore, comparison of nutrition at different periods may significantly add to our understanding of fundamental changes to the pattern of life, as in the transition from hunting and gathering to farming.

Malnutrition

What are the skeletal signs of malnutrition? So-called Harris lines, detected by X-rays on bones, indicate periods of arrested growth during development, and these are sometimes caused by malnutrition. A similar phenomenon occurs in teeth, where patches of poorly mineralized enamel, which a specialist can detect in a tooth-section, reflect growth disturbance brought about by a diet deficient in milk, fish, oil, or animal fats (or sometimes by such childhood diseases as measles). A lack of vitamin C produces scurvy, an affliction that causes changes in the palate and gums, and has been identified in an Anglo-Saxon individual from Norfolk, England, as well as in Peru, North America, and elsewhere.

The general size and condition of a skeleton's bones can provide an indication of aspects of diet. Sand in food, or the grit from grindstones, can have drastic effects on teeth. The excessive abrasion of teeth among certain California Native Americans can be linked to their habit of leaching the tannins out of acorns (their staple food) through a bed of sand, leaving a residue in the food.

Additional evidence for malnutrition can be obtained from art and literature. Vitamin B deficiency (beriberi) is mentioned in the *Su Wen*, a Chinese text of the 3rd millennium BC, and Strabo also refers to a case among Roman troops. Egyptian art provides such scenes as the well-known "famine" depicted at Saqqara, dating to around 2350 BC.

Chemical analysis of bone allows further insights. Much has been done with the stable isotopes of carbon and nitrogen (see Chapter 6), which vary among individuals according to what they ate. The carbon isotopes incorporated in bone – the stable ones, not 14C that is used for dating purposes – can be used to detect a diet high in certain plants or in marine resources. The consumption of maize,

Evidence for malnutrition: detail
of a wall relief from the complex
surrounding the pyramid of Unas, at
Saqqara in Egypt, depicting famine
victims, c. 2350 BC.

in particular, can be identified, so the method has been used to investigate
subsistence strategies in parts of the prehistoric New World. In eastern North
America, for example, a shift in the stable carbon isotope signature of human
bones about 1000 years ago corresponds nicely to a marked change in the
representation of maize in the plant remains from habitation **sites**. This is one
example where independent lines of evidence – the composition of bones and
the kinds of carbonized plant remains – complement one another, increasing
confidence in the inferences one makes about the past.

Cannibalism

Cannibalism – the eating of human flesh by humans – has often been claimed
to exist in different periods of the past, usually on the flimsiest of evidence.
Early scholars simply assumed that cannibalism was a "primitive" trait and
must therefore have existed in prehistory, but the traditional urge to uncover
cannibalism suffered a massive jolt with the appearance more than 30 years ago
of a groundbreaking work by anthropologist William Arens that, for the first
time, showed that the vast majority of claims for cannibalism in the ethnographic
or ethnohistorical record were untrustworthy. In recent decades, a better
understanding of taphonomy, greater familiarity with the huge variety of
funerary rituals around the world, and a more objective assessment of the facts,
have helped to weed out many claims for prehistoric cannibalism. Meanwhile
new claims have been put forward that rely on more plausible evidence.

At Atapuerca in northern Spain (see box, p.131), the bones of a human
ancestor called *Homo antecessor*, dating to perhaps 1 million years ago and found
in the Gran Dolina site, bear abundant cutmarks that, in the absence of any
evidence for funerary rituals or other secondary treatment of the dead, are most
likely butchery marks, which have therefore been interpreted as evidence for
cannibalism, and it is difficult to disagree with this inference. However, a later
site at Atapuerca, the Sima de los Huesos, also presents the earliest evidence
in the world for some kind of funerary ritual, perhaps some 600,000 years

Cutmarks on this human bone from Gran Dolina were almost certainly caused by butchering.

ago. We know from recent times that a huge variety of often bizarre funerary practices exists, some involving cutting, smashing, and burning of bones, either shortly after death or long afterwards. The archaeological record contains many instances from different periods, stretching back into prehistory, that can plausibly be attributed to such practices.

In order to decide whether human remains were produced by cannibalism or by funerary activities (or warfare, etc.), there are two main categories of evidence: the presence of human bones with marks of cutting, smashing, or burning, and the presence of human bones mixed with animal bones (i.e. the remains of food), with similar marks and treatment. However, one must avoid jumping to simplistic and "obvious" conclusions. The data are always ambiguous, and must be assessed carefully and objectively.

Dramatic claims have been made for cannibalism among the Ancestral Pueblo of the American Southwest, around AD 1100, including supposed human fecal material containing human tissue; but once again alternative explanations are available, involving not only funerary practices but also the extreme violence and mutilation inflicted on enemy corpses in warfare. The fecal material may actually be from a scavenging coyote.

The possibility remains that cannibalism may have existed occasionally, but even if that were true, the contribution of human flesh to diet must have been minimal and sporadic, paling into insignificance beside that of other creatures, especially the big herbivores.

Study Questions

- What physical attributes can be determined from human remains?
- How can archaeologists determine if two individuals are related?
- How are teeth used to assess how old an individual was at death?
- What are some of the methods archaeologists use to determine what people in the past looked like?
- What can human remains tell us about the lives of people living in the past?
- What is the evidence for prehistoric cannibalism? Do you believe it?

Summary

- The physical remains of past peoples provide direct evidence about their lives. Bioarchaeology is the study of human remains from archaeological sites. Though whole human bodies can be preserved in a variety of ways, including mummification and freezing, the vast majority of human remains recovered by archaeologists are in the form of skeletons and bone fragments.

- An important part of the analysis of human remains is the identification of physical attributes. The gender of skeletal remains, for example, can be determined through observing the shape of the pelvis as well as other bones. Teeth and bones can help establish an individual's relative age at death, namely whether they were young, adult or old. It is even possible to reconstruct what an individual looked like through careful analysis of skull features, or to assess the relationship between two individuals.

- Examination of human remains can also shed light on the more negative aspects of past lives – the diseases and deformites suffered, and sometimes an individual's cause of death. Study of bones and the chemical signatures within them provides evidence of ancient diet and nutrition (or malnutrition), and can even give clues as to whether early humans might have been eating each other.

Further Reading

The following provide an introduction to the study of the physical remains of humans:

Aufderheide, A.C. 2003. *The Scientific Study of Mummies*. Cambridge University Press: Cambridge.

Blau, S. & Ubelaker, D.H. 2008. *Handbook of Forensic Archaeology and Anthropology*. World Archaeological Congress Research Handbooks in Archaeology. Left Coast Press: Walnut Creek.

Brothwell, D. 1986. *The Bog Man and the Archaeology of People*. Harvard University Press: Cambridge, Mass.

Chamberlain, A.T. & Parker Pearson, M. 2004. *Earthly Remains. The History and Science of Preserved Human Bodies*. Oxford University Press: New York.

Donnan, C.B. 2003. *Moche Portrait Vessels from Ancient Peru*. University of Texas Press: Austin.

Larsen, C.S. 2002. *Skeletons in our Closet: Revealing our Past through Bioarchaeology*. Princeton University Press: New York.

Mays, S. 2010. *The Archaeology of Human Bones*. Routledge: London.

Waldron, T. 2001. *Shadows in the Soil: Human Bones and Archaeology*. Tempus: Stroud.

[See p. 345 for a list of useful websites]

What Did They Think?
Cognitive archaeology

The mental attributes of our ancestors are covered in this chapter. In Chapter 8 we examined their physical attributes, but of course the lives of ancient people who produced the archaeological record were not just about the physical aspects of existence: they had mental abilities, thoughts, and spiritual lives just as we do today.

We will begin this chapter by looking at **cognitive archaeology** – the study of past ways of thought from material remains – which is in many respects one of the newer branches of modern **archaeology**. Rather than simply "imagining" what people in the past must have thought or believed, it is possible to use the more disciplined techniques of cognitive archaeology to gain insights into these important aspects of the past: we can analyze the concepts people had and the way they thought.

We can, for example, investigate how people went about describing and measuring their world: as we shall see, the system of weights used in the Indus Valley civilization can be understood very well today. We can investigate which material goods people valued most highly, and perhaps viewed as symbols of authority or power. And we can investigate the manner in which people conceived of the supernatural, and how they responded to these conceptions in their ritual practice.

Cognitive Archaeology

It is generally agreed today that what most clearly distinguishes the human species from other life forms is our ability to use **symbols**. A symbol may be defined as the representation of an idea or of a concept, whether in verbal or in visual form. All intelligent thought and indeed all coherent speech are based on symbols, for words are themselves symbols, where the sound or the written letters stand for and thus represent (or symbolize) an aspect of the real world. Usually, however, meaning is attributed to a particular symbol in an arbitrary way. And that meaning is specific to a particular cultural tradition. It is usually impossible to infer the meaning of a symbol within a given **culture** from the symbolic form of the image or object alone. We have to see how that form is used, and to try to understand its meaning from the context in which it is used. Cognitive archaeology has thus to be very careful about specific contexts of discovery. There are very few symbols that have a universal meaning cross-culturally. It is the **assemblage** that matters, not the individual object in isolation.

Investigating How Human Symbolizing Faculties Evolved

The field of cognitive archaeology is concerned primarily with the cognitive behavior or our own species, *Homo sapiens*. Modern genetic studies suggest that we are all closely related, and that the innate cognitive abilities within any one regional group of our species, along with other behavioral attributes, are much like those in another. For instance, all human groups today have the capacity of complex speech, a capacity that in all probability we share with our ancestors of 80,000 to 60,000 years ago, the time of the first human dispersals out of Africa. Clearly, however, as we go back much further in time and consider earlier **hominin** species, whether *Homo habilis* or *Homo erectus*, we are dealing with creatures of more limited cognitive abilities. Their study represents an important subdivision of cognitive archaeology – the development of hominin cognitive abilities up to the emergence of our own species. It presents special problems, since for these earlier ancestors we cannot make the assumption that they had innate cognitive facilities much like our own. That is something that has to be investigated.

Language and Self-Consciousness. Most biological anthropologists agree that modern human abilities have been present since the emergence of *Homo sapiens* some 200,000–150,000 years ago. But as we look earlier, scholars are less united. Some archaeologists and biological anthropologists consider that an effective language may have been developed by *Homo habilis* around 2 million years ago, along with the first chopper tools, but others think that a full language capability developed very much more recently, with the emergence of *Homo sapiens*. This would imply that the tools made by hominins in the

Key Concepts
Early Human Symbolizing Faculties

- The development of language and self-consciousness

- Evidence of design in tool manufacture

- Evidence of the procurement of materials and planning

- The deliberate burial of human remains

- Representations and "art"

Lower and Middle **Paleolithic** periods were produced by beings without true linguistic capacities.

The origins of self-consciousness have been debated by scientists and philosophers, but with few definite conclusions. There is little evidence available to clarify the matter, but one philosopher, John Searle, has argued that there is no sudden transition, but rather a gradual development: he asserted, for example, that his dog Ludwig has a significant degree of self-consciousness.

There are several lines of approach into other aspects of early human abilities. One way that we can try to assess early human cognitive ability is by examining the way stone tools and other **artifacts** were made.

Design in Tool Manufacture.   Whereas the production of simple pebble tools – for instance by *Homo habilis* – may perhaps be considered a simple, habitual act, not unlike a chimpanzee breaking off a stick to poke at an ant hill, the fashioning by *Homo erectus* of so beautiful an object as an Acheulian **hand-axe** seems more advanced.

So far, however, that is just a subjective impression. How do we investigate it further? One way is to measure, by experiment, the amount of time taken in the manufacturing process. A more rigorous quantitative approach, as developed by Glynn Isaac, is to study the range of variation in an assemblage of artifacts. For if the toolmaker has, within his or her **cognitive map**, some enduring notion of what the end-product should be, one finished tool should be much like another. Isaac distinguished a tendency through time to produce an increasingly well-defined variety or assemblage of tool **types**. This implies that each person making tools had a notion of different tool forms, no doubt destined for different functions. Planning and design in tool manufacture thus become relevant to our consideration of the cognitive abilities of early hominins, abilities that moreover distinguish them from higher apes, such as the chimpanzee.

The production of a stone tool, a pot, a bronze artifact, or any product of a well-defined manufacturing process involves a complicated and often highly standardized sequence of events. For early periods, such as the Paleolithic, the study of the processes involved in making artifacts offers one of the few insights available into the way cognitive structures underlay complex aspects of human behavior. French prehistorians Claudine Karlin and Michèle Julien analyzed the sequence of events necessary for the production of blades in the Magdalenian period of the French Upper Paleolithic; many other production processes can be investigated along similar lines.

Procurement of Materials and Planning Time.   Another way of investigating the cognitive behavior of early hominins is to consider planning time, defined as the time between the planning of an act and its execution. For instance, if the raw material used to manufacture a stone tool comes from a specific rock outcrop, but the tool itself is produced some distance away (as documented by waste flakes produced in its manufacture), that would seem to indicate some enduring intention or foresight by the person who transported the raw material. Similarly, the transport of natural or finished objects, whether tools, seashells, or attractive fossils, as has been documented, indicates at least a continuing interest in them, or the intention of using them, or a sense of "possession." The study of such objects, by the techniques of **characterization** discussed in Chapter 7 and other methods, has now been undertaken in a systematic way.

Deliberate Burial of Human Remains.   From the Upper Paleolithic period there are many well-established cases of human burial, where the body or bodies have been deliberately laid to rest within a dug grave, sometimes accompanied by ornaments of personal adornment. Evidence is emerging, however, from even earlier periods. The act of burial itself implies some kind of respect or feeling for the deceased individual, and perhaps some notion of an afterlife (although that point is less easy to demonstrate). The adornment seems to imply the existence of the idea that objects of decoration can enhance the individual's appearance, whether in terms of beauty or prestige or otherwise. A good Upper Paleolithic example is the discovery made at Sungir, some 200 km (125 miles) northeast of Moscow and dating from *c*. 27,000 years ago: burials of a man and two children together with mammoth ivory spears, stone tools, ivory daggers, small animal carvings, and thousands of ivory beads.

In assessing such finds, we must be sure to understand the **formation processes** – in particular what may have happened to the burial after it was made. For example, animal skeletons have been discovered alongside human remains in graves. Traditionally this would have been taken as proof that animals were deliberately buried with the humans as part of some ritual act. Now, however, it is thought possible that in certain cases animals scavenging for food found their way into these burials and died accidentally – thus leaving false clues to mislead archaeologists.

Deliberate burial of the dead: a young girl (left, aged 9–10) and an adolescent boy (right, aged 12–13) buried head to head at Sungir, northeast of Moscow, *c*. 27,000 years ago. They wore a variety of pendants, bracelets, and other ornaments, their clothes were covered with thousands of ivory beads, and the boy wore a belt of fox teeth. The entire burial was covered in red ocher.

9 **What Did They Think?**

Piece of red ocher with abstract engravings, from Blombos Cave, South Africa, dating to c. 77,000 years ago.

Representations. Any object, and any drawing or painting on a surface that can be unhesitatingly recognized as a depiction – that is, a representation of an object in the real world (and not simply a mechanical reproduction of one, as a fossil is) – is a symbol. General questions about representations and depictions for all time periods are discussed in a later section. For the Paleolithic period, there are two issues of prime importance: evaluating the date (and hence in some cases the authenticity), and confirming the status as a depiction. Although it has long been believed that the earliest depictions are of Upper Paleolithic date and produced by *Homo sapiens*, increasing numbers of earlier examples are forcing us to re-examine this supposition.

So far the earliest well-dated product that might securely be described as "art," or at least as "graphic design" (of however modest a kind) is a piece of red ocher with an incised network pattern from the Blombos Cave, South Africa, dating to 77,000 years ago. It is believed to be the work of our own species *Homo sapiens*.

We should, however, note the enormous cognitive significance of the act of depiction itself, in all the vividness seen in the art of Chauvet or Lascaux in France, or Altamira in Spain. We do not yet understand very well, however, why such representation was rare in the Pleistocene (Ice Age) period, or what the significance to their creators of the remarkable depiction of animals in the painted caves of France and Spain may have been (see box overleaf).

Working with Symbols

We are interested in studying how symbols were used. Perhaps we cannot fully understand their meaning, if that implies the full meaning they had for the original users. Without going into a profound analysis, we can define "meaning" as "the relationship between symbols." We can hope to establish some, but by no means all, of the original relationships between the symbols observed.

Paleolithic Art

Cave Art

Much has been written about the Ice Age caves of western Europe, decorated with images of animals and with abstract markings. Clustered in specific regions – most notably the Périgord and Pyrenees in southwest France and Cantabria in northern Spain – they span the whole of the Upper Paleolithic, from about 30,000 BC onward. The majority of the art, however, dates to the latter part of the Ice Age, to the Solutrean and especially the Magdalenian period, ending around 10,000 BC.

The cave artists used a great range of techniques, from simple finger tracings and modeling in clay to engravings and bas-relief sculpture, and from hand stencils to paintings using two or three colors. Much of the art is unintelligible – and therefore classified by scholars as "signs" or abstract marks – but of the figures that can be identified, most are animals. Very few humans and virtually no objects were drawn on cave walls. Figures vary greatly in size, from tiny to more than 5 m (16.5 ft) in length. Some are easily visible and accessible, while others are carefully hidden in recesses of the caves.

The first systematic approach to the study of cave art ("parietal art") was that of the French archaeologist André Leroi-Gourhan, working in the 1960s. Following the lead of Annette Laming-Emperaire, Leroi-Gourhan argued that the pictures formed compositions. Previously they had been seen as random accumulations of individual images, representing simple "hunting magic" or "fertility magic." Leroi-Gourhan studied the

Principal locations of Paleolithic cave art in western Europe.

positions and associations of the animal figures in each cave. He established that horse and bison are by far the most commonly depicted animals, accounting for about 60 percent of the total, and that they are concentrated on what seem to

The spectacular paintings of Chauvet Cave (left), southern France, discovered in 1994, depict more than 440 animals.

An engraving of a mammoth (below) from Cussac Cave in the Dordogne, France.

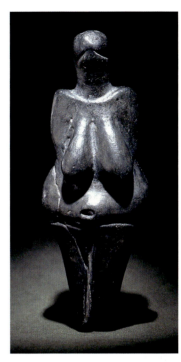

Portable art: three bone carvings from the cave of La Garma, northern Spain, and (right) a recently discovered "Venus" figurine in mammoth ivory from the open-air site of Zaraisk, near Moscow, Russia. (Far right) "Venus" figurine from Dolní Věstonice, Czech Republic.

be the central panels of caves. Other species (e.g. ibex, mammoth, and deer) are located in more peripheral positions, while less commonly drawn animals (e.g. rhinoceroses, felines, and bears) often cluster in the cave depths. Leroi-Gourhan therefore felt sure he had found the "blueprint" for the way each cave had been decorated.

We now know that this scheme is too generalized. Every cave is different, and some have only one figure whereas others (e.g. Lascaux in southwest France) have hundreds. Nevertheless, Leroi-Gourhan's work established that there is a basic thematic unity – profiles of a limited range of animals – and a clearly intentional layout of figures on the walls. Currently, research is exploring how each cave's decoration was adapted to the shape of its walls,

and even to the areas in the cave where the human voice resonates most effectively.

New finds continue to be made – an average of one cave per year, including major discoveries in France, such as Cosquer Cave (1991) near Marseilles, the Ice Age entrance of which is now drowned beneath the sea, and the spectacular Chauvet Cave (1994) in the Ardèche, with its unique profusion of depictions of rhinoceroses and big cats.

In the 1980s and 1990s, however, a series of discoveries also revealed that "cave art" was produced in the open air. Indeed this was probably the most common form of art production in the Ice Age, but the vast majority of it has succumbed to the weathering of many millennia, leaving us with the heavily skewed sample of figures that

survived more readily inside caves. Only a dozen sites are known so far, in Spain, Portugal, and France, but they comprise hundreds of figures, mostly pecked into rocks, which by their style and content are clearly Ice Age in date.

Portable Art

Ice Age portable ("mobiliary") art comprises thousands of engravings and carvings on small objects of stone, bone, antler, and ivory. The great majority of identifiable figures are animals, but perhaps the most famous pieces are the so-called "Venus figurines," such as the limestone Venus of Willendorf, from Austria. These depict females of a wide span of ages and types, and are by no means limited to the handful of obese specimens that are often claimed to be characteristic.

In the pages that follow we shall consider cognitive archaeology in terms of five different uses to which symbols are put.

1   A basic step is the establishment of place by marking and delimiting territory and the territory of the community, often with the use of symbolic markers and monuments, thereby constructing a perceived landscape, generally with a sacred as well as a secular dimension, a land of memories.
2   A fundamental cognitive step was the development of symbols of measurement – as in units of time, length, and weight – which help us organize our relationships with the natural world.
3   Symbols allow us to cope with the future world, as instruments of planning. They help us define our intentions more clearly, by making models for some future intended action, for example plans of towns or cities.
4   Symbols are used to regulate and organize relations between human beings. Money is a good example of this, and with it the whole notion that some material objects have a higher value than others. Beyond this is a broader category of symbols, such as the badges of rank in an army, that have to do with the exercise of power in a society.
5   Symbols are used to represent and to try to regulate human relations with the Other World, the world of the supernatural or the transcendental – which leads on to the archaeology of **religion** and cult.

No doubt there are other kinds of uses for symbols, but this rather simplistic listing will help us in our discussion of how we should set about analyzing them.

Establishing Place: The Location of Memory

One of the fundamental aspects of the cognition of the individual is the establishment of place, often through the establishment of a center, which in

Key Concepts
Working with Symbols

- The human species is distinguished from other life forms by its use of symbols

- Symbols are used by humans for a variety of purposes, some of which can be recognized in the archaeological record:

The marking of place and the definition of territory

The construction of systems of measurement

Design, mapping, and the planning of future actions

Shaping and reflecting social realities, including identity and power relationships

Communicating with supernatural powers in the Other World

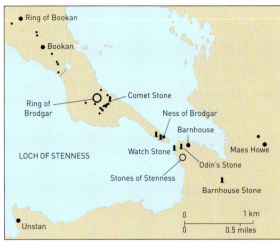

The ceremonial center of Orkney, a ritual landscape in which individuals lived and which in turn shaped their experience and world view. The Ring of Brodgar (left) was one element of a complex and rich sacred landscape (right), which demonstrates that not only large, organized state societies were capable of creating major public works.

a permanent settlement is likely to be the hearth of the home. For a community another significant place is likely to be the burial place of the ancestral dead, whether within the house or at some collective tomb or shrine. For a larger community, whether sedentary or mobile, there may be some communal meeting place, a sacred center for periodic gatherings.

These various **features**, some of them deliberate symbolic constructions, others more functional works that nonetheless are seen to have meaning – the home, the tilled agricultural land, the pasture – together constitute a constructed landscape in which the individual lives. As some archaeologists have pointed out, this landscape structures the experience and the world view of that individual. These observations are just as relevant to small-scale societies as to **state** societies. Many great cities from China to Cambodia and from Sri Lanka to the Maya lowlands and Peru are laid out on cosmological principles, allowing the ruler to ensure harmony between his subjects and the prevailing sacred and supernatural forces. But the sacred center can be important in smaller societies also, and many of those that appear to have had a corporate structure rather than a powerful central leader, were capable of major public works – the temples of Malta and the megalithic centers of Carnac and of Orkney are good examples, as well as Stonehenge and Chaco Canyon. Such monuments can also be used to structure time and can operate to facilitate access to the other, sacred world.

But these things operate also at a local level, not only at great centers. So the entire countryside becomes a complex of constructed landscapes, with meaning as well as of practical use. The landscape is composed of places bringing memories, and the history of the community is told with reference to its significant places. **Landscape archaeology** thus has a cognitive dimension, which takes it far beyond the preoccupation with productive land-use characteristic of a purely materialist approach: the landscape has social and spiritual meaning as well as utility.

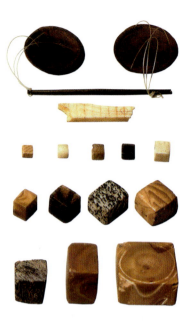

Units of weight: stone cubes from Mohenjodaro, Pakistan, were produced in multiples of 0.836 g (0.03 oz). Scale pans indicate the practical use to which the cubes were put.

Measuring the World

One aspect of an individual's cognition we can readily reconstruct is the way in which it copes with measurement or quantitative description. The development of units was a fundamental cognitive step. In many cases, they can be recovered archaeologically, especially in the case of units of time, length, and weight.

The measurement of time is implied whenever a calendrical system can be documented. It is implied also when alignment, preserving the direction of the sun (or moon) at one of the major turning points can be documented. That is well known to be the case for the major axis of Stonehenge, the great **Neolithic** monument in England, which is oriented toward the midsummer sunrise. Such is also the case for the stone tomb of Newgrange in Ireland, dating from *c.* 3200 BC, the entrance passage of which is oriented toward the midwinter sunrise.

The existence of measurements of weight can be demonstrated by the discovery of objects of standard form that prove to be multiples of a recurrent quantity (by weight), which we can assume to be a standard unit. Such finds are made in many early civilizations. Sometimes the observations are reinforced by the discovery of markings on the objects themselves, which accurately record how many times the standard the piece in question weighs. Systems of coinage are invariably graded using measurement by weight, as well as by material (gold, silver etc.), although their purpose is to measure differences in value. More directly relevant here are discoveries of actual weights.

An excellent example comes from the **site** of Mohenjodaro, a major city of the Indus Valley civilization around 2500–2000 BC. Attractive and carefully worked cubes of colored stone were found there. They proved to be multiples of what we may recognize as a constant unit of mass (namely 0.836 g, or 0.03 oz), multiplied by such integers as 1 or 4 or 8, up to 64, then 320 and 1600.

It can be argued that this simple discovery indicates:

1 that the society in question had developed a concept equivalent to our own notion of weight or mass;
2 that the use of this concept involved the operation of units of measure;
3 that there was a system of numbering, involving hierarchical numerical categories (e.g. tens and units), in this case apparently based on the fixed ratio of 16:1;
4 that the weight system was used for practical purposes (as the finding of scale pans indicates);
5 that there probably existed a notion of equivalence, on the basis of weight among different materials, and hence, it may follow, a ratio of value between them;
6 that this inferred concept of value may have entailed some form of constant rate of exchange between commodities.

Items 5 and 6 are more hypothetical than the others in the list. But it seems a good example of the way that superficially simple discoveries can, when subjected to analysis, yield important information about the concepts and procedures of the communities in question.

Planning: Maps for the Future

The cognitive map that each one of us carries in the "mind's eye" allows us to conceive of what we are trying to do, to formulate a plan, before we do it. Only rarely does the archaeologist find direct material evidence as to how the planning was carried out. But sometimes the product is so complex or so sophisticated that a plan prepared in advance, or a formalized procedure, can be postulated.

It is, of course, difficult to demonstrate purposive planning, if by that is meant the prior formulation of a conscious plan in the construction of some work. At first sight, a village like Çatalhöyük in Turkey (c. 6500 BC), or a sector of an early Sumerian town such as Ur (c. 2300 BC), suggest prior planning. But when we look at the operation of various natural processes we can see that effects of very high regularity can occur simply by repetition within a well-defined scheme. There is no need to suggest that the polyps in a coral reef, or the worker bees in a beehive, are operating according to a conscious plan: they are simply getting on with the job, according to an innate procedure. The layouts of Çatalhöyük and Ur may be no more sophisticated than that. To demonstrate prior planning it is necessary to have some clear evidence that the scheme of construction was envisaged at the outset. Such proof, however, is rarely forthcoming. A few actual maps have come down to us from prehistoric or early historic times; but most probably represent depictions or representations

(Below) The regularity in layout of the Indus Valley city of Mohenjodaro – with main streets approximately at right angles – hints at conscious town planning.

(Below right) The Çatalhöyük village layout (bottom) may have been no more consciously planned than the cells in a beehive (top).

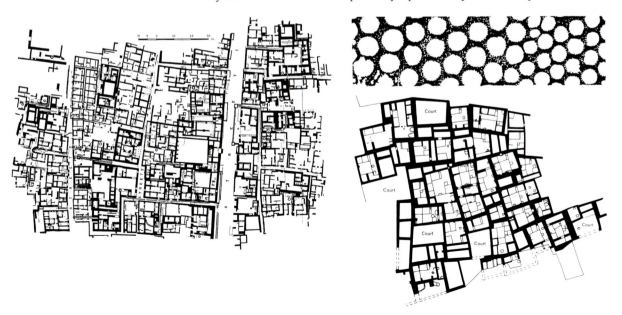

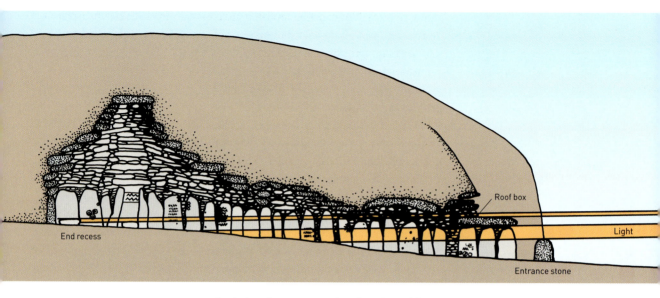

Labels on figure: End recess · Roof box · Light · Entrance stone

Deliberate alignment: the rays of the midwinter sun illuminate the passage and chamber at Newgrange, Ireland.

of existing features, not the planning of future ones. Just occasionally, however, we find models of buildings that may have been constructed before the building itself. There are five or six models of Neolithic temples on the Mediterranean island of Malta that might represent planning in this way: they certainly show close attention to architectural detail.

Such direct projections in symbolic form of the cognitive map of the designer are rare. Sculptors' trial pieces and models, such as have been found in the ancient Egyptian city at Tell el-Amarna, are likewise unusual discoveries.

An alternative strategy is to seek ways of showing that regularities observed in the finished product are such that they could not have come about by accident. That seems to be the case for the passage grave of Newgrange in Ireland, dating from *c*. 3200 BC. At sunrise on midwinter's day the sun shines directly down the passage and into the tomb chamber. There is only a low probability that the alignment would be by chance in the approximate direction of the sun's rising or setting at one of its two major turning points on the horizon. But it is unlikely also that, in terms of altitude, the passage of such a tomb would be aligned on the horizon at all. In fact, there is a special "roof box" with a slit in it, over the entrance, which seems to have been made to permit the midwinter sun to shine through.

Often, careful planning can be deduced from the methods used in a particular craft process. Any metal objects produced by the lost-wax method undoubtedly represent the result of a complex, controlled, premeditated sequence, where a version of the desired shape was modeled in wax before the clay mold was constructed round it, which then allowed the shape in question to be cast in bronze or gold. Another example is the standardization in many early metal-using communities of the proportions of different metals in objects made of alloyed metal. The constant level of 10 percent tin found in the bronze objects of the European Early Bronze Age is not fortuitous: it is evidently the result of carefully controlled procedures that must themselves have been the result of generations of trial and experiment. The use of a unit of length will also document some measure of planning.

Complete regularity in layout, where there is a grid of streets at right angles, evenly spaced, is also a convincing indication of town planning. Traditionally, it is claimed that the Greek architect Hippodamus of Miletus (in the 6th century BC) was the first town planner. But ancient Egypt furnishes much earlier examples – for instance, in the town built by pharaoh Akhenaten at Tell el-Amarna, which dates from the 14th century BC. And the cities of the Indus Valley civilization around 2000 BC show some very regular features. They are not laid out on an entirely rectilinear grid, but the main thoroughfares certainly intersect approximately at right angles. How much of this was deliberate prior planning, and how much was simply unplanned urban growth are questions that have not yet been systematically investigated.

A stronger case for deliberate town planning can be made when the major axis of a city is aligned on an astronomically significant feature, as discussed in the previous section, Measuring the World, and the great Mesoamerican and Andean centers. Paul Wheatley, in his influential book *The Pivot of the Four Quarters* (1971), has emphasized how the desire to harmonize the urban order with the cosmic order influenced town planning. This seems to be true not just for American civilizations but for Indian, Chinese, and Southeast Asian ones as well. The argument is reinforced when the urban order is supplemented by a rich cosmic iconography, as in such cities as Angkor, capital of the Khmer empire, in modern Cambodia.

Symbols of Organization and Power

Symbols are used for regulating and organizing people as well as the material world. They may simply convey information from one person to another, as with language or, as in the case of archival records, from one point in time to another. But sometimes they are symbols of power, commanding obedience and conformity, for example the giant statues of rulers found in many civilizations.

Power relations are sometimes documented graphically, as in the great statues of the Egyptian pharaohs, or on the splendid **stelae** and reliefs of the Maya. For example, Lintel 24 from Yaxchilan shows the ruler ("Shield Jaguar") and his wife during a blood-letting ritual (see overleaf). The glyphs that frame their images give details of their names, the calendar date, and a description of the rite. The images do of course have religious significance, but they also emphasize the role of the ruler and his family in subjecting themselves to this painful ritual for the good of the community. Shield Jaguar holds aloft a flaming torch. He has a magnificent headdress, with feathers at the rear and

5 Eb 15 Mac
9.13.17.15.12
(25 October
AD 709)

It is his
image in
penance

with a
fiery
spear

It is the
penance
of the
4 Katun
Lord

Shield Jaguar III
the captor of

captive's name
(undeciphered)

Divine Pa'chan Lord
(name of local dynasty)

It is her
image in
penance

Lady ?
Xook

Lady
K'abal
Xook

Ix
Kaloomte'
(title)

Lintel 24 from Yaxchilan showing
Shield Jaguar III and his wife,
Lady K'abal Xook, during a sacred
ritual. The glyphs that frame their
images give details of their names
and titles, the calendar date, and
a description of the rite.

the shrunken head of a past sacrificial victim tied to the top of his head by a
headband. The inscription indicates a date in the Maya Long Count calendar
equivalent to October 28, AD 709.

More often, however, power relations are not documented pictorially but
have to be inferred from the **association** of prestigious artifacts made, often with
beautiful craftsmanship, from exotic materials.

Archaeological evidence on its own can in fact yield evidence of scales of
value, as work on the analysis of finds from the late Neolithic cemetery at Varna
in Bulgaria, dating from *c.* 4000 BC, has shown. Numerous golden artifacts were
discovered in the cemetery, constituting what is the earliest known major find of
gold anywhere in the world. But it cannot simply be assumed that the gold is of
high value (its relative abundance in the cemetery might imply the opposite).

Three arguments, however, can be used to support the conclusion that the
gold here was indeed of great worth:

Deducing scales of value: the great worth of the gold from Varna, Bulgaria, is suggested by, among other things, its use to decorate significant parts of the body.

1 Its use for artifacts with evidently symbolic status: e.g. to decorate the haft of a perforated stone axe that, through its fine work and delicate nature, was clearly not intended for use.

2 Its use for ornaments at particularly significant parts of the body: e.g. for face decorations, for a penis sheath.

3 Its use in simulation: sheet gold was used to cover a stone axe to give the impression of solid gold; such a procedure normally indicates that the material hidden is less valuable than the covering material.

The demonstration that gold objects were highly valued by society at this time in ancient Bulgaria also implies that the individuals with whom the gold finds were associated had a high social status. The importance of burials as sources of evidence for social status and ranking was discussed in Chapter 5. Here we are more interested in the use of grave-goods, such as the Varna gold-covered axes, and other discoveries, as symbols of authority and power. The display of such authority is not very pronounced in such a society as the one excavated at Varna, but it becomes more blatant the more hierarchical and stratified the society becomes.

The Archaeology of Religion

One leading English dictionary defines religion as: "Action or conduct indicating a belief in, or reverence for, and desire to please, a divine ruling power." Religion thus involves a framework of beliefs, and these relate to supernatural or superhuman beings or forces that go beyond the everyday material world. In other words superhuman beings are conceptualized by humans, and have a place in the shared cognitive map of the world.

One problem that archaeologists face is that these belief systems are not always given expression in **material culture**. And when they are – in what can be termed the **archaeology of cult** – there is the problem that such actions are not always clearly separated from the other actions of everyday life: cult can be embedded within everyday functional activity, and thus difficult to distinguish from it archaeologically.

The first task of the archaeologist is to recognize the evidence of cult for what it is, and not make the old mistake of classifying as religious activity every action in the past that we do not understand.

Recognition of Cult. If we are to distinguish cult from other activities, such as the largely secular ceremonial that may attend a head of state (which can also have very elaborate symbolism), it is important not to lose sight of the transcendent or supernatural object of the cult activity. Religious ritual involves the performance of expressive acts of worship toward the deity or transcendent being. In this there are generally at least four main components (we will see below how these may then help us draw up a list of aspects that are identifiable archaeologically):

- *Focusing of attention* The act of worship both demands and induces a state of heightened awareness or religious excitement in the human celebrant. In communal acts of worship, this invariably requires a range of attention-focusing devices, including the use of a sacred location, architecture (e.g. temples), light, sounds, and smell to ensure that all eyes are directed to the crucial ritual acts.
- *Boundary zone between this world and the next* The focus of ritual activity is the boundary area between this world and the Other World. It is a special and mysterious region with hidden dangers. There are risks of pollution and of failing to comply with the appropriate procedures: ritual washing and cleanliness are therefore emphasized.
- *Presence of the deity* For ritual to be effective, the deity or supernatural force must in some sense be present. It is the divine as well as human attention that needs to be heightened. In most societies, the deity is symbolized by some material form or image: this need be no more than a very simple symbol – for instance, the outline of a sign or container, the contents of which are not seen – or it may be a three-dimensional cult image, such as a statue.
- *Participation and offering* Worship makes demands on the celebrant. These include not only words and gestures of prayer and respect, but also often active participation involving movement, perhaps eating and drinking. Frequently, it involves also the offering of material things to the deity, both by sacrifice and gift.

An excellent example of cult activity visible in the archaeological record is offered by the site of Göbekli Tepe in Turkey (see box overleaf). Another is the great ceremonial center at Chavín de Huantar in north-central Peru, which flourished from 850 to 200 BC. The most immediately obvious feature of the site is its imposing architecture, comprising a complex of stone-faced platforms built in the earliest phase on a U-shaped plan and set apart from living areas at the site. Ritual involving both conspicuous public display and hidden mysteries is implied by the presence of an open circular sunken plaza that could hold 300 participants, and hidden underground passageways, the most important of which led to a narrow chamber dominated by a 4.5-m- (14-ft-9-in-) high granite shaft known as the Lanzón (Great Image).

The carving on this shaft of a fanged anthropomorphic being, its location in a central chamber facing east along the temple's main axis, and its size and workmanship all suggest that this was the principal cult image of the site. Moreover, some 200 other finely carved stone sculptures were discovered in and around the temple, the **iconography** of which was dominated by images of caymans, jaguars, eagles, and snakes. A cache of more than 500 broken high-quality pots containing food found in an underground gallery may have been

SOUTH AMERICA
• Chavín de Huantar

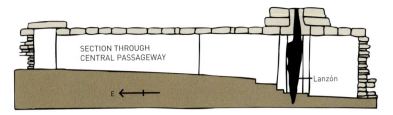

SECTION THROUGH CENTRAL PASSAGEWAY

E ←——

Lanzón

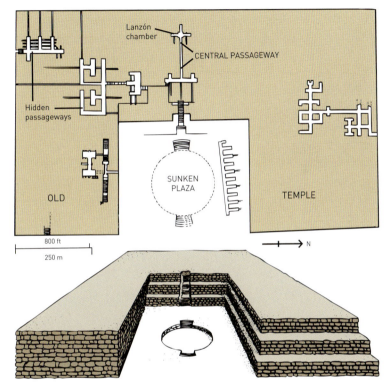

Lanzón chamber

CENTRAL PASSAGEWAY

Hidden passageways

SUNKEN PLAZA

OLD

TEMPLE

800 ft

250 m

N

Perspective and plan views of the early U-shaped platforms at the site, with a section through the central passageway showing the narrow chamber dominated by the Lanzón or Great Image.

Two views of the Lanzón or Great Image (top, complete image; above, rollout drawing), depicting a fanged anthropomorphic being.

Transformation of a masked shaman (left) into a jaguar (right). These sculptures were displayed on the outer wall of the temple, and hint at drug-induced rituals.

The World's Oldest Sanctuary: Gobekli Tepe

The site of Göbekli Tepe, near the town of Urfa in southeast Turkey, can lay claim to be the world's oldest sanctuary. Dating from between 9000 and 8000 BC, it is a large mound 300 m (1,000 ft) in diameter, containing a series of enclosures, perhaps as many as 20, of which 4 are under excavation by Klaus Schmidt of the German Archaeological Institute in Istanbul. Although radiocarbon dates set it contemporary with the very earliest Neolithic of the Levant, Pre-Pottery Neolithic A, there are no traces of cultivated plants at the site, and the fauna includes only wild species, such as gazelle, wild cattle, wild ass, red deer, and wild pig. The society that built and used the site was effectively one of hunter-gatherers. But this was not a settlement site.

Carved Pillars

The most characteristic feature of Göbekli Tepe are the pillars, arranged to create oval structures including up to 12 such pillars, interconnected by stone benches. Each is a T-shaped monolith of limestone standing several meters high and weighing up to 12 tons. The largest, not yet fully excavated, seems to be 5 m (16 ft) high.

Upon these pillars are carvings in relief of animals – lions, foxes, gazelle, wild boar, wild asses, aurochs, snakes, birds, insects, and spiders. The excavator suggests that the

A view of the excavations at Göbekli Tepe. Large T-shaped stone pillars connected by walls and benches form enclosures.

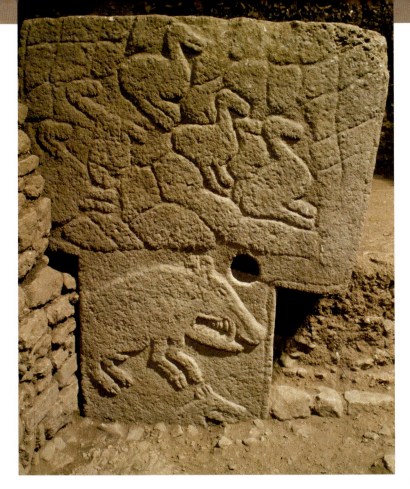

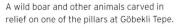
A wild boar and other animals carved in relief on one of the pillars at Göbekli Tepe.

pillars themselves represent stylized humans, the horizontal and vertical elements representing the head and body, for the pillars sometimes show arms and hands in low relief. There are also three-dimensional sculptures of animals, mainly boar, that seem to have been placed on the tops of walls.

Analysis

These enclosures certainly suggest the practice of ritual, with their special architectural forms, meeting the "focusing of attention" criteria discussed in this chapter. Moreover they are rich in animal symbolism. Klaus Schmidt suggests that funerary rituals were practiced there, which he suggests would account for the very considerable labor involved in the construction of each of the enclosures. But no burials have yet been found: Schmidt predicts that they will be discovered beneath the benches or behind the walls of the enclosures when those areas are excavated. Certainly it seems reasonable to suggest that Göbekli Tepe was a special central place, a ritual focus for the regional population. Contemporary villages are known

nearby: Nevali Çori, also excavated by Schmidt, was one such. In it was a small enclosure, likewise containing T-shaped megalithic pillars and life-sized limestone sculptures of humans and animals, which may be regarded as a small sanctuary.

But Göbekli Tepe was much larger and more specialized, lacking the residential accommodation of the village. Ritual practice at this special site seems highly likely. As we have seen, funerary ritual is possible, but not yet documented. Nor is there yet evidence of "deities" (in the sense of beings with transcendent powers) – no iconography to suggest supernatural beings. It is possible, of course, that the rituals at the site involved veneration for the ancestors. So it might be premature to speak of "cult" if that is taken to imply the worship of deities.

What is remarkable, however, is that the use of Göbekli Tepe seems to precede the development of farming in this area – although the site lies close to the region where einkorn wheat was first domesticated. It may have been visited seasonally and need not document a sedentary population. But for the archaeologist interested in the origins of farming in this very area, it is a notable and intriguing site.

offerings (though the excavator believes they were used for storage). There is some evidence for drug-induced rituals and the possibility that canals beneath the site were used for ritual washing and to create roaring sounds to heighten the impact of ceremonies.

The study of Chavín thus demonstrates that a careful archaeological and art historical analysis of different kinds of evidence can produce sound proof of cult activity – even for a site and society concerning which there are no written records whatsoever.

The Impact of Literacy

Symbols of depiction provide us with perhaps our most direct insight into the cognition of an individual or a society for pre-literate periods. Among literate communities, however, written words – those deceptively direct symbols used to describe the world – inevitably dominate the evidence. The locations and dates of the world's earliest writing systems are summarized on the map below.

Ancient literature in all its variety, from poems and plays to political statements and early historical writings, provides rich insights into the cognitive world of the great civilizations. But, to use such evidence accurately and effectively, we need to understand something of the social context of the use of writing in different societies.

The very existence of writing implies a major extension of human cognitive processes. Written symbols have proved the most effective system ever devised by humans not only to describe the world around them, but also to communicate with and control people, to organize society as a whole, and to pass on to posterity the accumulated knowledge of a society.

Map showing locations of the world's earliest writing systems.

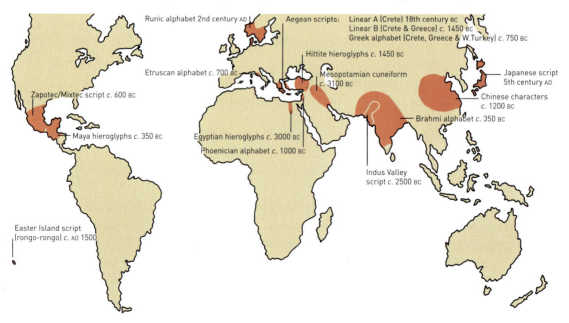

Runic alphabet 2nd century AD

Aegean scripts: Linear A (Crete) 18th century BC
Linear B (Crete & Greece) c. 1450 BC
Greek alphabet (Crete, Greece & W.Turkey) c. 750 BC

Hittite hieroglyphs c. 1450 BC

Etruscan alphabet c. 700 BC

Mesopotamian cuneiform c. 3100 BC

Japanese script 5th century AD

Zapotec/Mixtec script c. 600 BC

Chinese characters c. 1200 BC

Brahmi alphabet c. 350 BC

Maya hieroglyphs c. 350 BC

Egyptian hieroglyphs c. 3000 BC

Phoenician alphabet c. 1000 BC

Indus Valley script c. 2500 BC

Easter Island script (rongo-rongo) c. AD 1500

Literacy in Classical Greece

The importance of literacy is well illustrated by the case of Classical Greece, where literacy was widespread among the population. In several ancient civilizations writing was practiced only by a small segment of the population, notably scribes – for instance in Ancient Egypt or Mesopotamia, and the same was probably true in Mesoamerica. In Greece, however, it is likely that many of the people who had the status of citizens were able to read.

For extended texts, whether works of literature or accounts, the Greeks wrote on papyrus. Examples of such texts have been found at Pompeii and in the very dry conditions of the Faiyum depression in Egypt. For public inscriptions, the Greeks used stone or bronze, although notices that were not of permanent interest were put on display on whitened boards (the simple alphabetic script of the Greeks favored such relatively casual use).

Among the functions of Greek inscriptions carved on stone or bronze were:
- Public decree by the ruling body (council or assembly)
- Award of honors by the ruling body to an individual or group
- Treaty between states
- Letters from a monarch to a city
- List of taxes imposed on tributary states
- Inventories of property and dedications belonging to a deity
- Rules for divination (understanding omens), e.g. from the flight of birds
- Building accounts, records of specifications, contracts, and payments
- Public notices: e.g. list for military service
- Boundary stones and mortgage stones
- Epitaph
- Curse laid on whoever might disturb a particular tomb.

It is clear from this list what an important role writing had within the democratic government of the Greek states.

A better indication of literacy and of the role of writing in Greek daily life is given by the various objects bearing inscriptions, and by comments scrawled on walls (graffiti). One type of object, the *ostrakon*, was a voting ticket in the form of a fragment of pottery with the name of the individual – for (or against) whom the vote was being cast – incised on it. Many have been found in Athens where (by the system of "ostracism") public men could, by a vote of the assembly, be driven into exile. Other Greek uses of writing on a variety of objects were:
- On coins, to show the issuing authority (city)
- To label individuals shown in scenes on wall paintings and painted vases
- To label prizes awarded in competitions
- To label dedications made to a deity
- To indicate the price of goods
- To give the signature of the artist or craftsperson
- To indicate jury membership (on a jury ticket).

Potsherds (*ostraka*) inscribed with two famous Greek names: Hippokrates (above) Themistokles (below).

Many of these simple inscriptions enable us to glimpse aspects of everyday life in Ancient Greece, and even to identify and learn things about individuals. The British Museum has a black-figure drinking cup of *c.* 530 BC, made in Athens and imported to Taranto, Italy, bearing the inscription: "I am Melousa's prize: she won the maiden's carding contest."

It can be seen from this brief summary that writing touched nearly every aspect of Classical Greek life, private as well as public. The cognitive archaeology of ancient Greece thus inevitably draws to a great extent on the insights provided by such literary evidence – as will become apparent, for example, in our discussion of procedures for identifying supernatural beings in art and individual artists. But we should not imagine that cognitive archaeology is thus necessarily dependent on literary sources to generate or test its theories.

Textual evidence is indeed of paramount importance in helping us understand ways of thought among literate societies but, as we saw above for the Paleolithic period, there are in addition purely archaeological sources that may be used to create theories about the thought processes of ancient individuals and peoples, and purely archaeological criteria to judge their validity. Moreover, literary sources may themselves be biased in ways that need to be fully assessed before any attempt can be made to match such sources with evidence from the archaeological record.

Study Questions

- What are symbols and how do they relate to cognitive archaeology?
- What are some of the ways in which humans use symbols?
- How do archaeologists and anthropologists investigate the cognitive abilities of our hominin ancestors?
- What are some of the ways in which the people of the past measured their world?
- How do archaeologists recognize religion or cult in the archaeological record?
- What was the role of writing in Classical Greek daily life?

Summary

- In this chapter we have shown how archaeological evidence can be used to provide insights into the way of thinking of cultures and civilizations long dead.

- Whether it be evidence for measurement, means of organization and power, or cult activity – there are good archaeological procedures for analyzing and testing cognitive hypotheses about the past. An archaeological project may focus on one aspect of the way ancient people thought (for example, in the search for a possible standard unit of measurement), or it may be much broader (for example, the work at Chavín). While textual evidence may be of crucial importance in supporting or helping to assess cognitive claims – as in Mesoamerica or Mesopotamia – cognitive archaeology does not depend on literary sources for its validity.

Further Reading

The following provide an introduction to the study of the attitudes and beliefs of ancient humans:

Arsuaga, J.L. 2003. *The Neanderthal's Necklace: In Search of the First Thinkers*. Four Walls Eight Windows: New York.

Aveni, A.F. (ed.). 2008. *People and the Sky: Our Ancestors and the Cosmos*. Thames & Hudson: London & New York.

Bahn, P. G. 2014. *Images of the Ice Age*. Oxford University Press: Oxford.

Johnson, M. 2010. *Archaeological Theory*. Blackwell: Oxford.

Marshack, A. 1991. *The Roots of Civilization* (2nd ed.). Moyer Bell: New York.

Renfrew, C. & Zubrow E.B.W. (eds). 1994. *The Ancient Mind: Elements of Cognitive Archaeology*. Cambridge University Press: Cambridge & New York.

Renfrew, C. 2009. *Prehistory: Making of the Human Mind*. Modern Library: New York.

[See p. 345 for a list of useful websites]

Why Did Things Change?
Explanation in archaeology

10

To answer the question "why?" is the most difficult task in **archaeology**. We must go beyond simply describing the appearance of things and try to *understand* the pattern of events.

This is the goal motivating many who take up the study of the human past. There is a desire to learn something from a study of what is dead and gone that is relevant for the conduct of our own lives and our societies today. Archaeology, which allows us to study early and remote prehistoric periods as well as the more recent historical ones, is unique among the human sciences in offering a considerable time depth. Thus, if there are patterns to be found among human affairs, the archaeological timescale may reveal them.

There is no agreed and accepted way of setting out to understand the human past. A chapter such as this is therefore bound to be inconclusive, and certain to be controversial. But it is a chapter worth writing and worth thinking about, for it is in this area of inquiry that archaeological research is now most active. The main debates have developed over the past 40 years or so.

Traditional explanations of change in the past focused on the concepts of **diffusion** and migration – they assumed that changes in one group must have been caused either by the influence or influx of a neighboring and superior group. But in the 1960s the development of the **processual** approach of the so-called New Archaeology exposed the shortcomings of the earlier explanations. It was realized that there was no well-established body of theory to underpin archaeological inquiry (to a large extent this is still true, although there have been many attempts).

The early New Archaeology involved the explicit use of theory and of models, and above all of generalization. It was criticized, however, as being too much concerned with ecological aspects of adaptation and with efficiency, and with the purely utilitarian and functional aspects of living (in other words, it was too "functionalist"). Meanwhile, an alternative perspective, inspired by Marxism, was laying more stress on social relations and the exercise of power.

Strategies of Explanation

- *Migrationist and Diffusionist*: explanations rely on rather simple ideas of the supposed migrations of peoples, or the often ill-defined spread of ideas

- *Processual*: attempts to provide more general explanations (using, for instance, evolutionary theory), sometimes using law-like formulations, and (more successfully) framing hypotheses and testing deductions from these against the data

- *Postprocessual or Interpretive*: emphasizes the specific context, drawing sometimes on structuralist or neo-Marxist ideas, stressing often the role ("agency") of the individual, and avoiding the generalizations of the processual approach

From the 1970s, in reaction to the processual "functionalists," some archaeologists favored a **structuralist** archaeology and then a **postprocessual** one. These approaches stressed that the ideas and beliefs of past societies should not be overlooked in archaeological explanation.

Since that time archaeologists have given more systematic attention to the way humans think, how they make and use **symbols**, and to what may be described as cognitive issues. One approach, today termed "**cognitive archaeology**," seeks to work in the tradition of processual archaeology while stressing social and cognitive aspects.

So far there is no single, widely agreed approach.

Migrationist and Diffusionist Explanations

The New Archaeology made the shortcomings of traditional archaeological explanations much more apparent. These shortcomings can be made clearer in an example of the traditional method – the appearance of a new kind of pottery in a given area and period, the pottery being distinguished by shapes not previously recognized and by new decorative motifs. The traditional approach will very properly require a closer definition of this pottery **style** in space and time. The archaeologist will be expected to draw a distribution map of its occurrence, and also to establish its place in the stratigraphic sequence at the **sites** where it occurs. The next step is to assign it to its place within an archaeological **culture**.

Using the traditional approach, it was argued that each archaeological culture is the manifestation in material terms of a specific people – that is, a well-defined ethnic group, detectable by the archaeologist by the method just outlined. This is an ethnic classification, but of course the "people," being prehistoric, were given an arbitrary name. Usually, they were named after the place where the pottery was first recognized (e.g. the Mimbres people in the American Southwest), or sometimes after the pottery itself (e.g. the Beaker Folk).

Next it was usual to see if it is possible to think in terms of a folk migration to explain the changes observed. Could a convenient homeland for this group of people be located? Careful study of the ceramic **assemblages** in adjoining lands might suggest such a homeland, and perhaps even a migration route.

Alternatively, if the migration argument did not seem to work, a fourth approach was to look for specific features of the cultural assemblage that have parallels in more distant lands. If the whole assemblage cannot be attributed to an external source, there may be specific features of it that can. Links may be found with more civilized lands. If such "parallels" can be discovered, the traditionalist would argue that these were the points of origin for the features in our assemblage, and were transmitted to it by a process of cultural diffusion. Indeed, before the advent of **radiocarbon dating**, these parallels could also be used to date the pottery finds in our hypothetical example, because the features and traits lying closer to the heartlands of civilization would almost certainly already be dated through comparison with the historical chronology of that civilization.

It would be easy to find many actual examples of such explanations. For instance, in the New World, the very striking developments in architecture and other crafts in Chaco Canyon in New Mexico have been explained by comparisons of precisely this kind with the more "advanced" civilizations of Mexico to the south.

Traditional explanations rest, however, on assumptions that are easily challenged today. First, there is the notion among traditionalists that archaeological "cultures" can somehow represent real entities rather than merely the classificatory terms devised for the convenience of the scholar. Second is the view that ethnic units or "peoples" can be recognized from the archaeological record by equation with these notional cultures. It is in fact clear that ethnic groups do not always stand out clearly in archaeological remains. Third, it is assumed that when resemblances are noted between the cultural assemblages of one area and another, this can be most readily explained as the result of a migration of people. Of course, migrations did indeed occur (see below), but they are not so easy to document archaeologically as has often been supposed.

Finally, there is the principle of explanation through the diffusion of culture. Today, it is felt that this explanation has sometimes been overplayed, and nearly always oversimplified. For although contact between areas, not least through trade, can be of great significance for the developments in each area, the effects of this contact have to be considered in detail: explanation simply in terms of diffusion is not enough.

Nevertheless it is worth emphasizing that migrations did take place in the past, and on rare occasions this can be documented archaeologically. The colonization of the Polynesian islands in the Pacific offers one example. A complex of finds –

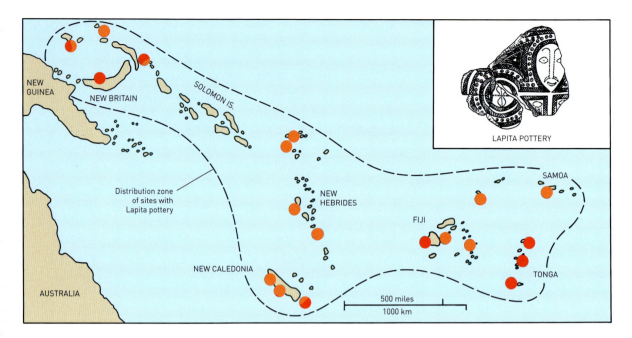

LAPITA POTTERY

Distribution zone
of sites with
Lapita pottery

500 miles
1000 km

Migration: a positive example. The question of first settlement of the Polynesian islands has apparently been resolved by the discovery of the Lapita culture, which is characterized in particular by pottery with incised decoration. Lapita sites provide a record of the rapid movement of islanders by boat, eastwards from the northern New Guinea region to as far as Samoa in western Polynesia, between 1600 and 1000 BC.

especially pottery with incised decoration – known as the Lapita culture provides a record of the rapid movement of islanders eastward across a vast uninhabited area, from the northern New Guinea region to as far as Samoa, between 1600 and 1000 BC (see above). Also, innovations are frequently made in one place and adopted in neighboring areas, and it is still perfectly proper to speak of the mechanism as one of diffusion (see illustration of the origins of the Roman alphabet, below). A good example of what was first a migrationist explanation, and then became a diffusionist explanation, until it was subsequently rejected, is offered by the case of Great Zimbabwe (see box opposite).

Diffusion: a positive example. One instance where an innovation in one place is known to have spread widely elsewhere through diffusion is that of the alphabet. Around the 12th century BC, on the Levantine coast, the Phoenicians developed a simplified phonetic script to write their Semitic language. By the early 1st millennium BC, the script had been adapted by the Greeks to write their language. Then the Greek alphabet was modified in Italy, to write Etruscan and Latin, the Roman language. It was through Latin that our own alphabet (known as the Roman alphabet) came to much of Europe, and later the rest of the world.

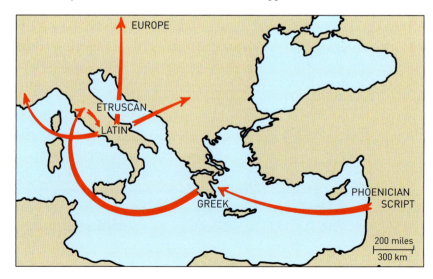

EUROPE

ETRUSCAN

LATIN

GREEK

PHOENICIAN
SCRIPT

200 miles
300 km

Explaining Great Zimbabwe

The remarkable monument of Great Zimbabwe, near Masvingo in modern Zimbabwe, has been the object of intense speculation ever since the region was first explored by Europeans in the 19th century. For here was an impressive structure of great sophistication, with beautifully finished stonework.

Early scholars ascribed the site to builders from "more civilized" lands to the north. During a visit by the British explorer Cecil Rhodes, the local Karange chiefs were told that "the Great Master" had come "to see the ancient temple which once upon a time belonged to white men." This was thus a migrationist view.

Systematic excavations were undertaken by Gertrude Caton-Thompson (p. 34), and she concluded her report in 1931: "Examination of all the existing evidence, gathered from every quarter, still can produce not one single item that is not in accordance with the claim of Bantu origin and medieval date." But despite this, other archaeologists continued to offer diffusionist explanations in speaking of "influences" from "higher centers of culture." Portuguese traders were one favored source of inspiration.

Subsequent research has backed up the conclusions of Caton-Thompson. Great Zimbabwe is now seen as the most notable of a larger class of monuments in this area.

The conical tower (right) is one of the most impressive features at the site.

Carved soapstone bird (below) found at Great Zimbabwe in 1903, and one of eight from the site. The motif adorns the modern Zimbabwean flag, banknotes, and coinage.

Archaeologists are now able to give a coherent picture of the economic and social conditions in the area in the 13th to 15th centuries AD that made the great achievement of the construction of the monument possible. Significant influence – diffusion – from more "advanced" areas is no longer part of that picture.

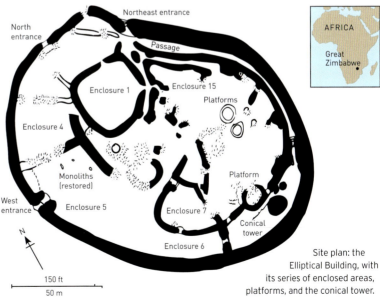

Site plan: the Elliptical Building, with its series of enclosed areas, platforms, and the conical tower.

The Processual Approach

The processual approach attempts to isolate and study the different processes at work within a society, and between societies, placing emphasis on relations with the environment, on subsistence and the economy, on social relations within the society, on the impact that the prevailing ideology and belief system have on these things, and on the effects of the interactions taking place between the different social units.

It is a characteristic of processual explanations that they have usually focused on ecological and social factors the operation of which can be analyzed in some detail. Sometimes a systems model is used, looking at the interaction of what may be defined as the subsystems of the culture system. A good early example of a processual explanation, even though today it is regarded as incomplete, is offered by Lewis Binford's explanation for the origins of sedentary society and of a farming economy.

In 1968, Binford published an influential paper, "Post-Pleistocene Adaptations," in which he set out to explain the origins of farming, or food production. Attempts to do this had been made by earlier scholars. But Binford's explanation had one important feature that distinguished it from earlier explanations and made it very much a product of the New Archaeology: its generality. For he was setting out to explain the origins of farming not just in the Near East or the Mediterranean – although he focused on these areas – but also worldwide. He drew attention to global events at the end of the last Ice Age (i.e. at the end of the Pleistocene epoch, hence the title of his paper).

Binford centered his explanation on demography: he was concerned with population dynamics within small communities, stressing that once a formerly mobile group becomes sedentary – ceases to move around – its population size will increase markedly. For in a settled village the constraints no longer operate that, in a mobile group, severely limit the number of small children a mother can rear. There is no longer the difficulty, for instance, of carrying children from place to place. Crucial to the question was the fact that in the Near East some communities (of the Natufian culture around 9000 BC) did indeed become sedentary before they were food-producing. He could see that, once settled, there would be considerable population pressure, in view of the greater number of surviving children. This would lead to increasing use of such locally available plant foods as wild cereals, which had hitherto been considered marginal and of little value. From the intensive use of cereals, and the introduction of ways of processing them, would develop the regular cycle of sowing and harvesting, and thus the course of plant-human involvement leading to domestication would be well underway.

But why did these pre-agricultural groups become sedentary in the first place? Binford's view was that rising sea levels at the end of the Pleistocene (caused by the melting of polar ice) had two significant effects. First, they reduced the extent of the coastal plains available to the **hunter-gatherers**. And second, the new habitats created by the rise in sea level offered to human groups much greater access to migratory fish and to migrant fowl. Using these rich resources, rather as the inhabitants of the Northwest Coast of North America have done in more recent times, the hunter-gatherer groups found it possible for the first time to lead a sedentary existence. They were no longer obliged to move.

In some respects Binford's explanation is seen today as rather too simple. Nevertheless, it has many strengths. Although the focus was on the Near East, the same arguments can equally be applied to other parts of the world. Binford avoided migration or diffusion, and analyzed the origins of farming in processual terms.

Marxist Archaeology

Following the upsurge in theoretical discussion that followed the initial impact of the New Archaeology, there was a reawakening of interest in applying to archaeology some of the implications of the earlier work of Karl Marx. Marx was an extremely influential 19th-century philosopher and political economist. Although his work covered a wide range of issues, he is most famous for his analysis of history in terms of conflicts between social classes.

The key feature of "**Marxist archaeology**," then, is that change within a past society was caused mainly by the contradictions that arise between the forces of production and social organization. Characteristically these contradictions emerge as a struggle between classes (if this is a society where distinct social classes have already developed). Emphasis on class struggle and internal differences is a feature of most Marxist explanations: this is a view of the world where change comes about through the resolution of internal dissent. It may be contrasted with the "functionalist" view favored by the early New Archaeology, where selective pressures toward greater efficiency are seen to operate and changes are often viewed as mutually beneficial.

In traditional Marxism the ideology of a society – the whole system of knowledge and belief – is seen as largely determined by the nature of the economic base. This point is disputed by the "neo-Marxists" who regard ideology and economics as interrelated and mutually influential, rather than one as dominant and the other subordinate.

There are many positive features that Marxist analyses share with processual archaeology, but, in comparison with the processual studies of the New Archaeologists, many such Marxist analyses seem rather short on the handling of concrete archaeological data. The gap between theoretical archaeology and field archaeology is not always effectively bridged, and the critics of Marxist archaeology sometimes observe that since Karl Marx laid down the basic principles more than a century ago, all that remains for the Marxist

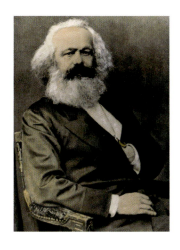

Karl Marx.

archaeologists to do is to elaborate them: research in the field is superfluous. Despite these differences, processual archaeology and Marxist archaeology have much in common.

Evolutionary Archaeology

Evolutionary archaeology explores the notion that the processes responsible for biological **evolution** (as set out by Charles Darwin) also drive culture change.

Proponents see the modern mind as the product of biological evolution, and argue that the only way so complex an entity can have arisen is by natural selection. In particular they argue that the human mind evolved under the selective pressures faced by hunter-gatherers during the Pleistocene period, and that our minds remain adapted to that way of life. Several writers have followed this lead, seeking to place the evolution of mind in an explicitly evolutionary framework. These are fascinating insights, but they have not yet been supported by any neurological analysis of the hardware of the brain and of its evolution.

Evolutionary archaeologists in the United States advocate the application of Darwinian evolutionary theory to the archaeological record. They can justifiably point to long-standing cultural traditions in different parts of the world that reflect the inheritance of cultural traits from generation to generation. It could be argued that they have shown how the transmission of human culture can validly be seen in Darwinian evolutionary terms. However, it is less clear that to analyze culture change in those terms offers fresh insights not already available to archaeologists. Evolutionary archaeology has not yet produced case studies of culture change that explain its processes more coherently or persuasively than other approaches: that is the challenge that it currently faces.

The Form of Explanation: Specific or General?

To understand these debates within archaeology it is useful to consider what exactly we mean by "explanation." The different things we try to explain might require different kinds of explanation.

There are two completely opposite forms of explanation. The first approach is specific: it seeks to know more and more of the details surrounding an event. It assumes that if we can establish enough of what led up to the event we hope to explain, then that event itself will become much clearer for us. Such explanation has sometimes been called "historical."

Some historical explanations lay great stress on any insights we can gain into the ideas of the historical people in question, and for that reason are sometimes termed idealist. If you want to know why an action was taken it is necessary to get inside the mind of the decision-maker, and thus to know as many of the surrounding details, and as much about his or her life, as possible.

The second form of explanation, that of the New Archaeology, lays much more stress on generalization. The early New Archaeologists sought for "regularities," for patterns in the data, and turned to the philosophy of science (of the time) for help. Unluckily, perhaps, they turned to the American philosopher Carl Hempel, who argued that all explanations should be framed in terms of natural laws. A lawlike statement is a universal statement, meaning that in certain circumstances (and other things being equal) X always implies Y, or that Y varies with X according to a certain definite relationship. Hempel argued that the events we might be seeking to explain could be accounted for by bringing together two things: the detailed circumstances leading up to the event, and the "law" that would allow us to forecast what actually happened.

A few New Archaeologists tried to write archaeology in the form of universal laws. Most, however, saw that it is very difficult to make universal laws about human behavior that are not either very trivial, or untrue. Some archaeologists, such as Kent Flannery, saw that when Hempel's approach was applied to archaeology, it produced only "Mickey Mouse laws" of little conceivable value. Flannery's favorite example was: "as the population of a site increases, the number of storage pits will go up."

One of the positive contributions of the New Archaeology, however, was in fact to follow the scientific convention of making specific and explicit, as far as is possible, the assumptions on which an argument rests. It makes very good sense to formulate a hypothesis, establish by **deduction** what would follow from it if it were true, and then to see if these consequences are in fact found in the archaeological record by testing the hypothesis against fresh data. Processual archaeologists argued that it is this willingness to test our beliefs and assumptions against real data that separates a scientific approach from mere uncontrolled speculation.

Explanation: One Cause or Several?

As soon as we start to address the really big questions in archaeology, explanation becomes a very complicated matter: many of the big questions refer not to a single event, but to a class of events.

One of the biggest questions, for example, is the development of urbanization and the emergence of **state** societies. This process apparently happened in different parts of the world independently. Each case was, in a sense, no doubt unique. But each was also a specific instance of a more general process. In just the same way, a biologist can discuss (as Darwin did) the process by which the different species emerged, without denying the uniqueness of each species, or the uniqueness of each individual within a species.

If we focus now on the origins of urbanization and the state as an example, we shall see that this is a field where many different explanations have been offered. Broadly speaking, we can distinguish between explanations that concentrate largely on one cause (**monocausal explanations**) and those that consider a number of factors (**multivariate explanations**).

Monocausal Explanations: The Origins of the State

If we look at different monocausal explanations in turn, we shall find that some of them are in their way very plausible. Often, however, one explanation works more effectively than another when applied to a particular area – to the emergence of the state in Mesopotamia, for instance, or in Egypt, but not necessarily in Mexico or in the Indus Valley. Each of the following examples today seems incomplete. Yet each makes a point that remains valid.

The Hydraulic Hypothesis. The historian Karl Wittfogel, writing in the 1950s, explained the origin of the great civilizations in terms of the large-scale irrigation of the alluvial plains of the great rivers. It was, he suggested, this alone that brought about the fertility and the high yields, which led to the considerable density of population in the early civilizations, and hence to the possibility of urbanism. At the same time, however, irrigation required effective management – a group of people in authority who would control and organize the labor needed to dig and maintain irrigation ditches, etc. So irrigation and "hydraulic organization" had to go together, and from these, Wittfogel concluded, emerged a system of differentiated leadership, greater productivity and wealth, and so on.

Wittfogel categorized the system of government characteristic of those civilizations founded on irrigation agriculture as one of "oriental despotism." Among the civilizations to which this line of thinking has been applied are:

- Mesopotamia: the Sumerian civilization from *c.* 3000 BC and its successors
- Ancient Egypt: the Valley of the Nile from *c.* 3000 BC
- India/Pakistan: the Indus Valley civilization from *c.* 2500 BC
- China: the Shang civilization, *c.* 1500 BC, and its successors

Internal Conflict. In the late 1960s the Russian historian Igor Diakonoff developed a different explanation for state origins. In his model, the state is seen as an organization that imposes order on class conflict, which itself arises from increased wealth. Internal differentiation within the society is here seen as a major causative element, from which other consequences follow.

Warfare. Warfare between adjacent groups is increasingly seen as an agent of change. While in some cases there were cyclical conflicts with little long-term effect, in others the result was conquest and the formation of larger, inclusive state societies. Kent Flannery has emphasized the historically documented role of individual military leaders in the initial formation of state societies (an example of the "agency" of the individual, see below).

Population Growth. An explanation much favored by many archaeologists focuses on the question of population growth. The 18th-century English scholar Thomas Malthus argued that human population tends to grow to the limit permitted by the food supply. When the limit or "carrying capacity" is reached, further population increase leads to food shortage, and this in turn leads to an increased death rate and lower fertility (and in some cases to armed conflict). That sets a firm ceiling on population.

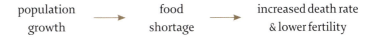

population growth → food shortage → increased death rate & lower fertility

Esther Boserup, in her influential book *The Conditions of Agricultural Growth* (1965), effectively reversed the position of Malthus. He had viewed food supply as essentially limited. She argued that agriculture will intensify – farmers will produce more food from the same area of land – if population increases. In other words, by shortening the periods during which land is left to lie fallow, or by introducing the plow, or irrigation, farmers can increase their productivity. Population growth can then be sustained to new levels.

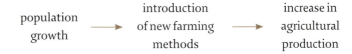

population growth → introduction of new farming methods → increase in agricultural production

So increase of population leads to intensification of agriculture, and to the need for greater administrative efficiencies and economies of scale, including the development of craft specialization. People work harder because they have to, and the society is more productive. There are larger units of population, and consequent changes in the settlement pattern. As numbers increase, any decision-making machinery will need to develop a hierarchy. Centralization ensues, and a centralized state is the logical outcome.

Environmental Circumscription. A different approach, although one that uses some of the variables already indicated, is offered by Robert Carneiro. Taking as his example the formation of state society in Peru, he developed an explanation that laid stress on the constraints ("circumscription") imposed by the environment, and on the role of warfare. Population increase is again an important component of his model, but the model is put together in a different way, and the development of strong leadership in time of war is one of the key factors.

External Trade. The importance of trading links with communities outside the homeland area has been stressed by several archaeologists seeking explanations for the formation of the state. One of the most elaborate of these is the model put forward by the American archaeologist William Rathje for the emergence of state societies in the Maya lowlands. He argued that in lowland areas lacking basic raw materials there will be pressure for the development of more integrated and highly organized communities able to ensure the regular supply of those materials. He used this hypothesis to explain the rise of the Classic Maya civilization in the lowland rainforest.

Multivariate Explanations: The Classic Maya Collapse

All the preceding explanations for the origins of the state primarily emphasize one chief variable, a principal strand in the explanation, even though there are several strands involved. In reality, when there are so many factors at work, there is something rather too simplified about such monocausal explanations. It is necessary somehow to be able to deal with several factors at once: that is why such explanations are termed multivariate. Of course, none of the explanations summarized above is so naive as to be truly monocausal: each involves a number of factors. But these factors are not systematically integrated. Several scholars have therefore sought ways of coping with a large number of variables that simultaneously vary.

One example of a multivariate explanation has been developed for the collapse of Classic Maya society in the 9th century AD (see box overleaf).

Postprocessual or Interpretive Explanation

After the mid-1970s, the early New Archaeology we can term here functional-processual archaeology came under criticism from several quarters. For example, early on it was criticized by Bruce Trigger in his book *Time and Tradition* (1978), who found the approach, which sought to formulate explanatory laws, too constraining. He preferred the broadly descriptive approach of the traditional historian. It was also criticized by Kent Flannery, who was scornful of the trivial nature of some of the so-called laws proposed and felt that more attention should be focused on the ideological and symbolic aspects of societies. Ian Hodder, likewise, felt that archaeology's closest links were with history, and wanted to see the role of the individual in history more fully recognized.

Hodder also very validly stressed what he called "the active role of material culture," emphasizing that the **artifacts** and the material world we construct are not simply reflections of our social reality that become embodied in the material record. On the contrary, material culture and actual objects are a large part of what makes society work: wealth, for instance, is what spurs many to work in a modern society. Hodder goes on to assert that material culture is "meaningfully constituted," or in other words that it is the result of deliberate actions by individuals whose thoughts and actions should not be overlooked.

Discussions of these issues led some archaeologists in Britain and in the United States to create the postprocessual archaeology of the 1990s, overcoming some of what they saw as the limitations of processual archaeology (and indeed much of traditional Marxist archaeology also). These debates are now largely over, but the result is a series of interesting approaches that together will shape the "interpretive archaeologies" of the early 21st century, operating alongside the continuing processual or **cognitive-processual** tradition.

Structuralist Approaches

Several archaeologists have been influenced by the structuralist ideas of the French anthropologist Claude Lévi-Strauss, and by the advances in linguistics of the American Noam Chomsky. Structuralist archaeologists stress that human actions are guided by beliefs and symbolic concepts, and that the proper object of study is the structures of thought – the ideas – in the minds of human actors who made the artifacts and created the archaeological record. These archaeologists argue that there are recurrent patterns in human thought in different cultures, many of which can be seen in such polar opposites as: cooked/raw; left/right; dirty/clean; man/woman, etc. Moreover, they argue that thought categories seen in one sphere of life will be seen also in other spheres, so that, for example, a preoccupation with boundaries in the field of social relations is likely to be detectable in other areas, such as "boundaries" visible in pottery decoration.

Critical Theory

Critical Theory is the term given to the approach developed by the so-called "Frankfurt School" of German social thinkers, which came to prominence in the 1970s. This stresses that any claims to seek "objective" knowledge are illusory. By their interpretive approach these scholars seek a more enlightened view, which will break out of the limitations of existing systems of thought. They see research workers (including archaeologists) who claim to be dealing in a scientific way with social matters as tacitly supporting the "ideology of control" by which domination is exercised in modern society.

This overtly political critique has serious implications for archaeology. For the philosophers of this school stress that there is no such thing as an objective fact. Facts only have meaning in relation to a view of the world, and in relation to theory. Followers of this school are critical of the criterion of testing as used by processual archaeologists, seeing this procedure as merely the importing into archaeology and history of "positivistic" approaches from the sciences. They call into question most of the procedures of reasoning by which archaeology has operated.

The Classic Maya Collapse

Contrary to widespread belief, Maya civilization did not suffer a single, sudden, and total collapse. When the Spaniards reached northern Yucatan in the early 16th century they found dense populations of Maya-speaking people living in hundreds of thriving local polities.

Archaeologists now know that cycles of collapse and recovery were common in Maya society for 1500 years. The earliest "big" collapse occurred in the Mirador Basin of northern Guatemala, where huge centers thrived in the Middle and Late Preclassic. By around AD 150 this region was largely abandoned (and never substantially recovered) and there is evidence that ecosystems there and elsewhere were increasingly degraded.

The Classic period (AD 250–900) southern Maya lowlands also saw many local collapses, as Maya capitals and their dynastic lines waxed and waned, as well as a final collapse in the 10th century.

Collapse in the Southern Lowlands

The final collapse in the southern lowlands has long been the most celebrated and difficult to explain because of its scale and because there was no recovery in that region. In AD 750 this vast area supported a population of at least several million people divided among 40–50 major kingdoms. But eight centuries later, when Europeans arrived, it was almost deserted. Explorers in the 19th century told of imposing and overgrown ruins, creating romanticized impressions of a catastrophic collapse. By the beginning of the 20th century scholars could decipher dates carved on Maya monuments. These suggested a steady expansion of and vigor in Maya civilization beginning in the 3rd century AD, peak activity around AD 790, and then a precipitous decline in monument building over the next 120 years, which signaled the collapse of centralized rulership. Although only elite activity was directly reflected in these data, in the absence of other information it was presumed that each Classic political system and population suffered a catastrophic collapse in one or two generations.

We now know that the collapse process was much more complicated and protracted. Most scholars agree that the decline began at least as early as AD 760, when centers in the west of the region were abandoned during well-documented cycles of destructive warfare. Centers elsewhere continued to erect monuments for some time, the last in about AD 909. Royal building projects ceased – sometimes very suddenly – and no more royal burials were interred. Although some polities and capitals collapsed abruptly and with clear signs of violence, others were abandoned more gradually (and apparently peacefully). If our perspective is the whole southern lowlands, the disintegration of centralized political institutions thus occurred over a period of roughly 150 years (although some imposing centers did somehow survive the troubles).

What happened to the populations associated with the defunct Classic capitals is a more controversial issue. Many regions do appear to have suffered abrupt demographic declines, but others did not. At Copan, for example, elite activity continued in some sub-royal palace compounds until about AD 1000, and the overall population dwindled away over some four centuries.

Explaining the Collapse

Any explanation of the collapse must account for all this complexity, and the best approach, before making broad generalizations, is to determine what happened to particular centers. Our efforts are also hindered by our ignorance (or disagreements) concerning Maya agricultural

Temple I at Tikal, Guatemala, built around AD 740–750. Tikal was one of the great Maya centers, but was almost completely deserted after AD 950.

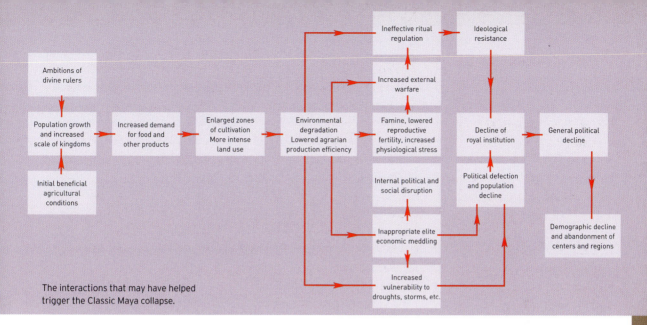

The interactions that may have helped trigger the Classic Maya collapse.

strategies, how people asserted claims to resources, and the details of social, political, and economic institutions. Nevertheless, archaeologists have discarded or demoted some influential earlier explanations, such as the idea that oppressive demands for labor caused peasants to rebel.

Most archaeologists do agree that no single cause can explain what happened. Instead, a set of interlocked stresses, such as overpopulation, deterioration of the agricultural landscape, famine, disease, warfare, internal social unrest, climate change, and ideological fatigue increasingly afflicted the Late Classic Maya (see diagram). None of these stresses was new, and earlier Maya kingdoms had survived them. The Late Classic Maya, however, were more numerous and contentious than ever, and had inherited an unusually fragile ecosystem shaped and degraded by centuries of human use. Populations peaked in the 8th

century, and over-shot the capacity of the agricultural landscape. The whole shaky edifice of Classic society came down, although it was more of a slump than a crash.

Some causes were certainly more important than others. Most recently, paleoclimatologists have postulated a series of droughts in the interval between AD 770 and 1100. Some believe this was the single most important trigger of the collapse, affecting food production in an increasingly damaged and vulnerable landscape. Others disagree because the climate data are inconsistent, and because the northern Maya, who lived in the driest part of the lowlands, still thrived – especially at Chichen Itza.

Although materialist stresses were probably most important, there were also social and ideological components to the collapse. Warfare intensified, and there are signs at some centers of internal unrest. Sub-royal elites in such kingdoms as

Copan became increasingly assertive and competitive. Evidence from some centers reveals the violent elimination of whole royal families, although it is not always clear by whom. The ancient Maya were also adaptively constrained by their own ideology, particularly their obsessive focus on maize not just as a food, but also as an almost mystical substance. Kingship, the central institution of Maya political life, stressed the supernatural potency of rulers. Kings projected themselves as the great guarantors of prosperity and stability, and manifestly were unable to deliver on these promises during the critical 8th and 9th centuries. Many things about the collapse were gradual, but the rejection of kingship and its monuments, art, burials, palaces, and inscriptions appears to have been everywhere abrupt. Even where Maya populations survived for centuries, they did not revive the old royal ways of Classic times.

The processualists' response to these ideas is to point out that to follow them seems to imply that one person's view of the past is as good as another's (so-called "relativism"), without any hope of choosing systematically between them. This would open the way to the "fringe" or "alternative" archaeologies discussed in Chapter 11, where explanations can be offered in terms of flying saucers, or extraterrestrial forces, or any fantasies that the human mind may conjure up. It is not entirely clear how the Critical Theorists can answer this criticism.

Neo-Marxist Thought

Neo-Marxist thought places a much greater emphasis on the significance of ideology in shaping change in societies than does traditional Marxism (which treats ideology as subordinate to economy). One example of a neo-Marxist approach is offered by the work of Mark Leone at Annapolis in Maryland, as part of a research project concerned with establishing a deeper historical identity for the area. His example is the 18th-century garden of William Paca, a wealthy landowner: the garden has been studied archaeologically and has now been reconstructed.

Leone examines the Annapolis garden in detail, and emphasizes the contradiction represented between a slave-owning society and one proclaiming independence in order to promote individual liberty, a contradiction seen also in Paca's life. "To mask this contradiction," Leone writes, "his position of power was placed in law and in nature. This was done both in practicing law and in gardening."

This neo-Marxist outlook has its echo in the emerging local archaeologies of some countries in the developing world, where there is an understandable desire to construct a history (and an archaeology) that lays stress on the local population and its achievements before the colonial era (see Chapter 11).

Cognitive Archaeology

During the 1980s and 1990s a new perspective emerged, which transcends some of the limitations of functional-processual archaeology of the 1970s. This new synthesis, known as cognitive archaeology (or "cognitive-processual" archaeology), while willingly learning from any suitable developments in postprocessual archaeology, remains in the mainstream of processual archaeology. It still wishes to explain rather than merely describe. It also still emphasizes the role of generalization within its theoretical structure, and stresses the importance not only of formulating hypotheses but also of testing them against the data. It rejects the total relativism that seems to be the end point of Critical Theory, and it is suspicious of structuralist (and other) archaeologists who claim privileged insight into "meaning" in ancient societies, or proclaim "universal principles of meaning."

Key Concepts
Cognitive Archaeology

Cognitive archaeology is the study of the ways of thought and structures of belief of past societies on the basis of their material remains. It:

- attempts to use the more rigorous and explicit methods of the processual approach

- applies these to symbolic and ideological issues, many of which were first addressed by postprocessual or interpretive approaches (e.g. questions of identity, gender, and religious belief in the past)

- shows willingness to address the symbolizing and reasoning abilities of hominins before the emergence of *Homo sapiens*, sometimes within an evolutionary framework

- accepts the postprocessual emphasis on the active role of material culture

- recognizes that cognitive developments are also social developments

Cognitive-processual archaeology differs from its functional-processual predecessor in several ways:

1 It seeks actively to incorporate information about the cognitive and symbolic aspects of early societies into its formulations (see overleaf).
2 It recognizes that ideology is an active force within societies and must be given a role in many explanations, as neo-Marxist archaeologists have argued, and that ideology acts on the minds of individuals.
3 Material culture is seen as an active factor in constituting the world in which we live. Individuals and societies construct their own social reality, and material culture has an integral place within that construction, as effectively argued by Ian Hodder and his colleagues.
4 The role of internal conflict within societies is a matter to be more fully considered, as Marxist archaeologists have always emphasized.
5 The rather limited view of historical explanation being entirely related to the human individual should be revised.
6 It can take account of the creative role of the individual without relying on intuition or becoming extremely subjective.
7 "Facts" can no longer be viewed as having an objective existence independent of theory.

This last point needs further discussion. Philosophers of science have long contrasted two approaches to the evaluation of the truth of a statement. One evaluates the statement by comparing it with relevant facts, to which, if true, it should correspond. The other evaluates the statement by judging whether or not it is consistent with the other statements that we believe to be true within our framework of beliefs. Although it might be expected that the scientist would follow the first of these two procedures, in practice any assessment is based on a combination of the two. For it is accepted that facts have to be based on observations, and observations themselves cannot be made without using some framework of inference, which itself depends on theories about the world. It is more appropriate to think of facts modifying theory, yet of theory being used in the determination of facts.

Cognitive-processual archaeologists, like their functional-processual predecessors, believe that theories must be tested against facts. They reject the relativism of the Critical Theory and postprocessual archaeology of the 1990s. They do, however, accept that the relationship between fact and theory is more complicated than some philosophers of science 40 years ago recognized.

Symbol and Interaction

The point has already been made that the early New Archaeology aspired to investigate social structures. But it was slow to explore symbolic aspects of culture, which is why cognitive-processual archaeology is a recent development.

The role of religious ritual within society has been investigated in a new way over the past 30 years by the cultural anthropologist Roy Rappaport. Instead of seeking to immerse himself in the agricultural society in New Guinea under study, becoming totally familiar with the meanings of its symbolic forms, he followed instead a strategy of distancing himself – of looking at the society from the outside, at what it actually does (not what it says it does) in its ritual behavior. This position is a convenient one for the archaeologist who is always outside the society under study, and unable to discuss issues of meaning with its participants. Rappaport has studied the way ritual is used within society and his focus is on the functioning of symbols rather than on their original meaning.

His work influenced Kent Flannery, one of the few of the original generation of New Archaeologists to concern himself in detail with symbolic questions. The book written by Joyce Marcus and Kent Flannery, *Zapotec Civilization* (1996), is one of those rare archaeological studies where symbolic and cognitive questions are integrated with subsistence, economic, and social ones to form an integrated view of society.

Quite clearly **religion** and such other ideologies as modern Communism have brought about great changes, not just in the way societies think but also in the way they act and behave – and this will leave its mark in the archaeological record. The whole field of official symbolism, and of religious symbolism within it, is now the focus of archaeological research in several parts of the world.

Postprocessual archaeology has not shown itself adept at explaining classes of events or general processes, since the focus in postprocessual thought is upon the specific conditions of the context in question, and the validity of wider or cross-cultural generalizations is not accepted. Cognitive-processual archaeology on the other hand is very willing to generalize, and indeed to integrate the individual into the analysis as an active agent.

Two studies in the mainstream processual tradition exemplify well the emphasis that is now placed upon the cognitive dimension. Timothy Earle in *How Chiefs Come to Power* devotes successive chapters to economic power, military power, and ideology as a source of power, utilizing three widely separated case studies situated in Denmark, Hawaii, and the Andes.

And, likewise treating the subject within a comparative perspective, Richard Blanton has examined the sources of power in early states, contrasting the "cognitive-symbolic base of power" with what he terms the "objective base of power." The study fully integrates the cognitive dimension into the analysis, alongside economic issues. In such works the limitations of the earlier processual archaeology have been transcended and the roots of change are investigated with full weight being given to the cognitive and the symbolic dimensions.

Agency and Material Engagement

In the past decade or so archaeologists working in different conceptual traditions have sought in various ways to integrate the cognitive and symbolic on the one hand with the practical and productive on the other. One aim is to reconcile the short-term intentions or agency of the individual with the long-term and often unintended consequences of cumulative actions. Archaeologists who take this approach hope to combine a broad outline of processes of change with the finer texture of specific culture histories.

Agency

The concept of agency has been introduced to permit discussion of the role of the individual in promoting change, but the scope of the term is not always clear, particularly when used, as by some anthropologists, as a quality that can be assigned to artifacts as well as to people. The various discussions of agency attempt to illuminate the role of the individual, but it is very difficult to determine clearly how the actions of one individual had a wider and longer-term impact.

Material Engagement

A related notion, that change arises from conscious and often purposeful human activities, is associated with the recently developed concepts of material engagement or materialization. These seek to overcome the duality in discussions of human affairs between the practical and the cognitive, the material and the conceptual. Indeed most innovations and long-term changes in human societies, even technical ones, have a symbolic dimension as well as a material one, involving what the philosopher John Searle terms "institutional facts," which are themselves social creations.

The material engagement approach is one of several that gives greater attention to things and the material properties of things, and the different interactions between humans and the material world that come about through developing technologies and changing social and economic relations.

There is still a tension also between those using archaeology to write culture history (usually of a single society) and those using evolutionary thinking to analyze long-term change. Each perspective has clear coherence and validity, but the two rarely seem to mesh together.

In these different approaches to the explanation of change there is some commonality of aspiration and this may yet lead to interesting new developments. But there is no single theoretical perspective that commands universal or even widespread respect.

Study Questions

- Why is archaeology unique among the human sciences?
- What are the key differences between processual and postprocessual archaeology?
- What is Marxist archaeology and how is it different from the New Archaeology?
- What are some monocausal explanations for the origins of the state?
- What is Critical Theory and what are its implications for archaeology?
- Is there a correct way to explain change in the past?

Summary

- It is difficult to explain *why* things happened in the past, yet this must be one of the key tasks of archaeology.

- Explanations in terms of the migrations of people or using the rather vague idea of the "diffusion" of culture used to be very popular: today they are less frequent.

- The processual approach has consistently tried to see broader patterns and general explanations. In general, multivariate (several-factor) explanations work better than monocausal (single-factor) explanations for such complex outcomes as the origins of state societies.

- Interpretive explanations, on the other hand, usually emphasize the specific context. Both approaches converge toward a cognitive archaeology that acknowledges the role of human intelligence, creativity, and initiative.

- Yet there remain several different approaches to the difficult task of explanation. Some scholars advocate the notion of human agency, others analyze the knowledgeable engagement between humans and the material world. This remains an under-developed area of archaeological theory.

Further Reading

The broad topics covered in this chapter are explored in:

DeMarrais, E., Gosden, C. & Renfrew, C. (eds). 2004. *Rethinking Materiality, the Engagement of Mind with the Material World*. McDonald Institute: Cambridge.

Earle, T. 1997. *How Chiefs Come to Power, the Political Economy in Prehistory*. Stanford University Press.

Gamble, C. 2007. *Origins and Revolutions: Human Identity in Earliest Prehistory*. Cambridge University Press: Cambridge & New York.

Hodder, I. 2004. *Reading the Past* (3rd ed.). Cambridge University Press: Cambridge & New York.

Malafouris, L. 2013. *How Things Shape the Mind: A Theory of Material Engagement*. MIT Press: Cambridge, Mass.

Mithen, S. 1999. *The Prehistory of the Mind*. Thames & Hudson: London & New York.

Renfrew, C. 2003. *Figuring It Out – the Parallel Visions of Artists and Archaeologists*. Thames & Hudson: London & New York.

Renfrew C. 2007. *Prehistory: Making of the Human Mind*. Weidenfeld & Nicolson: London; Modern Library: New York.

Shennan, S. 2002. *Genes, Memes and Human History*. Thames & Hudson: London & New York.

Webster, D.L. 2002. *The Fall of the Ancient Maya*. Thames & Hudson: London & New York.

[See p. 345 for a list of useful websites]

Whose Past?
Archaeology and the public

This book is concerned with the way that archaeologists investigate the past, with the questions we can ask, and our means of answering them. But the time has come to address much wider questions: Why, beyond reasons of scientific curiosity, do we want to know about the past? What does the past mean to us? What does it mean to others with different viewpoints? Whose past is it anyway?

These issues lead us to questions of responsibility, public as well as private. For surely a national monument, such as the Parthenon in Athens, means something special to the modern descendants of its builders? Does it not also mean something to all humankind? If so, should it not be protected from destruction, in the same way as endangered plant and animal species? If the looting of ancient **sites** is to be deplored, should it not be stopped, even if the sites are on privately owned land? Who owns, or should own, the past?

These very soon become ethical questions – of right and wrong, of appropriate action and reprehensible action. The archaeologist has a special responsibility because **excavation** itself entails destruction. Future workers' understanding of a site can never be much more than our own, because we will have destroyed the evidence and recorded only those parts of it we considered important and had the energy to publish properly.

The past is big business – in tourism and in the auction rooms. But by their numbers tourists threaten the sites they seek to enjoy; and the plunder of looters and illegal excavators finds its way into private collections and public museums. The past is politically highly charged, ideologically powerful, and significant. And the past, as we shall see in the next chapter, is subject to increasing destruction through unprecedented commercial, industrial, and agricultural exploitation of the earth's surface and through damage in war.

The Meaning of the Past: The Archaeology of Identity

When we ask what the past means, we are asking what the past means for us, for it means different things to different people. An Australian Aborigine, for example, may attach a very different significance to fossil human remains from such an early site as Lake Mungo, or to paintings in the Kakadu National Park, than a white Australian. Different communities have very different conceptions about the past that often draw on sources well beyond **archaeology**.

At this point we go beyond the question of what actually happened in the past, and of the explanation of why it happened, to issues of meaning, significance, and interpretation. And it is at this point, therefore, that many of the concerns that have become explicit in archaeology over the past couple of decades become entirely relevant. How we interpret the past, how we present it (for instance in museum displays), and what lessons we choose to draw from it are to a considerable extent matters for subjective decision, often involving ideological and political issues.

For in a very broad sense the past is where we came from. Individually we each have our personal, genealogical past: our parents, grandparents, and earlier kinsfolk from whom we are descended. Increasingly in the Western world there is an interest in this personal past, reflected in the enthusiasm for family trees and for "roots" generally. Our personal identity, and generally our name, are in part defined for us in the relatively recent past, even though those elements with which we choose to identify are largely a matter of personal choice. Nor is this inheritance purely a spiritual one. Most land tenure in the world is determined by inheritance, and much other wealth is inherited: the material world in this sense comes to us from the past, and is certainly, when the time comes, relinquished by us to the future.

Either Philip II of Macedon, father of Alexander the Great, or Philip III, Alexander's half-brother, was buried in a gold casket decorated with an impressive star. This was adopted as the national symbol of the Former Yugoslav Republic of Macedonia, as seen on one of their stamps.

Nationalism and its Symbols

Collectively our cultural inheritance is rooted in a deeper past: the origins of our language, our faith, our customs. Increasingly archaeology plays an important role in the definition of national identity. This is particularly the case for those nations that do not have a very long written history, though many consider oral histories of equal value to written ones. The national emblems of many recently emerged nations are taken from **artifacts** seen as typical of some special and

early local golden age: even the name of the state of Zimbabwe comes from the name of an archaeological site.

Yet sometimes the use of archaeology and of images recovered from the past to focus and enhance national identity can lead to conflict. In the 1990s a major crisis related to the name and national emblems adopted by the then newly independent Former Yugoslav Republic of Macedonia. For in Greece, immediately to the south, the name Macedon refers not only to contemporaneous provinces within Greece, but also to the ancient kingdom of that famous Greek leader, Alexander the Great. The affront that the name caused in Greece was compounded by the use by the FYR Macedonia of a star as a

(Left) The larger of the colossal Buddhas of Bamiyan, carved from the cliff face in perhaps the 3rd century AD, and now destroyed. (Center) The moment of destruction. (Right) What remains of the statue today.

national symbol, using the image on a gold casket found among the splendid objects in a tomb from the 4th century BC at Vergina, a tomb located well within modern Greek territory, thought to have belonged either to Philip II of Macedon, the father of Alexander, or to Philip III, Alexander's brother. Territorial claims can sometimes be based on contentious histories, and some Greeks thought that the FYR Macedonia was seeking not only to appropriate the glorious history of Macedonia but perhaps also to incorporate Greece's second city, Thessaloniki, within its territorial boundaries. Riots ensued, based, however, more on inflamed ethnic feelings than upon political reality.

Archaeology and Ideology

The legacy of the past goes beyond sentiments of nationalism and **ethnicity**. Sectarian sentiments often find expression in major monuments, and many Christian churches were built on the site of deliberately destroyed "pagan" temples. In just a few cases they actually utilized such temples – the Parthenon in Athens is one example – and one of the best preserved Greek temples is now the Cathedral in Syracuse in Sicily.

Religious extremism is responsible for many acts of destruction. The senseless demolition in March 2001 by the Taliban of the two giant Buddhas carved into the sandstone cliffs at Bamiyan, in the Hindu Kush, perhaps in the 3rd century AD, shocked the world. The only motivation seems to have been that these were religious images not in accordance with the faith of the Taliban. Despite a delegation from the Islamic Conference, at which 55 Islamic nations were represented, the destruction went ahead. Standing 53 and 36 m high (174 and 118 ft), these were the tallest standing Buddhas in the world; explosive charges destroyed them almost totally.

3 That world vanished in a catastrophe of cosmic proportions.

4 Nothing of that original homeland is available for scientific examination, nor are any artifacts surviving.

The basic structure of Donnelly's argument was repeated with variants by Immanuel Velikovsky (meteors and astronomical events) and recently by Graham Hancock (who sites his lost continent in Antarctica). A popular alternative, elaborated with great financial profit by Erich von Däniken, is that the source of progress is outer space, and that the advances of early civilizations are the work of aliens visiting earth. Ultimately, however, all such theories trivialize the much more remarkable story that archaeology reveals – the history of humankind.

Fraud in Archaeology. Fraud in archaeology is nothing new and takes many forms – from the manipulation of evidence by Heinrich Schliemann to such infamous cases of fakery as Britain's Piltdown Man. It has been suggested that more than 1200 fake antiquities are displayed in some of the world's leading museums. A particularly serious example came to light as recently as 2000, when a leading Japanese archaeologist admitted planting artifacts at excavations. Shinichi Fujimura – nicknamed "God's hands" for his uncanny ability to uncover ancient objects – had been videotaped burying his "discoveries" before digging them up again as new finds. He admitted having buried dozens of artifacts in secret, claiming that it was the pressure of having to discover older sites that forced him to fake them by using artifacts from his own collections.

Of 65 pieces unearthed at the Kamitakamori site north of Tokyo, Fujimura admitted to having faked 61, together with all 29 pieces found in 2000 at the Soshinfudozaka site in northern Japan. He later admitted having tampered with evidence at 42 sites; but in 2004 the Japanese Archaeological Association declared that all of the 168 sites he dug had been faked. Japanese archaeological authorities are understandably worried about the potential impact on evidence for the Early **Paleolithic** period in Japan unearthed since the mid-1970s.

A cluster of handaxes at Kamitakamori faked by Japanese archaeologist Shinichi Fujimura.

It seems that this phenomenon may currently be on the rise. Some of this can be blamed on the increased "mediatization" of the field, where, as in Japan, it can be important to generate publicity to further one's career, and scientific publication often takes a back seat to press conferences where the latest finds are trumpeted. Spectacular discoveries are now sometimes seen as more important than scholarly debate or critical review. Nevertheless, the actual fabrication or planting of fake objects is an extreme form of fraud. Japanese archaeologists are worried that there may be other fraudulent artifacts, yet to be unearthed, a situation that has been likened to "archaeological landmines," ready to wreak havoc on future generations of scholars.

The Wider Audience.   Although the immediate aim of most research is to answer specific questions, the fundamental purpose of archaeology must be to provide people with a better understanding of the human past. Skillful popularization – using site and museum exhibits, books, television, and increasingly the Internet – is therefore required, but not all archaeologists are prepared to devote time to it, and few are capable of doing it well.

Excavators often regard members of the public as a hindrance to work on-site. More enlightened archaeologists, however, realize the financial and other support to be gained from encouraging public interest, and they organize information sheets, open days, and on long-term projects even fee-paying daily tours, as at the Bronze Age site of Flag Fen in eastern England. In Japan, on-the-spot presentations of excavation results are given as soon as a dig is completed. Details are released to the press the previous day, so that the public can obtain information from the morning edition of the local paper before coming to the site itself.

Clearly, there is an avid popular appetite for archaeology. In a sense, the past has been a form of entertainment since the early digging of burial mounds and the public unwrapping of mummies in the 19th century. The entertainment may now take a more scientific and educational form, but it still needs to compete with rival popular attractions if archaeology is to thrive.

Who Owns the Past?

Until recent decades, archaeologists gave little thought to the question of the ownership of past sites and antiquities. Most archaeologists themselves came from Western, industrialized societies the economic and political domination of which seemed to give an almost automatic right to acquire antiquities and excavate sites around the world. Since World War II, however, former colonies have grown into independent nation states eager to uncover their own past and assert control over their own heritage. Difficult questions have therefore arisen. Should antiquities acquired for Western museums during the colonial era be returned to their lands of origin? And should archaeologists be free to excavate the burials of groups whose modern descendants may object on religious or other grounds?

Museums and the Return of Cultural Property

At the beginning of the 19th century Lord Elgin, a Scottish diplomat, removed many of the marble sculptures that adorned the Parthenon, the great 5th-century BC temple that crowns the Acropolis in Athens. Elgin did so with the permission of the then Turkish overlords of Greece, and later sold the sculptures to the British Museum, where they still reside, displayed in a special gallery. The Greeks now want the "Elgin Marbles" back.

The Greek claim for the return of the Acropolis marbles from the British Museum has been given greater force by the construction of the new Acropolis

Museum. Plaster casts of all the "Elgin Marbles" now take their places in the appropriate positions in the original sculptural scheme, along with those sculptures that remained in Athens. These now sit there, patiently awaiting the hoped-for return of their long-lost relatives. That in essence is the story so far of perhaps the best-known case where an internationally famous museum is under pressure to return cultural property to the country of origin.

But there are numerous other claims directed at European and North American museums. The Berlin Museum, for example, holds the famous bust of the Egyptian queen Nefertiti, which was shipped out of Egypt illegally. The Greek government has officially asked France for the return of the Venus de Milo, one of the masterworks of the Louvre, bought from Greece's Ottoman rulers. And Turkey has recently been successful in recovering art treasures, including the "Lydian Hoard," from New York's Metropolitan Museum of Art (which has also returned the now infamous "Euphronios Vase" to Italy, see p. 312), and may now pursue Turkish statuary and objects in European countries, including the British Museum.

(Top) The New Acropolis Museum in Athens, built to house the marbles from the Parthenon (seen through the window) that are still in Athens and, one day (it is hoped), the "Elgin Marbles" too. (Above) Part of the "Elgin Marbles" in the British Museum: a horseman from the frieze of the Parthenon in Athens, c. 440 BC.

Excavating Burials: Should We Disturb the Dead?

The question of excavating burials can be equally complex. For prehistoric burials the problem is not so great, because we have no direct written knowledge of the relevant **culture**'s beliefs and wishes. For burials dating from historic times, however, religious beliefs are known to us in detail. We know, for example, that the ancient Egyptians and Chinese, the Greeks, Etruscans, and Romans, and the early Christians all feared disturbance of the dead. Yet it has to be recognized that tombs were falling prey to the activities of robbers long before archaeology began. Egyptian pharaohs in the 12th century BC had to appoint a commission to inquire into the wholesale plundering of tombs at Thebes. Not a single Egyptian royal tomb, including that of Tutankhamun, escaped the robbers completely. Similarly, Roman carved gravestones became building material in cities and forts; and at Ostia, the port of ancient Rome, tomb inscriptions have even been found serving as seats in a public latrine!

The Native Americans.   For some Native Americans in North America, archaeology has become a focal point for complaints about wrongdoings of the past. They have expressed their grievances strongly in recent years, and their political influence has resulted in legal mechanisms that sometimes restrict or prevent archaeological excavations, or provide for the return to Native American peoples of some collections now in museums. Apart from the question of returning and/or reburying material, sometimes there have been vehement objections to new excavations. The Chumash, for example, refused permission for scientists to remove what may be the oldest human remains in California, even though an offer was made to return and rebury the bones after a year's study. The bones, thought to be about 9000 years old, were eroding out of a cliff on Santa Rosa Island, 100 km (62 miles) west of Los Angeles. Under California's state laws the fate of the bones lay with their most likely descendants – and the Chumash were understandably angry about past treatment of their ancestors' skeletons, with hundreds of remains scattered in various universities and museums. They preferred to see the bones destroyed "in accordance with nature's law" than to have other people interfere with them. In other cases, however, Native American communities have provided for the systematic curation of such remains once they have been returned to them.

As in Australia (see overleaf), there is no single, unified indigenous tradition. Native Americans have wide-ranging attitudes toward the dead and the soul. Nonetheless demands for reburial of ancestral remains are common. The solution to the problem has been found to lie in acquiescence, compromise, and collaboration. Often archaeologists have supported the return of remains of fairly close ancestors of living people. Material has also been returned that had no archaeological **context** and was thus of minimal value to science.

Repatriation of older and more important material is a difficult issue. The longstanding position of the Society for American Archaeology is that scientific and traditional interests in archaeological materials must be balanced, weighted by the closeness of relationship to the modern group making a claim and the scientific value of the remains or objects requested. With the Society's support, in 1990 the Native American Graves Protection and Repatriation Act (NAGPRA) was passed. It requires some 5000 federally funded institutions and government agencies to inventory their collections and assess the "cultural affiliation" of Native American skeletons, funerary and sacred objects, and items of cultural patrimony. If cultural affiliation can be shown, the human remains and objects must, on request, be returned to the affiliated Native American tribe or Native Hawaiian organization. Difficult problems lie in interpreting key terms in the law, such as "cultural affiliation," and in weighing diverse forms of evidence in the context of prehistoric material. In addition to archaeological and historical information, the law explicitly recognizes the validity of oral traditions. This has led to broad expectations by tribes that prehistoric remains can be claimed if their oral traditions say that its people were created in the same region where the remains were found. However, when these expectations were tested in court it was found that the law requires a balanced consideration of oral tradition with scientific evidence.

An amendment to the NAGPRA regulations in 2010 extended rights to culturally unaffiliated remains as long as these were found on tribal lands or areas of aboriginal occupation. This means that US museums will now have to relinquish control of many more human remains to tribal groups.

Controversy and a legal battle dogged the bones of "Kennewick Man," found in 1996 in Washington State, and radiocarbon dated to 9300 BP. Eight prominent

(Left) Seminole bones from Florida are reburied in 1989 by archaeologists and Native Americans at Wounded Knee.

(Right) Facial features of Kennewick Man during reconstruction, with muscles added in clay.

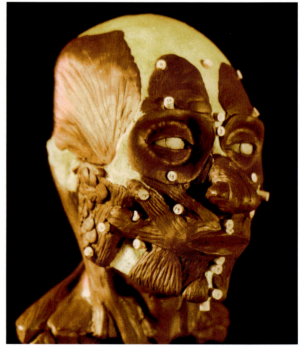

anthropologists sued the Army Corps of Engineers, which has jurisdiction over the site, for permission to study the bones, but the Corps wanted to hand the skeleton to the local Native American Umatilla Tribe for reburial, in accordance with NAGPRA. The scientists were extremely anxious to run tests, since preliminary examination had suggested that Kennewick Man was a 19th-century settler; its early date raises complex, important and fascinating questions about the peopling of the Americas. The Umatilla, on the other hand, were adamantly against any investigation, insisting that their oral tradition says their tribe has been part of this land since the beginning of time, and so all bones recovered from here are necessarily their ancestors – and must not be damaged for dating or genetic analysis. In 2002 a magistrate affirmed the right of the scientists to study the bones and, despite subsequent legal appeals, in June 2005 the battle (which cost millions of dollars in legal fees) was finally won, and analysis began in earnest.

The Australian Aborigines.   In Australia, the present climate of Aboriginal emancipation and increased political power has focused attention on wrongdoings during the colonial period, when anthropologists had little respect for Aboriginal feelings and beliefs. Sacred sites were investigated and published, burial sites desecrated, and cultural and skeletal material exhumed, to be stored or displayed in museums. The Aborigines were thus, by implication, seen as laboratory specimens. Inevitably, the fate of all this material, and particularly of the bones, has assumed great symbolic significance. Unfortunately, here as in other countries, archaeologists are being blamed for the misdemeanors of the non-archaeologists who obtained most of the human remains in question.

The view of Aborigines in some parts of Australia is that all human skeletal material (and occasionally cultural material too) must be returned to them, and then its fate will be decided. In some cases they themselves wish the remains to be curated in conditions that anthropologists would consider to be satisfactory, usually under Aboriginal control. Since the Aborigines have an unassailable moral case, the Australian Archaeological Association (AAA) is willing to return remains that are either quite modern or of "known individuals where specific descendants can be traced," and for these to be reburied. However, such remains are somewhat the exception. The University of Melbourne's Murray Black Collection consists of skeletal remains from more than 800 Aborigines, ranging in date from several hundred years to at least 14,000 years old. They were dug up in the 1940s without any consultation with local Aborigines. Owing to a lack of specialists the collection has still by no means been exhaustively studied – but nevertheless it has been returned to the relevant Aboriginal communities. In 1990 the unique series of burials from Kow Swamp, 19,000 to 22,000 years old, were handed back to the Aboriginal community and reburied; more recently the first skeleton found at Lake Mungo, the world's oldest known cremation

(26,000 years BP), was returned to the custody of the Aborigines of the Mungo area; and Aboriginal elders have announced they may rebury all the skeletal material (up to 30,000 years old) from Mungo.

Archaeologists are understandably alarmed at the prospect of having to hand over material many thousands of years old. Some also point out that the Aborigines – like indigenous peoples elsewhere – tend to forget that not all of their recent forebears took pious care of the dead. But, not least in the light of Aboriginal sufferings at European hands, their views are entitled to respect.

The Responsibility of Collectors and Museums

It has become clear in recent years that private collectors and even public museums, for centuries regarded as guardians and conservators of the past, have become (in some cases) major causative agents of destruction. The market in illegal antiquities – excavated illegally and clandestinely with no published record – has become a major incentive for the looting of archaeological sites. The looting is funded, whether directly or indirectly, by unscrupulous private collectors and by unethical museums. All over the world looters are continuing their destructive work. Several languages have a word for them: in Greece they are *archaiokapiloi*, in Latin America *huaqueros*. Italy has two special words: *clandestini* and *tombaroli*. They unearth beautiful, salable objects. But deprived of their archaeological context, these objects no longer have the power to tell us much that is new about the past. Many of them end up on display in some of the less scrupulous museums of the world. When a museum fails to indicate the context of discovery, including the site the exhibit came from, it is often a sign that the object displayed has come via the illicit market.

One such *clandestino*, Luigi Perticarari, a robber in Tarquinia, Italy, published his memoirs in 1986 and makes no apology for his trade. He has more first-hand knowledge of Etruscan tombs than any archaeologist, but his activity destroys the chance of anyone sharing that knowledge. He claims to have emptied some 4000 tombs dating from the 8th to the 3rd centuries BC in 30 years. So it is that, while the world's store of Etruscan antiquities in museums and private collections grows larger, our knowledge of Etruscan burial customs and social organization does not.

The same is true for the remarkable marble sculptures of the Cycladic islands of Greece, dating to around 2500 BC. We admire the breathtaking elegance of these works in the world's museums, but we have little idea of how they were produced or of the social and religious life of the Cycladic communities that made them. Again, the contexts have been lost.

In the American Southwest, 90 percent of the Classic Mimbres sites (c. AD 1000) have now been looted or destroyed (see box opposite). In southwestern Colorado, 60 percent of prehistoric Ancestral Pueblo sites have been vandalized. Pothunters work at night, equipped with two-way radios, scanners, and

Destruction and Response: Mimbres

UNITED STATES
• Mimbres

The Mimbres potters of the American Southwest created a unique art tradition in the prehistoric period, painting the inside of hemispherical bowls with vigorous animal and human forms. These bowls are now much admired by archaeologists and art lovers. But this fascination has led to the systematic looting of Mimbres sites on a scale unequaled in the United States, or indeed anywhere in the world.

The Mimbres people lived along a small river, the Río Mimbres, in mud-built villages, similar in some respects to those of the later Puebloans. Painted pottery began, as we now know, around AD 550, and reached its apogee in the Classic Mimbres period, from about AD 1000 to 1130.

Systematic archaeological work on Mimbres sites began in the 1920s, but it was not in general well published. Looters soon found, however, that with pick and shovel they could unearth Mimbres pots to sell on the market for primitive art. Nor was this activity necessarily illegal. In United States law there is nothing to prevent excavation of any kind by the owner on private land, and nothing to prevent the owner permitting others to destroy archaeological sites in this way (although some state laws, in New Mexico and Arizona, for example, now protect human burials on both private and state land).

In the early 1960s, a method of bulldozing Mimbres sites was developed that did not destroy all the pottery. The operators found that by controlled bulldozing they could remove a relatively small depth of soil at a time and extract many of the pots unbroken. In the process, sites were of course completely destroyed, and all hope of establishing an archaeological context for the material was lost.

Since 1973 there has at last been a concerted archaeological response. The Mimbres Foundation, under the

(Top) Mimbres bowl from the Classic period, showing a ritual decapitation. (Above) Animalian forms were a popular Mimbres subject. The "kill" hole allowed the object's spirit to be released.

direction of Steven LeBlanc, was able to secure funding from private sources to undertake excavations in the remains of some of the looted sites. It also made good progress in explaining to the owners of those sites how destructive this looting process was to any hope of learning about the Mimbres' past. From 1975 to 1978 a series of field seasons at several partially looted sites succeeded in establishing at least the outlines of Mimbres archaeology, and in putting the chronology upon a sure footing.

The Mimbres Foundation also reached the conclusion that archaeological excavation is an expensive form of conservation, and decided to purchase a number of surviving (or partially surviving) Mimbres sites in order to protect them. Moreover, this is a lesson that has been learned more widely. Members of the Mimbres Foundation have joined forces with other archaeologists and benefactors to form a national organization, the Archaeological Conservancy. Several sites in the United States have now been purchased and conserved in this way. The story thus has, in some sense, a happy ending. But nothing can bring back the possibility of really understanding Mimbres culture and art, a possibility that did exist at the beginning of the 20th century before the wholesale and devastating looting.

Unfortunately, in other parts of the world there are similar stories to tell.

lookouts. It is very difficult to prosecute them under the present legislation unless they are caught red-handed, which is almost impossible.

The *huaqueros* of Central and South America, too, are interested only in the richest finds, in this case gold – whole cemeteries are turned into fields of craters, with bones, potsherds, mummy wrappings, and other objects smashed and scattered. The remarkable tombs excavated between 1987 and 1990 at Sipán, northwest Peru, of the Moche civilization, were rescued from the plunderers only by the persistence and courage of the local Peruvian archaeologist, Walter Alva.

So far as illicit antiquities are concerned, the spotlight has indeed turned upon museums and private collectors. Many of the world's great museums, following the lead of the University Museum of Pennsylvania in 1970, now decline to purchase or receive by gift any antiquities that cannot be shown to have been exported legally from their country of origin. But others, such as the Metropolitan Museum of Art, New York, have in the past had no such scruples: Thomas Hoving, at that time Director of the museum, stated: "We are no more illegal in anything we have done than Napoleon was when he brought all the treasures to the Louvre." The J. Paul Getty Museum, with its great wealth, has a heavy responsibility in this, and has recently adopted a much more rigorous acquisition policy.

Such museums as the Metropolitan Museum of Art, which in 1990 put on display the collection of Shelby White and the late Leon Levy, and the Getty Museum, which in 1994 exhibited (and then acquired) that of Barbara Fleischman and the late Lawrence Fleischman – both collections with a high proportion of antiquities of unknown **provenience** – must share some responsibility for the prevalence of collecting in circumstances where much of the money paid inevitably goes to reward dealers who are part of the ongoing cycles of destruction, and thus ultimately the looters. The responsibility borne by collectors who, in buying such works, indirectly fund the looting process, is also now being recognized. It has been argued that "Collectors are the real looters." Peter Watson, in his revealing survey *The Medici Conspiracy* (2006), has outlined the surprising events that led the Italian government to bring criminal charges against the former curator of antiquities at the Getty, and to recover from the Metropolitan Museum of Art one of their most celebrated antiquities, the "Euphronios Vase," for which they had in 1972 paid a million dollars, but without obtaining secure evidence of its provenience. As the Romans had it: "caveat emptor" ("buyer beware").

It remains a real paradox that collectors, who often have a genuine feeling for the antiquities that they amass, are ultimately funding the looting that is the main threat to the world's archaeological heritage.

There are signs that things may be improving, however. The Dealing in Cultural Objects (Offences) Act was approved by the United Kingdom Parliament in 2003. For the first time it is now a criminal offence in the UK knowingly to deal in illicitly excavated antiquities, whether from Britain or overseas. And in New

The "Weary Herakles": the lower part, excavated in Turkey in 1980, and the upper part, which was exhibited in the Boston Museum of Fine Arts, are now reunited in Turkey.

York in June 2003 the United States Court of Appeals upheld the conviction of the antiquities dealer Frederick Schultz for conspiring to deal in antiquities stolen from Egypt. Schultz is a former president of the National Association of Dealers in Ancient, Oriental, and Primitive Art and has in the past sold antiquities to some leading museums in the United States. A jail term for so prominent a dealer will send a clear message to some conspicuous collectors and museum directors that they should be more attentive in future in the exercise of "due diligence" when acquiring unprovenienced antiquities.

Recent cases include:

The "Weary Herakles." Two parts of a Roman marble statue of the 2nd century AD surfaced separately: the lower part was excavated at Perge in Turkey in 1980 and was moved to the Antalya Museum, while the joining upper part was purchased by the late Leon Levy and was for some years exhibited at the Boston Museum of Fine Arts, to which Levy gave a half share. The museum and Levy's widow Shelby White initially resisted Turkish claims to the piece, but it has now been returned to Turkey.

The Sevso Treasure. A splendid late Roman assemblage of silver vessels was acquired as an investment by the Marquess of Northampton, but was subsequently claimed in a New York court action by Hungary, Croatia, and Lebanon. Possession was awarded to Lord Northampton, who then found the treasure unsaleable and sued his former legal advisors in London for their poor advice at the time of purchase; an out-of-court settlement, reportedly in excess of £15 million, was agreed on confidential terms in 1999. Hungary is now seeking

A splendid silver dish (right) from the looted Sevso Treasure, one of the major scandals in the recent story of illicit antiquities.

to obtain this material, and perhaps Lord Northampton will sell his treasure after all. It was exhibited at a private viewing at Bonham's, the London auctioneers, in 2006, and nothing has been heard of it since.

The Getty Affair. The J. Paul Getty Museum in Los Angeles found itself in the spotlight of publicity in 2005 when its Curator of Antiquities, Marion True (subsequently fired), went on trial in Italy on charges relating to the purchase by the Getty of antiquities allegedly illegally excavated in Italy. The trial ran out of time, without verdict, but the Getty Museum meanwhile by agreement returned many looted antiquities to Italy. The Getty Museum has also now adopted a strict acquisition policy fully in line with the 1970 UNESCO Convention.

Aramaic incantation bowl from the 6th to 7th century AD with a text, written in black ink, intended to bind demons, deities, and other hostile forces who might harm the owner.

The UCL Aramaic Incantation Bowls. In 2005 University College London established a Committee of Inquiry into the provenience of 654 Aramaic incantation bowls (dating to the 6th to 7th centuries AD, and believed to come from Iraq) that had been lent for purposes of study by a prominent Norwegian collector, Martin Schøyen. It did so following claims that the bowls had been illegally exported from their country of origin. UCL received the Report of the Committee in July 2006, but subsequently returned the bowls to Schøyen with whom it had concluded a confidential out-of-court settlement preventing publication of the Report, and agreeing to pay an undisclosed sum to Schøyen. This episode highlights the need for "due diligence" when antiquities are accepted, on loan as well as through gift or purchase, by public institutions. The full story of the UCL Aramaic incantation bowls remains to be told.

It is ironic that a love and respect for the past and for the antiquities that have come down to us should lead to such destructive and acquisitive behaviour. "Who owns the past?" is indeed the key issue if the work of archaeology is to continue, and to provide us with new information about our shared heritage and about the processes by which we have become what we are. In that sense we may well ask "Does the past have a future?" That is the theme addressed in our final chapter.

Study Questions

- Who owns the past?
- What are some ways in which symbols from the past have led to conflict?
- What are ethics? What sorts of ethical issues do archaeologists encounter?
- Why are many archaeologists critical of "pseudoarchaeology"?
- What are illicit antiquities?

Summary

- The past has different meanings for different people, and often personal identity is defined by the past. Increasingly archaeology is playing a role in the definition of national identity, where the past is used to legitimize the present by reinforcing a sense of national greatness. Ethnicity, which is just as strong a force today as in earlier times, relies upon the past for legitimization as well, sometimes with destructive consequences.

- Ethics is the science of what is right and wrong, or morality, and most branches of archaeology are seen to have an ethical dimension. Until recent decades archaeologists gave little thought to such questions as "who owns the past?" Now every archaeological decision should take ethical concerns into account.

- We cannot simply dismiss the alternative theories of fringe archaeology as farcical, because they have been so widely believed. Anyone who has read this book, and who understands how archaeology proceeds, will already see why such writings are a delusion. The real antidote is a kind of healthy skepticism: to ask "where is the evidence?" Knowledge advances by asking questions – that is the central theme of this book, and there is no better way to disperse the lunatic fringe than by asking difficult questions, and looking skeptically at the answers.

- The archaeology of every land has its own contribution to make to the understanding of human diversity and hence of the human condition. Although earlier scholars behaved with flagrant disregard for the feelings and beliefs of native peoples, interest in these matters today is not an attempt further to appropriate the native past.

- Perhaps the saddest type of archaeological destruction comes from the looting of sites. Through this act, all information is destroyed in the search for highly salable artifacts. Museums and collectors bear some of the responsibility for this. Museums are also under increasing pressure to return antiquities to their lands of origin.

Further Reading

General introductions to the topics covered in this chapter include:

Brodie, N., Kersel, M., Luke, C. & Tubb, K.W. (eds). 2008. *Archaeology, Cultural Heritage, and the Antiquities Trade*. University Press of Florida: Gainsville.

Burke, H., Smith, C., Lippert, D., Watkins, J.E. & Zimmerman, L. 2008. *Kennewick Man: Perspectives on the Ancient One*. Left Coast Press: Walnut Creek.

Feder, K. 2008. *Frauds, Myths, and Mysteries: Science and Pseudoscience in Archaeology*. McGraw-Hill: New York.

Greenfield, J. 2007. *The Return of Cultural Treasures* (3rd ed.). Cambridge University Press: Cambridge & New York.

Lynott, M.J. & Wylie, A. 2002. *Ethics in American Archaeology* (2nd ed.). Society for American Archaeology: Washington D.C.

Renfrew, C. 2009. *Loot, Legitimacy and Ownership: The Ethical Crisis in Archaeology*. Duckworth: London.

Watson, P. 2006. *The Medici Conspiracy*. PublicAffairs: New York.

[See p. 345 for a list of useful websites]

The Future of the Past
Managing our heritage

12

The Destruction of the Past

The Response: Survey, Conservation, and Mitigation

- Survey
- Conservation and Mitigation
- The Practice of CRM in the United States
- International Protection

Publication, Archives, and Resources

What Use Is the Past?

Building a Career in Archaeology

Study Questions
Summary
Further Reading

What is the future of archaeology? Can our discipline continue to produce new information about the human past, the **evolution** of our species, and the achievements of humankind? This is one of the dilemmas that currently confront all archaeologists, and indeed all those concerned to understand the human past. For just as global warming and increasing pollution threaten the future ecology of our planet, so the record of the past is today faced by forces of destruction that demand a coherent and energetic response.

Some of those forces of destruction have been discussed earlier, and others are confronted here. The big question continues to be: what can be done? That is the problem that faces us, the solution to which will determine the future both of our discipline and of the material record that it seeks to understand. Here we review two parallel approaches: conservation (protection) and mitigation. The two, working together, have generated in recent years new attitudes toward the practice of **archaeology**, which may yet offer viable solutions.

The Destruction of the Past

There are two main agencies of destruction, both of them human. One is the construction of roads, quarries, dams, office blocks, etc. These are conspicuous and the threat is at least easily recognizable. The other, agricultural intensification, is slower but much wider in its extent, thus in the long term far more destructive. Elsewhere, reclamation schemes are transforming the nature of the environment, so that arid lands are being flooded and wetlands, such as those in Florida, are being reclaimed through drainage. The result is the loss of remarkable archaeological evidence. A third agent of destruction is conflict, the most obvious current threat being in the war zones of the Middle East.

There are two further human agencies of destruction that should not be overlooked. The first is tourism, which, while economically having important effects on archaeology, makes the effective conservation of archaeological sites more difficult. The second, as we have seen in Chapter 11, is not new, but has grown dramatically in scale: the looting of archaeological **sites** by those who dig

The Warka Vase (below) was looted from the Iraqi National Museum, Baghdad, during the invasion of Iraq in 2003. Fortunately it was recovered (bottom) and though in pieces, these were probably ancient breaks.

for monetary gain, seeking only salable objects and destroying everything else in their search. More ancient remains have been lost in the last two decades than ever before in the history of the world.

Agricultural Damage. Ever increasing areas of the earth, once uncultivated or cultivated by traditional non-intensive methods, are being opened up to mechanized farming. In other areas, forest plantations now cover what was formerly open land, and tree roots are destroying archaeological sites.

Although most countries keep some control over the activities of developers and builders, the damage to archaeological sites from farming is much more difficult to assess. The few published studies make sober reading. One shows that in Britain even those sites that are notionally protected – by being listed on the national Schedule of Ancient Monuments – are not, in reality, altogether safe. The position may be much better in Denmark and in certain other countries, but elsewhere only the most conspicuous sites are protected. The more modest field monuments and open settlements are not, and these are the sites that are suffering from mechanized agriculture.

Damage in War. Among the most distressing outrages of recent years has been the continuing destruction, sometimes deliberate, of monuments and **artifacts** in the course of armed conflict. Already, during World War II, historic buildings in England were deliberately targeted in German bombing raids.

In war the sentiments are sometimes national or ethnic, rather than religious. Such was the case in the civil war in Yugoslavia, although it also had religious overtones. The bridge at Mostar in Bosnia, built by the Ottoman Turks in 1566 and a symbol of Bosnian identity, was destroyed by Croatian forces in 1993. Although it has now been rebuilt, the loss of the original structure was one of the most tragic acts in Europe since World War II: the deliberate destruction of cultural heritage on purely ethnic grounds.

The failure of Coalition forces in the invasion of Iraq in 2003 to secure the Iraqi National Museum in Baghdad allowed the looting of the collections, including the celebrated Warka Vase, one of the most notable finds from the early Sumerian civilization – although, like many other important antiquities, this was later returned to the museum. The failure was all the more shocking since archaeologists in the United States had met with representatives of the Defense Department some months prior to the war to warn of the risk of looting in museums and at sites, and archaeologists in Britain had similarly indicated the dangers to the British government months before the war began. Only parts of the collection were taken, and it seems that it was the work both of looters from the street, who smashed cases, decapitated statues, and trashed offices, but also perhaps some well-informed individuals who knew what they were looking for and who had access to storeroom keys. It is these who are likely to have taken

Objects from Tutankhamun's tomb looted from the Cairo Museum in 2011, and subsequently recovered by Egyptian authorities.

the museum's collection of Mesopotamian cylinder seals, the finest in the world, for sale to collectors overseas.

In 2011, during the "Arab spring" in Egypt, civil unrest gave the opportunity for thieves to break into the Cairo Museum and steal a number of significant antiquities, although the authorities rapidly restored order. Continuing conflict in Syria and Egypt is having a devastating effect on archaeology, with widespread looting of sites as well as thefts from museums. The effects are especially serious for Egypt, which relies so heavily upon archaeological tourism. In August 2013 the archaeological museum in Malawi, in Egypt's Minya region, was destroyed and looted – sarcophagi and statues were damaged, and curators revealed that 1040 of 1080 objects in the collection were missing, presumably now heading for the burgeoning trade in illicit antiquities.

It seems all the more extraordinary that the United States and the United Kingdom have still not ratified the 1954 Hague Convention for the Protection of Cultural Property in the Event of Armed Conflict, or its protocols. The British Government has announced its intention of doing so, but claims – some 50 years after the initial drafting of the Convention – that "to do so will require extensive consultation on legal, operational, and policy issues relating to the implementation of the Protocol."

The Response: Survey, Conservation, and Mitigation

In many countries of the world where the material remains of the past are valued as an important component of the national heritage, the response has been the development of a public archaeology: the acceptance that the public and therefore both national and regional government have a responsibility to avoid unnecessary destruction of that heritage. And of course there is an international dimension also. This acceptance implies that steps should be taken to conserve what remains, often with the support of protective legislation. And when development is undertaken, which is often necessary and inescapable – to build freeways for instance, or to undertake commercial development, or to bring land into cultivation – steps need to be taken to research and record any archaeological remains that in the process are likely to be destroyed. In this way the effects of development can be mitigated.

These approaches have highlighted the need, in advance of any potential development, for reliable information concerning whatever archaeological remains may be present. This puts crucial emphasis on one of the key developments in the archaeological methodology of the late 20th century: site location and survey. The actions undertaken in response to the threat to the heritage need have a logical and natural order: survey, conservation, mitigation.

Within the United States, what are termed "preservation" laws to protect heritage resources do not guarantee that archaeological remains will be preserved. The laws mandate a weighing of options and dictate the process by which the value of the resource is assessed against the value of the development.

In rare cases, the value of a site is so great that it will be preserved and a project canceled or re-routed. In the vast majority of cases, though, sites are excavated, recorded, and destroyed: a compromise between development and heritage needs.

Survey

Before major developments are undertaken, a key part of the planning phase must be a survey or assessment of the likely effects of such development upon what may be termed the archaeological resource. Such an assessment extends beyond archaeology to more recent history and other aspects of the environment, including threatened plant and animal species. The cultural heritage, and especially its material remains, needs to be carefully assessed.

Such assessment today will often involve the use of satellite imagery as well as aerial photography. It requires mapping with the aid of GIS. And it also needs to involve field survey, using on-the-ground evaluation through field walking (sometimes called "ground truthing") so that unknown archaeological sites – and extant historical buildings and infrastructure, historic landscapes, and traditional cultural properties – can be located and evaluated before development begins.

Conservation and Mitigation

Most nations today ensure a degree of protection for their major monuments and archaeological sites. In England, as early as 1882, the first Ancient Monuments Act was passed and the first Inspector of Ancient Monuments appointed: the energetic archaeologist and pioneer excavator General Pitt-Rivers (see pp. 22–24). A "schedule" of ancient monuments was drawn up, which were to be protected by law. Several of the most important monuments were taken into "guardianship," whereby they were conserved and opened to the public under the supervision of the Ancient Monuments Inspectorate.

In the United States, the first major federal legislation for archaeological protection, the American Antiquities Act, was signed into law in 1906 by Theodore Roosevelt. The act set out three provisions: that the damage, destruction, or excavation of historic or prehistoric ruins or monuments on federal land without permission would be prohibited; that the president would have the authority to establish national landmarks and associated reserves on federal land; and that permits could be granted for the excavation or collection of archaeological materials on federal land to qualified institutions that pursued such excavations for the purpose of increasing knowledge of the past and preserving the materials.

The American Antiquities Act set the foundation and fundamental principles for archaeology in the United States. These include that federal protection is limited to federal land (although some individual states and local governments have their own laws), that **excavation** is a permitted activity for those seeking to learn and conduct research in the public interest, that unpermitted archaeological activities and vandalism are criminally punishable, and that archaeological resources are important enough that the president may create reserves for protection independent of the other branches of government. These principles continue through the many other federal laws that followed. Today, the principal laws that practicing archaeologists must know and follow include the National Historic Preservation Act of 1966, the National Environmental Policy Act of 1969, the Archaeological Resources Protection Act of 1979, the Abandoned Shipwrecks Act of 1987, and the Native American Graves Protection and Repatriation Act of 1990. These laws, and a host of others, updated and expanded the basic principles and practices of protecting, preserving, and managing archaeological resources on federal lands in the United States (see the following section on **Cultural Resource Management**).

Similar provisions hold for the major monuments of many nations. But in the field of heritage management it is with the less obvious, perhaps less important sites that problems arise. Above all, it is difficult or impossible for sites to be protected if their existence is not known or recognized; this is why the role of survey is so crucial.

The conservation of the archaeological record is a fundamental principle of heritage management. It can be brought about by partnership agreement with the landowner – for instance to avoid plowing on recognized sites. Measures can be taken to mitigate the effects of coastal erosion (although this can be very difficult) or inappropriate land use. And above all, effective planning legislation can be used to prevent commercial development in sensitive archaeological areas. Indeed, increasingly, the approach is to think of entire landscapes and their conservation, rather than focusing upon isolated archaeological sites.

When considering the impact of commercial or industrial development, one aspect of mitigation is the carefully planned avoidance of damage to the archaeological record. A well-considered strategy in advance of development will usually favour this approach. In some cases, however, the development necessarily involves damage to the archaeological record. It is at this point that salvage or **rescue archaeology** becomes appropriate. Rarely, when particularly

Conservation in Mexico City: The Great Temple of the Aztecs

When the Spanish Conquistadors under Hernán Cortés occupied the Aztec capital, Tenochtitlan, in 1521, they destroyed its buildings and established their own capital, Mexico City, on the same site.

In 1790 the now-famous statue of the Aztec mother goddess Coatlicue was found, and also the well-known Calendar Stone, but it was not until the 20th century that more systematic archaeological work took place.

Various relatively small-scale excavations were carried out on remains within the city as they came to light in the course of building work. But in 1975 a more coherent initiative was taken: the institution by the Department of Pre-Hispanic Monuments of the Basin of Mexico Project. Its aim is to halt the destruction of archaeological remains during the continuing growth of the city. In 1977, a Museum of Tenochtitlan Project was begun, with the aim of excavating the area where remains of what appeared to be the Great Temple of the Aztecs had been found in 1948. The project was radically transformed early in 1978 when electricity workers discovered a large stone carved with a series of reliefs. The Department of Salvage Archaeology of the National Institute of Anthropology and History took charge. Within days, a huge monolith, 3.25 m (10 ft 7 in) in diameter, was revealed, depicting the dismembered body of the Aztec goddess Coyolxauhqui who, according to myth, had been killed by her brother, the war god Huitzilopochtli.

The Museum of Tenochtitlan Project, under the direction of Eduardo Matos Moctezuma, became the Great Temple Project, which over the next few years brought to light one of the most remarkable archaeological sites in Mexico.

No one had realized how much would be preserved of the Great Temple. Although the Spaniards had razed the standing structure to the ground in 1521, this pyramid was the last of a series of re-buildings. Beneath the ruins of the last temple the excavations revealed those of earlier temples.

In addition to these architectural remains was a wonderful series of offerings to the temple's two gods, Huitzilopochtli and the rain god Tlaloc – objects of obsidian and jade, terracotta and stone sculptures, and other special dedications, including rare coral and the remains of a jaguar buried with a ball of greenstone in its mouth.

A major area of Mexico City has now been turned into a permanent museum and national monument. Mexico has regained one of its greatest pre-Columbian buildings, and the Great Temple of the Aztecs is once again one of the marvels of Tenochtitlan.

The Great Stone, found in 1978, provided the catalyst for the Great Temple excavations. The goddess Coyolxauhqui is shown decapitated and dismembered – killed by her brother, the war god Huitzilopochtli.

MEXICO

Mexico City

The skeleton of a jaguar (above) from a chamber in the fourth of seven building stages of the Great Temple. The jade ball in its mouth may have been placed there as a substitute for the spirit of the deceased.

The Great Temple excavation site (right), with stairways visible of successive phases of the monument. The building was originally pyramidal in form, surmounted by twin temples to the war god Huitzilopochtli and the rain god Tlaloc. Conservation work is in progress here on the Coyolxauhqui stone, just visible at the center of the image at the base of a flight of steps.

A recent discovery: this massive stone slab (below) depicting the god Tlaltecuhtli ("Lord of the Earth") was found at the site in 2006. The monolith was moved to the Templo Mayor Museum in 2010.

important archaeological remains are unexpectedly uncovered, development may be halted entirely (for an example, see box on pp. 322–23).

It is inevitable in the case of major developments, for instance the construction of a freeway, that many archaeological sites, major as well as minor, will be encountered. In the survey stage of the planning process, most of these will have been located, observed, noted, and evaluated. A mitigation plan addresses what steps are required to protect the archaeological record or recover significant information if it cannot be protected by avoidance. In some cases it may be possible to alter the route of the freeway: that is one aspect of mitigation. But usually, if the project is to go ahead, the "preventive" archaeology will involve the investigation of the site by appropriate means of sampling, including excavation.

In many countries a significant proportion of the budget available for archaeological research is now deliberately assigned to these projects, where damage to the archaeological record seems inevitable and where it can be mitigated in this way. There is a growing presumption that sites that are not threatened should not be excavated if there is a potentially informative site that can provide comparable excavation, the future of which is threatened by damage through development. It is increasingly realized that important research questions can be answered in the course of such mitigation procedures.

The Practice of CRM in the United States

Over the past four decades American archaeology has become embedded in Cultural Resource Management (CRM), a complex of laws, regulations, and professional practice designed to manage historic buildings and sites, cultural landscapes, and other cultural and historic places. The practice of CRM is often known as "applied archaeology."

The National Historic Preservation Act and the National Environmental Policy Act are the major legal bases for CRM. These laws require agencies of the US government to consider the environmental impacts of their actions (through an "environmental assessment," which may lead to an "environmental impact statement"), including effects on historical, archaeological, and cultural values. The role of "State Historic Preservation Officer" (SHPO) was created in each US state. Each agency runs its own compliance program.

Projects in which US government agencies are involved – whether on federal land or on other lands but federally funded or requiring a federal permit – must be reviewed to determine their effects on environmental, cultural, and historical resources. CRM programs in state and local governments, federal agencies, academic institutions, and private consulting firms have grown out of this requirement. The SHPOs coordinate many CRM activities, and keep files on historic and prehistoric sites, structures, buildings, districts, and landscapes.

Section 106 of the National Historic Preservation Act requires federal agencies to identify historic places of all kinds (archaeological sites, historic buildings, Native

Key Concepts
CRM in the USA

- CRM (Cultural Resource Management) or "applied archaeology" accounts for more than 90 percent of the field archaeology carried out in the USA today

- *Legal Basis*: under Section 106 of the National Historic Preservation Act (NHPA), archaeological investigation is often carried out in advance of projects on federal land, using federal funds, or requiring a federal permit

- *Funding*: generally speaking, the proponent of the construction or land-use project pays for the work, whether that party is a federal, state, or local agency, or a private developer

- *Compliance*: project proponents fund legally required compliance work that includes inventory (survey), evaluation of a resource's importance, assessment of impacts to important resources, and mitigation (which may include avoidance, excavation, and conservation)

- *Outcome*: the fieldwork typically results in at least a report filed with the SHPO and data entered in government and other databases. Many CRM projects also result in published journal articles, monographs, and books

American sites, etc.) that may be affected by their actions, in consultation with SHPOs, tribes, and others. They then have to determine what to do about project effects – all in consultation with SHPOs and other interested parties. Identification often requires archaeological surveys both to find and evaluate archaeological sites. Evaluation involves applying published criteria to determine eligibility for the National Register of Historic Places – the US schedule of significant historic and cultural land areas, sites, structures, neighborhoods, and communities.

If the agency and its consulting partners find that significant sites are present and will be adversely affected, they seek ways to mitigate the effect. Often this involves redesigning the project to reduce, minimize, or even prevent the damage. Sometimes, where archaeological sites are concerned, the decision is taken to conduct excavations to recover significant data before they are destroyed. If the parties cannot agree on what to do, an independent body known as the Advisory Council on Historic Preservation makes a recommendation and then the responsible federal agency makes its final decision.

Most surveys and data recovery projects in the USA are carried out by private firms – sometimes companies that specialize in CRM work, but otherwise by branches of large engineering, planning, or environmental impact assessment companies. Some academic institutions, museums, and non-profit organizations also carry out CRM work. CRM-based surveys and excavations now comprise at least 90 percent of the field archaeology carried out in the USA.

The review system under Section 106 can produce excellent archaeological research, but research interests must be balanced with other public interests, especially the concerns of Native American tribes and other communities. The quality of work depends largely on the integrity and skill of the participants – agency employees, SHPOs, tribal and community representatives, and private-sector archaeologists. Among the recurring problems are quality control in fieldwork, applying the results of fieldwork to important research topics, publication and other dissemination of results, and the long-term preservation and management of recovered artifacts.

One good example of this process is the vast Tennessee-Tombigbee Waterway project (see box opposite), although not all CRM projects are so well managed. Particularly in the case of small projects, which are carried out by the thousands, it is easy for very shoddy work to be done and little useful data to be produced. But on the other hand, large excavation projects find huge numbers of artifacts, and these have to be carefully stored – and this becomes more and more of a problem as time passes and new excavations are conducted. Large-scale CRM excavations also tend to be underfunded. Since Tennessee-Tombigbee and other similar projects in the 1970s and 1980s, the emphasis has certainly shifted toward remote sensing and planning for the management of archaeological resources in ways that minimize the need for excavations. The Society for American Archaeology has also helped to fund a Register of Professional Archaeologists in an attempt to improve standards. Professional requirements and qualifications have been established by the Department of the Interior, various land-managing agencies, and even some local governments. Permits to undertake archaeological work require credentials, experience, and acceptable past performance.

International Protection

Since world government is currently based upon the effective autonomy of the nation states of the United Nations, measures of conservation and mitigation likewise operate at the level of the nation states. Only in a few cases does some broader perspective prevail, often through the agency of UNESCO (The United Nations Educational, Scientific and Cultural Organization).

The World Heritage List.   Under the World Heritage Convention of 1972, the World Heritage Committee can place sites on the World Heritage List. At the time of writing there are 759 cultural sites on the list (some of which are illustrated overleaf), along with more than 200 natural and mixed sites. Although being on the list does not in itself afford protection, and certainly does not bring additional international resources to assist in conservation, it does act as an incentive for the responsible nation state to ensure that recognized standards are met.

There is in addition a World Heritage in Danger List that highlights the needs of specific threatened sites. The ancient city of Bam in Iran, seriously damaged

CRM in Practice: The Tennessee-Tombigbee Waterway Project

At the time the largest earth-moving project ever undertaken, the Tennessee-Tombigbee Waterway connects those two rivers with a 234-mile-long series of canals running through Mississippi and Alabama. A CRM survey of the huge area of land involved identified 682 sites; it was determined that 27 would be affected by waterway construction. Of these, 17 had good research potential, and another 24 sites were selected for data recovery. Some 12 sites could be preserved by altering the construction program.

Excavation was designed to investigate the evolution of cultures in the area, with emphasis on sampling a good range of sites. The largest site was Lubbub Creek, the only major settlement in the threatened area belonging to the Mississippian culture (AD 900–1450). It includes a major ceremonial mound surrounded by a fortified village. The work undertaken in mitigation of environmental impact gave an excellent opportunity for systematic excavation of both settlement and cemeteries.

(Left) An aerial view of the Lubbub Creek site on the Tombigbee River, Alabama. (Right) Two of the salvage archaeologists carefully cleaning a large urn.

by an earthquake in December 2003, is a case in point, as is the Bamiyan Valley in Afghanistan, which has suffered sadly through war and unrest (see p. 301). The walled city of Baku in Azerbaijan is another major site, damaged by earthquake in November 2000 and now receiving support.

Countering the Traffic in Illicit Antiquities.   The principal international measure against the traffic in illicit antiquities is the 1970 UNESCO Convention on the Means of Preventing the Illicit Import, Export and Transfer of Ownership of Cultural Property. But its principles are not directly enforced by international law, and depend rather on national legislation and on bilateral agreements between nations. The responsibilities of collectors and museums were reviewed

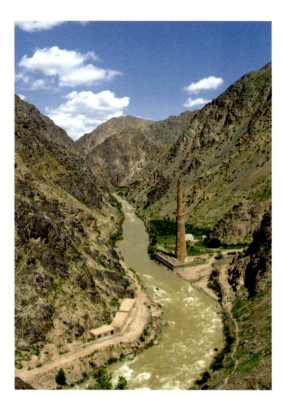

UNESCO World Heritage Sites:

(Clockwise from left): A 12th-century minaret at Jam, Afghanistan, decorated with stucco and glazed tile; one of 500 statues of Buddha at the 8th-century Buddhist temple at Borobodur, Indonesia; 12th-century rock-cut Ethiopian orthodox church at Lalibela; the oval "pyramid" at the wonderfully preserved Maya city of Uxmal, Mexico; a spiral minaret, part of the great 9th-century mosque at Samarra, Iraq; Fatehpur Sikri, India, capital city of the 16th-century Mughal emperor Akbar.

in Chapter 11. There are signs that it is becoming more difficult to sell recently looted antiquities on the open market, at any rate in some countries, but the problem remains a massive one.

Protecting the Cultural Heritage in Times of War. The 1954 Hague Convention for the Protection of Cultural Property in the Event of Armed Conflict and its protocols in principle offer a degree of protection. In practice, however, they have not been effective and, as noted earlier, have not yet been ratified by the United Kingdom or by the United States of America. Both nations were criticized for their shortcomings during the invasion of Iraq in 2003.

These international initiatives are all important, and potentially significant. But at present they are very limited in their effectiveness. In the future they may be better supported, but most of the effective measures safeguarding the future of the past still work primarily at a national level.

Publication, Archives, and Resources

The pace of discovery through the surveys conducted to assess environmental impact and the excavation procedures undertaken in mitigation is remarkable. But the results are often not well published or otherwise made available either to specialists or to the public. In the United States there is an obligation that

environmental impact statements and a summary of any measures taken in mitigation should be lodged with the state archive, but not that they should be published. In Greece the government has for some years failed to fund publication of the Archaiologikon Deltion, the official record of nationally funded excavations. The record is better in France and to some extent in Germany. But few countries can boast effective publication of the quite considerable activities undertaken, generally with a measure of state funding.

In some countries this has led to a division between the practice of academic archaeologists (working in universities and museums) and of those undertaking **contract archaeology**, whether funded by the developer or by the state, but in both cases working to mitigate the impact of development. The work of the former is supposed to be problem-oriented and often does indeed lead to publication in national or international archaeological journals and in detailed monographs. The work of the contract archaeologist is sometimes carefully coordinated, leading to informative regional and national surveys. But in too many instances its publication is not well coordinated at all.

The solution to these problems is not yet clear. But one possibility is certainly emerging: online publication. In this respect some of the major museums have led the way, making the catalogs of their collections available online. Few contract archaeologists currently make their environmental impact statements or mitigation reports available in that way, but this may one day become a requirement: a condition for funding in the first place. In the United Kingdom an important initiative has been taken by the national archaeological Find Reporting Scheme. There the practice of metal detecting in the search for archaeological artifacts is not prohibited by law, as it is in many countries, and this has been a concern to professional archaeologists. But at least state funding has been established for a scheme whereby metal detectorists can voluntarily report their finds to a reporting officer, and many in fact do so. In particular the results are being made available online, with a significant increase in information about the distributions of particular classes of artifact. Thus some of the traditional barriers between professional researchers and the wider public are breaking down. It is likely that in the future excavation data will also become available online and thus more rapidly accessible than is often currently the case. The obligation to inform the public, who ultimately provide the resources for much of the research, is being met.

What Use Is the Past?

The popularity of archaeology has markedly grown in recent years, if television programs and magazine articles are used as a measure. Certainly the number of archaeology students in university courses has increased greatly in many countries. And the world's great museums have ever-increasing visitor numbers. As we have seen, in many countries public resources are invested in conservation, and developers are obliged to ensure that proper measures are undertaken in mitigation of their impact upon the cultural environment. But are these resources expended simply to satisfy the idle curiosity of the world's citizens? Is their main purpose simply to create agreeable historic sites to visit?

We think that there is more at work than this. It can be argued that there is today a growing awareness that humankind needs to feel and to know that it has a past – a past that can be documented securely by concrete material evidence that we can all access, examine, and assess. For without our roots we are lost. Over recent generations those roots are well represented by our friends, by our families, and by our existing communities. But in a deeper sense, and in a deeper past, we are all in this together. The different **religions** of the world provide meaning for the lives of many people. But they do not all agree, or so it might seem, about some of the questions of human origins and early history that we have been discussing here. Some offer creation stories that are profound and illuminating. Each of these can be enriched by knowledge of the material evidence for early human development. The finds are there, in every part of the world. And more finds continue to be made.

It is abundantly clear, from the pace of archaeological discovery, that there is more to learn. That is one reason why the subject is so interesting. And it always will be. So long as the practices of conservation and mitigation are maintained we shall continue to learn more about the human past, and in that sense about what it means to be human. We hope that such will be the future of the past. And we do not doubt that it will be useful.

Building a Career in Archaeology

There are a variety of careers in archaeology – whether, for example, in the field of archaeological research (in a university or as an independent researcher), or in a more administrative capacity as a government employee, or in the business of heritage tourism. To show how an archaeological career could develop, we have invited four professionals, all earning a living by doing archaeology, to tell his or her own story.

Each is an established archaeologist but at a different stage in his or her career. Their backgrounds are also different. Yet most of them have something in common: they came to archaeology fortuitously, by chance, as it were. This is hardly surprising, since the practice of archaeology is not a major profession, such as medicine or the law or retail selling. But each of them, by some means, caught the bug. That bug, that fascination with the human past, is what drives them. The joy they express is not simply discovering and uncovering objects that have lain hidden for thousands of years. It is the pleasure of making sense of the data, making sense of the past.

Two of the authors work in countries (Thailand and South Africa) outside of the transatlantic axis, between Europe and the United States, which was so significant in the early development of archaeology. It may be relevant that each did his or her postgraduate training at centers within that axis (Michigan and London respectively). Yet each now teaches graduate students in their own country – students who will themselves become the new generation of searchers, developing a world archaeology that will be fully international.

Part of that internationalism is indeed the rich experience of working in places and with people who lie outside of one's previous existence. Many of us are born and brought up in cities, so that archaeological fieldwork brings a welcome first experience of living and working with hunter-gatherers or with rural farmers in an environment very different from that of city or university.

Each of the authors is also concerned with the present and with the future, and aspires to make a difference to that future. Lisa J. Lucero hopes that her work on the demise of the Classic Maya, apparently through long-term drought, can inform our current understanding of the impact of climate change. Each sees it as part of their job both to interact with scholars in other countries, and to communicate with a wider public in his or her own homeland. The archaeologist of today, as of yesterday, is a person of wide horizons, with knowledge of the human past, and with a concern for the human future.

Lisa J. Lucero: University Professor, USA

How I Was Inspired to Become an Archaeologist

Even at high school I always wanted to know how much of a movie or book supposedly based on history was based on fact. This interest led me to obtain an anthropology degree at Colorado State University. I attended graduate school at UCLA, where the atmosphere in the Archaeology Program was positively electric. My interest – encouraged by my peers and professors – was to explore the foundation of political power. In the case of the Classic Maya (c. AD 250–900) the power of rulers rested on the labor of the majority commoners and farmers. The only way to reveal their story is to excavate commoner houses, which I have done over the years. It is amazing to peel back the layers of Maya mounds representing centuries of habitation and rebuilding by Maya families.

How I Got My First Job

It took a few interviews before I was offered my first job at New Mexico State University, where I stayed for 10 years, until I was recruited by the University of Illinois at Urbana-Champaign. I truly enjoy the academic atmosphere – I must, since I have never been out of it! I spend most of my time on various research projects as well as teaching.

The Most Rewarding Thing I Have Discovered

There is not one particular thing that I have discovered in my more than 20 years of conducting archaeology. What is rewarding are the questions I feel more and more qualified to address about human societies, including my own. What amazes me is the resilience of our species; we have overcome so much in our

Lisa J. Lucero
University of Illinois at
Urbana-Champaign
Email: ljlucero@illinois.edu

Lisa J. Lucero excavating at the Maya center of Yalbac, in the jungles of central Belize.

history. People of the past, however, have also faced challenges that they could not overcome. It is hugely valuable to identify those strategies of the past that did not work, so as to avoid history repeating itself.

What Do I Research and How Can it Make a Difference?

In the last 10 years, I have been interested in how climate change – in this case, a long-term drought – played a role in the demise of the Classic Maya. In an area without permanent surface water, large and powerful centers relied on complex reservoir systems to supply water during the annual dry season, but long-term drought rapidly brought this to an end. Within several decades farmers in the southern Maya lowlands went back to living in small communities, or migrated in all directions. And this is where I can make a difference as an archaeologist – applying lessons from the past to current problems resulting from global climate change. I am involved in several organizations that bring together scholars focusing on issues of climate change and sustainability in the tropics. Our goals are twofold: avoid past missteps and highlight how ancient societies practiced sustainable ways of living.

Rasmi Shoocongdej: University Professor, Thailand

How I Was Inspired to Become an Archaeologist

I initially thought about journalism as a career choice, but then became interested in archaeology. In my junior year at Silpakorn University, I wrote an article on Thai cultural heritage for a student newsletter, helped establish an archaeology club, and created a mobile exhibition on cultural heritage for schools in rural areas. These activities constituted a crucial turning point in my archaeological career: I was enjoying becoming a journalist of the past.

How I Got My First Job

In 1984, after working as a research assistant in the Archaeology Division of the Fine Arts Department at Silpakorn, I went to study at the University of Michigan; there was no graduate program in anthropological or prehistoric archaeology in Thailand. While studying at Michigan, I applied for a lectureship at Silpakorn University (one of the few teaching positions in Thailand), and returned to Thailand in 1987 to begin teaching archaeology.

What Do I Do Now?

I am currently an Associate Professor of Archaeology and Chair of the Department of Archaeology at Silpakorn University. I devote much of my time to students, aiming to develop their awareness of cultural heritage and a sense of responsibility to society, and to public campaigns for the conservation of Thai and other ethnic groups' heritages in Thailand. I am also engaged in a long-term project in highland Pang Mapha in northwestern Thailand, which began in 1998.

My Research Interests

My research focuses on understanding hunter-gatherer mobility organization, specifically of foragers of the late- to post-Pleistocene period (c. 32,000–10,000 BP)

Rasmi Shoocongdej
Silpakorn University
Email: Bangkokrasmi@su.ac.th
Website: www.rasmishoocongdej.com

Rasmi Shoocongdej presenting the Pang Mapha project at the 11th International Conference of the European Association of Southeast Asian Archaeologists, Bougon, France, in 2006.

in the western border area of Thailand. Other interests include nationalism and archaeology, archaeology and multi-ethnic education, looting, and archaeology and the arts. My field experiences include projects in northern, western, central, and southern Thailand; Cambodia; southwestern USA; and southeastern Turkey.

The Most Rewarding Thing I Have Done or Discovered

From the Pang Mapha project, two discoveries are highly significant (particularly as there are very few late Pleistocene sites currently known in Thailand): remains of the two oldest *Homo sapiens* found in northern Thailand (c. 13,000–12,000 BP), and the largest stone tool workshop in Thailand (c. 32,000–12,000 BP).

As I believe that the past can serve the present and the future, also rewarding is that part of the Pang Mapha project that has involved working closely with the local communities to help connect them to their archaeological heritage, such as through art-related activities to present the history, beliefs, and meanings of the coffins that are still on site.

Why Being an Archaeologist Matters to Me and How I Make a Difference

I believe in searching for the truth of humankind, so I am fulfilling my dream to be a journalist of the past by doing archaeology. My search for indigenous and local archaeological knowledge and appropriate methodologies will enable me to develop an archaeology in my country that can contribute to "world archaeologies." I also hope that my work on heritage management with local communities will increase cooperation in fighting against the illegal antiquities trade and the destruction of archaeological sites.

Douglas C. Comer: CRM Archaeologist, USA

How I Was Inspired to Become an Archaeologist

Douglas C. Comer
Cultural Site Research and Management, Baltimore
Email: dcomer@culturalsite.com
Website: www.culturalsite.com

I knew early on that I would be a scientist, and I was inspired to become an archaeologist not because of any strong interest in artifacts or history, but because I had a need to understand how I might be connected to other humans. In an Anthropology course at Grand Valley State University, I was introduced to the work of Leslie White. He had huge ideas: culture was an extra-somatic adaptation to the environment; life was the process that counteracted the Second Law of Thermodynamics. He argued that these basic processes would be quantified as the field matured. To me, this suggested that by analyzing data, we would be able to isolate the factors that made us who we were.

How I Got My First Job

As I finished my Master's degree in Anthropology, the National Historic Preservation Act of 1966 was being implemented in earnest. I immediately found employment with the Colorado State Highway Department, first doing salvage archaeology. I was then loaned to the Forest Service to survey areas in the White River National Forest that were to be timbered. I had the opportunity to analyze and write up the results of some of these surveys, and on the strength of that found permanent employment with the National Park Service.

Douglas C. Comer in the field in Jordan, verifying the location of antiquities seen in satellite imagery.

Shadreck Chirikure
University of Cape Town
Email: Shadreck.Chirikure@uct.ac.za

What Do I Do Now?

I now run a CRM consulting firm, Cultural Site Research and Management (CSRM). I have always been convinced that the management of cultural resources should be based in scientific research and analysis, in particular, the collection of relevant data that can be quantified and analyzed in replicable ways. And, being a nerd, I have enthusiastically embraced geospatial analysis technologies as they have emerged. CSRM has been active in Southeast Asia, the Middle East, the United States, Africa, and Central and South America.

My Research Interests

My research interests revolve around the ways in which humans utilize and structure space at all scales, including the site and the landscape. I would like to refine further the use of aerial and satellite remote-sensing technologies in archaeology and cultural resource management. We cannot hope to protect archaeological resources until we know where they are.

The Most Rewarding Thing I Have Done or Discovered

Truthfully, everything that I have ever found on the ground or in aerial and satellite imagery has been interesting to me, but I'm particularly interested in the sorts of discoveries that suggest new avenues of research for archaeology.

Why Being an Archaeologist Matters to Me and How I Make a Difference

We live in a time in which information is far more readily available than at any time in the past. Yet while there is much more information that purports to be relevant to why people behave as they do, it has become increasingly difficult to differentiate fact from fantasy. Archaeology draws upon a reliable tradition of scholarship that includes rigorous documentation and verification procedures. As anthropologists, we know that human groups define themselves and set a course for the future by means of an imagined past. Archaeology deals with the material evidence of the past and a scientific analysis of it that can be used to bring our imaginings more in line with the realities of the world, and so make us better able to cope with those realities. It is intensely interesting and somewhat humbling to play a role in this.

Shadreck Chirikure: Archaeometallurgist, South Africa
How I Was Inspired to Become an Archaeologist

If I had been asked 15 years ago whether I wanted to become an archaeologist, I would have said NO. My dream was to work in the finance industry. I entered into archaeology by pure chance. It all started with studying the degrees of BA General and BA Special Honours in Archaeology at the University of Zimbabwe between 1997 and 2001. We studied great civilizations, we studied humanity's progress over time, and we studied archaeology's potential to unlock development in host communities. In no time, I wanted to be part of this discipline that combined the thrill of discovery with learning and solving community problems.

Shadreck Chirikure in the Materials Laboratory at the University of Cape Town.

In 2001, I was awarded a joint English Heritage and Institute for Archaeometallurgical Studies Scholarship to study for an MA in Artefact Studies at University College London. I was already imagining how much I would have missed out if I had ended up in finance! At MA level, I started working in archaeometallurgy on pre-industrial metal production in Africa. Generous grants enabled me to expand this research at PhD level.

How I Got My First Job

On graduating with a PhD in Archaeology in 2005, I assumed a postdoctoral research position at the University of Cape Town's Department of Archaeology, becoming a lecturer in 2007. My main responsibilities include research, teaching, administration, and running the Materials Laboratory, which is Africa's only facility of its kind. The Materials Laboratory is dedicated to the study of pre-industrial technologies in Africa, such as metalworking and ceramics. Our projects range from studying the technology of metal production (iron, tin, copper, bronze, etc.) to understanding the social context of the technology. I collaborate with leading researchers based overseas, and I have won awards for research papers and participated in award-winning documentaries.

The Most Rewarding Thing I Have Done or Discovered

The success of my work in the Materials Laboratory led to my appointment as the head of a team of international experts working on the conservation and protection of the world-famous Oranjemund shipwreck discovered in Namibia in 2008. This 16th-century shipwreck contained large amounts of treasure: 28 kg (60 lb) of Spanish and Portuguese gold coins, 4 kg (9 lb) of Spanish and Portuguese silver coins, 20 tons of copper ingots, 6 tons of unworked elephant ivory, and many more artifacts together with the superstructure of the ship itself.

Why Being an Archaeologist Matters to Me

From time to time, I write newspaper articles on archaeology and also feature on radio programs and in magazines discussing topical issues and careers in archaeology. Being an academic archaeologist allows me to contribute to national discourse through heritage protection programs, research programs, community learnership, and heritage entrepreneurship projects.

Study Questions

- What are some of the ways that humans damage or destroy archaeological sites?
- In the United States, what are the key pieces of legislation that relate to archaeological protection, conservation, and mitigation?
- What is Cultural Resource Management (CRM)? What percentage of archaeological work in the USA can be considered CRM?
- Why is the publication of archaeological information so important?
- How is archaeology relevant to today's world?

Summary

- Many nations believe that it is the duty of the government to have policies with regard to conservation, and these conservation laws often apply to archaeology. Construction, agricultural intensification, tourism, and looting are all human activities that damage or destroy sites.

- Built on a strong legal foundation, CRM or "applied archaeology" plays a major role in American archaeology. When a project is on federal land, uses federal money, or needs a federal permit, the law requires that cultural resources are identified, evaluated, and if they cannot be avoided, addressed accordingly in an approved mitigation plan. A large number of private contract archaeology firms employ the majority of archaeologists in the US. These firms are responsible for meeting mitigation requirements, overseen by a lead agency and an SHPO. Publication of final reports is required, but the variable quality and usually limited dissemination of these reports remain a problem.

- Archaeologists have a duty to report what they find. Since excavation is, to a certain extent, destructive, published material is often the only record of what was found at a site. Perhaps up to 60 percent of modern excavations remain unpublished after 10 years. Governments and professional organizations are taking a harsher stance against archaeologists who do not publish and often will not grant digging permits to those who have unpublished work. The Internet and the popular media can help to fulfil one of the fundamental purposes of archaeology: to provide the public with a better understanding of the past.

Further Reading

The following books are useful introductions to heritage management:

Carman, J. 2002. *Archaeology and Heritage, an Introduction*. Continuum: London.

King, T.F. 2008. *Cultural Resource Laws and Practice, an Introductory Guide* (3rd ed.). Altamira Press: Walnut Creek.

King, T.F. 2005. *Doing Archaeology: A Cultural Resource Management Perspective*. Left Coast Press: Walnut Creek.

Sabloff, J.A. 2008. *Archaeology Matters: Action Archaeology in the Modern World*. Left Coast Press: Walnut Creek.

Smith, L. & Waterton, E. 2009. *Heritage, Communities and Archaeology*. Duckworth: London.

Sørensen, M.L.S. & Carman, J. 2009. *Heritage Studies: Methods and Approaches*. Routledge. London.

Tyler, N., Ligibel, T.J. & Tyler, I. 2009. *Historic Preservation: An Introduction to its History, Principles and Practice* (2nd ed.). W.W. Norton & Company: New York.

[See p. 345 for a list of useful websites]

Glossary

(Terms in *italics* are defined elsewhere in the glossary)

absolute dating The determination of age with reference to a specific time scale, such as a fixed calendrical system; also referred to as chronometric dating.

aerial survey An important technique, primarily employing aerial and satellite imagery, used in the discovery and recording of archaeological *sites* (see also *LIDAR* and *reconnaissance survey*).

alloying Technique involving the mixing of two or more metals to create a new material, e.g. the fusion of copper and tin to make bronze.

ALS (Airborne Laser Scanning) see *LIDAR*.

annealing In copper and bronze metalworking, this refers to the repeated process of heating and hammering the material to produce the desired shape.

anthropology The study of humanity – our physical characteristics as animals, and the unique non-biological characteristics we call *culture*. The subject is generally broken down into three subdisciplines: *biological (physical) anthropology*, *cultural (social) anthropology*, and *archaeology*.

archaeobotany See *paleoethnobotany*.

archaeological culture A constantly recurring *assemblage* of *artifacts* assumed to be representative of a particular set of behavioral activities carried out at a particular time and place (*cf. culture*).

archaeology A subdiscipline of *anthropology* involving the study of the human past through its material remains.

archaeology of cult The study of the material indications of behavior undertaken in response to religious beliefs.

archaeomagnetic dating Sometimes referred to as paleomagnetic dating, this technique is based on the fact that changes in the earth's magnetic field over time can be recorded in such materials as baked clay structures (ovens, kilns, and hearths).

archaeozoology Sometimes referred to as zooarchaeology, this involves the identification and analysis of faunal species from archaeological *sites*, as an aid to the reconstruction of human diets and to an understanding of the contemporary environment at the time of deposition.

artifact Any portable object used, modified, or made by humans; e.g. stone tools, pottery, and metal weapons.

assemblage A group of *artifacts* recurring together at a particular time and place, and representing the sum of human activities.

association The co-occurrence of an *artifact* with other archaeological remains, usually in the same *matrix*.

attribute A minimal characteristic of an *artifact* such that it cannot be further subdivided; attributes commonly studied include aspects of form, *style*, decoration, color, and raw material.

Australopithecus A collective name for the earliest known hominids emerging about 5 million years ago in East Africa.

band A term used to describe small-scale societies of *hunter-gatherers*, generally fewer than 100 people, who move seasonally to exploit wild (undomesticated) food resources. Kinship ties play an important part in social organization.

bioarchaeology The study of human remains (but in Europe it is sometimes applied to other kinds of organic remains, such as animal bones).

biological anthropology A subdiscipline of *anthropology* dealing with the study of human biological or physical characteristics and their *evolution*.

characterization The application of techniques of examination by which characteristic properties of the constituent material of traded goods can be identified, and thus their source of origin; e.g. *thin-section analysis*.

chiefdom A term used to describe a society that operates on the principle of ranking, i.e. differential social status. Different *lineages* are graded on a scale of prestige, calculated by how closely related one is to the chief. The chiefdom generally has a permanent ritual and ceremonial center, as well as being characterized by local specialization in crafts.

chronometric dating See *absolute dating*.

classification The ordering of phenomena into groups or other classificatory schemes on the basis of shared *attributes* (see also *type* and *typology*).

cognitive archaeology The study of past ways of thought and symbolic structures from material remains.

cognitive map An interpretive framework of the world that, it is argued, exists in the human mind and affects actions and decisions as well as knowledge structures.

cognitive-processual approach An alternative to the materialist orientation of the functional-processual approach, it is concerned with (1) the integration of the cognitive and symbolic with other aspects of early societies; (2) the role of ideology as an active organizational force.

computerized (computed) axial tomography (CAT or CT scanner) The method by which scanners allow detailed internal views of bodies, such as mummies. The body is passed into the machine and images of cross-sectional "slices" through the body are produced.

conjoining See *refitting*.

context An *artifact*'s context usually consists of its immediate *matrix* (the material around it e.g. gravel, clay, or sand), its *provenience* (horizontal and vertical position in the matrix), and its *association* with other artifacts (with other archaeological remains, usually in the same matrix).

contract archaeology Archaeological research conducted under the terms of federal or state legislation, often in advance of highway construction or urban development, where the archaeologist is contracted to undertake the necessary research.

coprolites Fossilized feces; these contain food residues that can be used to reconstruct diet and subsistence activities.

core A lithic *artifact* used as a blank from which other tools or flakes are made.

Critical Theory A theoretical approach developed by the so-called "Frankfurt School" of German social thinkers, which stresses that all knowledge is historical, and in a sense biased communication; thus, all claims to "objective" knowledge are illusory.

cultural anthropology A subdiscipline of *anthropology* concerned with the non-biological, behavioral aspects of society; i.e. the social, linguistic, and technological components underlying human behavior. Two important branches of cultural anthropology are *ethnography* (the study of living cultures) and *ethnology* (which attempts to compare cultures using ethnographic evidence). In Europe, it is referred to as *social anthropology*.

cultural ecology A term devised by Julian Steward to account for the dynamic relationship between human society and its environment, in which *culture* is viewed as the primary adaptive mechanism.

cultural resource management (CRM) The safeguarding of the archaeological heritage through the protection of *sites* and through *salvage archaeology* (rescue archaeology), generally within the framework of legislation designed to safeguard the past.

culture A term used by anthropologists when referring to the non-biological characteristics unique to a particular society (cf. *archaeological culture*).

culture-historical approach An approach to archaeological interpretation that uses the procedure of the traditional historian (including emphasis on specific circumstances elaborated with rich detail, and processes of *inductive* reasoning).

deduction A process of reasoning by which more specific consequences are inferred by rigorous argument from more general propositions (cf. *induction*).

deep-sea cores Cores drilled from the sea bed that provide the most coherent record of climate changes on a worldwide scale. The cores contain shells of microscopic marine organisms (foraminifera) laid down on the ocean floor through the continuous process of sedimentation. Variations in the ratio of two oxygen isotopes in the calcium carbonate of these shells give a sensitive indicator of sea temperature at the time the organisms were alive.

dendrochronology The study of tree-ring patterns; annual variations in climatic conditions that produce differential growth can be used both as a measure of environmental change, and as the basis for a chronology.

diatom analysis A method of environmental reconstruction based on plant microfossils. Diatoms are unicellular algae, whose silica cell walls survive after the algae die, and they accumulate in large numbers at the bottom of rivers and lakes. Assemblages directly reflect the composition of the water's extinct floral communities, as well as the water's salinity, alkalinity, and nutrient status.

diffusionist approach The theory (popularized by V.G. Childe) that all the attributes of civilization from architecture to metalworking had diffused from the Near East to Europe.

DNA (Deoxyribonucleic acid) The material that carries the hereditary instructions (the "blueprint") that determine the formation of all living organisms.

earth resistance survey A method of *subsurface detection* that measures changes in conductivity by passing electrical current through ground soils. These changes are generally caused by moisture content, and in this way, buried features can be detected by differential retention of groundwater.

ecofacts Non-artifactual organic and environmental remains that have cultural relevance, e.g. faunal and floral material, as well as soils and sediments.

electrical resistivity See *earth resistance survey*.

electrolysis A standard cleaning process in archaeological conservation. *Artifacts* are placed in a chemical solution, and by passing a weak current between them and a surrounding metal grill, the corrosive salts move from the cathode (object) to the anode (grill), removing any accumulated deposit and leaving the artifact clean.

electron spin resonance (ESR) Enables trapped electrons within bone and shell to be measured without the heating that *thermoluminescence* (TL) requires. As with TL, the number of trapped electrons indicates the age of the specimen.

environmental archaeology A field of interdisciplinary research – *archaeology* and natural science – that is directed at the reconstruction of human use of plants and animals, and how past societies adapted to changing environmental conditions.

environmental circumscription An explanation for the origins of the *state* propounded by Robert Carneiro that emphasizes the fundamental role exerted by environmental constraints and by territorial limitations.

ethnicity The existence of ethnic groups, including tribal groups. Though these are difficult to recognize from the archaeological record, the study of language and linguistic boundaries shows that ethnic groups are often correlated with language areas.

ethnoarchaeology The study of contemporary *cultures* with a view to understanding the behavioral relationships that underlie the production of *material culture*.

ethnography A subset of *cultural anthropology* concerned with the study of contemporary cultures through first-hand observation.

ethnology A subset of *cultural anthropology* concerned with the comparative study of contemporary cultures, with a view to deriving general principles about human society.

evolution The process of growth and development generally accompanied by increasing complexity. In biology, this change is tied to Darwin's concept of natural selection as the basis of species survival. Darwin's work laid the foundations for the study of artifact *typology*, pioneered by such scholars as Pitt-Rivers and Montelius.

evolutionary archaeology The idea that the processes responsible for biological *evolution* also drive culture change, i.e. the application of Darwinian evolutionary theory to the archaeological record.

excavation The principal method of data acquisition in *archaeology*, involving the systematic uncovering of archaeological remains through the removal of the deposits of soil and the other material covering them and accompanying them.

experimental archaeology The study of past behavioral processes through experimental reconstruction under carefully controlled scientific conditions.

fall-off analysis The study of the way in which quantities of traded items found in the archaeological record decline as the distance from the source increases. This may be plotted as a fall-off curve, with the quantities of material (Y-axis) plotted against distance from source (X-axis).

feature A non-portable *artifact*; e.g. hearths, architectural elements, or soil stains.

fission-track dating A dating method based on the operation of a radioactive clock, the spontaneous fission of an isotope of uranium present in a wide range of rocks and minerals. As with *potassium-argon dating*, with which its time range overlaps, the method gives useful dates from rocks adjacent to archaeological material.

flotation A method of screening (sieving) excavated *matrix* in water so as to separate and recover small *ecofacts* and *artifacts*.

fluxgate magnetometer A type of magnetometer used in *subsurface detection*, producing a continuous reading.

forensic anthropology The scientific study of human remains in order to build up a biological profile of the deceased.

formation processes Those processes affecting the way in which archaeological materials came to be buried, and their subsequent history afterwards. Cultural formation processes include the deliberate or accidental activities of humans; natural formation processes refer to natural or environmental events that govern the burial and survival of the archaeological record.

frequency seriation A *relative dating* method that relies principally on measuring changes in the proportional abundance, or frequency, observed among finds (e.g. counts of tool types, or of ceramic fabrics).

functional-processual approach See *processual archaeology*.

Geographic Information Systems (GIS) GIS are software-based systems designed for the collection, organizing, storage, retrieval, analysis, and displaying of spatial/digital geographical data held in different "layers." A GIS can also include other digital data.

geomagnetic reversals An aspect of *archaeomagnetism* relevant to the dating of the Lower Paleolithic, involving complete reversals in the earth's magnetic field.

gift exchange See *reciprocity*.

ground reconnaissance A collective name for a wide variety of methods for identifying individual archaeological *sites*, including consultation of documentary sources, place-name evidence, local folklore, and legend, but primarily actual fieldwork.

half-life The time taken for half the quantity of a radioactive isotope in a sample to decay (see also *radioactive decay*).

hand-axe A Paleolithic stone tool usually made by modifying (chipping or flaking) a natural pebble.

hoards Deliberately buried groups of valuables or prized possessions, often in times of conflict or war, and that, for one reason or another, have not been reclaimed. Metal hoards are a primary source of evidence for the European Bronze Age.

hominins The subfamily to which humans belong, as opposed to the "hominids," which incude not only humans but also gorillas and chimps, and "hominoids," which group these with gibbons and orang-utans.

hunter-gatherers A collective term for the members of small-scale mobile or semi-sedentary societies, whose subsistence is mainly focused on hunting game and gathering wild plants and fruits; organizational structure is based on *bands* with strong kinship ties.

hypothetico-deductive explanation A form of explanation based on the formulation of hypotheses and the establishment from them by *deduction* of consequences that can then be tested against the archaeological data.

ice cores Borings taken from the Arctic and Antarctic polar ice caps, containing layers of compacted ice useful for reconstructing paleoenvironments and as a method of *absolute dating*.

iconography An important component of *cognitive archaeology*, this involves the study of artistic representations that usually have an overt religious or ceremonial significance; e.g. individual deities may be distinguished, each with a special characteristic, such as corn with the corn god, or the sun with a sun goddess, etc.

induction A method of reasoning in which one proceeds by generalization from a series of specific observations so as to derive general conclusions (*cf. deduction*).

interaction sphere A regional or inter-regional exchange system, e.g. the Hopewell interaction sphere.

isotopic analysis An important source of information on the reconstruction of prehistoric diets, this technique analyzes the ratios of the principal isotopes preserved in human bone; in effect the method reads the chemical signatures left in the body by different foods. Isotopic analysis is also used in *characterization* studies.

landscape archaeology The study of individual *features* including settlements seen as single components within the broader perspective of the patterning of human activity over a wide area.

LIDAR (Light Detection and Ranging) A *remote sensing* technique using the same principle as radar. The instrument transmits light to a target, some of which is reflected back to the instrument. The time for the light to travel out to the target and back is used to determine the range to the target.

lineage A group claiming descent from a common ancestor.

market exchange A mode of exchange that implies both a specific location for transactions and the sort of social relations where bargaining can occur. It usually involves a system of price-making through negotiation.

Marxist archaeology Based principally on the writings of Karl Marx and Friedrich Engels, this posits a materialist model of societal change. Change within a society is seen as the result of contradictions arising between the forces of production (technology) and the relations of production (social organization). Such contradictions are seen to emerge as a struggle between distinct social classes.

material culture The buildings, tools, and other *artifacts* that constitute the material remains of former societies.

matrix The physical material within which *artifacts* are embedded or supported, e.g. gravel, clay, or sand.

Mesolithic An Old World chronological period beginning around 10,000 years ago, between the *Paleolithic* and the *Neolithic*.

metallographic examination A technique used in the study of early metallurgy involving the microscopic examination of a polished section cut from an *artifact*, which has been etched so as to reveal the metal structure.

microwear analysis The study of the patterns of wear or damage on the edge of stone tools, which provides valuable information on the way in which the tool was used.

Midwestern taxonomic system A framework devised by McKern (1939) to systematize sequences in the Great Plains area of the United States, using the general principle of similarities between artifact *assemblages*.

monocausal explanation Explanations of culture change (e.g. for *state* origins) that lay stress on a single dominant explanatory factor or "prime mover."

multivariate explanation Explanations of culture change (e.g. the origin of the state) that, in contrast to monocausal approaches, stress the interaction of several factors operating simultaneously.

Neolithic An Old World chronological period characterized by the development of agriculture and, hence, an increasing emphasis on sedentism.

Neolithic Revolution A term coined by V.G. Childe in 1941 to describe the origin and consequences of farming (i.e. the development of stock raising and agriculture), allowing the widespread development of settled village life.

New Archaeology A new approach advocated in the 1960s that argued for an explicitly scientific framework of archaeological method and theory, with hypotheses rigorously tested, as the proper basis for explanation rather than simply description (see also *processual archaeology*).

non-probabilistic sampling A non-statistical sampling strategy (in contrast to *probabilistic sampling*) that concentrates on sampling areas on the basis of intuition, historical documentation, or long field experience in the area.

obsidian A volcanic glass, the ease of working and characteristically hard flint-like edges of which allowed it to be used for the making of tools.

off-site data Evidence from a range of information, including scatters of such *artifacts* and *features* as plowmarks and field boundaries, that provides important evidence about human exploitation of the environment.

Oldowan industry The earliest toolkits, comprising flake and pebble tools, used by hominids in the Olduvai Gorge, East Africa.

open-area excavation The opening up of large horizontal areas for *excavation*, used especially where single period deposits lie close to the surface as, for example, with the remains of American Indian or European Neolithic long houses.

paleoentomology The study of insects from archaeological *contexts*. The survival of insect exoskeletons, which are quite resistant to decomposition, is important in the reconstruction of paleo-environments.

paleo-ethnobotany (archaeobotany) The recovery and identification of plant remains from archaeological *contexts*, used in reconstructing past environments and economies.

Paleolithic The archaeological period before *c.* 10,000 BC, characterized by the earliest known stone tool manufacture.

paleomagnetism See *archaeomagnetic dating*.

palynology The study and analysis of fossil pollen as an aid to the reconstruction of past vegetation and climates.

physical anthropology See *biological anthropology*.

plating A method of bonding metals together, for instance silver with copper or copper with gold.

polity A politically independent or autonomous social unit, whether simple or complex, which may in the case of a complex society (such as a state) comprise many lesser dependent components.

pollen analysis See *palynology*.

postprocessual explanation Explanation formulated in reaction to the perceived limitations of functional-processual *archaeology*. It eschews generalization in favor of an "individualizing" approach that is influenced by *structuralism*, *Critical Theory*, and neo-Marxist thought.

potassium-argon dating A method used to date rocks up to thousands of millions of years old, though it is restricted to volcanic material no more recent than *c.* 100,000 years old. One of the most widely used methods in the dating of early hominid *sites* in Africa.

prehistory The period of human history before the advent of writing.

prestige goods A term used to designate a limited range of exchange goods to which a society ascribes high status or value.

probabilistic sampling Sampling method, using probability theory, designed to draw reliable general conclusions about a *site* or region, based on small sample areas; 4 types of sampling strategies are recognized: (1) *simple random sampling*; (2) *stratified random sampling*; (3) *systematic sampling*; (4) *stratified systematic sampling*.

processual archaeology An approach that stresses the dynamic relationship between social and economic aspects of *culture* and the environment as the basis for understanding the processes of culture change. Uses the scientific methodology of problem statement, hypothesis formulation, and subsequent testing. The earlier functional-processual archaeology has been contrasted with *cognitive-processual archaeology*, where emphasis is on integrating ideological and symbolic aspects.

provenience The place of origin or (earliest) known history of something; also the horizontal and vertical position of an *artifact*, *ecofact* or *feature* within a *matrix*.

pseudoarchaeology The use of selective archaeological evidence to put forward nonscientific, fictional accounts of the past.

pyrotechnology The intentional use and control of fire by humans.

radioactive decay The regular process by which radioactive isotopes break down into their decay products with a *half-life* that is specific to the isotope in question (see also *radiocarbon dating*).

radiocarbon dating An absolute dating method that measures the decay of the radioactive isotope of carbon (^{14}C) in organic material (see *half-life*).

ranked societies Societies in which there is unequal access to prestige and status, e.g. *chiefdoms* and *states*.

reciprocity A mode of exchange in which transactions take place between individuals who are symmetrically placed, i.e. they are exchanging as equals, neither being in a dominant position.

reconnaissance survey A broad range of techniques involved in the location of archaeological *sites*, e.g. the recording of surface *artifacts* and *features*, and the sampling of natural and mineral resources.

redistribution A mode of exchange that implies the operation of some central organizing authority. Goods are received or appropriated by the central authority, and subsequently some of them are sent by that authority to other locations.

refitting Sometimes referred to as conjoining, this entails attempting to put stone tools and flakes back together again, and provides important information on the processes involved in the knapper's craft.

relative dating The determination of chronological sequence without recourse to a fixed time scale; e.g. the arrangement of *artifacts* in a typological sequence, or *seriation* (cf. *absolute dating*).

religion A framework of beliefs relating to supernatural or superhuman beings or forces that transcend the everyday material world.

remote sensing The imaging of phenomena from a distance, primarily through airborne and satellite imaging. "Ground-based remote sensing" links geophysical methods, such as radar, with remote sensing methods applied at ground level.

rescue archaeology See *salvage archaeology*.

research design Systematic planning of archaeological research, usually including (1) the formulation of a strategy to resolve a particular question; (2) the collection and recording of the evidence; (3) the processing and analysis of these data and their interpretation; and (4) the publication of results.

resistivity meter See *soil resistivity*.

salvage archaeology The location and recording (usually through excavation) of archaeological *sites* in advance of highway construction, drainage projects, or urban development.

segmentary societies Relatively small and autonomous groups, usually of agriculturalists, who regulate their own affairs; in some cases, they may join together with other comparable segmentary societies to form a larger ethnic unit.

seriation A *relative dating* technique based on the chronological ordering of a group of *artifacts* or *assemblages*, where the most similar are placed adjacent to each other in the series. See *frequency seriation*.

side-scan sonar A survey method used in underwater archaeology that provides the broadest view of the sea-floor. An acoustic emitter is towed behind a vessel and sends out sound waves in a fan-shaped beam. These pulses of sonic energy are reflected back to a transducer – return time depending on distance traveled – and recorded on a rotating drum.

simple random sampling A type of *probabilistic sampling* where the areas to be sampled are chosen using a table of random numbers. Drawbacks include (1) defining the site's boundaries initially; (2) the nature of random number tables results in some areas being allotted clusters of sample squares, while others remain untouched.

simulation The formulation and computer implementation of dynamic models, i.e. models concerned with change through time.

site A distinct spatial clustering of *artifacts*, *features*, structures, and organic and environmental remains – the residue of human activity.

social anthropology See *cultural anthropology*.

soil resistivity See *earth resistance survey*.

state A term used to describe a social formation defined by distinct territorial boundedness, and characterized by strong central government in which the operation of political power is sanctioned by legitimate force. In cultural evolutionist models, it ranks second only to the empire as the most complex societal development stage.

stela (pl. stelae) A free-standing carved stone monument.

step-trenching *Excavation* method used on very deep *sites*, such as Near Eastern *tell* sites, in which the excavation proceeds downwards in a series of gradually narrowing steps.

stratification The laying down or deposition of strata or layers (also called deposits) one above the other. A succession of layers should provide a relative chronological sequence, with the earliest at the bottom and the latest at the top.

stratified random sampling A form of *probabilistic sampling* in which the region or *site* is divided into natural zones or strata, such as cultivated land and forest; units are then chosen by a random number procedure so as to give each zone a number of squares proportional to its area, thus overcoming the inherent bias in *simple random sampling*.

stratified systematic sampling A form of *probabilistic sampling* that combines elements of (1) *simple random sampling*, (2) *stratified random sampling*, and (3) *systematic sampling*, in an effort to reduce sampling bias.

stratigraphy The study and validation of *stratification*; the analysis in the vertical, time dimension, of a series of layers in the horizontal, space dimension. It is often used as a *relative dating* technique to assess the temporal sequence of *artifact* deposition.

structuralist approaches Interpretations that stress that human actions are guided by beliefs and symbolic concepts, and that underlying these are structures of thought that find expression in various forms. The proper object of study is therefore to uncover the structures of thought and to study their influence in shaping the ideas in the minds of the human actors who created the archaeological record.

style According to the art historian Ernst Gombrich, style is "any distinctive and therefore recognizable way in which an act is performed and made." Archaeologists and anthropologists have defined "stylistic areas" as areal units representing shared ways of producing and decorating *artifacts*.

subsurface detection Collective name for a variety of *remote sensing* techniques operating at ground level, and including both invasive and non-invasive techniques.

surface survey Two basic kinds can be identified: (1) unsystematic and (2) systematic. The former involves field-walking, i.e. scanning the ground along one's path and recording the location of *artifacts* and surface features. Systematic survey by comparison is less subjective and involves a grid system, such that the survey area is divided into sectors and these are walked systematically, thus making the recording of finds more accurate.

symbol representation (by word or visual image) of an idea or concept. The capacity to use symbols is a defining feature of human cognition.

systematic sampling A form of *probabilistic sampling* employing a grid of equally spaced locations; e.g. selecting every other square. This method of regular spacing runs the risk of missing (or hitting) every single example if the distribution itself is regularly spaced.

systematic survey See *surface survey*.

taphonomy The study of processes that have affected organic materials, such as bone after death; it also involves the microscopic analysis of tooth marks or cut marks to assess the effects of butchery or scavenging activities.

tectonic movements Displacements in the plates that make up the earth's crust.

tell A Near Eastern term that refers to a mound *site* formed through successive human occupation over a very long timespan.

temper Inclusions in pottery clay that act as a filler to give the clay added strength and workability and to counteract any cracking or shrinkage during firing.

thermoluminescence (TL) A dating technique that relies indirectly on *radioactive decay*, overlapping with *radiocarbon dating* in the time period for which it is useful, but also has the potential for dating earlier periods. It has much in common with *electron spin resonance* (ESR).

thin-section analysis A technique whereby microscopic thin sections are cut from a stone object or potsherd and examined with a petrological microscope to determine the source of the material.

Three Age System A *classification* system devised by C.J. Thomsen for the sequence of technological periods (stone, bronze, and iron) in Old World prehistory. It established the principle that by classifying *artifacts*, one could produce a chronological ordering.

total station An electronic/optical instrument used in surveying and to record excavations.

trace-element analysis The use of chemical techniques for determining the incidence of trace elements in rocks. These methods are widely used in the identification of raw material sources for the production of stone tools.

tree-ring dating See *dendrochronology*.

tribes A term used to describe a social grouping generally larger than a *band*, but rarely numbering more than a few thousand; unlike bands, tribes are usually settled farmers, though they also include nomadic pastoral groups whose economy is based on exploitation of livestock. Individual communities tend to be integrated into the larger society through kinship ties.

type A class of *artifacts* defined by the consistent clustering of *attributes*.

typology The systematic organization of *artifacts* into *types* on the basis of shared *attributes*.

underwater reconnaissance Geophysical methods of underwater survey include (1) a proton magnetometer towed behind a survey vessel, to detect iron and steel objects that distort the earth's magnetic field; (2) *side-scan sonar* that transmits sound waves in a fan-shaped beam to produce a graphic image of surface features on the sea-bed; (3) a sub-bottom profiler that emits sound pulses that bounce back from features and objects buried beneath the sea floor.

uniformitarianism The principle that the *stratification* of rocks is due to processes still going on in seas, rivers, and lakes; i.e. that geologically ancient conditions were in essence similar to or "uniform with" those of our own time.

uranium series dating A dating method based on the *radioactive decay* of isotopes of uranium. It has proved particularly useful for the period before 50,000 years ago, which lies outside the time range of *radiocarbon dating*.

varves Fine layers of alluvium sediment deposited in glacial lakes. Their annual deposition makes them a useful source of dating.

Wheeler box-grid An excavation technique developed by Mortimer Wheeler from the work of Pitt-Rivers, involving retaining intact baulks of earth between excavation grid squares, so that different layers can be correlated across the *site* in the vertical profiles.

zooarchaeology See *archaeozoology*.

Illustration Credits

Abbreviations: a=above, b=below, l=left, c=center, r=right

(Unless otherwise indicated, coloring of illustrations for this edition was undertaken by Drazen Tomic and Ben Plumridge.)

10a Museum of London Archaeology Service; 10bl Çatalhöyük Research Project, Cambridge; 10br David Anderson; 11a Franck Goddio/Hilti Foundation, photo Christophe Gerigk; 11bl Johan Reinhard; 11cr Kenneth Garrett; 11br Imaginechina/Corbis; 16 O. Louis Mazzatenta/National Geographic/Getty Images; 18 Wiltshire Heritage Museum, Devizes; 19 Private Collection/Archives Charmet/Bridgeman Art Library; 20 F. Catherwood, *Views of Ancient Monuments in Central America, Chiapas and Yucatán*, London 1844; 21cr National Anthropological Archives, NMNH, Smithsonian Institution, Washington, D.C.; 21br Courtesy the Peabody Museum of Archaeology and Ethnology, Harvard University; 22a St. Louis Art Museum, Eliza McMillan Fund; 22cl Grand Canyon National Park Museum; 22bl National Anthropological Archives, NMNH, Smithsonian Institution, Washington, D.C.; 23a A. Pitt-Rivers, *Excavations in Cranborne Chase*, 1893–1898; 23b Petrie Museum of Egyptian Archaeology, University of London; 24ar Archaeological Survey of India; 24bl Museo Nacional de Antropologia, Arqueologia e Historia, Lima, Peru; 25al Courtesy the Peabody Museum of Archaeology and Ethnology, Harvard University; 26 The Royal Commission on Ancient and Historical Monuments of Scotland; 28 Ray Smith; 34bl Courtesy Mrs Mary Allsebrook, Oxford; 34br The Principal and Fellows of Newnham College, Cambridge; 35al University of Colorado Museum of Natural History, Boulder; 35ac Jericho Exploration Fund; 35ar Courtesy the Peabody Museum of Archaeology and Ethnology, Harvard University; 35br Jen and Des Bartlett and Bruce Coleman Ltd; 40–41 ML Design (after A. Sherratt (ed.) *Cambridge Encyclopedia of Archaeology*, 1980, fig. 20.5); 44 John Sibbick; 45 Sue Cawood; 46 Annick Boothe (adapted from W. Rathje & M. Schiffer, *Archaeology* 1982, fig. 4.11); 49 Fototeka Hrvatskoga restauratorskog zavoda and Robert Sténuit; 52ar Sandro Vannini/Corbis; 52cl Egyptian Museum, Cairo; 52b Drazen Tomic (after Ian Bott); 54bl Vienna Report Agency/Sygma/Corbis; 54br South Tyrol Museum of Archaeology, Bolzano/Wolfgang Neeb/Bridgeman Art Library; 55 Drazen Tomic (after Tracy Wellman); 56al After Rudenko; 56bl Johan Reinhard; 58 National Museum of Ireland, Dublin; 59 Ruth Kirk; 64 best-photo/istockphoto.com; 65 Wolfgang Kaehler/Corbis; 69 Annick Boothe (after Flannery (ed.) 1976); 70 Photos Shannon P. McPherron; 72a Annick Boothe (after Connah & Jones, in Connah 1983, p. 77); 72b Timothy E. Black; 73 Annick Boothe (after Oxford Archaeological Unit); 74 Rog Palmer; 75 Crown Copyright, Forestry Commission; 76a © Marty Sedluk; 76b Courtesy John Weishampel, Caracol Archaeological Project; 77l USGS; 78 Courtesy USGS and Jason Ur; 79 NASA; 80 Drazen Tomic (after Tracy Wellman); 82 Giza Plateau Mapping Project (with thanks to Camilla Mazzucato, Farrah Brown La Pan, and Freya Sadarangani); 85a René Millon; 85b OGphoto/istockphoto.com; 86 Mandy Mottram; 90 Courtesy Dean Goodman, Geophysical Archaeometry Laboratory, University of Miami, Japan Division; 91a Abingdon Archaeological Geophysics; 91b GSB, Bradford; 94 Drazen Tomic (after M. Carver, *Underneath English Towns* 1987, fig. 2); 96, 97 Photos Jamestown Rediscovery, courtesy William M. Kelso; 99l Robin Coningham; 99r Center for American Archaeology, Kampsville Archaeological Center; 100 Annick Boothe (after *The*

Courier, Unesco Nov. 1987, p. 16, drawing by M. Redknap); 101al Annick Boothe (after *National Geographic*, supplement Jan. 1990); 101b Courtesy Robert Grenier; 103 Annick Boothe (after J. Deetz, *Invitation to Archaeology*, Natural History Press/Doubleday & Co., New York 1967); 110 Wheeler, *Ancient India*, 3 Jan. 1947; 111 Annick Boothe; 112 Annick Boothe (after Rathje & Schiffer, *Archaeology* 1982, fig. 4.17); 113l ML Design; 113r Kevin Fleming/Corbis; 114 E.R. Degginger/Science Photo Library; 117 Corpus of Maya Hieroglyphic Inscriptions and Gordon R. Willey Laboratory for Mesoamerican Studies, Peabody Museum of Archaeology and Ethnology, Harvard University; 119 Michael Worthington, Oxford Tree-Ring Laboratory; 120 Simon S.S. Driver (information from Bannister & Smiley in *Geochronology*, Tucson 1955); 123a Annick Boothe; 123b Annick Boothe (123bl after Hedges & Gowlett in *Scientific American* 254 (1), Jan. 1986, p. 84); 126, 127 Courtesy Tom Higham; 128a David Hurst Thomas & the American Museum of Natural History; 128b P. Deliss/Godong/Corbis; 130 Dr Andrew Carter; 131 Javier Trueba/Madrid Scientific Films; 134 Brett Eloff courtesy Lee R. Berger and the University of the Witwatersrand; 135a Drazen Tomic (adapted from Stringer & Andrews 2011, pp. 12–13); 135b John Sibbick; 137al Michael S. Yamashita/Corbis; 137ar Irmgard Groth Kimball; 137cl Photo Heidi Grassley © Thames & Hudson Ltd., London; 137cr Interfoto/Alamy; 137bl Walter Wust; 138–39 Simon S.S. Driver (with amendments by Drazen Tomic); 145 Simon S.S. Driver; 150 Annick Boothe (after Johnson 1972); 152 Tracy Wellman (after Isaac); 153 Robert Foley; 154 From B. Fagan, *In the Beginning* (6th ed.) 1988, fig. 16.4 (after Winter in Flannery (ed.) 1976, fig. 2.17); 156 Christopher Peebles; 159al, 159ar Charles Higham; 159b Dmitry Rukhlenko/istockphoto.com; 160a Simon S.S. Driver (after Renfrew); 160b Jeremy Walker/Alamy; 161b Bryan Busovicki/istockphoto.com; 162 Paolo Matthiae; 163 Gary Urton; 164al Musée du Louvre, Paris; 164b British Museum, London; 166l Lewis Binford; 166br Peter Johnson/Corbis; 167 Nigel Pavitt/JAI/Corbis; 169 John Milner Associates; 170 Chester Higgins; 171 Courtesy Landesdenkmalamt Baden-Württemberg-Archäologische Denkmalpflege; 173l From Gimbutas 1974, p. 163, drawing by Linda Mount-Williams; 173r Caroline Malone and Simon Stoddart (courtesy National Museum of Archaeology, Malta); 174l Musée du Pays Châtillonnais – Trésor de Vix, Châtillon sur Seine, Côte d'Or, France; 174r The Art Archive/Alamy; 179a Lucy Maw; 182l Annick Boothe (after Shackley 1981, fig. 4.3); 182r Annick Boothe (after Scarre (ed.) 1988, p.107); 184 Philip Winton (after Piperno and Ciochon, *New Scientist* 10/11/90); 185 Philip Winton; 187 Janette Deacon; 189 After A. Marshack, *The Roots of Civilization* 1972, fig. 78b; 192 Institute of Archaeology, Chinese Academy of Social Sciences, Beijing; 195 Annick Boothe (after J. Greig, Plant Foods in the Past, *J. of Plant Foods* 5 1983, 179–214); 197 After Mangelsdorf; 198 akg-images; 201a Pat Shipman and Richard Potts; 201b Photo Curtis Marean © Dikika Research Project; 202, 203 Thomas F. Kehoe; 205 British Museum, London; 212 Peter Bellwood; 213 Annick Boothe; 214a Drazen Tomic (after Bruce Bradley); 214b Béatrice Schmider; 216a Ingenui/istockphoto.com; 218 World History Archive/Alamy; 222 Kenneth Garrett; 223al Kunsthistorisches Museum, Vienna; 223ar Palace Museum, Beijing; 223cl British Museum, London; 223c National Archaeological Museum, Athens; 223cr Ulmer Museum, Ulm; 223bl Ohio Historical Society, Columbus; 223bc Werner Forman Archive; 225l ML Design (after Peacock 1982, fig. 80); 227 ML Design (after Renfrew); 229 Annick Boothe (after Pires-Ferreira in Flannery (ed.) 1976, fig.

10.16); 230a George Bass/Cemal Pulak, Institute of Nautical Archaeology, Texas; 230b ML Design (after Bass); 231 George Bass/Cemal Pulak, Institute of Nautical Archaeology, Texas; 235 Jonathan Blair/Corbis; 236 Annick Boothe; 237al Archäologisches Landesmuseum, Schloss Gottorf, Schleswig; 237ar Çatalhöyük Research Project, Cambridge; 237bl The Sutton Hoo Society; 238, 239 British Museum, London; 240 Annick Boothe (after Brothwell 1981, fig. 3.4); 241 Tracy Wellman (after Houghton 1980); 243a Christian Kober/Robert Harding World Imagery/Corbis; 243c British Museum, London; 243bl Antti Korpisaari; 243bc Elizabeth Daynès/National Geographic Image Collection; 243br Griffith Institute, Ashmolean Museum, Oxford; 244l, 244r British Museum, London; 245l Christian Meyer; 245ar Landesamt für Denkmalpflege und Archäologie Sachsen-Anhalt. Photo Juraj Lipták; 245br Landesamt für Denkmalpflege und Archäologie Sachsen-Anhalt. Drawing by Karol Schauer; 247 Oriental Institute, University of Chicago; 249 Photo Services des Antiquités de l'Egypte; 250 Javier Trueba/MSF/Science Photo Library; 256 Kenneth Garrett; 257 Reproduced by permission of Chris Henshilwood, African Heritage Research Institute, Cape Town, South Africa; 258bl Ministère de la culture et de la communication, Direction régionale des affaires culturelles de Rhone-Alpes, Service régionale de l'archéologie; 258br Anonymous/AP/PA Photos; 259l&c Pablo Aries and Sergey Lev; 259r Natural History Museum, London; 261l Henry Chaplin/istockphoto.com; 261r Philip Winton; 263l Annick Boothe; 263r Lucy Maw (after Mellaart); 264 Annick Boothe (after O'Kelly); 266 British Museum, London; 267 Musée des Antiquitiés Nationales, St. Germain-en-Laye; 269l Annick Boothe; 269ar Annick Boothe (after Burger); 269b Museo de Chavin de Huantar, Ancash, Peru; 270, 271 DAI, Photo Nico Becker; 272 ML Design; 273 Photo Scala, Florence; 280a Annick Boothe (after Kirch); 280b Annick Boothe (after Gelb); 281c Colin Hoskins/Alamy; 281b ML Design (after Garlake); 283 akg-images; 290 Craig Chiasson/istockphoto.com; 300a Courtesy Serbian Stamps Shop, Belgrade; 300b Hellenic Ministry of Culture and Tourism; 301 Jean-Claude Chapon/AFP/Getty Images; 301c CNN/Getty Images; 301r Saeed Khan/AFP/Getty Images; 303 Robert Harding Picture Library/Alamy; 304 Hiroshi Kasiwara; 306a Peter Eastland/Alamy; 306b British Museum, London; 308l Paul Bahn; 308r Emmanuel Laurent/Eurelios/Science Photo Library; 313a Antalya Museum and Museum of Fine Arts, Boston; 313b By courtesy of the Trustee of the Marquess of Northampton 1987 Settlement; 314 British Museum, London; 318a National Museum, Baghdad; 318b Marc Deville/Gamma-Rapho/Getty Images; 319 STR/AFP/Getty Images; 322 National Geographic Image Collection/Alamy; 323al, 323ar Courtesy Great Temple Project, Mexico City; 323b Eduardo Verdugo/AP/PA Photos; 327 Christopher Peebles; 328al David Adamec; 328ar Kirill Trifonov/istockphoto.com; 328bl Nickolay Stanev/istockphoto.com; 328br Robert Harding Picture Library/Alamy; 329l Dmitry Rukhlenko/istockphoto.com; 329r Jon Arnold Images/Alamy; 332 Courtesy Lisa J. Lucero; 333 Courtesy Rasmi Shoocongdej; 335 Courtesy Douglas C. Comer; 336 Courtesy Shadreck Chirikure.

All locator maps: Ben Plumridge © Thames & Hudson Ltd, London.

Text credits
The following serves as an extension of the information on page 4. The textual contributions below are copyright © Thames & Hudson Ltd, London: pp. 96–97 and 331–36.

Useful Websites

Wikipedia archaeology portal
http://en.wikipedia.org/wiki/Portal:Archaeology
Open Directory Project: Archaeology
http://www.dmoz.org/Science/Social_Sciences/Archaeology/
Archaeology newsletter: Explorator
https://groups.yahoo.com/group/Explorator/

Organizations and Societies:

Archaeological Institute of America
http://www.archaeological.org/
Canadian Archaeological Association
http://www.canadianarchaeology.com/
Society for American Archaeology
http://www.saa.org/
American Anthropological Association
http://www.aaanet.org/
Institute for Archaeologists
http://www.archaeologists.net/
Society for Historical Archaeology
http://www.sha.org/
Biblical Archaeology Society
http://www.bib-arch.org/
Association for Environmental Archaeology
http://www.envarch.net/
World Archaeological Congress
http://www.worldarchaeologicalcongress.org/
Society for Archaeological Sciences
http://www.socarchsci.org/

American Schools of Oriental Research
http://www.asor.org/

Magazines:

Archaeology
http://www.archaeology.org/
Online journal finder
http://journalseek.net/

Other:

Archaeology links
http://ari.asu.edu/archnet/
http://www.anthropologie.net/
The Archaeology Channel
http://www.archaeologychannel.org/
Human evolution
http://humanorigins.si.edu/
http://www.talkorigins.org/
Egyptology
http://www.guardians.net/egypt/
Aboriginal Studies
http://www.ciolek.com/WWWVL-Aboriginal.html
Mesoamerican Archaeology
http://www.famsi.org
Center for Archaeoastronomy
http://www.wam.umd.edu/~tlaloc/archastro/
European Megalithic Monuments
http://www.stonepages.com/

Index